Vernal Equinox

A VICTORIAN GRIMOIRE

Karen A. Cooper
430 Van Ness Ave.
Santa Cruz, CA
95060

About the Author

Patricia Telesco is an ordained minister with the Universal Life Church and a Senior Editorial Advisor for the Wiccan-Pagan Press Alliance. Her hobbies include Celtic illumination, playing harp and dulcimer, historical costuming, writing and singing folk music, sufi dancing, historical herbalism studies, carving wood and soapstone, poetry, and the Society for Creative Anachronism (a historical recreation group). Many of these activities have extended themselves into her small mail order business called Hourglass Creations. Her articles and poems have appeared in journals such as *Circle, The Unicorn, Moonstone* (England), *Demeter's Emerald, Silver Chalice,* and Llewellyn's *New Worlds of Mind and Spirit* (formerly *New Times*), and she is also the author of a children's book *The Wings of Disrael.* She welcomes the opportunity to do workshops and lectures. Patricia lives in Buffalo, New York, with her husband, young son, dog and five cats.

To Write to the Author

If you wish to contact the author or would like more information about this book, please write to the author in care of Llewellyn Worldwide, and we will forward your request. Both the author and publisher appreciate hearing from you and learning of your enjoyment of this book and how it has helped you. Llewellyn Worldwide cannot guarantee that every letter written to the author can be answered, but all will be forwarded. Please write to:

Patricia Telesco
c/o Llewellyn Worldwide
P.O. Box 64383-784, St. Paul, MN 55164-0383, U.S.A.
Please enclose a self-addressed, stamped envelope for reply, or $1.00 to cover costs.
If outside U.S.A., enclose international postal reply coupon.

Free Catalog from Llewellyn

For more than 90 years Llewellyn has brought its readers knowledge in the fields of metaphysics and human potential. Learn about the newest books in spiritual guidance, natural healing, astrology, occult philosophy and more. Enjoy book reviews, new age articles, a calendar of events, plus current advertised products and services. To get your free copy of Llewellyn's *New Worlds of Mind and Spirit,* send your name and address to:

Llewellyn's New Worlds of Mind and Spirit
P.O. Box 64383-784, St. Paul, MN 55164-0383, U.S.A.

A Victorian Grimoire

Enchantment ❧ Romance ❧ Magic

Patricia Telesco

1992
Llewellyn Publications
St. Paul, Minnesota 55164-0383, USA

FIRST EDITION

Cover collage © **Sandra Starck**
 Special thanks to A FINE ROMANCE – 2912 Hennepin Avenue South, Minneapolis, MN 55408 – for the use of their Victorian artifacts in the creation of the cover art. Thanks to artist Joelle Nelson for her kind assistance.

Book design and layout by Terry Buske, Marilyn Matheny and Deborah Chapdelaine.

Cover photograph by Michael Yencho

Poetry border design by Robin Wood

Library of Congress Cataloging-in-Publication Data
Telesco, Patricia 1960–
    A Victorian grimoire / by Patricia Telesco
        p.   cm.
    Includes bibliographical references and index.
    ISBN 0-87542-784-7
    1. Magic 2. Magic--History--19th century.   I. Title
BF1595.T485 1992
133.4' 3' 09034--dc20   92-20393
                                                          CIP

Llewellyn Publications
A Division of Llewellyn Worldwide, Ltd.
P.O. Box 64383, St. Paul, MN 55164-0383, U.S.A.

Acknowledgements

Many people helped make this book a reality. First and foremost among those to be thanked are my husband and son, the former for his pride in my work and his reminders to me to rest periodically, and the latter for teaching me how to play again.

Second in line are the members of my family, my friends, and co-workers, who support me even when they do not always understand what I am trying to do. Specifically, I want to thank my mother, who taught me the wonders of earth and how to reach for the stars; my sisters, who don't know how many times they have influenced my life for the better; and Zane, a man who has been a companion through thick and thin, even across the miles. Thanks especially to Jody, my favorite chaplain of chocolate, who knows me better than I know myself. A dearer friend for many lives, none could have or hope for.

Third are the many great men and women in this world who paved the way for all those of alternative faiths (sometimes with blood) by their words, wisdom, and a strength of will. They stood up for what they believed. Without them and without people who continue their work, we would not be able to say, "never again, the burning."

I would like to take this opportunity to thank Lisa Iris, who kicked me in the butt and told me to send this manuscript in to the publisher. I also want to thank Nancy Mostad, a fellow cat lover with very special vision, and Lisa Peschel, who has a gift for listening. All three of these women stood by me, gave me the foundation from which to build my dream, and patiently nursed me through my insecurity via 100 phone calls. A person would be very blessed to have but one of these women grace their lives, let alone all three.

Appreciation also goes to Blythe, a goddess of coffee; Patty, the priestess of pizza; Lynn and Terry, for sharing their family stories with me; Dave K., for being an incredible research assistant; and particularly to the many talented spiritual writers whose dedication to down-to-earth magical education stands as an inspiration to all of us.

To the gentles of the SCA, specifically Clan IronHawk and House Atai, in whom I have often found a kind hand, loving heart, and a dream to live (if only for a moment), I give my sincere thanks. In the persona of Lady Marian LoreSinger, I thoroughly enjoy the creative outlet and special friends which SCA provides. During the magical moments of events, I learned that "living" history can not only be educational but fun, and found a strong foundation from which to build my book.

To the readers and supporters of *The Magi*, many of whom have become friends: thanks for putting up with the typos, spelling errors and just standing by me for the last four years. You are a great blessing to me. Specifically to the people at Moon Circles, Rowan Tree Church and The Aquarian Church in Texas who had more faith in this newsletter than I did when it began, and who have always lent a hand with a smile and a good word—thanks.

And lastly, to myself. For the first time in my life I have followed a longtime dream with conviction and hope to its fulfillment. In this book, I have seen the magic of self-love, determination, and creativity born into my life in a way I never knew possible. To those of you who walk through these pages and try to find your way, may your path be filled with light and may it not be too rocky. May you come to find that inner knowingness that lets you say without fear, "I am a Witch/Pagan . . . and that is exactly what I should be."

Forthcoming Books

The Victorian Flower Oracle
The Urban Pagan

Dedicated To

The spirit of the Law, not the letter of it. The ability to do and be, not look and judge. The love that asks nothing but to give. The joy of children laughing. The peace this Earth must some day come to know, and the very special magic in all of us.

❦

In Memory Of

My father, Karl Kroldart, who did not live to see me fulfill this dream, but whose love of the arts inspires me to this day. The creative minds of Jim Henson and Gene Roddenbury, whose light-filled vision for tomorrow continue to give many hope and joy today. Merry part.

TABLE OF CONTENTS

PREFACE

Writing is not unlike giving birth. You go through months (sometimes years) of carrying the idea in your heart and mind, until finally the baby is born. For *A Victorian Grimoire*, the labor pains were not easy or expected. In delivery, the original manuscript was less than half the size of this one with a slightly different facade. After review, it was felt that there was potential for this child, but a new focus was added, that of Victorian history.

Now, I know the Middle Ages like the back of my hand. I am even somewhat familiar with ancient traditions, but the Victorian era was something that never really "tickled my fancy." So when Llewellyn suggested this approach, I kind of hemmed and hawed, and to be honest, was less than thrilled with the whole idea. Yet, writing is the one dream, the one great love in my life I have never given up. I simply couldn't overlook the opportunity being presented to me, no matter how unfamiliar the open door seemed. So, I dove head first into the swirling pool of time. Little did I know then the kind of wonderful waters I was about to encounter.

When I began, I knew literally nothing about the Victorian era, other than some pretty ornaments I had seen at Yule. In order to obtain the information needed for an undertaking of this nature I started "dating" my local library rather seriously. As I explored the books, I realized there was much more to this era than the repressive primness we usually think of when the word "Victorian" is used in conversation. Before I knew it, and much to my amazement, I was actually enjoying the research.

After pouring over one hundred texts, doing five hundred hours of study, and getting a severe case of writer's cramp, I sat back and said, "wow." A new appreciation for those times had grown in my heart. Even though I never really wanted to learn about Victorianism, when I looked at it through eyes which sought more than just the negative aspects, I found rich and diverse traditions which changed my reality. The Buffalo Public Library became the surrogate father of my growing baby, my book.

Now, in addition to writing, I am also an herbalist with a small business on the side called Hourglass Creations. As I began to compile my notes for the book, I realized how incredibly helpful much of this information could be to my herbal work. The Victorian recipes, ideas and methods were filling my mind, and not long thereafter, my shelves! What before had only been a medievally based hobby for our historical re-enactment group took on new meaning within the boundaries of my own century.

This was not the only way this book affected me. As I read about the turn of the century, I began to understand more of my "today" better. Historical foundations gave me a clearer perspective to discern both the good and bad in our heritage. I found myself looking at older people with a new appreciation for the wisdom they have to share, and the amazingly agile minds they must have had to bring about our technology. Traditions, which I never thought much about, took on new life with the added flavor the Victorian era gave them. Then, finally, my magic began to reflect the peaceful beauties found throughout the pages of time.

While these changes were taking place within, my world without was also transforming. New, unexpected, and very precious friendships formed between myself and three women who are, quite literally the godparents for this project. They watched over me and it with a gentle love and contagious enthusiasm that helped me over the mountains and molehills. Likewise my other friends, and especially my husband, came forward to voice their support for a project that I, for an instant or two, considered saying "no" to.

So this book, in published form, is also a testimony to learning and growth. Life presents many opportunities to us, but they don't always come in the wrappings we expect. My package came to me with hundreds of questions, many doubts, and a lot of hard work to make the dream a reality. While I was writing this book, I filed the chapters under "victory" in my computer system so that each time I worked on a section, I could literally retrieve victory into my life. As I look back over the last few months, I realize that even if this book had not been published, it would have been worth the effort for the gifts of knowledge, understanding and simple loveliness it has brought to me. It is my sincere prayer that these pages carry the same treasures to your life, on wings of peace. Blessed Be.

INTRODUCTION

The Victorian era was filled with romance. Everything carried a special smell, look and touch, rich with the flavors of hearth, home and love. During this time, there was no need for what we now call Kitchen Witchery because their lives were the magic, their home and family the center of attention, and their kitchen a playground for creativity and love.

Now our lives are so complex and busy that we are left to wonder if the special magic of days gone by can be recaptured in our modern life, homes, and circles without being outmoded. We also cannot simply ignore the changes that modern technology has brought to us.

We can return to this simpler school of magic, this magic that begins in our own back yard and blends the old with the new. But first we need to change our perspectives of ourselves, our lives, the world around us, and magic itself. Everyday we are bombarded with portraits of the status quo—and these are rarely positive. The pictures painted for those in the Craft are even less so. No matter how hard we try, these images affect us to the point where we sometimes expect our magic to be spectacular.

Real magic can be something unpretentious, soft, and part of every corner of our reality. For example, if my child cries out of his concern for me, I will take that tear and mix it with water for drinking, the metaphor being that his healing love will flow into me through that tear. This type of symbolic magic is very powerful, and much more meaningful because it is a direct result of the experience of living.

If we were to define and describe for a moment a modern version of the Victorian enchantments, they would be unique and individual combinations of common sense, science, humor, herbalism, faith, cooking, creativity, and love. They are the sorts of things that spring from our every day life, with few fancy words or rituals. Indeed, from this perspective, life itself becomes the ritual, and anything you add to that is like icing on the cake! This way of thinking also tends to promote the belief that anything which can be used should be used, so there is no waste. In this case, a Witch with a modernized Victorian attitude is far more likely to use her athame (or sacred knife) as a cutting tool in the kitchen (in contrast to a tradition which puts it aside strictly for magical use) because it is clean, sharp and available.

This does not mean that "high magic" and its customs do not have a place. Wicca and Paganism have a rich and diverse history which should not be ignored. Yet, in the intricacy of today's world, sometimes we seek something simpler, something which expresses what we feel when we feel it—regardless of what phase the moon is in or what time of day it is. A Victorian enchantment embodies this individual flair and therefore it can augment any path with which you are working.

I call it magic for lack of a better word, but some of what I share with you is anything but supernatural. Some of it comes from learning to be a good listener (in order to read people better), and some of it comes from knowing yourself. Some of it comes from a willingness to try new things, trust your talents, and take a little extra time to make things at home instead of hopping in your car to buy them at the local supermarket. Other portions have to do with sensitivity, learning to let go, and having fun. Oh, yes, there is enough of what we call meditation, visualization, ritual, spell, and invocation blended in to help our minds refocus on something other than the mundane, but ultimately *real magic comes from you*. It is deep within like a spark, just waiting for expression.

The art of *A Victorian Grimoire* is the art of releasing that spark into your everyday life, into every situation, no matter how common. From doing the dishes, to making soap, to a game for young ones, each portion of our world should be magical. It takes a little effort and creativity to let that specialness out, but once you get the hang of it, you will find it becomes second nature, until every measure of your being cannot help being changed. Then you can grow and become a reflection of something far greater—the Divine in all of us.

Magic is not just going to Circle and having a few crystals scattered around your home. If it does not change how you live, express yourself, and how you look at the world, you are not doing it right. This book is set up in such a way as to help you take your tradition in hand and weave it into every corner of your reality daily, until outwardly everything you touch reflects the light growing within.

For those who find their lives do not always allow for long, time-consuming rituals, this book will allow you to continue practicing and expressing your magic through common, everyday situations. In some instances you will notice that I have used a cliche, superstition or "old saying" as a component in magic. This is because of the power and degree of truth these things often carry. Aphorisms can be very helpful in triggering just the right mental and emotional responses for magic, since your mind reacts to the phrases and ideas like a well-known friend.

You will also notice that some recipes are magically inclined, but many of them are also practical and useful. History shows us that our Craft often came from the village wise person who knew how to heal with her hands as well as with a spell. The Victorian era was likewise imminently pragmatic, yet it was an age in which people gave homage to the spirit of beauty. So as we go about our daily activities, let's learn from their example. Why not stir in an incantation, fold in a magically blessed herb, bake up a visualization, or whatever it takes to bring a bit of resplendence and balance back to ourselves and our world?

Please note that while this book is set up by topic, you can use any of the recipes anytime. Please experiment, change and adapt them to find what works best for you.

I should note here that while I am aware that not all aspects of the Victorian era were positive, no period in history is "picture perfect." However, I firmly believe that we have studied and read enough about past wars, pestilence and violence in our life times. Now we have the opportunity to shift our attention and awareness to the positive features history can offer, especially with regard to working towards global healing. By bringing the flavor of the Victorian era into the New Age we can begin to refocus and augment our appreciation of the home, family, and Earth.

This knowledge encourages us to waste less and recycle more by thinking of practical ways to reuse what might normally just be tossed aside (often saving money and having fun in the process). It inspires us to find a little bit of happiness in each day no matter how bad things may seem. Most of all, modern Victorian enchanters say, "Be yourself, express yourself, and become the magic." It is wonderful to wake up everyday and know that every thing you do is more than just a "job" or "chore." You can make it special and productive. You can bring to each living experience that special spark of magic already within you.

Special Note:

For those of you who are new to Wicca and magical ideals, there are three sections in the back of this book which will help make this text more useful to you. Appendix A shares a little of the history of magic since the 1800's to give you a broader perspective on the roots of "The Craft." Appendix B explains the basics tenants of Wicca, including ritual, tools, and spells. Appendix C gives names and addresses of companies that supply magical goods. And finally, the Glossary supplies a working knowledge of magical terminology. You may want to read these segments first as a means of enhancing the significance of the pages which follow, especially as they pertain to your life.

A thing of beauty is a joy forever
Its loveliness increases;
It will never pass into nothingness;
But will keep a bower quiet for us,
And a sleep full of sweet dreams,
And health, and quiet breathing.
— Percy Bysshe Shelley

CHAPTER ONE

Through the Keyhole: A Historical Peek at the Victorian Era

There was a door to which I found no key,
There was a veil through which I could not see.
— Edward Fitzgerald

To understand the spirit of any period of history, we first need to take a look at the events that shaped people's lives. In this respect, the Victorian era was both beautiful and confusing. Fashion, personal perspectives, social structures, and industry were changing much more rapidly than in the past. In America, women were suddenly thrust into the labor force, while their husbands or fathers were fighting the Civil War. This particular event was probably one of the most influential in establishing the Women's Prosperity Act of 1870, which allowed married women to own property for the first time. It is not surprising then, that it is also during this period that there is an increase in the establishment of female colleges and a greater concern for women's literacy is expressed.

In 1876, America celebrated its 100th birthday with a special exposition in Philadelphia. The Expo was financed predominantly by women's fund raising efforts and there was a special building to display and commemorate the advancement of women as a group. This may have been the first sense of sisterhood reclaimed by American women. This did not lessen the attachment to fashion in the least, though. In the same year, the tortoise shell comb was heralded in "Young Ladies Journal" as being among the prettiest novelties for the year.

In 1879, the Brooklyn Bridge was completed, the Statue of Liberty unveiled, and the first skyscraper built. 1861 saw the death of the Duchess of Kent and Prince Albert, followed by a long period of mourning in England. 1887 relieved this feeling with the Queen's Year of Jubilee, celebrating fifty years on the throne. War changed the mood yet again in 1898 when America went to battle with Spain.

By the turn of the century, America was still strongly rural. Over 11 million people made their living as farmers. Yet, there was a swelling interest in urbanization. This odd combination of rural and urban dwelling was characterized best by the kinds of goods listed in the Sears Catalogue issued in 1900. The catalogue listed food items, homeopathic cures, a veterinary department, hair restorers, and remedies for everything from obesity and ague to "female diseases."

We can see by this overview how many social situations were affecting the people of this era, and consequently their roles in the community. Even so, there was a special charm, warmth, and charisma about these days that is irresistibly alluring. American writers were reflecting romance, nature, man, society and idealism, while in Europe we see such classical authors as Browning and Fitzgerald come on the scene. This is the age when Alice in Wonderland and Huck Finn gave children everywhere something to dream about.

Middle class values were predominantly respected and encouraged. Religion, the family, the spirit of endeavor, morality, moderation, respectability—all played a vital part. Domestic life became the foundation for national greatness, the repository for the highest teachings of knowledge. Elegance and virtue were available at the fireside.

These values were reflected in magazines of the time. They devoted much space to home life and the extended family. Their covers depicted close-knit families, warmly decorated homes, effective homemakers, and welcome guests. The paintings and other art forms were now of a more tender style, romancing the viewer with apple blossoms, waving horse chestnut leaves, and hollyhocks. Virginity and harmony were accented. Art flourished in the Victorian home in almost every corner. It reflected their ideals and brought a feeling of grandeur to the entire living space.

The Victorian era was a time when small family businesses often became the strongholds for a town; horseback riding and biking became fashionable; and for the first time there was a new awareness and desire for individuality. Reading and writing became more important, especially for women. This was evidenced by more newlyweds being able to sign their marriage certificates and carve their initials lovingly into trees and rocks. Literacy also began to increase steadily, due to the commencement of mail delivery.

With more people reading and writing, the interest in books was heightened. Even so, books were an expensive and precious commodity, and they usually had to be ordered by mail. Small public libraries began to form around 1870, but many of them lacked funds. Most books stayed in the home or were restricted to a professional domain.

The limited amount of books that were available in a lending library were shelved according to how "age appropriate" they were. This meant that the books for general reading were on the lower shelves and the "private" ones, the ones deemed scandalous or injurious to young virtue, (any book remotely connected to sex) were confined to the higher shelves. As Somerset Maugham once put it, "The Victorian era, where an asterisk was followed after a certain interval with a baby . . . ." However shocking the book, the mischievous, curious or enterprising child was not about to be stopped when a simple step stool could quickly remedy this out-of-reach situation. They often teamed up with friends or siblings in order to attain their forbidden goal. Some things never change.

Technology during the Victorian period was growing by leaps and bounds. The telegraph, telephone, steamboats, railroad, and even an internal combustion engine for the automobile propelled America into an industrial evolution which is still going on today. With improved technology, the entertainment industry was not far behind. The waltz was still a very popular form, but with the advent of rag time and jazz, a lighter sound was heard in the land. New dances and new attitudes came with it, along with a colorful array of personalities ranging from the infamous Jessie James to the courageous Helen Keller.

A review of fashion brings to light many interesting ideals and charming stories. Women's clothes reflected their place in society. They were forbidden fruit. Every part of the body except the face was covered, usually in layers. Even indoors, the hands were seldom openly viewed, being hidden neatly in gloves. Although women were constrained by fashion, so were men. There were complaints from men of the time (noted in diaries) about how their clothing seemed drab and uninteresting by comparison. I have a feeling they would have quickly changed their minds after one day in a boned bodice, but even so, men's fashions changed very little. The standard men's ensemble of shirt, cuff links, tie or scarf, vest, coat, hat and pants, together with gloves, tie pins, signet rings, watches, and chains stayed fairly consistent with only minor alterations, while women's clothing saw revisions with each decade.

Certain items such as the crinoline (support skirt) and bustle appeared and reappeared with the changing trends. These hoops and bumps made great entertainment for humorists of the time, because they knocked over knick-knacks and tea cups and often got tangled in each other. There was a short reprieve from the mid 1860s–1880s when skirts were tighter and soft color modes became less scandalous. By this time gloves, which up till now were worn constantly by men and women alike, were starting to disappear despite the etiquette books. The high necked blouse gave way to a slightly more open neckline, and much to the amazement of all, sometimes short sleeves!

Unfortunately, in the 1880s the bustle returned with a fury. A dress was even presented to the Queen for her jubilee which held a specially designed music box in the rear. Each time she sat down, the box played "God save the Queen." This devise was most tiring, as of course she would immediately have to rise and so would everyone in the room with her. The 1880s also saw the opening of tea shops in London for working women. And, just to show fashion and taste have little in common, the women in France were wearing vegetables and stuffed birds on their hats.

By 1890, there was an increase in masculine styles for women including ties, coats, and cuff links. This was most predominant among working women, while housewives were content to stay with what was considered a more traditional style. To give you a better idea of the intri-

cate nature of these clothes, I happened on a Victorian slip at an antique shop which I purchased and wear unashamedly as a skirt. The piece is beautiful and flowing, with eyelet style lace at the bottom, but even with a modern iron it takes 20 minutes to get all the wrinkles out! Add to this the layers and yards of material common to the Victorian dress and you begin to have a whole new respect for the homemaker of the day.

No matter what the apparel, throughout the era it was always adorned with some type of jewelry. Lockets, hair pins, necklaces, chokers, rings, buckles, cameos, and plumes bedecked every head, neck, and hand. It is odd that such a conservative people were so enamored of shiny trinkets, but enamored they were. Some quality costume jewelry was available by this time, but most was made from real gold, silver, bronze, and any number of valuable jewels.

Unlike their finery, fabric colors were rather bland until after 1900. The most popular colors were crisp blacks for winter and whites for summer, although variations of dark blue and grey were also common. Color itself was questionable and disreputable. Too much

ornamentation or color was considered a sign of easy virtue. Even with the emphasis on appearance and presentation, makeup was definitely frowned upon as being injurious to the complexion.

Even though the Victorian era is often considered to have a stoic demeanor, like any age, Victorianism had its fair share of free thinking, bohemian types. The feminists, artists and other philosophical "riffraff" were more than happy to try and upset the apple cart by wearing fashions which contradicted what the majority of the populace thought prudent. During the popularity of the top hat, they wore wide brimmed, low-crowned hats. It never even seemed to occur to them to dispense with the accessory altogether.

This dichotomy was occurring in religion as well. The average person still frequently followed superstitions and old sayings, went to seances, marked the moon phases, and even believed that the body mirrored the order of the cosmos. Perhaps not everyone who lived their life by these notions called them magic, but the interest and practices were prevalent, especially among "common" folk. Homeopaths, psychics, and healers were listed openly in the yellow pages (along with Coke, which was a fuel, not a soda then). Psychic talent was linked to physical care, and with the emergence of psychology as a science, people began to recognize that their appetites came from the self instead of the external world. This marks a very important change in perspective from a people who once felt themselves left to the whims of fate.

By 1889 public exhibitions of mind reading became commonplace. Even the great Houdini was trying his hand at it until 1898. Eva Fay was the most accomplished female spiritualist at the time, performing in music halls. As the demand for this entertainment grew, so did con artists. In reviewing the times, it seems that most people on the stage were frauds, pandering to the people's need for distraction.

A few, however, such as Wolf Messing (a projection telepathist), were quite remarkable in their talents, appearing genuine even under the scrutinizing eye of Einstein and Freud. People like these helped bring about the founding of the Theosophical Society in 1875 and the American Society for Psychical Research in 1885. Both these organizations were dedicated to studying all manners of phenomena—including automatic writing, out of body experiences, mind reading, and reincarnation. It is well worth noting that some of our most admired psychics and Witches (Leland, Murray, Gardner and Cayce), lived during the early 1900s. Most of what would be considered "the Craft" in America at this time (Craft meaning the magic that Witches practice) was centered mostly around the "Old Ways," the folk and practical magics, with a healthy helping of fairy magics.

It would be unfair of me to paint a perfect portrait of Victorianism. There were many things about the period which were difficult, individually restrictive, and harsh. Life spans were shorter, (the average life span was under fifty years) some of the fashions were physically dangerous, children were more frequently abused, and working conditions were unsafe, just to name a few. Perhaps this is why the other side of Victorian life, the quaintness, was necessary. Their almost mystical fascination with beauty and nature was a way to bring symmetry to otherwise erratic times.

The growing interest today in Victorianism leads me to believe that the picturesque essence of this era, its pleasantries, are still important for the here and now. It may well be that we, like them, need a new symmetry. In reading about this period, it is impossible not to notice that there was a special power to the romance, to the urban and home rituals, and to the sensuality of the day which is incredibly captivating.

Today, we seem to yearn to grasp a small nugget of our Victorian history because it is perceived as being less complicated and more self sufficient, a time which by its very nature feels magical on many levels. Not necessarily the magic of organized Circles (a group of people who meet regularly to perform rituals), but instead the simple magic of celebrating the seasons, knowing the Earth, using resources with wisdom and prudence, reclaiming our bodies as something sacred, looking at our children as our future, and just generally making an effort to bring beauty, self-reliance, simplicity and balance back to our world on a daily basis.

So the attempt is made herein to blend the best of the old and new together into a charming harmony; one that sings the songs of the land, the individual, the family, and every corner of our mundane lives. One that takes these songs and makes them uniquely ours, full of the reality of our existence mingled with the stardust of our dreams. One that, most importantly, allows us to reclaim the magic today, tomorrow and everyday.

Whate'er the theme, the Maiden sang
As if her song could have no ending.
I saw her singing at her work
And o'er the sickle bending
I listened, motionless and still
And as I mounted up that hill
The music in my heart I bore
Long after it was heard no more.
—William Wordsworth

CHAPTER TWO

Victorian Symbols for Modern Magic

There is a sweet music here that softer falls
than petals from blown roses on the grass.
—Alfred, Lord Tennyson

The Victorian era was full of magic, from the focus on the stage magician and mind readers to the subtle symbolism embodied in what they wore, how they stood, and even what they said. These things were like emblems which came directly out of the way life was lived, out of common attitudes. They were influenced by what limited technology the era had. Even more importantly, the symbols were terribly logical and made sense, considering their reality. For example, the cat-o-nine tails, a whip with nine knotted cords fastened to a handle, represented discipline because of its frequent application to the bottoms of ill-behaved children. Layered drapes denoted respectability, prosperity, and privacy. People with this type of decor would have had the means to afford it, therefore the prosperity is evident. The layering effect gives greater privacy, a highly valued commodity of the day.

Trees, in the parks or near the house, were standing reminders of long life and endurance. The roll-top desk spoke of locked secrets, solidity, and a sense of purpose. In considering how to use Victorian symbolism in modern magic, we need to think first about the original meanings and feelings they inspired, then bring them into perspective for a new and very different century.

BAUBLES, BANGLES, AND JEWELS

Gems and precious metals of all sorts, including moonstone, emerald, garnet, jet, diamond, ruby, tortoise shell, ivory and opal were very much a part of the Victorian era. Their adornment was not only a show of "finery," but was also part of courtship and marriage rituals. Children, dead relatives, and even pets were remembered through jewelry. Locks of hair were braided or worked into lockets and rings as forget-me-nots; portraits and silhouettes

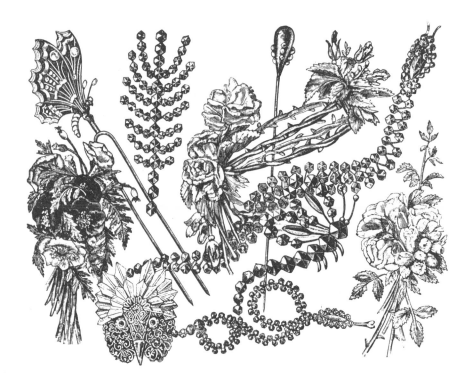

were affectionately placed in framed pins; pocket watches and cuff links were engraved—almost everything a person wore carried a personal story or a memory. These things gave a sense of warmth to the rather neutral colors evidenced in clothing.

Today, we continue this tradition not only with jewelry, but by carrying and using crystals of all sorts as a focus for magic and meditation. One of the best known traditions is that of possessing the birth stone for luck, life and health. According to this custom, it is best if the gem is received as a gift. The following list gives each month and its corresponding stone. Also noted is any information regarding folklore and common magical characterizations which can readily be implemented for symbolic magical tools, visualizations, or spell components.

Birthstones and Their Attributes

January — Garnet
According to traditional beliefs, it protects the wearer against lightning. It is considered a truth stone, one which allows for consistency and faith. If your convictions are on tumultuous ground, try visualizing yourself surrounded by the garnet. Allow light to pour through it into your being to give strength to your foundations and illuminate the shadows. Carry this stone in a medicine pouch to encourage truthfulness with self, or make it the center of a wreath to help protect your home against storm.

February — Amethyst
A good dreaming stone, it was also thought to bring peace of mind and aid a sense of humor. Place it under your pillow to bring a pleasant night's sleep, or give it to a loved one

as a symbol of keeping your union alive. If you happen to enjoy drinking now and again, you may wish to have an amethyst mounted on your cup, as wive's tales claim it keeps you from drunkenness.

March — Aquamarine, Bloodstone

These are stones of protection, cleansing, and motivation. Use these any time you seem to need incentive. Place a stone under your pillow to bring visionary dreams, or give it as a gift, signifying long life and health. Leave it on top of any project that you have been putting off as a gentle reminder to keep you going.

April — Diamond

Because of its strength and the length of time it takes to form (centuries) the diamond has come to symbolize patience, wisdom and fortitude. It is also an excellent stone to commemorate a union, because it is said to bring couples the virtues needed for any relationship. Since real diamonds are very expensive, you may wish to get a Herkimer (a quartz crystal that looks similar to a diamond) for your magical collection.

May — Emerald

A stone of romance, this is also a good gem to give for a handfasting. It is said to bring peace to any home and quiet storms both natural and emotional. If you find you need grounding, sit with this (or a piece of cloth which is emerald colored) under a tree. Cup the stone in the palm of your hands and allow the energy to flow downwards through you, bringing your foundations back into balance.

June — Pearl, Moonstone, Alexandrite

These stones are wonderful for peacefulness, compassion, healing, and increasing psychic ability. Try placing a moonstone on your third eye while meditating, or holding a pearl in your hand. Charge any of these stones with healing energy to give to a friend in need. Pearl and moonstone are also excellent goddess stones, for connecting with the Full Moon aspect of the Divine and bringing fertility to any effort.

July — Ruby

For clarity of thought and success, the ruby is unmatched. To banish negative energy or bring new balance to your life, try visualizing white light poured through the deep crimson stone into your being. Allow it to build and refresh your creativity and bring a broader perspective to any situation.

August — Peridot, Sardonyx

These are stones of change and financial matters. In some traditions, these stones are used for special talismans which are believed to allow the wearer to walk without a trace in any environment. They may also be applied to banish fear. If you are feeling too visible, have financial needs, or desire real change in your life, focus your needs on either stone, then carry it with you and keep it in the center of your altar until your situation changes.

September — Sapphire
The jewel of faithfulness, truth, and enlightenment, a sapphire is a wonderful stone to use in visualization when you desire to increase your magical knowledge. It will balance truth and wisdom with your learning. You may also use a sapphire-colored candle or piece of fabric as a focus.

October — Opal, Tourmaline
These stones are best used when you need to improve your self-awareness, self-esteem or find yourself feeling hopeless. The color of the stones reflect the brilliance of the Full Moon, a time when we can come to find the fullness of self without judgement. If you find you are feeling negative about yourself, try a visualization where you are in the center of a bright fire opal, filled to overflowing with the light around it. Allow your negative feelings to pour out like dark clouds and replace them with the opal's radiant joy.

November — Topaz
To ease a saddened heart, find rest, or be revitalized, carry a piece of blessed topaz (best if given from a dear friend). It is the bearer of the sun's energy, warming the coldest of situations and allowing us to lounge for a while in restful bliss.

December — Turquoise (undyed), Zircon
For hundreds of years, these stones have been used for protection on all levels of our being. Place pieces around your home, car, office and anywhere you wish their guardian powers to stand watch when you cannot. For enhanced effect, as you position the stones, you may wish to visualize them forming a net of white-light energy which completely surrounds the area.

Other Decorative and Symbolic Materials

Mosaics were special souvenirs for travelers. Talented artisans would create intricate designs of local attractions by cutting malachite, carnelian, and other stones, and then fitting them together on a black background. The final effect was so astounding that it could not be told from a painting without close inspection. If you are fortunate to find good mosaic work today, try using it for safe, enjoyable travel spells by visualizing white light pouring from the stone over your vehicle, then carrying the mosaic with you on your trip.

Another application might be for those times when you are feeling too visible. In that case, before you enter the situation again, visualize yourself as part of a mosaic. Then slowly allow the outline of your image to blend into the background in your mind's-eye. The idea behind this visualization is to help draw your personal energy in, and allow it to mingle wherever you are without static. Thus, your noticeability will decrease.

Pique and tortoise shell were favored for their ability to be molded into any form. They were most commonly used for intricate hair combs. Carry a charged piece of this for times when you need adaptability and positive change, or simply leave it on your altar to remind you of the valuable lessons of flexibility.

One note here, since the tortoise is an endangered species, be sure the item you get is antique or a good replication out of consideration for our natural environment.

Jet was used during times of mourning because of its color and the strict rules regarding proper mourning periods. Use jet on your altar when remembering a loved one, or carry it with you during times when you need strength to endure drastic changes.

I also feel jet could be useful in recognizing the "dark" side of self, and dealing constructively with it. In this instance, sit with the stone beneath you as you meditate. Consider all the habits or thought patterns in your life which are negative. (Or, just consider the ones you are ready to deal with now.) Take a moment to examine why they are a part of you and decide if you wish to release them. If so, allow them to pour into the stone below like black, muddy water. When you feel almost empty of this negativity, take the stone and throw it into a stream that is rushing away from you. Those parts of the past will likewise flow away.

Metals: Gold is aligned with the more masculine side, the symbol of the sun, fire and success. Historically, it adorned magical wands and was a symbol of leadership. Silver is aligned with the feminine, the moon, and water. Silver balances gold, because it reflects the inner self and the unseen world. Silver is often used for ritual cups, sea salt containers, and herbs set aside for magical use. Copper is associated with Earth and conduction, which is why it is often used to create magical wands. It is a good stabilizer, and a good focus for energy. Lead is for grounding; so when you are day-dreaming too much, put a little piece in your shoe to help keep your feet on the ground. Finally, tin is a metal of good fortune so you may wish to make it part of luck sachets, and have a little piece to adorn your altar . . . after all, a little serendipity never hurts!

Feathers: A favorite touch for finishing off a hat, feathers appeared in a multitude of colors and sizes. For magic, the feather is easily associated with the element of air and may be used as a standard in the East quadrant of a magic Circle, or as a means of moving the incense around your sacred space. Many people burn sage and then use a feather to fan the smoke.

An individual who does auric cleansing may employ a feather. It can be helpful when softly urging physical energies into proper balance to use the feather to trace the aura, instead of the hands. If you try this on yourself, begin by closing your eyes. Sense the light, cool air as the feather moves across the surface of your skin, and visualize the light energy of your body smoothing out to an even level and a consistent color. Continue in this manner until you feel more balanced, centered, and calm.

General: If you enjoy collecting jewelry, the Victorian age offers a wide variety of beautiful pieces which are not overly expensive. Acorns, leaf sprays and rose buds were common configurations in silver and gold which can be used to enhance your ritual robes, magical pouches and sacred space for various seasons.

Since many of the items mentioned above are rather expensive by nature, check your local gift shops. Many today are selling numerous colors of candles (a corresponding color may act as a substitute for a stone), and others stock candles with powdered gemstone in the wax. These candles are far less costly than the actual stone and just as useful. Dress your candle with matching herbal oils for increased effectiveness.

Sweet is the lore which nature brings,
Our meddling intellect mis-shapes
The beauteous form of things
We murder to dissect.
Enough of science and of art
Close up these barren leaves
Come forth and bring with you a heart
That watches and receives.
— William Wordsworth

DOLLS

By 1824, some ingenious German had found a way to make a doll say "ma-ma." By early 1900, Raggedy Ann was one of the most popular dolls sold. Dolls were important to Victorian atmosphere because they reflected the ideals of the day. For the most part, dolls were dressed just like little women or girls with all the frills and accoutrements. Children would use them to act out what they saw every day. The dolls helped teach role-modeling and assissted in bringing the young person "properly" into adulthood.

We are able to use homemade dolls to adorn our altar with images of the Divine. God/dess dolls can be created out of corn husks, cloth or lacy hankies, then decorated and anointed to adorn the sacred space of any season.

The Corn Husk Dolls

Often seen commercially as "kitchen witches" or knick-knacks, you can easily make these yourself. First, you will need to gather corn husks, trimming off the butt end and getting rid of the very coarse outer ones. Natural husks are creamy in color, so they are easy to dye by putting them in water tinted with food coloring. Other items needed for your creation include: glycerine (to soften the husks), thread, small balls of Styrofoam, and pipe cleaners.

Begin by soaking the corn husks until pliable in warm water and glycerine. (One quart of water to two teaspoons glycerine is a good ratio). Put them on an absorbent towel. Fold part of the towel over them so that they remain damp while you work with them.

To create the head for a doll that will be 6 inches tall when finished, take 4 inches of pipe cleaner and a Styrofoam ball that measures about 3/4 inches in diameter and connect the two. Next, take two pieces of husk and cross them over the top of the Styrofoam ball (the head). Wrap the corn husks around the ball and secure them with some thread, tying them off at the bottom. Trim off the excess at the neck (or bottom of the ball).

Another 4 inch piece of pipe cleaner may be employed for the arms. First cover your pipe cleaner tightly with a piece of husk equal in length and about 1 inch wide. Tie this about 1/4 inch from each end to make a wrist. To create the puffed sleeves, take another piece of husk 3 inches wide and 3 inches long. Attach this husk to the area just above the wrist, wrapping it tightly with thread. Turn the husk inside-out. This way, when you turn it right side in it will appear to be a puffed sleeve. Do this on both ends of the arm piece.

Now, put the two pieces (the arms and the head/torso) together and attach them about half-way from the head, wrapping the thread neatly around the adjoining parts, criss-crossing about 15 turns. Then tie it tightly.

For the upper body, use two pieces of husk, 2 x 2 inches in size. Tie it on just under the arms. When the pieces that form the upper body are folded up toward the head, they should extend 1-1/2 inches above the head. Take the front portion and pull the husk down so you can insert some padding (a little extra fabric or cotton) to create a bust line. Hold this tightly while you bring the back piece down. Gather both at the "waist" and tie securely.

Now, bend her arms up alongside the head. Take 5 or 6 wider strips of husk and overlap them at the waist, with wider end up towards the head. Tie these pieces as tightly as possible, then bring the layers down to make the skirt. From this point on, the way you decorate your Goddess figure is purely personal. Place a garland of daisies around her neck

Making a Corn Husk Doll

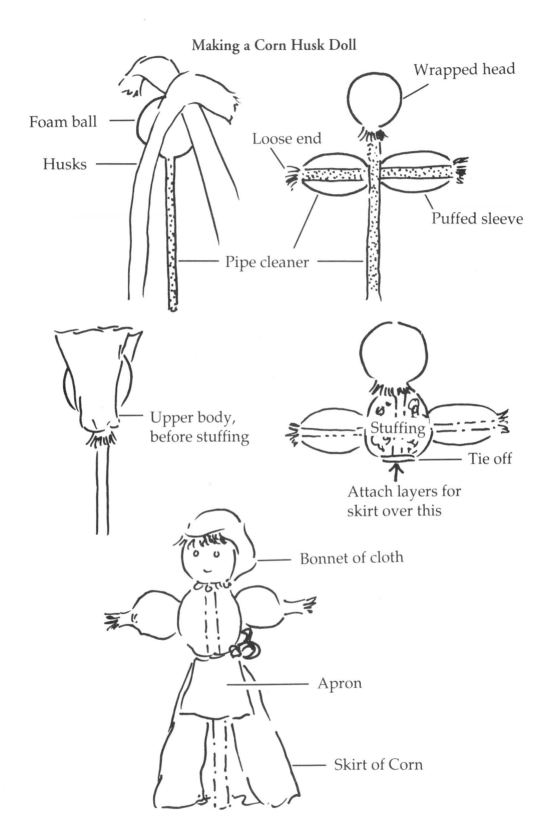

Foam ball

Husks

Pipe cleaner

Wrapped head

Loose end

Puffed sleeve

Upper body, before stuffing

Stuffing

Tie off

Attach layers for skirt over this

Bonnet of cloth

Apron

Skirt of Corn

in spring, or lay her gently in a pool of colorful leaves come fall. Sew her a ritual robe, or let her stand as she is for your autumn altar.

The Handkerchief Goddess

If you are like me and do not have the patience for the aforementioned procedure, the handkerchief God/dess is made in far fewer steps, with just a few twists and a little stuffing. Take the top of the hankie and fold it down, putting a little stuffing in the middle. Tie this off to make a head. The two sides are then gathered up and knotted for arms, with the bottom staying open for a skirt-like effect. Using this method also allows you to choose colors appropriate to your season. You can even decorate it with a few fruits or flowers to match the altar. In the fall, make her a garland of chestnuts and an apron from golden leaves. Come spring, crown her with early-blooming flowers!

Handkerchiefs were also a part of the language of love in the Victorian era. Dropping one invited a meeting and one over the shoulder meant, "follow me." Because of this, your handkerchief goddess might serve you well if placed on your altar for rituals or spells of union—especially during the month of February, which is traditionally the month when the emotion of love is venerated.

A special note here: if, when reading the rituals or spells you find any terminology which is unfamiliar to you, please refer to the Glossary.

Here is a spell to create a deeper emotional bond. It is meant to be done between a man and woman already romantically involved. Each person should begin by making an image of themselves. Follow the same procedure given for a handkerchief God/ess, but add a piece of personal jewelry or something else which represents you. The corn God/dess and the Poppet may be used in this ritual if you prefer.

With hair taken from each of you, fashion a long braid. Then, after creating sacred space and casting your circle, each of you should take a spot, your doll in hand, by the element that most represents you. If you are a gentle, healing sort, stand by the Western point of water. If your partner tends to be capricious, let them take a place near the altar designated for air.

Next, focus your attention on your desire to deepen your relationship. Visualize a reddish-purple light between you, drawing you together. Begin walking slowly towards each other until you and your images (dolls) meet in the center of the magical space.

Each of you should take an end of the hair braid and help secure it around both dolls. Make sure the dolls face each other. Tie the braid loosely. (Love should not be constraining.) Put the two dolls on your altar. Take a moment to voice your feelings to each other, then kiss gently. Before you close the ritual, you may want to just sit quietly together, enjoying the special connection of spirit this ritual offers. When you dismiss the sacred space, keep your dolls in a safe, clean place where they will come to no harm and can help protect that union.

Sacred Goddess, Mother Earth,
Thou from whose immortal bosom
Gods and men and beasts have birth,
Leaf and blade and bud and blossom
Breath thine influence most divine.
                    —Percy Bysshe Shelley

Poppets

Another popular kind of homemade doll is the poppet, a little stuffed figurine used largely in love magic. However, it is also used in symbolic magic for healing. For example, if you have a friend who has been plagued by colds, sew up a little figurine filled with herbs of healing and revitalization (eucalyptus and lemon are especially good for colds). In all good conscience, you should first ask your friend's permission to help, so that you can personalize the poppet to represent him/her. While you work on the figurine, you should visualize the sickness of your friend being poured into it, even as you stuff the herbs. Next, chant a small verse, something like, "With love you are stitched, with love you are made, all sickness I banish, instead health now inlaid. As a needle to thread, be this poppet to _____, so that (he/she) may rise joyfully out of their bed."

Depending on your viewpoint, you can now do one of two things with the poppet. One is to give it to the intended individual that they might carry their health with them. The second is to bury the poppet, thus burying the sickness. Either method is equally effective; the only difference is which one makes more sense to you. Additional information on the use of poppets, specifically in love magic, is available in *The Complete Book of Witchcraft* by Raymond Buckland.

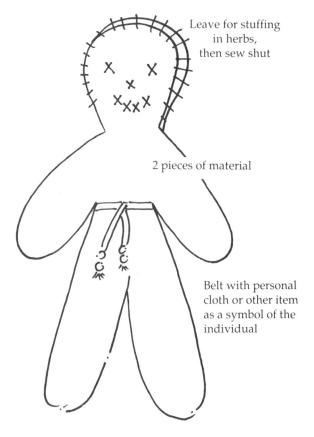

Leave for stuffing in herbs, then sew shut

2 pieces of material

Belt with personal cloth or other item as a symbol of the individual

FAN MAGIC

Since Queen Elizabeth I occupied the throne of England, the hand-held fan became an item of fashion, taking on many forms—from cloth, to wood, to feathers. By the time Queen Victoria ascended the throne, she made it quite clear that she disliked men carrying them anymore, but that for a lady the fan was an invaluable accessory. As time went on, an entire book was written on "fanology," including an intricate alphabet. This system was so complicated as to require a great deal of concentration. Even so, fans became an important silent tradition, often mysterious to all but the informed, practiced observer.

The messages conveyed through the fan ranged from the subtle to the sublime. For example, the time of a meeting was told by the number of sticks showing on the fan. A woman could chastise an imprudent guest by shutting her fan quickly and pointing their direction. Other communications included:

- Covering your left ear to request your secret be kept.
- Half opened fan to the lips to give permission to kiss.
- Drawing the fan across the eyes by way of apology.
- Twirling the fan in your left hand to warn of being watched.
- Dropping the fan in sign of friendship.
- Presentation of the shut fan to ask if love could be found here.

Today, we have electrical fans, but that does not lessen the beauty of hand-held ones, or their usefulness as symbols. They can be put in the Eastern part of your magic Circle (often known as the "Eastern Watchtower") to symbolize the element of air. Or, because of its long association with romance, the fan might be employed as a focus for love spells.

Here's an example of a love spell that uses a fan. Write your wish for a romantic partner on the right hand side of the fan. Next, light a red candle to symbolize tender love. Hold the open fan sideways so that the rounded edge is to your left. As you focus your desire on the fan, slowly begin to close it up from the bottom edge, thus slowly bringing your written wish physically and symbolically closer to you. When the fan is closed, hold it

for a moment longer, continuing to think about the attributes of an ideal mate, then place the fan in a special place, perhaps even under your pillow. Allow the candle to burn out naturally, trusting that the energy of your work will find the intended person. (As a safety precaution, never leave a burning candle unattended.)

The closed fan can be operated like a wand to elegantly scribe the magical Circle. This is especially handy in late summer, when it can later be utilized simply to keep cool! A fan may also be used in place of a feather to gently move incense around the participants of a circle instead of the sometimes uncomfortable application of a sparking smudge stick (a cluster of dried cedar and sage bound together and often burned to disburse negative energy before magical workings).

The silent language of fans could be learned by people who are members of magical orders, people who value secrecy in their tradition. They will find this to be a splendid form of communication. They would not have to rely on the traditional language of fans, but could instead create one of their own more suitable to their rituals and teachings. If a group were to employ such a method, I would highly suggest making the fan an intricate part of rituals, and giving it a special place of honor for seasonal fans on their altar. However you decide to use a fan, once it is personalized you should consider placing an identifying mark on it and then keep it in a special place, as you would any magical tool. You can also hang feathers, beads, crystals and other objects off the end of it (as you might on a wand or staff) to create an instrument which is both useful and beautiful for solitary and group workings.

FIREWOOD

The Moon showeth her power most evidently in those bodies which have neither sense nor lively breath; for carpenters reject the timber of trees fallen in the full-moon, as being soft and tender . . .

— Plutarch

Firewood, piled neatly at the back door, was not a luxury to the Victorian home but a necessity for cooking and warmth. Most schools of thought held that it should be cut at the waning moon, being most durable when cut in winter.

Wood may be used as a component in modern magic for any spells relating to durability, strength and security. For example, if you feel your finances are on shaky ground, you may want to try placing a silver coin inside a cedar box as a way of symbolically safeguarding your monetary well-being. Sympathetic magic such as this will not make you rich, that is not the intention. Instead, this is a magical way to help meet your needs when times are rough. As with any magic of this nature, don't expect your spell to be effective if you are not making an honest effort on the mundane level to solve your problems too!

Fire is also an excellent focus for scrying and vision quests. To scry or meditate by fire-light, begin by gathering a small stack of fallen, dried wood and shavings, as you would for any fire. If possible, try to light the fire using paper instead of lighter fluid. The chemicals are not conducive to good results on a spiritual level. Also, make sure you have a trench around your fire for safety reasons.

Once the wood is burning fairly evenly, get as comfortable as possible. If you are using the fire to scry, I suggest having a container of sandalwood, nutmeg, mugwort, or lemongrass (for psychic awareness) to toss on the flames. These types of herbs help keep bugs away and are conducive to divination. Sometimes the smoke actually becomes the conduit for your forecast, the images being formed in the air instead of by the flames themselves.

Next, take a few moments to calm your mind and focus on the question at hand. If you are simply meditating, allow your eyes to watch the flame, somewhat distractedly, and concentrate on breathing in a slow, all-connected manner. Watch the fire dance. If you are relaxed enough, you may actually see the fire elementals known as Salamanders which form the flames. Listen to the breathing of the wood as it crackles and feel its warm energy covering your skin. If you are focusing on a question, now is the time to add your herbs to the fire. If not, just close your eyes and continue to sense the fire through smell, hearing and even tasting the fire in the air. You will find this is a very soothing way to meditate. Sometimes you will fall asleep, which is why I issued the caution that you build a trench around your fire.

Finally, if scrying, you may see images form in the flames, or in the sparks and smoke. It may only be nuances, or a symbolic representation of an answer to your question. If you are unsure of what the results mean, write them down and sleep on them. Eventually their significance will be revealed.

Wood is good for more than just being fuel for the fire. In magic circles, ritual tools are often made out of wood (preferably made from fallen timber instead of harvested), especially by people who have strong attachments to the natural world. The type of wood used very often has to do with personal preference and traditional correlations. Woodruff is for joy, willow is for protection and magical wands, and pine is often employed for cleansing.

FRIENDSHIP CLOTHS

There was a marvelous tradition born from the working of quilts during the Victorian days. Some quilts were made from bits of cloth saved carefully from the family members' clothing to mark special occasions. Others, called Friendship cloths, were made by collecting a square of silk, which was painted or embroidered with a flower or other ornamentation, then signed by close friends. As enough squares were collected, they were hand stitched tenderly together into a lap blanket or quilt to keep both the body and heart warm for years to come.

For the solitary practitioner, a Friendship cloth would indeed have to be collected from friends. While still small, this cloth could be used as a special covering for prized magical tools or as a central part of the altar. For the coven, however, I see a beautiful way to literally sew the members together into a visual harmony.

As new members are initiated into the order, they would be required to bring their square to add to the cloth, which could then be the cover for the altar or a vestment for the Priest/ess at all gatherings. Their pieces could be embroidered or painted with a personal rune or message, and sewn into the cloth after initiation. If anyone ever leaves the group, the square remains behind as a permanent record, a living history if you will, for the coven.

For a group that adopts this type of idea, I would suggest creating a special ritual for connecting the pieces together. This ritual should be linked to the times when new members join. This way the members are not only united in word and deed, but symbolically as well. The altar cloth or vestment could be presented to each Priest/ess of the order each time a member is dedicated. In this manner it would act as a token of their position, to be a visual reminder of the people who's spiritual welfare and guidance are trusted to them.

Show thy heart's secret to an ancient Power
Who hath forsaken old and sacred thrones
For prophecies of thee, and for the sake
Of loveliness new-born.

—John Keats

GIFT BASKETS

At the turn of the century, neighbors were not just people, but a very important part of daily life. It was not uncommon for one neighbor, when in need, to find a heaping basket of goodies on their doorstep after church. The women of an area usually knew who might need a little extra, and often got together to prepare the baskets, usually beginning in November and continuing until Spring granted fruitfulness again.

Such openness and consideration is something we have lost in our society, and something which I feel can be reclaimed by those of spiritual callings. If you work in a coven, make it your responsibility to know who has needs, and help see that those needs are met, if only on the level of emotional support. If you are a solitary, use your talents and sensitivity to enrich the lives of those around you.

For instance, say someone is having trouble sleeping. Make a little basket filled with a dream pillow, some valarian or catnip tea, a crystal charged with restful energy (leave it out under a new moon), a tape with soft music, or other items you think may help. Bundle it up in a wicker basket lined with a pretty linen napkin and deliver it yourself or anonymously. The gesture will be appreciated greatly, believe me.

The wonderful things about these gift baskets is the fact that they combine practicality, magic, and a wonderful gesture. If we give of what we have to those in need, sharing of Earth's bounty, we will never want.

GLOVES

A hand displayed with many a little art . . . .
— Alfred, Lord Tennyson

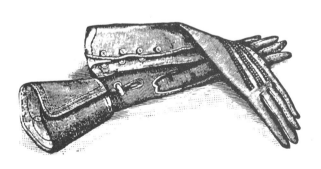

The symbolism of the glove far predates their favor in the Victorian era. Originally the glove was used in the shield for protection, in solemn pledges of loyalty, as a challenge, and sometimes even as a symbol of welcoming. Sir Walter Scott once said that "the glove is a symbol of faith." Because of this, it has long been associated with affairs of royalty and chivalry.

During Victorian times, short gloves were considered day wear, long ones were worn at night, and soiled gloves were completely distasteful. The creation of snap gloves in the 1890s lead to many a young girl being chastised for disrupting church services. Grande Dames and young women alike would not appear in polite company without gloves. Therefore they also carry a tone of propriety.

Some of these traditions may have actually been an extension of the medieval custom of favor-giving. A medieval damsel would often give her scarf or glove as a favor to a man, to protect him in battle. Swearing by the glove was a custom in conversation then, much as someone today might swear by "all that is holy." A person's gloves might be removed from them as a sign of degradation or disapproval by a superior. Also, a personal glove was sometimes sent as a sign of consent to a particular proposal. Many of these traditions were popular until about 1925.

For modern magic, I suggest the glove be used for a focus in matters of protection, love, honor, and propriety. To protect someone, first make a poppet in her/her name. Then place a blessed, clean white glove around the poppet and leave it where it will be undisturbed. For affairs of love, put a rose on a glove in the center of your altar, as if you are extending a hand full of affection. If you feel someone has wrongfully accused you, or spoken ill behind your back, you might drop a glove in the center of your circle and ask the fates to "take it up," allowing the negative energy to be returned to the sender.

HANDCRAFTS

Many types of handcrafts were not only a pastime for the Victorians but also a means of income. Arts were learned from parents and grandparents until certain techniques and skills could be recognized as belonging to a specific household. These techniques, such as forging, glass blowing, and rug looms, required years of patient training by deft hands to achieve a product worthy for sale in the eyes of the self-sufficient, quality-minded American.

For sympathetic magic, any of the symbols for handcrafts can be used to create powerful visualizations that are helpful when you are working for positive changes, inspiration, and patience in your life. Good examples of this would be to see yourself forging a piece of metal with the word "integrity" on it to shape that quality into your life, or to envision yourself at a potter's wheel making a vessel named "persistence."

On another level, items made by hand are much nicer for magical use. This is not to say the machine made athame you may own is not as effective as a handmade one, it is just different. There is a special energy that tools take on when created by a hand that is magically guided and proficient in its craft. It is even more magical if you are able to make things yourself. Many people today are relearning these somewhat "lost" arts in an effort to reclaim the history and knowledge that has been misplaced by technology.

Some of us do not have the knowledge or time to forge a knife, so, for assistance, we can turn to the local artisans who have a sensitivity to psychic energy. If they cannot teach you how to devise your tool from beginning to end, they may be able to make one to your specifications. Check the bulletin boards at your local health food shops, cooperatives, and bookstores. Check the advertisements in Pagan/Wiccan/New Age newsletters, and ask other people in your magical community if they can recommend someone for whatever goods you seek. If you do not have anyone nearby to consult, send off a few letters of inquiry to publishing houses or groups outside your area who may be able to get you more information and hopefully help you network with some other people closer to home.

HATS

Hats of all shapes and sizes were a long-lasting aspect of the Victorian age. A person simply did not go out in public without appropriate head wear. To the modern Witch or Pagan, the most important hat of this time is that of the stage magician. During a magic show, people in Victorian times allowed themselves to view what was considered miraculous and mystical, putting aside their toils for a few moments. Because of this, I suggest using the hat as a magical focus for seemingly impossible situations. When circumstances are almost overwhelming, write down everything that burdens you and place this paper within a hat. Sprinkle lady's mantle and sage (for positive transformation and strength) over the paper, leaving it in the light of a waning moon to help ease the difficulties and bring some rest. The visualization of "pulling a rabbit out of the hat," and substituting whatever you need in place of the rabbit, may be equally useful.

You can use hats in rituals for sanctuary and any magics dealing with protection, shelter or security. Hats may also be employed in any spell where you wish to make a habit or negative feeling "disappear." For instance, you could place on your altar an item symbolizing the feeling or habit. Then, during your ritual cover it with a hat. This action on your part is a outward indication that you are ready to release yourself from this difficulty, and leave it behind you. Sometimes it works to tie a cord around the symbol, hide it under the hat, and then cut it. This can give you the inner strength to cut that fixation out of yourself.

If possible, have someone else take the hat off after the ritual and dispose of the item so that you personally do not see it again. If circumstances do not allow for this, look away from the item and cover it with a cloth before ritually burying or burning it. This way, for you, the symbol of your problem has literally disappeared.

KNOTS

Good day Mr. Elder, here I bring my fever,
I tie it to you and go on my way.

— Heraklas

The history of knots and knot magic is far older than the Victorian era. The word itself comes from a Greek term meaning spell or charm. The use of knots or weavings in magic is apparent in many cultures and various traditions. Some people believe that certain aspects of the rosary and abacus may have had their beginnings in knots.

The Victorians were no less interested in this device. A rope with twenty-one knots would be hung under the eves of a house to restrict rain. Or, should some moisture be needed, one of the knots would be loosed. Nine slip knots would be placed in a string for luck and protection.

Another common folk remedy was to take a rope to the person with ills and speak this while tying a knot, "I do not bind thee, knot, but _____ (fill in appropriate ailment)." These types of cures and unique magical correspondences are seen in books such as *Black's Folk Medicine* from the turn of the century.

This tradition has carried over into modern magic, with all manner of string and knot spells used today. To illustrate: garlands of red flowers are often wrapped around the arms of a couple who are being hand-fasted (married) as an emblem of the beauty of their new oneness, and their healthy passion. On a more personal level, if there is a negative feeling you have in your life, one way to help release it is to take some string and loosely bind a dark feather to a tree. Allow the wind to eventually free it, moving it away from you. By these two examples we see that the original symbolism of binding, connecting, releasing, gathering, safety, and fortune utilized by our forefathers has changed little—except in instances where color, herbal or other symbolisms are added to intensify the energy.

PICNICS

Our blankets spread on a mushroom's head
while the laughing stars do shine . . .
— Louisa Twamley

During the Victorian era, the picnic almost became a national institution. Victorians loved to socialize, spend time in the great outdoors, and eat good food. They would get their wicker baskets and stuff them full of chicken, fresh bread, pies and an assortment of store-bought luxuries, and—at the slightest excuse—head for the country. Here the children could play hide and seek, tag, and run merrily through the fields while adults enjoyed light-hearted conversations under a sunny sky. The countryside, dotted with bluebells, briar roses and lavender brought a sweet scent to the air, perfect for daydreaming or visiting with friends.

Since our world today is so busy, we have in some instances lost sight of the simple pleasures, such as a country picnic. Not only do picnics have great aesthetic value, but they are good for our spirits as well. Gandhi once said that, "there is more to life than increasing its speed." Picnics represent a perfect opportunity to slow down for a few moments and enjoy the Earth. Whether we go alone or with some cherished friends, this is an excellent time to do grounding work, focus on our connection to Mother Earth, and re-establish the priority of inner health for ourselves and each other.

Nature provides us with vast amounts of healthy visualization and meditation material from the well-rooted oak, the gentle healing of the stream, or the freedom of a bird in flight. Lie on the ground, or sit against a tree and breathe deeply of life. Take time for a well-deserved outing and return refreshed. Sample meditations/visualizations which can be used during your outings can be found in Chapter Nine.

SWORD CANES

There is no use for life and death, save to enjoy the interval.
— G. Santayana

The walking stick has long been a part of men's apparel, being both functional and decorative. At the turn of the century, the most popular type of walking stick was a sword cane. This was a cane of hardened bamboo with a secret compartment for everything from a stiletto to a full rapier. These blades were definitely a throw back to the time of dueling, honor, and chivalry. They were an effective means of self-defense. As an interesting aside, I owned one which was found hidden in the wall of a Victorian home here in Buffalo. Apparently it had been used in self-defense and then concealed by the owner. The top was made from hardened rosin and decorated with brass. An Italian stiletto was hidden neatly within the cane portion.

If you are fortunate enough to find a sword cane, please check the laws in your state, as in some cases it may be illegal for all but the licensed collector to possess one. If permissible, the sword cane makes the perfect combination of a wand and athame. For those who practice ceremonial magic, the sword cane has the added benefit of being "safe" in that it has its own light-weight, readily available sheath.

Because sword canes were used for personal security, they may be used as a focus for protective magic. Stand in the center of your sacred space and begin to visualize the white light surrounding you, as shown in Appendix B. Then take your cane and allow the light to move through it in your mind's eye while scribing a circle around, above and below yourself. It's exactly like drawing on paper, only using your imagination and the sword cane as your pencil in the air!

TEAS

In happy homes where tea is brewed at five o'clock,
or where, indeed, it is always on tap, life is a success.
— Mrs. John Sherwood,
From *Manners and Social Usage*, 1884

Even after the Boston Tea Party, the American love for tea as a social contrivance certainly did not lessen. Having a tea in the greenhouse, inviting friends for tea and sweet cakes, came to mean a moment to sit and enjoy idle conversation.

Entire books were dedicated to the proper manners for tea. It was felt that one should not apply too much cream or mounds of sugar lest the taste be hampered. Tea was to always be of a good quality, and poured out properly among guests. No matter what the means of service, however, tea appeared at almost all social functions. Partly, this had to do with the relaxing nature of tea itself, but even more important was the almost ritualistic setting aside of time just for peacefulness.

Tea was usually placed on a freshly laundered cloth adorned with china, napkins, a lemon dish, the creamer, the sugar bowl, triangular pieces of toast, wafer thin cucumber sandwiches, sweet cakes, servers, and usually an array of seasonal flowers. Depending on where the tea was held, such as the garden or veranda, the cloth and ornaments would be changed to suit the ambiance of the setting.

Teas were so much a part of the Victorian way that signs saying "out to tea" were common at mercantiles during lunch hour. There were even specially designed mustache tea cups so hostesses could be assured that their male guests would not have damp mustaches while they conversed. Tea time also became the ideal opportunity for young men and women to meet unchaperoned, during an innocent hour of the day, and enjoy each other's company.

During the early 1900s, tea dances became the rage. People were frolicking to the music that was commonly played at noon-time tea. The daring nature of some of these dances caused fifteen women to be "sacked" from the prim and proper "Ladies Home

Journal" for doing the Turkey Trot, a risque dance that allowed the partners to be in close proximity to each other.

Some of this sentiment toward tea has continued to this day. I remember as a child my elderly neighbor introducing me to tea. While we sipped the hot, lightly sweetened liquid, she also managed to sneak in conversation on proper table manners! In my own home we continue to drink tea when we are weary or sick, or after a long tense day. We also offer it to guests. By so doing, we can add a little spark of magic to that moment. Some of my personal favorite tea blends are:

- **For colds and sore throat:** 1/2 teaspoon orange rind, 1/4 teaspoon lemon rind, a touch of cinnamon, 3 to 4 eucalyptus leaves, 1 teaspoon honey.

- **For pure enjoyment:** 1/4 teaspoon cinnamon, 1 slice of orange squeezed, 1/4 teaspoonginger, 1 teaspoon chamomile.

- **For children's tummy aches:** 1 teaspoon peppermint, 1 teaspoon chamomile, 1/2 teaspoon catnip, touch of honey.

- **Before rituals:** Make a light tea of cloves for kinship, apple for wisdom, and coffee for insight.

- **To simulate the mind, bring money or courage:** plain black tea.

- **For flu:** 1/4 teaspoon cinnamon, 1/4 teaspoon basil, 1/2 teaspoon catnip, 1/4 teaspoon goldenseal, 1/2 teaspoon mint.

❧ **Sleep (to aid):** 1/4 teaspoon each valerian root, red clover, hops and anise.

❧ **Protection:** 1/4 teaspoon each angelica, basil, fennel, rosemary and/or any other herbs which are considered "spicy."

❧ **Before divination (to increase awareness):** 1/2 teaspoon black tea, 1/4 teaspoon cinnamon, 1/4 teaspoon cloves.

Because of its long-standing associations, tea may also be brought to your altar, used as a spell component and added to incense mixes which you prepare. Its symbolism is specifically good for magic regarding social occasions, communication, rest, success or harmony in your home.

THE TEA CEREMONY

Humanity has met in a teacup.
—Okakura Kakuzo

To the Western mind, the Japanese tea ceremony takes great patience, self control, and discipline to master, yet it is one of great beauty. Underneath the drama, unfolded through the implements, the tea, the flowers and the paintings, is something of an ancient Buddhist ritual. Here the Tea Master becomes a kind of priest conducting a sacrament, where each motion of the ceremony reflects a law of the universe. It is interesting to note that the Japanese tea rooms during the Victorian era had no colors or sounds to distract the weary traveler from enjoying the "art" before them.

It is said that a proper tea for the Victorian lady, (especially the "High Teas" of English renown), would be one presented in the most perfect, polite, graceful, and charming manner possible. This has partially to do with the modes and manners of the era, but I also feel a bit of this comes from the Victorian fascination with Eastern culture. While the Victorian woman may not be performing an age-old rite, the success of her teas were no less important, and no less of an art.

By combining the Eastern and Western ideals regarding tea, it occurred to me that something like a Victorian Tea Ritual would be a wonderful way to renew or refresh kinship, especially for people just being reunited after a long period apart.

For this ritual, I suggest that you make your kitchen or dining room table into the "altar" space (a round table is especially nice), spreading a cloth over it that you reserve for very special occasions. Set out matching cups and decorate the table in a manner befitting the occasion with fresh flower buds, personally prepared incense, gourmet tea, and your companions' favorite homemade snack. You should note that while this ritual is rather intimate, it can easily be performed with large groups, if table space allows.

Light one pink candle (the color of love and friendship) for *each* person participating in the ritual. Put them on the table near each person's place setting. Put another candle near the center of the table. This candle (which signifies your fellowship), remains unlit. Once everyone is gathered, join hands. The person who is host/ess should be prepared to create the sacred space in a way that will be meaningful to the people participating. The host/ess should also pour out the tea once the Circle is cast, the four guardians are called, and everyone is seated. I caution you not to fill the cups much further than half full. Nothing disrupts a moment like this more than hot tea accidentally spilled on someone's lap! To avoid this, prepare the tea a little ahead of time so it will be comfortable to drink.

To show their acceptance of the hospitality offered through the tea, each person should drink fully of his/her cup. In certain cultures not to do so is considered an insult or challenge to the friendship. At this point all of the people at the table should take a turn expressing how they feel, and what this occasion means to them. When everyone is finished, all in unison take their candles to the central one, lighting it as they chant thrice together, "Unity, devotion and trust, God/dess, bring them among us."

After this, place the candles back in their respective places and enjoy some long-awaited comradery while munching on your snacks and having more tea. When the time comes to close, everyone should embrace, as the host/ess dismisses the sacred space. Keep those hugs close to your heart as you go, knowing you have kindled even stronger bonds in the spirit of perfect love.

❧

There are few hours in life more agreeable than the hour dedicated to the ceremony known as afternoon tea.
— Henry James

❧

"TRAMPS" IN THE WOODS

*She must speak to you through your heart. The woods and fields
must melt into your mind, dissolved by your love for them.*
—John Burroughs

The Victorian mind believed deeply that it was better to gratify the eye and the soul than the appetite. Since to their thinking nature was God-written poetry, what better place to go for contemplative "tramps" than the woods? Very often the Victorian lady would go on her spring excursion to check the progress of wild flowers, only to be distracted by intricate ivy growing on a wall, and completely forget about the book in her apron pocket, or the time for that matter.

In the summer, the senses are overwhelmed by bees, flowers in full bloom, and song birds, celebrating the rays of sunlight warming their nests. Come autumn the air will slowly change to harvest-time scents, rolling from the winds through every glen. No matter what the season, Victorian people enjoyed it, taking every opportunity to walk and experience each sight and sound that casually floated their way.

I feel we could learn much from them in this matter. Unlike the 20th century mindset, which mistakes leisure for laziness, our ancestors knew the value of bringing modest delights to each day. Since happiness is one of the most powerful magics I know, my suggestion is to try and set aside one day out of every season to get out into a natural setting. You may want to combine this time with that of your traditionally observed Rites (see also Chapter Two: The Wheel of the Year) so you can go to your magical space already attuned to the subtle changes in the music of Earth. Whether you go and catch guppies in a nearby stream, sing to the trees, take a walk, or just sit, take time to enjoy and reacquaint yourself with the nontechnical world. There is great peace to be found there.

UMBRELLAS

One of the most popular accessories of this time was a parasol or umbrella. Some clever inventors even created ways to place them in walking sticks and have them whistle when opened. In 1870 Queen Victoria spent 52 pounds on umbrellas, one of which was lined with chain maille for protection!

Bedecked with ribbons and lace, handles of wood, ivory, bone and precious stones, the parasol became so much a part of life that by 1880 the first superstitions regarding umbrellas were developing. In the 1890s U. S. Calvary men in Maine carried cream-colored parasols as part of their kit. Even the British army allowed their officers to have them in Africa and Asia, to help prevent sun stroke.

As was the case with the fan, a representative language developed for the umbrella which was the aid to many romantic causes. To get a date, many young men would ask to carry a lady's umbrella. To decisively snap open an umbrella was a show of disapproval in the topic of conversation, or a way to admonish a suitor who was being too forward. To retire behind the umbrella was to ask your suitor to leave or stop being so flirtatious.

Red umbrellas were carried in Germany to announce weddings and at the turn of the century poems were appearing with parasols scattered merrily through them. Here is one attributed to many people, including the Bishop of London:

The rain, it raineth every day,
On the just and unjust fella,
But chiefly on the just because,
The unjust have the just's umbrella!

Today, the umbrella may be used as a focus for love and communication spells. One such spell is for both. For this enchantment, obtain some water-soluable markers. Using the markers, write on the umbrella the name of the person with whom you hope to open the lines of romantic discourse. Let this dry, then close the umbrella and prepare your magical space. Have a little cache of rosemary, lavender, marjoram, rose and basil on your altar. These herbs are specifically for inspiring love and openness.

Sit down in your circle and think about this individual and your feelings toward him/her. Allow yourself to relax and be somewhat impartial. Visualize your feelings for him/her as a purplish-red light pouring from your hand to the umbrella before you. Then sprinkle the herbs over it saying:

"S/he loves me, s/he loves me not, the magic spell which I have wrought,
will open doors and light the way, I pray to hear from you in _____ days."

After saying this, open the umbrella. Opening the umbrella is a symbol of opening the lines of conversation between the two of you.

Please remember with spells of this nature that you are dealing with another human being. Your magic is not meant to manipulate them into caring about you, but instead simply to open the doors for opportunity. From there, the rest is up to you and nature!

The umbrella is probably the most powerful tool for weather magic. As the old saying goes, carry an umbrella and it won't rain. For a ritual in which you want to bring rain, try using an upside down, open umbrella as the center of your sacred space. It will make a cup-like shape to receive the bounty of the sky. Also, I can think of no lovelier way to cast a spring circle than by using a closed parasol in place of a wand. If you are outdoors, umbrellas of different colors may be set open on appropriate points to represent the elements. Have one decorated especially for the spring altar (perhaps it can be made by the children of your group or home).

WEATHER VANES AND LIGHTNING RODS

From our earliest history, we humans have wanted to know which way the winds blow, whether it was to keep the smoke from the fire out of our faces, or to predict the weather. While the earliest weather vane appears in Greece in the first century, their popularity in the Victorian era is well worth noting.

Made from pine, zinc, iron, copper, bronze, and tin, weather vanes and lightning rods were often combined on the top of nearly every home. The craftsmen of these decorative attachments had to make the pointer of the vane (be it tail feathers or a piercing beak) large enough to catch the surface of the breeze until the pointer swung around to point into the wind.

Even though the popularity of the lightning rod occurred a little later than that of the weather vane, the two were part of a new spirit emerging in the United States, a belief that people could begin to take control, or at least be more aware of, what fate planned to hand them. This was especially true with the lightning rod because it was constructed solely to protect the home from fire by grounding the energy of a storm.

For the modern magician, the best application for the weather vane is to determine the direction of the winds. This can be useful when when working with a specific element as a part of your rituals or spells. We know that the East wind is typically one of refreshment, giving strength to body and mind. It is also the wind of new beginnings, so it is best used for magic concerning drastic change. The North wind is for cooling harsh feelings, for rest, and sometimes for blunt realizations. If you feel your mind somewhat addled, the brisk nature of this wind may be very helpful. The South wind, since it is associated with fire, is excellent for adding energy to almost any spell. The West winds are best employed for fertility, healing and cleansing due to their association with water (see Chapter One). My only caution in using winds as a focus for magic is that they are very changeable and almost whimsical in nature. Because of this, your results may reflect the personality of this element.

Weather vanes are frequently constructed in such a manner that they visually represent the eight major points on our magical calendar (the eight major directions). Others are made to look like cats, dogs, birds, and any other form which could represent your personal

Magical Holidays and Eight Directions

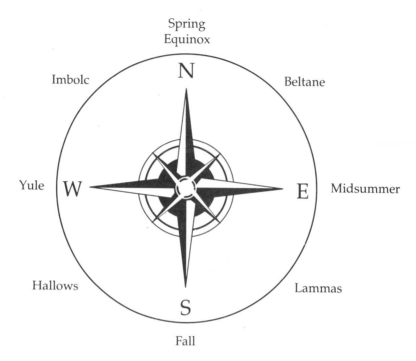

power animal or the guardian spirit for your home. For the person who enjoys working with wood or metal, patterns can be found in many instruction manuals, especially those manuals that pertain to country crafts or antique replication. You might find them at your local bookstore or library.

By obtaining a pattern, you could construct a weather vane which is specifically designed to aid your magical work. If you don't want to make one of your own, I suggest checking farm and antique shops in rural areas. If these stores don't carry weather vanes, the owners will likely know where to send you to find one.

The lightning rod is a good focal point for any type of protection magic (especially from the elements), for grounding visualizations, and for increased power. To use it magically, you might take an old lightning rod and have it cut down to use as a wand for directing magical energy. Another application would be to hold it to the ground while you meditate, allowing its natural conductive properties to draw negative energy away from you and into the soil. Because of the nature of this tool, however, prudence dictates that you do not use a lightning rod (even one of reduced size) outside during a storm; the results could be quite unpleasant.

From this chapter, you can see how many items and pastimes from our history, and indeed the world around us, can be used to bring more power, beauty and creativity to magic. But this is only the beginning. By learning to look at our environment with more inventive eyes, we can quickly find other ways that Victorian enchantments can be ours, starting with the holidays.

Oh, Earth! Thy face hath not the grace
That smiling Heaven did bless
When thou wert "good" and blushing stood
In thy young loveliness.
And, mother dear, the smile and tea
In thee are strangely met,
Thy joy and woe together flow
But ah! We love thee yet.

We bless thee now for gifts that thou
Hast freely on us shed,
For dews and showers and beauteous bowers
And blue skies overhead,
For man's perfume, and midday's bloom
And evening's hour of mirth,
For glorious night, for all things bright
We bless thee, Mother Earth!

    —Sara Jane Lippincott
     From *Invocation to Mother Earth*

CHAPTER THREE

Celebrating the Seasons: The Wheel of the Year

Thy voice is on the rolling air,
I hear thee where the waters run,
Thou standest in the rising sun,
And in the setting art thou fair.
—Alfred, Lord Tennyson

Holiday observances are a unique reflection of religion and mores. In Victorian households, most holiday celebrations centered around their children. The year began on January first, with people paying calls on close relatives to offer greetings and the special gifts prepared by children for their parents. Families might throw a snow party to relieve the quiet, long winter days.

February brought potluck suppers with friends, as a way of sharing what little bounty the home might have left. Valentine's Day was celebrated with great fancifulness and lavish romance. Lace cards, candies, and assorted trinkets were exchanged. Meanwhile, chickens began to lay eggs, as if to promise spring was just ahead.

Next came March, and with it a surge of cleaning. It was the month to warm up and prepare for the busy season of planting soon to come. April was the month for frolic and fun, marked on the first day with many a prank, and giggling children. As this toned down, and thoughts moved to preparing the land, May Day moved in with baskets of flowers mysteriously left on doorsteps as a gift from Spring, and the sound of bells tied on the children's legs to protect them from the faerie folk (Faeries are suspected to be very active at such times). A May Queen would be chosen and little sweets would be available in almost every home.

Easter was a holiday only to be surpassed in splendor by Christmas. Because of its strong association with fertility and birth, eggs were the center of festivities. There were egg hunts, egg jewelry, and egg-shaped boxes. Everyone put on their new clothes. Even the drapery of the house was changed to reflect the lighter moods and warm weather.

Spring and summer were the times of simple pleasures and light breezes. Days were filled with blossoms of all sorts, ice cream socials, and demure dances. Long strolls in the park with a favored friend or pet, daydreaming on swingsets, delicious teas and other quiet

41

activities were enjoyed to their fullest right up until the end of fall, when cold weather once again arrived at the doorstep.

In August and September, the country fair would come to town and women everywhere would begin their canning. Children whose families did not need them at home would return to school. In those days, education still took a back seat to necessity. October saw an end to the garden with many vegetable soups, stews, and yet more canning.

All Saints Day (November first) marked the beginning of winter and time to don dark colors once again. This was a day to remember the dead and bring out the warmer outer wear for the snows to come. Come November the family would have to finish curing their meats, and the smell of spices and mincemeat were heavy in the air.

Finally, the year ended at Christmas, with sprigs of holly and fir decorated with candy for the children. Pastries were a favorite tradition and Father Christmas slowly took over as the giver of gifts from the infant Jesus.

People in the Victorian era enjoyed celebrating the year by marking the holidays and the months in special ways. In 1866, a floral calendar came out giving each month a special plant or flower to commemorate it as follows:

January — Snowdrop
February — Primrose
March — Violet
April — Daisy
May — Hawthorn
June — Honeysuckle
July — Water Lily
August — Poppy
September — Morning Glory
October — Hop
November — Chrysanthemum
December — Holly

In marking our magical calendar, it is interesting to note that many of the herbs and plants recommended for our celebrations still follow this calendar. Also, it is good to remember that Christian holidays were originally placed near their Pagan counterparts to encourage participation (and hopefulyl conversion) by the common folk. That is why there are many overlapping symbols and holidays such as the egg, May Day and the Yule Log.

THE MAGICAL CALENDAR

Calendar books of all sorts, embellished with floral paintings and dreamy landscapes, were very popular in the Victorian home. The magical calendar is a little different, but it is filled with just as much beauty and warmth.

The magical calendar is a circle with no real beginning or end, distinguished not so much by dates as by the rhythm of the Earth as it moves through the heavens. Each tradition has different ways of greeting the seasons. Most commonly, though, Sabbats are the mid-points of the wheel and usually celebrated at night. Equinoxes and Solstices should be enjoyed by day to mark the progress of the sun as it dances through the sky. As Milton said, "Now the bright morning star, day's harbinger, comes dancing from the East . . ."

The ritual material provided in this book acts a little like the black lines in a coloring book. It is only a sketch to which you must bring color, feeling and life. I recommend that before each observance, you prepare yourself properly in body, mind and spirit. You may wish to take an herb bath (with magically prepared soap) meditate, and then create your sacred space. The area you use should be clean and free of clutter or anything which may distract you from the matter at hand. Your ritual space and frame of mind need to reflect the ideal behind the magical Circle itself. This does not mean being stoic or pristine, but I do believe the way we approach our magic can affect the outcome tremendously.

The information given in this chapter is meant to augment your celebrations, bringing the flavor of Victorianism with scents, decorations, and tasty treats. Recipes for the cakes and wines, anointing oils, ritual bath soaps, and incense can be found in Chapter Six.

If you do not wish to make the components for your rituals, I suggest checking New Age shops, crystal stores, cooperatives, health food shops, and herbal outlets for some of your supplies. Also, ask members of your community where they purchase various items so that you know where to find quality goods and prices.

I also suggest you refer to Llewellyn's annual *Astrological Calendar, The Moon Sign Book, The Sun Sign Book,* and *The Magical Almanac* for the exact dates and times for each celebration. These celebration times change slightly with each passing year.

By all means, consider these written rites as guidelines only. Be creative with your workings. If you feel a different herb, decoration, food, or invocation should be included in the ritual, do so! Ritual should express your individual or group vision so that the harvest of your efforts is beautiful magic in its most powerful, yet gentle movements.

Spring Equinox—March 21st

VERNAL

> *Come fill this cup and in the fire of Spring,*
> *the winter garment of repentance fling . . .*
> —Edward Fitzgerald

We begin our year with the turning of the wheel towards the sun. This is a time when light triumphs over darkness, a season for new beginnings and freedom from bondage. It is said that now the Lord of the Sun reaches a gentle hand to the Maiden Moon. As the bouquet of spring rains fill the air, the two begin to waltz together. As they move over the land, the first spring flowers break through the Earth and bloom beneath their feet. Wherever they travel, hopelessness becomes delight and dark clouds are hurled away to bring glorious warmth. Join in their happiness as the Earth is reborn with the dawn!

Invocation

> *In place beyond all space and time*
> *Tis to thee we come to find,*
> *To bless the work from out our hands*
> *And loose the ties that bind.*
>
> *Within this circle drawn round*
> *Your power now unfolds,*
> *As wondrous secrets ever young*
> *Bequeathed from times of old.*
>
> *Round fires burning towards the moon*
> *With pentacle and candles bright,*
> *Are we in working magics here*
> *As dancers in the night.*
>
> *To join our voice with ageless chants*
> *Of cup and sword, day and dark,*
> *The Gods preserve the Craft as we*
> *Merry Meet and Merry Part.*

Prayer

> *Spring air,*
> *Rise with loving rains,*
> *Greet the dawn o'er hill and plains,*
> *Bring your song, pray come again.*
> *Touch the dews with scents of myrrh,*
> *Wings of peace in our hearts stir,*
> *N'er cease your praise of her.*

Activities

A good time to exchange eggs as an emblem of life and fertility. The druids often dyed eggs red in honor of the sun, and various cultures represent the Divine as a great bird. To this day, the egg is often given as an amulet of prosperity, fertility, protection. With it comes the promise of life. Because of the strong symbolism of new beginnings that comes with spring, bless your seeds before planting. Liberate yourself from an old habit or idea and spend time outside enjoying the awakening world.

Tools and Ritual Components

Incense — A base of sandalwood with iris, dogwood bark, mint and cinquefoil makes a wonderful incense which will charge your space with prosperity and protection.

Ritual Soap — Violet, for simplicity, serenity, and peace. Violets were originally the gift of the Nymphs.

Anointing Oil — Jasmine, for manifestation.

Ritual Cup — Jasmine tea or wine punch.

Altar Decorations — Honeysuckle, dogwood, daffodils, bulbs, acorns, seeds, tansy, violet and any early blooming flowers. Amber may be used on the altar to bring success and good fortune to the year, and coral can be added as a water stone to thank the sky for spring rains.

Clothing — Wear a daisy chain necklace to commemorate the spring. Light robes and pastel colors are best for the season.

Cakes — Mint tea cakes decorated with a violet petal make a tasty treat for your gathering.

And the Spring arose on the garden fair,
Like the spirit of love felt everywhere
And each flower and herb on Earth's dark breast
Rose from the dreams of its wintry rest.
The snowdrop and then the violet
Arose from the ground with warm rain wet
And their breath was mixed with sweet odour sent
From the turf, like the voice and the instrument.
— Percy Bysshe Shelley

Beltane—May 1st

Then let us welcome lovely spring,
And still the flowery tribute bring,
And still to thee our carol sing, O lovely May!
— Mrs. Hemans, 1793–1835

Now is the time of the sacred marriage, fire festivals, Maypoles, and the dance of life. This is when we celebrate the return of life and fertility to the world. The sap in the trees has started to run, and with it new energy is brought to our magic. In days of old, May dew was believed to beautify the skin. And the smoke of a Beltane fire brought protection, especially to animals.

Invocation

> *Feathered winds come dance with me*
> *Lift me from the ground.*
> *Join my waltz, my spirit, freed*
> *As we're upward bound.*
>
> *Tongues of flame come jump with me*
> *Ye purifying fires,*
> *Join my joy, my playful glee*
> *As we move yet higher.*
>
> *Tears from seas, come sing with me*
> *Roll from out the caves,*
> *Join my verse, my body cleansed*
> *In your healing waves.*
>
> *Mother Earth come laugh with me*
> *Set aside your toils,*
> *Join my chant of forest green*
> *Secure me in rich soil.*
>
> *Earth and Air, Fire and Sea*
> *I call you all, come dance with me!*
> *Grant me now a sacred space*
> *While working magic in this place.*

In this invocation, each verse is designed for a cardinal point of the altar. At each of these four directions, a candle of the appropriate color should be lit, and a symbol of the element blessed as indicated in each verse. This is meant to be a celebration of life, so dance and sing around your circle. Don't be afraid to get inspired!

Activities

During the Maypole dance, think about what you wish to weave into or out of your spirit. The Maypole is an ancient symbol of the male aspect of the Divine, while the ribbons are strands of life. Have small baskets of goodies around the room to symbolize the coming abundance and to enjoy after the Circle. Magic is hungry work.

Small pieces of jade should be blessed, taken home, and planted to bring flourishing gardens. Topaz may be passed around the circle to help bring everyone into harmony with the radiant sun energy.

Tools and Ritual Components

Incense — Frankincense, rose and bluebells make a lovely scent to appease the Fey and bring trust and purification to your gathering.

Ritual Soap — Thyme and rose for balance and beauty, and to tempt the faerie folk into joining your celebration.

Anointing Oil — Lily of the valley, a traditional May Day flower.

Ritual Cup — Woodruff wine to banish negativity, or red clover tea, a Victorian favorite for spring.

Altar Decorations — Ivy, rose, and hawthorn adorn the altar, while fresh marigold petals form the outer circle. Garnet is a symbol of union and may be placed central to the altar for fidelity, and friendship.

Clothing — Crown yourself with a wreath of ivy. Wear bright, lively colors, especially the green of the forest to honor life and vitality.

Cakes — By May, strawberries have come into season. Why not enjoy them with Victorian popovers and a little cream? It's one way of thanking the Earth for her bounty. Candied violets are also a traditional Victorian treat for this holiday.

From my wings are shaken the dews
That waken the sweet buds every one,
When rocked to rest on their Mother's breast
As She dances round the sun.
— Percy Bysshe Shelley

Summer Solstice—June 21st

Good temper, like many a sunny day,
Sheds brightness on everything.
It is the sweetener of toil
And the soother of disquetude.
— Irving

Corresponding to St. Peter and Paul's day on the Christian calendar, Summer Solstice (or mid-summer or Litha as it is sometimes called) is the longest day of the year. Now is when the powers of light are invoked; the God/dess dances high in the sky and beckons us to join Her. It is an excellent time to work magics involving protection, strength, energy, and clear sight—for the light has come to banish any shadows in your life.

Invocation

Fireflies and summer sun,
In circles round we become as one.
Singing songs at magic's hour
We bring the winds and timeless power.
Turning inward, hand to hand
We dance the hearth to heal our land.
Standing silent beneath the sky
We catch the fire from out God's eye.
Swaying breathless beside the sea
We call the Goddess, so mote it be!

A drum is an wonderful accompaniment to this invocation. A circle dance, moving sunward, can also be done while it is chanted.

Prayer

Summer sun, with warmth do shine,
Greet the noon and fill the pines,
Sing your tune to wondering eyes,
Touch the flames with mustard-gold.
Healing fires our hands enfold,
Upon this pyre, Her story's told.

Activities

The cauldron, which held fire for Beltane, now holds water with which to bless the coven. Traditionally, a heather branch is used. It is believed that walking naked in a garden on Litha night insures fertility, although I suspect the gentleman watching is more responsible than any magic might be.

Now is the season to harvest your magical herbs, know the gentleness of summer breezes, and bring wisdom to your life though meditation. Toward these ends, a blue stone called lapis lazuli may be passed among your members to help increase psychic energy.

Tools and Ritual Components

Incense — Fennel, lemon verbena, and orange for fertility, romance, and love. Clover, marjoram, and chamomile are also excellent additions.

Ritual Soap — Lavender, which may also be used to asperge the Circle (asperging means to sprinkle water or wine around the circle to bless and purify it). Using lavender will bring stability, purity, protection and a growing awareness.

Anointing Oil — Heather, for greater understanding of self and a reconnection to the universe.

Ritual Cup — A pinch of mugwort and cinquefoil added to rose petal liquor makes a lovely drink for protection and awareness. As an alternative, make use of those pesky dandelions and put together a lovely wine to use next year.

Altar Decorations — Elder, thorn, yellow and gold flowers on the altar, and perhaps red, orange and yellow balloons for the outer circle. A red-orange stone called carnelian can be added to the sanctuary to bring you into harmony with the sun's energy.

Clothing — Simply because of the weather, this is the best time of the year for sky-clad rituals. If you prefer to be robed, wear the colors of the sun, and join in its radiance.

Cakes — Since just about every type of fruit is now available, instead of cakes why not have a fruit salad? Share with your group what each fruit represents so they may internalize the magic.

What was Summer chanting?
O'ye brooks and bird,
Flash and pipe in happiness
Stirring hearts that cares oppress,
Into shining words!
Here's a maze of butterflies
Dancing over golden gorse,
Here's a boat of grassy spies.
Sunshine has set free, of course!
Wonder at the wind that blows
Odours from the forest sweet,
Marvel at the honeyed rose, heaping petals at her feet.
Hark at wood nymphs rustling thro'
Brakes and thickets tender knee'd,
Hark! Some shepherd pipe there blew!
Was it Pan upon a reed?

Oh, the pinks and garden spice
Nature's every fair device
Mingled in a scented board,
Expected, longed-for and adored—
Summer's come!

     —Norman Gale

Lammas, Lughnasad—August 1st

Move eastward happy Earth, and leave yon orange sunset waning low.
—Alfred, Lord Tennyson

The wheel of the year now begins giving way to the dark. Days are growing shorter, a slightly cooler wind has begun to blow. This is first harvest, and a festival to celebrate the prosperity and generosity of the Mother.

Invocation

Ashes to ashes, dust to dust
We shall go as we can and do as we must.
The body may die but the spirit is free
To do greater wonders, so mote it be!

Ashes to ashes, clay to clay
We shall seek for our center and find our own way.
The flesh may be blind but the spirit can see
The God within all men, so mote it be!

Ashes to ashes, sand to sand,
We will use all our talents to heal our great land.
The flesh may be weak but the spirit in me
Is full with Her blessings, so mote it be.

This is actually performed as a chant, begun as a whisper and grows naturally louder to enable a cone of power to grow. Keep in mind the goal of your energy as you chant. When the power is released by the group leader, the verse may be repeated three times in a quiet voice to help ground people once more.

Activities

Lammas is a time to be thankful for your bounty. It is also the season when you can release old forms of thinking and harvest something fresh for your life. Perhaps you can share some of your garden treats with a neighbor, or invite a friend to dinner. Make some new acquaintances and watch the fruits of your labors come into fullness.

Tools and Ritual Components

Incense — Heather, frankincense and oak for awareness, balance and protection.

Ritual Soap — Oatmeal, in honor of the harvest.

Anointing Oil — Lilac, for clarity and harmony.

Ritual Cup — Rich honey mead or Horilka, the harvest of both bees and flowers, made carefully by your hands.

Altar Decorations — Sunflowers, wheat, rye, corn, and baked bread can be spread on your altar, while late-blooming flowers can be strewn to make the outer circle. Moonstone may be added to the decorations for peace, good fortune, and joy. Agate is also an especially good stone for Lammas as it is the stone of good harvests.

Clothing — Colors may be toned down now, becoming more reflective of the fall. Wear a sunflower in your hair to smile upward at the waning light.

Cakes — Just as oatmeal was a suggested ingredient for your soap, I suggest preparing an oatmeal or graham bread to mark the first harvest.

Fairest of the months, ripe Summer's Queen
The hey-day of the year
With robes that gleam with sunny sheen
Sweet August doth appear.
—R. C. Miller

Autumn Equinox—September 21st, approximately

On either side of the river lie long fields of barley and of rye,
that clothe the world and touch the sky.
—Alfred, Lord Tennyson

Now comes the dusk of the Sun, the second harvest and a time of banishing and cleansing before the winter snows. Fall's theme is rest after labor and contemplation. Think about what changes you want to make within, while without the world sleeps. Then, come the spring, both may be born anew.

Invocation

Call the winds, chant the rite,
Dance the fires, reclaim the night,
Asperge the circle, draw it round
Salt of earth with water bound.

Bring the censor, bless the Grail,
Raise your voice the Goddess hail,
Light the brazier, carve the runes,
Reach the stars, draw down the moon.

Wind Father, Lord of Suns
Move your power, become as one.
Earth Mother, Lady Sea
Share your magic, blessed be.

Many verses and music can easily be added to this chant. I recommend a low, steady drum beat as accompaniment and a spiralling circle dance. Accompaniment has been written for this, and may be obtained by sending SASE to the author via Llewellyn Publications, P. O. Box 64383, St. Paul, MN 55164.

Prayer

Autumn brook with crisp waves flow,
Greet the eve let willows blow,
A spell to weave, a love to grow
Touch the cup to lily ponds,
With lotus blooms and driftwood wand,
The Mother's womb renews her bond.

Activities

This is a harvest celebration to which an offering of a shell, cloth, grain, yarn and feathers is often brought. Since this is also the time when winter's night and summer's day are in perfect balance, magic that deals with mediation, symmetry, and overcoming and releasing bondage is especially effective.

Tools and Ritual Components

Incense — Combining benzoin, myrrh, honeysuckle bark, cinnamon, and vanilla creates a light, aromatic scent to bring balance, cleansing, and the mysteries of the Grail to our lives.

Ritual Soap — Marigold for concentration and purification.

Anointing Oil — Myrrh and vanilla for awareness.

Ritual Cup — Sage combined with white rose water, so that we may drink our fill of wisdom and strength for the months ahead.

Altar Decorations — Acorns, gourds, thistle, and late blooming flowers decorate the altar, while fresh ferns may be crossed on the floor for the outer circle. Bloodstone and malachite may be brought into the magical space to promote wisdom and healing.

Clothing — Bedeck yourself with the colors of fall—burnt orange, light brown, vibrant red. Wear a wreath of waxed leaves and enjoy the refreshing winds of change.

Cakes — Apples are still fresh off the trees. An apple pie or goodie made with vanilla, cinnamon, and ginger promises health and abundance over the winter. Corn bread is also a nice alternative.

While ripening corn grew thick and deep
And here and there men stood to reap,
One morn I put my heart to sleep
And to the meadows took my way.

The goldfinch on a thistle head
Stood scattering seedlets as she fed,
The wrens their pretty gossip spread
Or joined a random roundelay.
—Jean Ingelow

Hallows, Samhain—October 31st

Now the new year reviving old desires
And the thoughtful soul to solitude retires.
—Edward Fitzgerald

Although many people today would call it Halloween (a contraction of Hallowed Eve), the Victorians may have called this holiday Snap Apple Night or Nut Crack Night because of the traditional divination games played with nuts or apple peelings to determine the initials of future bridegrooms. Practical jokes were also a favorite diversion. Some people would use the cover of darkness to play pranks that were only discovered the next morning. A householder might find his/her wagon on the barn roof, and the perpetrator might be standing nearby saying something like, "The goblins must have done it" with a sneaky grin. Legend has it that faeries hold a grand anniversary this eve, and mischief making is a-foot!

For the user of magic, Samhain or Halloween is the in-between time, the time of the dead. The new year and the old swing on the same hinge, and the veil between worlds grows thin. This is also the time of the final harvest, when we gather and preserve our crop. At this time, our spiritual energy should be refilled to ensure sustenance for the winter.

Invocation

Apostle of the Ancients
Chant from your willow scroll,
Call Artemis to share Full Moons
And bless the silver bowl.

Guardian of the Fabled Book
Bow down your ear to hear
The cries of those within this womb
Whose birth to light is near.

Avatars of times now past
And times still yet to be,
Reveal our paths from out the mists
Pay heed, our augury.

Deities from days of old
Carve out our misplaced pride,
That we might rise among the stars
And there our souls abide

Apostle of the Ancients
Burn now the candles bright
Let spirits soar on seas of joy
And grant rebirth this night.

This invocation takes into consideration the heightened amount of spiritual activity of this night on the Wheel. Respect for the dead should be paid, and perhaps even a little offering of food. As you say each stanza of the invocation, light candles for each of the elements. Make sure you light your central altar candles first.

Activities

This is the best time of the year to do any type of divining magic. Also, an offering of first fruits is often made as a way of asking for a gentle winter. In Ireland, a bread made of dried fruit, nuts, and honey is baked together with tokens that symbolized good or bad luck. For example, a ring meant marriage while a pea meant poverty. This time of year is also a wonderful opportunity to leave an offering of honey and flower water for the Fey (or faery realm). Because it is a time when the veil between the worlds is thin, best be sure your offering is a tasty one!

Tools and Ritual Components

Incense — Sage, oak and fumitory, for releasing negative energy, protection and grounding.

Ritual Soap — Apple, cinnamon and ginger to commemorate the harvest and bring health for the winter.

Anointing Oil — Patchouli for awareness of the Divine spark within.

Ritual Cup — Apple ginger beer—it is a warm, fun drink to make and enjoy.

Altar Decorations — Apples, cornstalks, acorns and oak leaves may be placed on the altar. Pumpkins can be carved with designs appropriate for the cardinal points. The two best stones to employ during your work are obsidian (to control random energy) and jasper (to protect the meeting from unwanted spirits).

Clothing — Dressing in costume is perfectly acceptable. You may want to have a "theme" circle where everyone dresses like legendary beasts, characters, etc.

Cakes — A pumpkin pie with all the fixings. A pumpkin is a moon fruit, symbolizing fullness of psychic awareness, which is a helpful aid to Samhain night.

Upon that night, when fairies light
On Cassilis Downans dance
Or ow're the lays, in splendid blaze
On sprightly coursers prance
Or for Colian the route is ta'en
Beneath the moon's pale beams
There up the cove to stray and rove
Amang the rocks and streams.
— Robert Burns

Yule —December 21st

Jack Frost was in the garden,
I saw him there at dawn.
He was dancing round the bushes
And prancing on the lawn.
He had a cloak of silver,
A hat all shimm'ring white,
A wand of glittering stardust,
And shoes of sunbeam light.
— J. Smeeton

This is the longest night of the year and the time for awakenings. Fires are kindled to give the sun strength for its long voyage back to the skies. Fires also invoke the magic of protection and fortitude. Victorian ornaments depicted fruits, nuts, and berries, which were reminiscent of the earliest ornaments made and were meant to appease the tree spirits and bring fruit back to the bare branches.

Invocation

What is this dream that comes to me,
This longing in the spring
To whisper with a playful glee
Of Magic, wondrous things?

So it is that I am born
The Child with gossamer wings
Appearing with a sounding horn
And ageless songs to sing.

I ring the bells amidst the green
I spread the drew drops round
I become the Faerie Queen
And dance with holly crowned.

What is this dream that comes to me
These thoughts on summer days?
To wish that I were flying free
In forests filled with Fey.

So it is that I am born
The Lass with harp in hand
Strumming tunes to grow the corn
And bring life to the land.

I move the winds all through the glade
I dance the noon-gold sun
I become the Merry Maid
And dance till day is done.

What is this dream that comes to me
This muse as fall draws nigh?
To speak of things still yet to be
As winds that bend and sigh.

So it is that I am born
The Woman at the well
With songs of love upon this morn
And stories yet to tell.

I aid the ladies giving birth
I harvest ripened fields
I become as Mother Earth
And dance till daylight yields.

What is this dream that comes to me,
Reflections in the white
To share of things that I have seen
Of grails still shining bright.

So it is that I am born
The Old One close to death
With wisdom writ on pages worn
And humor in each breath.

I speak now with a quiet tone
I look with inner sight
I become the Ancient Crone
And dance with darkest night.

This invocation is a celebration of the Goddess in all her aspects, including the dark that now covers the Earth. It speaks of the cycle of hope, and the knowledge of the dawn still to come. There is music to this particular piece which may be obtained by sending a SASE to the author via Llewellyn Publications.

Prayer

Winter's quiet with blowing snows,
Greets the night and halts all foes,
Till comes the light and She who knows.
Touch the stones with crystal veils,
The stag returns to tell a tale,
With lessons learned, the Goddess Hail!

Activities

A season for new awareness is upon us, calling us to take on new projects and make changes. The world is still in hibernation, but each time the ground is warmed something starts to grow. Plant a seed in the rich soil of self and nurture it until spring. Light a Yule log to warm both home and heart and spend time with old friends.

Tools and Ritual Components

Ritual Soap — Frankincense and myrrh with a hint of bayberry.

Anointing Oil — Pine and anise to repel negative energy and herald the return of joy.

Ritual Cup — Egg nog decorated with a sprig of holly.

Altar Decorations — Evergreens, holly and mistletoe can bedeck the halls while pine branches may be placed to mark the circle. Aquamarine placed on the altar will bring motivation and courage, while an opal passed hand-to-hand shares hope for the spring to come.

Clothing — Stay warm! Wear heavy robes of green and red to help the sun continue its journey.

Cakes — Cookies! Nothing warms the child within like good, old-fashioned sugar cookies with anise frosting. Gingerbread and plumb pudding were also Victorian favorites.

This Lady never slept, but lay in trance
All night within the fountain, as in sleep,
Its emerald crags glowed in her beauty's glance.
Through the green splendor of the water deep
She saw the constellations reel and dance
Like fireflies and withal did ever keep
The tenour of her contemplations calm
With open eyes, closed feet and folded palm.
                  —Percy Bysshe Shelley

Candlemas, Imbolc—February 1st

> *Make thou my spirit pure and clear as are the frosty skies.*
> —Alfred, Lord Tennyson

Imbolc is a period of rest and a time when we should replenish the well of self for magic. It is the season for contemplation, inspiration, healing and contacting the muse. Take some time to work on your Book of Shadows; think about creating new rituals or spells; tend to your physical needs with devotion, and take a deep, cleansing breath before spring chores are knocking at your door once more.

Invocation

I am the cup,
The chalice of life
Ever-filled, ever-flowing
Molded by what I hold
Shaping what I pour
I am the waters of creation.

I am the sword,
Giver of death and spring
Ever-sharp, ever-piercing
Edged by what is true
Cutting what is not
I am the fires of rebirth.

I am the censer,
Keeper of the air
Ever-fresh, ever-blowing
Scented by what I touch
Moving with my will—
I am the winds of change.

I am the salt,
Purifier of Earth
Ever-seasoned, ever-healing,
Birthed by what is rock
Growing with the world
I am the spice of Mother.

I am the pentacle,
Circle of the void
Ever-changing, ever-returning
Pointed by the elements
Beginning with my end
I am the essence of magic.

This invocation is meant to help you center yourself on the senses, and bring heightened awareness. Although it is written for the solitary, it can easily be changed for group use by changing "I" to "we." The five elements are represented; four cardinal points then the center (the center is your altar). Light the candles at the Watchtowers (or each of the four directions) while speaking each verse.

Activities

Have a large candle or fire set up. As each person enters the circle, they bring with them a candle and light it from the original, sharing with the group a need they have. The energy of this night can be released in your Rites, bringing light to any dark clouds hanging over you.

Find a safe place to leave the candles burning until you have finished your ritual work, then blow them out as a symbol of completion and fulfillment.

Tools and Ritual Components

> **Incense** — Bay and basil for vision, courage and meditation.
>
> **Ritual Soap** — Heather to bring a greater sense of yourself and your place in the universe.
>
> **Anointing Oil** — Sandalwood and vanilla to bring greater concentration, increase psychic ability, and help any magical working. Touches of jasmine and balm are also nice.
>
> **Ritual Cup** — Angelica tea to encourage good fortune and health.
>
> **Altar Decorations** — Except for candles, the altar is unadorned at this time of year to signify rest. Should you desire, amethyst may be brought into the sacred space for peace of mind, and jet can be used to give heightened intuition and inner sight.
>
> **Clothing** — A white robe to match the candles makes for a beautiful ritual, accentuating the increasing brightness of days ahead.
>
> **Cakes** — Something light and simple, perhaps rose water and some angelica wafers or biscuits.

> *If Candlemas day be fair and bright,*
> *Winter will have another flight*
> *If Candlemas day be clouds and rain,*
> *Winter is gone, and will not come again.*
> —E. Holden

MOON MAGIC

*Yon rising moon looks for us again. How oft hereafter will she wax
and wane, how oft hereafter to look for us through this same garden.*
— Edward Fitzgerald

For as long as the moon and stars have existed, people have looked to the sky with wonder
and awe. Knowing the seasons of the stars, and the changes of the moon were important—
especially to farmers. Farmers timed their harvests less by the calendar and more by the sky
and the signs around them. They paid special attention to what sign the moon was in, since
that seemed to affect the plants.

Phases of the Moon

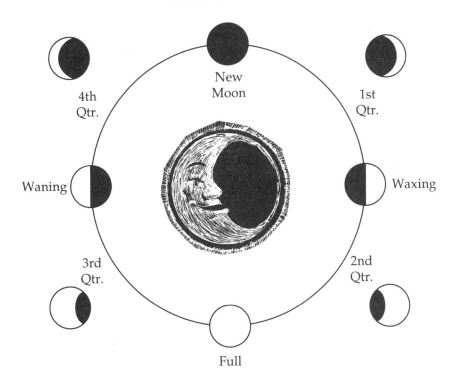

New
Moon

4th
Qtr.

1st
Qtr.

Waning   Waxing

3rd
Qtr.

2nd
Qtr.

Full

The use of the moon in magic is still well known today. We employ the symbolism of
a Waxing Moon for spells and rituals to bring things into our lives, for growth and positive
change, and to bless seeds or creative efforts of any kind. The Full Moon is one of power,
fruitfulness, abundance, psychic awareness, and fertility. The opposite of the Waxing Moon
(a waning crescent) can be used for banishings and things we want removed from our
lives—such as bad habits and outmoded, negative thought patterns. Finally, the New
Moon, (also called the Dark Moon) speaks of secrets, the death of the old man, rest, and
dealings with the dark side of self.

The first quarter of the moon starts when the moon and sun are in conjunction (New Moon). Here the moon is not visible, but towards the termination of the phase, the first bit appears. The initial sliver of the moon often allows for another phenomena known as "Earth Shine" to be seen. This is when a slight grey-white halo appears to emanate from the points of the crescent moon all around the rest of the sphere. Nights like these are incredibly beautiful, and they are excellent times for doing any magic dealing with spiritual endeavors.

The second quarter is between the New Moon and Full Moon, or when the sun and moon are at 90 degree angles to each other. The third quarter begins with three days of a Full Moon, the sun now being opposite in the sky to light it fully. Finally, the fourth quarter is the waning moon, moving us back to where we began.

TABLE OF TERMS REFERRING TO LUNAR PHASES				
Sun-Moon Angle	Llewellyn Terms	Common Terms Division by:		
		2	4	8
0-90° after Conjunction	First Quarter	Increasing Waxing Light New	New Moon	New Moon
				Crescent
90-180°	Second Quarter		First Quarter	First Quarter
				Gibbous
180-270°	Third Quarter	Decreasing Waning Dark Old	Full Moon	Full Moon
				Disseminating
270-360°	Fourth Quarter		Last Quarter	Last Quarter
				Balsamic

Any ritual can be intensified by following the moon and using its cycles to enhance the effect of your magic. For example, you could begin an artistic effort during a ritual held under the Full Moon of spring. During the rite, you might invoke the blessings of the Divine on your work, then dance sunward (clockwise) around the project to mark the natural creative cycle and bring fullness to that endeavor.

In times past, Full Moons marked various seasons and their characteristics. These may also be used to reinforce magical works. For example, the Chaste moon of late February represents the purity of spring and might be used for cleansing. The Indians called this the Snow Moon, for obvious reasons. The Seed or Worm Moon in March marks the beginning of the growing season, when the worms begin to surface. It is a good time to consider what you want to cultivate in your life. The Pink Moon of April, so named for the flowers abundant during this month, is a time for love magic. Come May, the Corn Moon tells us it is time to plant. The Mead or Strawberry Moon of June is a time to do your brewing and enjoy the rich fields, the Thunder Moon of July tells us of sudden storms, and come August, the Barley Moon tells us it is time to harvest what we sowed in March.

Snow Moon and Hunter's Moon of October reminds us that the cold is soon to come, and we should check our inner resources to be sure we are taking care of the temple of self. Finally, the Wolf or Cold Moon of December urges us to remember our animal friends in the wild, many of whom will die because of the lack of food. Lay out your bread crumbs in the forest, and share of what you have.

Invocation

This invocation may be used during any moon phase to help focus the lunar energy on the goals of your ritual.

I come into your garden fair,
To waltz upon the dew,
To look upon your handiwork,
While morning still is new.

I come into your meadow fair,
To laugh upon the lawn,
To stare upon a red-blue sky,
Working magic come the dawn.

I come into your forest fair,
To sing among the trees,
To sway carefree amidst the leaves,
At the time of the noon-day breeze.

I come into your greenwood fair,
To watch the sunlight play,
As it dances towards the dusk,
And sparkles like the Fey.

I come into your grove so fair,
The cloak of night comes round,
To gather stars within its sweep
And shine upon the ground.

I come upon your world so fair,
And think on what I've seen
Then fall to sleep with gods of old,
And dream on moon-beam wings.

LUNAR ASTROLOGY

As the moon moves through the signs of the zodiac and its phases, we can use its influence in our gardening techniques and our rituals. To find out what sign or phase the moon is in, simply check a good magical almanac or lunar calendar. Most regular calendars usually note by word or picture what phase the moon is in; an almanac will be more detailed, and an astrological calendar is probably your best bet for accurate information in this regard.

To write this section of the book, I gathered information from various sources and combined it with my own insight to provide a guideline. This guideline is meant to demonstrate the astrological significance of Lunar phases for certain magical applications. Since it is the symbolism which is important, I must stress that your own intuition should be trusted over anything written for the timing of any ritual or spell.

Moon in Aries — A good time to harvest or plant something special in your garden for magical use. Also a cycle for cultivating talents and knowledge. A good period to begin school work, foster friendships, and enhance any ability which you may have neglected.

Moon in Taurus — A season to allow growth, encourage vitality, and increase energy. If you have been overtaxing yourself lately, take this opportunity to meditate by moonlight and refill the well of self. An excellent period for spells pertaining to development and maturity of any project, including legal matters.

Moon in Gemini — Weeding, fertilizing, and general clean-up is called for. Don't ignore the little things which have been bothering you. Instead deal with them, then move on. Begin a banishing ritual for a negative attitude during the waning phase, then finish it come the New Moon. Add a little energy to any ambition to keep it fruitful.

Moon in Cancer — A great time to transplant anything, since this is not only the moon of growth and nurturing but also movement and encouragement. Magic pertaining to anything which has been stagnant in your life is indicated. Even love gone stale may find new freshness with ritual and spell work during this moon.

Moon in Leo — Time for both harvest and caution. The lion is a creature of fire, who tells us that while things are abundant now, winter still comes both spiritually and physically. You may want to do some canning now, give thanks for what you have, and consider how you are using your psychic gifts. They are jewels not to be scattered hastily.

Moon in Virgo — Another good period to plant and water anything. Start something new or breath some freshness into a lingering task. Magics dealing with intuition, attention to detail, discipline, healing, and rejuvenation are best started at waxing to Full Moon.

Moon in Libra — A sign of beauty and fruitfulness, Libra gives us the opportunity to sow flowering seeds and bring a little charm to the world. A healthy time for woolgathering, visualizations for positive change, and any magic concerning success.

Moon in Scorpio — Like Leo, we see here a caution towards prudence and stocking up. While it is a good time to plant, consideration should be given to any warning signs around you. If weather is ill, it may be best to wait instead of rushing forward either with your gardening or spiritual pursuits. Work on rituals or spells pertaining to wisdom, psychic attunement and discernment in all matters.

Moon in Sagittarius — Your imagination takes wing! Cultivate and develop anything which you have begun. Give foundations to your dreams. Now is the time when sturdy plants put down even firmer roots, so reflect this in your life with grounding, centering and a little stubborn will power to bring your vision into reality.

Moon in Capricorn — A season of feminine virtues, healing, and fertility. Anything which needs nurturing and structure, be it yourself, a friend or a project, do so now. Focus on magic to increase the instinctive side of yourself, psychic gifts, and the gentler qualities within.

Moon in Aquarius — A balance to Capricorn, this is the more mental, male energy. Time to plant anything that enjoys dry soil. Spiritually, likewise things may seem a little dry, but it is a good opportunity to discover your inner strength. The sun dances high, and the rational mind is sharp. An excellent chance to study your Craft from a more scientific angle.

Moon in Pisces — This is a good time to water and nurture your garden somewhat liberally. In your own life, it is a good time for ritual or spell work pertaining to conflicts which may have held you back. The encouraging energies of this cycle will help you get past your doubts, and lend extra power for magic. A season to reorganize and reconsider the circumstances around you.

A special note here: There is a difference between what constellation the moon appears in and the actual astrological significance. For example, your almanac may say that the moon is in Taurus, when actually for astrological purposes it is Gemini (30 degrees difference). Therefore, consult an astrological calendar or book for this information instead of a common almanac.

Sole watcher of the Dusky bower, I joy to be
and conscious feel the pale moon shower, Her light on me.
— Rebecca Hey

OTHER ANNUAL OBSERVANCES

The modern calendar is full of many other observances, ranging from Secretarial Day to President's Day. When these commemorations come around, consider what you can do magically to enhance them. On Arbor Day, the Victorian family used to go for a trip to the woods. Should a magical person do any less? Why not use that opportunity to reconnect with the land, and specifically the spirit of the trees.

On President's Day, do a ritual to bring wisdom to our leaders. For Memorial Day, pray for the eternal rest of the spirits whose lives ended in battle, and pray for lasting peace to come. On Valentine's Day, renew your bonds to friends and loved ones. No matter what the holiday, make it special by adding to it the flower of magic growing in your heart.

Then let winged Fancy wander
Through the thought still spread beyond her
Open wide the mind's cage-door
She'll dart forth and cloud-ward soar . . .

Fancy, high-commission'd—send her!
She has vassals to attend her
She will bring, in spite of frost
Beauties that the earth hath lost.

She will bring thee, all together
All delights of summer weather
All the buds and bells of May
From dewy sward or thorny spray.

All the heaped Autumn's wealth
With a still, mysterious stealth
She will mix these pleasures up
Like three fit wines in a cup.

—John Keats

CHAPTER FOUR

Garden of Delights

The Groves were God's first temples.
— W. C. Bryant
From *Forest Hymn*

The twentieth century has seen an impressive increase in the love of outdoors. It seems we are rediscovering what our Victorian ancestors knew all along, the delightful rewards of working the earth, feeling the sun and wind on our face, and just generally finding pleasure and lessons in our own back yard.

The gardens of Victorian days were magnificent, to say the least. They were embellished with summer houses, touched with lattice work, and graced with arches for climbing plants, garden seats, sundials, swings, fountains, and tables for teas. Some were so elaborate, they even included a lawn tennis court!

The Victorian lady of means didn't have to worry about cleaning the house, so she had more time to devote to colors and landscaping for personal expression, indoors and out. Red was the most favored color of flower, but every hue was used to create various designs. Clocks, flags, and other patterns were formed on lawns, with a heavy emphasis on Oriental and Italian styles. On the East coast, the most popular garden was one created from herbs intricately patterned with clipped trees of boxwood and privet, wired into topiary animals to guard the land. The truly industrious Victorian would also use seasonal blooms so that the garden would never be bare until the snow fell, and even then gourds and figs would pour over the arbor like a water fall.

Gardening was often a family pastime, considered to teach virtue. After my first year with a full garden of my own, I can honestly see where this idea originated. It takes patience and loving care to keep the simplest of gardens growing well, but the work is well worth the rewards. I cannot tell you the ecstasy of picking your own radishes and eating them fresh from the garden. It is a simple diversion and a divine one. It is in this spirit that this chapter examines magic, muse, beauty and utility for the grounds around our homes.

MAKING CHORES MAGICAL

*In one direction the earnest workers are probing the
secrets of nature, and unravelling one-by-one the
mystic threads that run through her fabrications.*

—Shirley Hibberd

Chores were not considered so much an inconvenience as they were a necessity in Victorian days. The Puritan work ethic still lay heavy in the hearts of the people. Many sincerely believed that idle hands were a lure for temptation and misconduct. Chores were a part of the daily routine to keep the house, grounds and fields in order for days ahead. Getting behind could not only make future work extremely difficult to catch up on, but also prove a social faux pas if any part of the home was found disorderly.

We have been rather spoiled by modern conveniences. Mind you, I don't plan on throwing mine away, but instead I think we should try to reevaluate our tasks and approach them with a more positive mind set. Any time you carry an affirmative attitude with you to a chore, that energy will affect not only how the work gets done, but the atmosphere of that area long after you have left it. Adopting a positive method is healthier and more productive in the long run, and it is definitely more reflective of magical living.

While I am on this subject, let me say that a change in attitude should not be limited to the outdoors. Carry it with you into your home and into everything you do so that when you are finished the light which lingers is full of life, love and magic for those that follow.

Picking up the Lawn

*What is more refreshing to the eye when walking than the nicely kept
and prettily stocked garden of the cottager with its various flowers!
How desirable to induce the working man to attend his little plot
and desert the beer shop . . .*

—Thomas Edward

Spring was a time of preparation for the Victorians. The soil and the house needed to be readied for the busy season ahead. This included lawn care. Cleaning the old dirt and debris from winter off of your lawn makes everything look fresh. On a spiritual level, it lightens the heaviness that the winter snows brought. It also hastens the process of bringing new life to the land and helps begin the process of "spring cleaning" for your entire home.

Before you compost all the remains raked from your yard, however, check through the pile for any broken branches. These boughs are like driftwood because they have been sitting in snow all winter, and are charged with the energy of water. In many cases, the bark will have soaked totally off, leaving a soft, naturally sanded wood which can be worked into a staff, wand, or even a set of pick-up-sticks for the children.

These bits of branches have many naturally formed nooks and crannies that can become cradles for crystals, shells, and other personal decorations. To make the holes a little deeper for the setting, you can use any carving tool. If you want to glue some decorations to the branch, make it from tree sap mixed with powdered herbs of your choice.

Once completed, you should treat the wood periodically with lemon oil to keep it from cracking. You can then hang coral, beads, herb bags, and even small gourds from it to add the finishing touches to your magical creation. The final product is one that is a gift from the trees in your own yard, and made by the love of your hands, so I can almost promise it will be a cherished possession for years to come. Also, consider making them for friends.

Planting

Spring has moved with a gentle breeze into your life. The time has come to do all of those physical chores—mow the lawn and weed and plant your garden—but how can you also make the most of your time outdoors on a spiritual level?

Planting offers us a special form of magic. Many old folk spells you come across deal with seeds, soil and/or flowering plants. The one which follows is the simplest, but can readily be adapted to suit your needs on a more personal level. Remember, the Victorian spirit says be creative!

Begin by writing what you need or want in your life on a piece of paper. Fold this paper three times and soak it in water. When it has dried, burn it, allowing the smoke to rise to the four winds with your wish. Finally, take the ashes and plant them with a flower-bearing seed. Legend says that when the plant comes to bloom, you should see the beginnings of the changes you wished for.

Another version of this spell is to follow much the same procedure, except this time you put the ashes of your wish inside a blown-out egg shell, then plant the wish, (egg and all) into the garden. For one thing, eggshells are wonderful for the soil. On a magical level, the natural course of time will break down the barrier between you and your desire until it grows in rich soil. Also, the egg is the symbol of fertility and life, bringing that power to your magical work.

Please note that as with any "wish" type magic, effort is required. Do not wish for prosperity then sit home instead of looking for a job. Good intentions mean little unless they are followed by action. If your wish is answered in an unexpected way, try not to be disappointed. Instead, try to understand the lesson you have been given.

Listening to my sweet pipings,
The winds in the reeds and the rushes,
The bees on the bells of thyme
And the birds on the myrtle bushes.
— Percy Bysshe Shelley

Nature also provides us with multiple opportunities to reawaken our senses. Listen closely to things you might normally ignore while you work the land. Smell the rich and diverse scents in the air, feel the unique textures of trees, and stones. Look closely at the world you have been given as a child might, even try tasting a rose (they are edible).[1]

Harken to the winds, which are the breath of the world. As you labor, breath deeply, visualizing oxygen being carried to every part of your body that needs it. Watch the insects, learn the seasons and take this chance to reexperience the classroom of earth.

Weeding

Don't be discouraged by all your weeds. Many are trying to tell you things about your soil, and others can even be beneficial. Nettles, for example, can be very helpful to an aromatic herb garden because they can discourage certain insects. Dandelions, a Victorian favorite, can be used in salads, as an ingredient in certain herbal remedies, and to make wines. They are also effective for replenishing certain minerals leached out of your soil. To learn more about the value of weeds, consult *Weeds and What They Tell* by Dr. E. Pfeffer. This book is well worth reading if you plan to be a serious gardener or herbalist.

There is also a magical application for weeds. As you pull weeds from the soil in your garden, it is also a good time to pull them from your life. Name your weeds so that they correspond to habits, feelings, and other things about yourself you don't like. As you toss aside the weed, visualize this habit leaving you. Do not look to see where the plant has landed, just release it, continuing until you are finished. Then put the whole pile of weeds in the compost. Sometimes, it helps if you name every weed the same thing to reinforce the effect.

GLORIOUS GARDENS

Make up your beds early in the morning; sew buttons on your husband's shirts; do not rake up any grievances; protect the young and tender branches of your family; plant a smile of good temper in your face, and root out all angry feelings, and expect a good crop of happiness.
— Robert B. Thomas, 1862

Paging through picture books of Victorian gardens can almost inspire you to run out to your city apartment balcony and put up a rose-covered trellis, just to have a little bit of flowering life somewhere close at hand. The colors are so rich, the blossoms so plentiful, that everywhere you could look there is a veritable feast for the eyes. Add to this the lavish diversity each garden presented, and we are left with a history which can give our imaginations endless amusement in considering options for our yards.

---

1 Before tasting anything, please check a good field guide to plants. For everything we can eat, there is at least one type of vegetation we cannot, and some are lethal.

Butterfly Gardens

Perhaps the Victorian love of grace was most reflected in the simple but elegant shape found in the butterfly. The butterfly garden was one of many specialty gardens that were favorite pastimes—there was no end to the creative expressions which gardening took. A true tribute to loveliness and ingenuity, the floral tapestries necessary to attract butterflies were unique because butterflies have certain requirements. First, a certain amount of shelter is needed from the wind, which can be provided by trees or a house wall. Next, there should be a good combination of sun and shade, along with a rocky area and a picturesque picket fence for the delicate winged visitors to land upon. Butterflies also require puddling areas in sand or mud.

Should you desire to make a butterfly garden of your own, and can meet the aforementioned criteria with the space at hand, all that is left is to put in the flowers to attract them. Begin with a base of meadow grass, planting your taller plants in back and shorter ones in front to create a terrace effect. A stone garden is a comely way of making a rocky space for them, and any number of wild or cultivated flowers will tempt them towards your creation. Marigolds, zinnias, baby's tears, sweet alyssum, milkweed, passion flower, daisy, lavender, verbena, boneset, clover and thistle are all excellent choices that can be arranged for a multitude of patterns, and will also fare well in most any soil. You may, for example, want to place your tall milkweeds in back, with the alyssum all the way in the front, followed by marigolds and then daisies.

When your garden is full grown, take out a folding chair and sit quietly to watch it. Observe the lightness of the butterfly as it moves from flower to flower, gathering nectar. Allow your tensions to fly away on their wings. Breathe in new energy with each light breeze, carrying hints of the sweet smells that your hands have helped bring to life. Enjoy a little Victorian leisure.

Clock Gardens

> *There groups of merry children played,*
> *There youths and maidens dreaming strayed,*
> *Oh precious hours, Oh golden prime*
> *And affluence of love and time.*
> *Even as a miser wants his gold,*
> *These hours the ancient time pieces told.*
> — Henry Wadsworth Longfellow

Some of the more interesting Victorian gardens were not only designed to look like clocks, but they could also keep time! There are old calendars which show the following correspondences for flowers and the times when they would open. Consult the "Flowers and Their Hours" chart to see how to plant a clock garden. Each letter of the alphabet corresponds to a section in the garden design.

The Victorians believed in the punctuality of the garden so much so that they would regulate the time of their meals by it, and some flowers would be named after their timeliness such as "Jack go to bed at noon." It must have taken great patience for any gardener to

Flowers and Their Hours

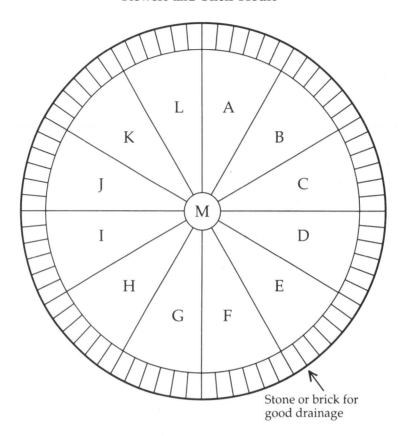

Stone or brick for
good drainage

A. Budding Roses — First Hour
B. Heliotrope — Second Hour
C. White Roses — Third Hour
D. Hyacinth, Dandelion — Fourth Hour
E. Lemons, Poppy, Day Lily — Fifth Hour
F. Lotus — Sixth Hour
G. Lupins, Garden Lettuce, Water Lily —
Seventh Hour

H. Oranges — Eighth Hour
I. Olive, Field Marigolds, Chickweed —
Ninth Hour
J. Poplar — Tenth Hour
K. Marigold — Eleventh Hour
L. Pansy, Violet — Twelfth Hour
M. A nice addition to this garden is a
central sundial.

plant an accurate clock, considering that correspondences vary greatly depending on your location, soil, availability of sun, and even sometimes on the seeds used.

This problem is no less so for the modern gardener. Creating your own clock garden will take some time and experimentation. Your first year, plant several types of seeds in a flower box. Keep a diary of their growth and habits. By the next season, you should have enough information to plant your seeds in a circle and mark the day with opening blooms.

Until you have it down to a science, you can use the times the flowers are meant to open for an hourly or planetary analogy. For example, if you have a spell that calls for working it at 1:00 a.m., and you have to get up by 5:00 a.m. for work, why not replace the actual time with a rose bud? Or, if you need to work when a planet is in a specific phase in the sky, but don't have enough time, you can pick one of your flowers during that phase and return to do your ritual later.

The idea with the clock garden is to allow you greater flexibility in your ritual and spells, without loosing the symbolism. I also think that anything grown by your own hands is going to be more personally significant, and therefore a greater asset to your magic.

*And there my heart with pleasure fills
And dances with the daffodils...*
— William Wordsworth

Crystal Gardens

We know that the Victorian lady loved gems and sparkling things of all sorts. We also know that the gardens of this time tried to emulate the oriental styles as much as possible, with what information they could obtain. One type of garden which had its origins in the East was the rock garden. In Japan, this was popularized by Zen philosophers who placed the stones in such a way as to reflect natural rhythms exhibited in nature.

Many Victorians partook in actually creating full rock gardens. These gardens were considered a novelty. Farmers who uncovered large stones while plowing would often use them to mark the boundaries of their land. They would also use them as a tether for a horse, or just as a place to go sit alone in the field and think. Like the flourishing oasis the urban Victorian created, any opportunity to use a natural object for ornamentation was not overlooked. They would often collect stones from outings and place them in patterns for pleasing results. These patterns could expand themselves to become a whole garden for the serious collector, but more frequently stones were used as ornamentation in landscaping.

In the New Age, we have seen a new focus on using stones in gardening, not only for comeliness but to enhance the soil, help the plants grow, keep away insects, and a number of other, more mystical applications. Stones and crystals are very attractive additions to the garden. If you can afford to get larger crystals, they can be placed to appear as if they are growing from the ground along with the plants, as if they are watchtowers jetting into the sky. If not, you can simply place smaller stones directly in the soil beneath or adjacent to the seeds which have the same planetary and lunar vibrations. Or choose ones which create a harmony together, and may be magically paired for increased effect.

One type of crystal garden that I personally enjoy is patterned in the form of a mandala. Here, different types of crystals are placed in a circle in such a manner that they correspond to the four directions. Since the study of the crystals and their correspondences is rather lengthy, and opinions vary, I suggest getting a couple of books which discuss crystals and compare notes. Then, use your own intuition for the final decision on which stones to place where, for each element and each of the four directions. Since each crystal can have a totally unique function above and beyond the normal magical parallels, your personal views of it will, in almost all cases, be just as important and useful to your gardening as any book.

Crystal Mandala Garden

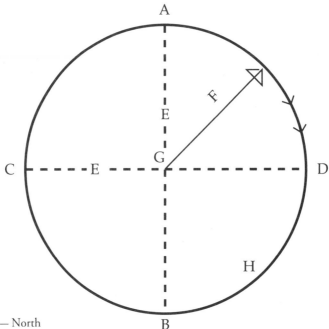

A. EARTH — North
B. FIRE — South
C. WATER — West
D. AIR — East
E. Dividing Line
F. Marking Rope
G. Center Point

EARTH: Ferns, Honeysuckle, Magnolia, Patchouli, Primrose, Tulip.
AIR: Clover, Lavender, Lemon grass, Mint, Lily of the Valley.
FIRE: Cactus, Thistle, Marigold, Snapdragon, Sunflower, Clove.
WATER: Aster, Daffodil, Daisy, Iris, Lilac, Rose.

To create a crystal mandala garden, you should get a good compass so that you can mark the four directions on the land first. Decide the size of your garden and create the circle using a long rope tied to a pole where the center will be. Extend the rope to its full length, with a sturdy stick on the end, and walk around from this point, drawing in the earth. This gives you your outline. Next, set four larger crystals where the four major compass points will be. Between these you can scatter various smaller stones in the outline of a circle as you deem appropriate. The four large stones, however, should be left sticking out of the ground as reference points.

From here, you divide your circle into four quarters. In each quarter you can plant flowers which correspond to that element either by their color or magical symbolism. For example, you may choose bright red roses for fire, even though they are often considered a "water" flower. I have listed some more common plants and their correspondences as suggestions.

If you have the time and space, a beautiful way of extending these correspondences is to set up a bird bath in the West for water, a brazier in the South for fire, a tree or large rock in the North to represent the earth, and finally a rod with feathers and bells in the East to depict the wind, or air. I can't begin to tell you the kind of wonderful energy a garden like this gives to any piece of land, especially while the flowers are in bloom. When the buds die off in the fall, the circle becomes a natural place for outdoor ritual.

The Faerie Garden

Up the airy mountains, down the rushy glen,
We daren't go a hunting for fear of little men.
—W. Arlington

The little people of mythical lore had many a place in the Victorian home and story book. Even the morning dew was believed to be touched with life by the Fey. The poetry of this age especially seemed to reflect the amusement and love that these wingedfolk inspired. Here is an example of such a poem:

The Flowers

All the names I know from nurse —
Gardener's garters, Shepherd's purse,
Bachelor's buttons, Lady's smock
And the Lady Hollyhock.

Fairy places, fairy things
Fairy woods where the wild bee wings,
Tiny trees for tiny dames
These must all be fairy names!

Tiny woods below whose boughs
Shady fairies weave a house
Tiny tree-tops, rose or thyme
Where the braver fairies climb!

Fair are grown-up people's trees
But the fairest woods are these
Where if I were not so tall
I should live for good and all.
—by R. L. Stevenson

If you find that such tales and poetry inspire you to make a fairy garden of your own, you can start almost anywhere in your yard. Hang some ribbons and little bells off of small trees to invite your fairy guests (who can use flower stems for a staircase and leaves for their canopy). Fashion tiny chairs from birch twigs, lilac branches and scraps of fabric tied neatly together with thread and place them comfortably around some of the favorite wee-folk herbs.

Although it is believed that circles of moss and mushrooms are their homes, you can make an enclosure for your friends in much the same way, applying mosses to the outside of a cardboard or plywood structure so it becomes a living chateau. Put this in a picturesque spot, remembering to leave an offering of sweet breads and honey inside to help attract them to your handiwork. Also, some of the handcrafted wooden doll furniture will work for a garden such as this if you find you have difficulty making small items. In this case, I suggest you treat the furniture with a water resilient finish so that it won't be damaged by seasonal changes.

If you have a large tree in your yard, plant a circle of annual flowers at its base, making a floral fairy ring. Doll house furniture can be added to this for a charming effect. Then, on May Day you can mimic the Victorian ladies by baking little sweet cakes the night before and placing them in your garden near the thyme (or beneath the leafy home you have created for them). Since it is believed the Faerie folk are most active at that time, you can hope to have a few of them see your talents and treats, and come to live in this whimsical abode. Go out early on the next morn and see if they have been eaten! If so, it is a definite sign that you have new guests.

Thorn, ash and oak are their favorite trees,
So perhaps you could circle the boughs with these:
Some foxglove for thimbles, some thyme for a treat,
Bluebells for their magic and logs for a seat!
Plant primrose and eat them if you dare by the day,
And it is said by the evening you'll glance a few Fey!
—Marian Loresinger

Kitchen Gardens

Also called an olitory, a kitchen garden was exactly what the name implied. Located near the kitchen door, this miniature grove was stuffed full of herbs, edible flowers, and posies used for decorating the home. This way, the homemaker could literally take two steps to pick a fresh bouquet or spice for dinner.

A common kitchen garden might have basil, dill, tarragon, chives and garlic for cooking; lavender and other aromatic herbs for potpourri; medicinal herbs and lemon verbena for a soothing bath; and a few other stewing herbs to keep summer bugs out of the pantry. Even as the century progressed, and the family doctor became more popular, this garden still remained for medicinal and culinary purposes. The "simples" (medicinal herbs) would often be gathered from the fields just to have them handy.

Because of space limitations, you may not be able to have a garden outside your kitchen, but perhaps you can set some magical, medicinal, or seasoning herbs in soil on your window sills throughout the house. They will lend their energy to each room, give off more healthy oxygen to your home, and also smell good. You can then pick off little bits and pieces and have fresh herbs anytime (for inspired "cooking" of any kind). The only caution here is to be certain none of your indoor plants are hazardous to pets, and that they are kept well out of reach of children.

If you are fortunate enough to have a yard, you will want to consider what kinds of herbs and flowers to place in your olitory. Begin by making lists of your cooking herbs, medicinal herbs, aromatics, and preferred flowers for potpourri and decoration. From this list, you will want to choose those plants which have more than one application in your home, and ones which have similar needs for water and sunlight. This way your garden does not have to be large to be extremely useful. You can then stock it with the appropriate herbs for its location (e.g. how much sunlight the area receives daily, the type of soil needed and if it is well irrigated).

Most herbs are best started indoors a few weeks before your growing season, then transplanted into their designated spot in the garden. Generally this will give you a longer period for harvest.

Kitchen Garden

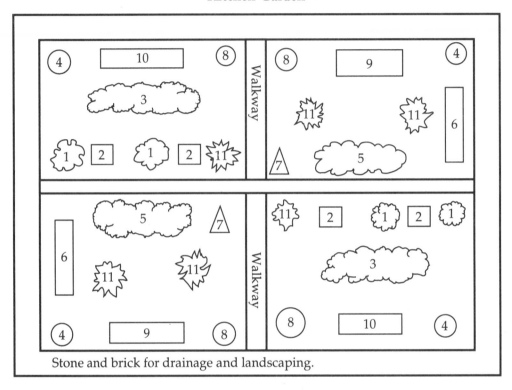

Stone and brick for drainage and landscaping.

1. Dark Opal Basil planted on 1' centers, annual, full aroma.
2. Sage planted on 1' centers, perennial.
3. Thyme planted on 1-1/2' centers, perennial.
4. Chives planted on 1-1/2' centers, harvest before flowering.
5. Peppermint planted on 2' centers, gather seeds in fall for next planting.
6. Dill planted on 2' centers, harvest before flowering, annual.
7. Tarragon planted on 2' patch, cuttings best taken in fall.
8. Garlic planted in late fall for next season, 4 to 5 cloves in 1' area about 2" apart.
9. Lemon Balm planted in 1' radius, annual.
10. Catnip planted on 1-1/2' radius, annual.
11. Spare room for flowers or other herbs.

Please note that the sizes of any of these may be adjusted to meet the space you have available. It is best, however, to plant several seeds in one spot to ensure a good harvest and be able to spot them more readily. In designing your herb garden, also take care that taller plants are placed where they will not shade-out the smaller ones.

Winter Gardens

Tonight the winds begin to rise,
And roar from yonder dripping day,
The last red leaf is whiled away,
The Rooks are blown about the skies.
—Alfred, Lord Tennyson

The Victorian home was a sacred place where the people were constantly engrossed in activities to make the everyday life more pleasant and comfortable. For them, no home could be complete without flowers, so as the cold winter months began to approach, thoughts turned to bringing the gardens of outdoors, indoors! Everything that could survive transplanting from geraniums and lemons, to ivy and ferns would be put into pots and planters of all shapes and sizes. These served to decorate each table and window.

The containers used ranged from the simple clay pot and coconut shells to an elegant porcelain jardiniere, placed conspicuously in the drawing room. One enterprising five year old child, as recounted by "Vick's Magazine" in September 1881, even thought of making one out of a good size gourd, carved properly and decorated by his own hand. The end result of this was that the child spent much time with the indoor plants, and made sure every visitor knew which plants were his!

The more rustic containers were placed in the living room and library, while the fanciful ones were in the parlor and dining room. Some of the little baskets and bundles would be changed by competent hands to reflect the seasons, while others were left to sit in their perch, merrily blooming. In this manner, the contemplative beauties and balm of nature were made a permanent part of Victorian living year round.

The Fernery

Inside the Victorian home could often be found an interesting device called a fernery. This was a miniature greenhouse comprised of pieces of glass. It was designed for ferns, pines, and other plants that only need a little dampness to thrive. The creativity expressed in these was nothing short of amazing. Some incorporated fountains, some were shaped like cathedrals, and others were worked into window boxes in the tradition of Victorian splendor.

Inside of these ferneries, a nymph-like world was created, complete with mossy basins, stained glass, lace and many other lavish accoutrements. This was one of the most popular ways for the Victorians to bring snippets of ferns, mosses and other unusual plants (such as the Venus Fly Trap) into their homes to enjoy.

A fernery can be made today by any number of methods, the easiest of which is to use a covered fish bowl. Place some small rocks (magically charged crystals look lovely) in the bottom then add to this some rich top soil and moss. Ferns, tiny bits of ivy and any plants with smaller root systems can be put in the soil, then sprinkled with water. Finally, small mythical or religious figurines can be placed within the design, the cover put on securely, and you will have a maintenance-free world in miniature to savor.

Another version of the fernery can be made using a clear glass Yule ornament. Follow the same procedure as above, except you will need tweezers to get the plants down through the small opening of the ornament. Once they are in place, you can decorate the outside of the bulb by spraying a little bit of false snow, or gluing a little glitter. Now you have a living decoration for your tree!

Gardening Hints

In creating your garden, it is important to bear in mind that the larger it is, the more work it will be. Work out your design(s) on paper first, being certain to give each plant adequate space and sunlight. Also leave enough space for walkways so you can harvest and weed without damaging your handiwork. During this process consider what theme, if any your garden will have, then choose the plants accordingly.

Once you have your garden planted, you can turn to the Victorians for some helpful hints on its care. Because they worked the land every day, the people of the late 1800s made some very useful observations. For example, they discovered that things like wormwood tea, astrums, garlic, black hellebore, and tobacco smoke discouraged pests in their gardens. This kind of knowledge is especially useful to the gardener who wants to work in a chemical-free environment. Other techniques the Victorian's employed which we can still use include:

- To discourage bugs, sprinkle plants with water which has been boiled with tomato leaves.
- In early spring, mix together and boil: 1 gallon of light mineral oil, 1 pound of soap and a half gallon of water. Spray this on your trees, especially fruit trees, before they flower. This non-toxic oil will discourage many chewing insects in the egg stage.
- For a great fertilizer, mix the soil with ground fresh bone, along with left over coffee grounds, egg shells, and hard wood ash. They also used manure mixed with other natural materials (leaves, grass, wood chips, weeds, sawdust etc.) through composting. If you decide to compost, please check the laws in your area. In certain urban districts it is against city codes.
- If you are having trouble with rabbits, ask one of your local barbers to save you some hair. Placing these clippings at the base of your plants often keeps rabbits away, and sometimes other animals as well.
- Use chicken wire and bells to keep the birds from snacking on your berries.
- Chamomile and/or rosemary tea sprinkled on plants inhibits insect infestation.

Our ancestors also discovered that certain plants seemed to fare better if planted during certain phases of the moon. During the first quarter, when the moon is just starting to be seen, think Green! Plant cabbage, broccoli, asparagus, celery, cucumbers, lettuce, parsley, and/or spinach. In the second quarter, the moon is moving towards full, so consider your round vegetables. Sow melons, beans, peppers, squash, tomatoes and peas. As the moon begins to wane, fill your garden with any root vegetable such as turnips, beets, carrots and radishes. The fourth phase of the moon is a fallow period. This is said to be the best time to weed and turn your soil.

If you are going to be gardening on a regular basis, I suggest you get a couple of books on companion gardening and pest control through herbs and other natural substances. One such book is *Rodale's Illustrated Encyclopedia of Herbs*. It includes medicinal use, legends, name origins, insect regulation and much more than I could easily mention here. Such a book is of endless use to the magical gardener.

Nature has but a few simple materials and yet with this poverty does she trick out all the world in scenes of delicious beauty.
—Shirley Hibberd

FLOWER FANCY

Love's language may be talked with these.
—Elizabeth Barrett Browning

Flowers and plants of all kinds—whether they are fresh, painted, porcelain, cloth or of any other nature were scattered about the Victorian home as leaves on a forest floor. The flower became so adored by people of this era that in 1879 an entire book by Miss Corruthers of Inverness was dedicated to the language of flowers. This book became the standard source for flower symbolism both in England and the United States.

In some respects, the flower (like the fan) afforded a silent language, especially for lovers, that allowed them to communicate many sentiments that the propriety of the times would not normally allow. Also, anything that carried the scent of a particular plant was considered to carry the same message. So should a young lady drop her rosemary-scented handkerchief, it might be considered to say, "my friend, remember me."

In reviewing the list of plants and their associations, the amount of information is almost overwhelming and could easily fill a book. So, listed herein are some of the more frequently noted plants and their meanings. The applications to modern magic are as limitless as your own imagination. Several methods to help get you started are:

- Add the dried plant to an incense being used for an appropriate ritual or spell. For example, add zinnias to your incense if doing a spell to aid a dear friend.
- Add the dried plant to sachets, or make them into oils for magical use. According to the Victorian language, a love sachet or perfumed oil might contain myrtle, acacia, almond and clover for love, hope, and luck. Anointing oils can likewise be made from almond, fennel, chamomile, and yew (for example) for watchfulness, strength, energy and faith.

❧ If you can not always work during specific hours or moon phases, flowers and plants may be harvested during those times for the effect you need. Just remember to mark your jars according to the hour, moon phase and planetary correspondences (if known). The plant may then be used in lieu of working at that specific time. Or, if you can work at the correct moment, the harvesting will only increase the power of the magic.

❧ Look up your plants in a good herb book. Use them according to their gender, color correspondence, folklore etc. In this case, say you don't have the red candle your spell calls for but you do have a bright orange marigold. Use the marigold in place of the candle as your focus! Scott Cunningham has several excellent books available on this subject through Llewellyn Publications.

❧ It should be noted that you can reverse the direction of the flower (e.g. the bloom facing downward) to reverse the intended meaning and energy of the plant, For example, if you wish to stop hatred within yourself, try crushing basil during your spell or ritual as a symbol of breaking that negative and destructive attitude.

Planetary Correspondences for Common Plants

Sun — Orange, saffron, chamomile, sunflower, rosemary, marigold, day lily.
Moon — Melon, pumpkin, water lilies, lettuce, willow, wintergreen.
Mercury — Carrot, marjoram, caraway, parsley, fennel.
Venus — Primrose, periwinkle, violet, apple, strawberry, tomatoes.
Mars — Coriander, garlic, onion, pepper, radish, basil, tarragon.
Jupiter — Fig, clove, anise, oak, nutmeg, sage, dandelion.
Saturn — Elm, pine, barley, cypress.

Please note that Uranus, Neptune and Pluto are not included here because they were undiscovered at this time in history. It is an interesting bit of folklore to note that most people believed plants carried a physical resemblance to the planetary sign governing them.

The Language of Flowers

After the advent of Miss Corruther's books, many other little cards, fans, and books appeared discussing this fragrant language. Listed below are some of the most commonly occurring plants and flowers given in these books. Their messages varied a little here and there with personal perspectives, but for the most part the interpretations were consistent so that the language could be used by any who knew it. For more detailed information on flowers, their language and use throughout history, consult *The Magic Garden* by A. Mercatante and *The Victorians and their Flowers* by Nicollette Scourse.

The Fragrant Language of Flowers

Acacia — Secret love.
Almond — Hope, watchfulness, haste.
Aloe — Superstition.
Aspen — Fear, sensibility.
Balm — Sympathy.
Basil — Hatred.
Bay Leaf — Change.
Birch — Grace.
Buttercup — Riches.
Carnation — Admiration.
Chamomile — Energy.
Cedar — Strength.
Clover — Fertility, luck.
Daisy — Innocence.
Dandelion — Oracle.
Elder — Compassion.
Evergreen — Worth.
Fennel — Strength.
Fir — Time.
Foxglove — Ambition.
Geranium, (silver) — Recall.
Hawthorn — Hope.
Heather — Solitude.
Holly — Foresight, good wishes.
Honeysuckle — Fidelity.
Horse Chestnut — Luxury.
Iris — Hope, messages.

Ivy — Friendship.
Jasmine — Amiability.
Lavender — Answers.
Lilac — First love.
Lily — Purity, joy.
Marigold — Sorrow.
Mistletoe — Overcoming difficulties
Moss — Maternal love.
Myrtle — Love.
Nightshade — Secrets.
Oak — Hospitality.
Pansy — Thoughtfulness.
Periwinkle — Friendship.
Poppy — Sleep, comfort.
Primrose — Consistency.
Rose — Beauty, love.
Rose, (burgundy) — Simple pleasures.
Rose, (versicolor) — Mirthfulness.
Rose, (moss) — Merit.
Sweet William — Treachery.
Thistle — Defiance.
Thyme — Courage.
Sweet William — Treachery.
Violet — Steadfastness.
White Poplar — Time.
Yew — Faith, rebirth.
Zinnia — Friendship.

Flower Books

Another favorite way to dabble away the hours in the parlor was with a flower album. This was a special book of pressed plants, gentle poetry, thoughts of romance and a little botany mixed in for good measure. Once the flowers and plants were dried, they would often be secured to a page with a prettily written bit of wisdom as an accompaniment.

For the creative Witch, this tradition could easily be carried on with your personal diary or Book of Shadows. In some respects, this is not unlike compiling a cook book except that it is a magical one interlaced with pressed flowers, waxed leaves, and matching scented oils—until you have created a very intimate grimoire that reflects all of your vision.

To begin your book, get yourself a blank diary or small notebook from a stationary shop which can be carried with you and a good three-ring binder with dividers. Some of the sections you will probably want to make for yourself include: music, chants, spells, invocations, recipes, food, herbals, lore, meditations, sayings, definitions, rituals, blessings, etc. No matter what sections you set up, always organize your binder in such a way so that you know immediately where to look for each item you might place there.

I suggest that each spell, recipe, etc. should be placed on a separate sheet of paper, then alphabetized within the subdivision. This is for two reasons. First, it allows you to easily remove the paper to make changes, updates, corrections and/or copies for friends. Second, and perhaps more importantly, you can find them more quickly this way.

Keep your smaller diary with you as much as possible. Write in this book your ideas, observations, dreams, etc. When you are with friends discussing magic, make note of their good ideas, recipes, spells and so forth. This may seem rather silly, but more often than not when I don't write them down, I forget and then am angry with myself for missing a good opportunity. Likewise, if you write a ritual or spell for something special, make sure to get an extra copy for your book at home. There is no telling how often you might have the chance to share it with another person or group.

Some people like to use onion skin paper in their binders, then hand calligraph the information for a special flair. If you are looking for special paper, most art supply stores will carry various colors and textures. You can also use spray-applied sealant to protect your work, and your dried flowers. As an alternative to using the spray, you could buy the clear plastic protectors for each page. They are available at most places which carry school supplies.

Another nice touch is to use scented inks which correspond to the magics you are writing about. For this, pour 2 to 3 teaspoons of a strong herbal infusion into a bottle of ink. This proportion should allow the scent to remain on the paper for quite some time. The overall effect of this is not unlike aromatherapy, where particular scents trigger a mental reaction to help prepare you for that specific spell, ritual or whatever. In this instance you may use the language of flowers, a magical herb book or inspired intuition to choose your scents.

About once a month, you should transfer things which will be used on a regular basis out of your traveling note book and into the permanent binder. You may also want to transfer items found in books, if you use them frequently. The idea is to have your favorite and most valued information all in one spot, instead of having to rummage through 18 different volumes. If you are consistent about this, the binder will fill up with wonderful magics from you and your friends in no time!

I can not tell you how often I refer to mine, but it is at least daily. When questions come by the phone or mail, or when other magical people are visiting, it sits center-table as a handy reference and aid. It is also nice to take it out periodically, light a candle and some incense, and sit quietly in my study paging through the beauty of the Goddess in word and thought.

While winking mary-buds begin to open their golden eyes,
With everything that pretty bin, my Lady, sweet, arise!
                                                            —E. Holden

Pressing Plants

Almost all wildflowers and ferns will begin to wilt if carried by hand for too long. Because of this, it is best to lay them between sheets of blotting paper as soon as possible. Also, be sure that any moisture on the leaves is dried off so that they do not discolor or mold.

Arrange your plants with care, according to their texture and color. Ferns can not be too firmly pressed, nor can any flower with more pithy textures. You should change the blotting paper at least twice in a two week period for best results. If any of your plants try to adhere to the paper, a simple tap on the back of the page should loosen them. Mosses and seaweed are about the only exceptions to this rule, the former needing only to be placed in thick paper for pressing once, and the later dried quickly by the fire so it would not loose its color.

Your pressing device may also be of Victorian fashioning. Take a wooden board and several sheets of paper. Layer the plants in between the sheets of paper, making certain there are at least 4 to 6 pieces of paper between each layer. Then place another piece of wood on top and strap the two together to look like a bound book (old belts work exceptionally well for this). You may remove the straps in about 14 days, but the plants should be left to sit for another 48 hours before exposing them to air.

A charming by-product of the Victorian pressings was a moss covered frame for preserving illuminated texts, engravings, or any type of prized art. To create one of these frames, the lady would go to the woods and collect her mosses from dead tree trunks and dry them in a dark, cool area of the home. She would then prepare a very thick paste of flour and water to apply to a wooden frame chosen for its size and shape. Gradually, the entire frame would be covered with the mosses, allowing them to overlap as they do in the wild, with the occasional longer piece making a fern like spray in the background. This is a very simple technique which can be used in your home to make special, nature-based gift items or to keep for your personal decorating.

WEATHER MAGIC

And so whatever the plow-shares run,
The clouds run overhead,
And the soil that works and lets in the sun,
With water is always fed.
                              —Dana Wilber, 1880

It is not surprising that there were quite a few armchair scientists in the Victorian days trying to devise methods to make rain. If they succeeded, they could prevent drought and get rich. Hundreds of people attempted different methods, including one where a small explosive devise was sent up into the clouds via balloon! Besides these efforts, some of the most common superstitions had to do with the foreshadowing of rain and drought, the two things that farmers had to be intimately aware of. Signs of rain included sheep bleating or skipping about, doves coming late in the evening, swallows flying low on the water, fleas biting and toads hopping home.

In a modern city, it is difficult to observe such things. We are left to our senses and our local weather station to indicate the weather ahead. However, during periods of drought or extreme storms and high winds, we may feel guided to work a positive ritual by way of assistance. A good rule of thumb with weather magic is to release the energy to the Divine and let Her decide how best to use it. Remember, you are tampering with the weather patterns of a whole planet.

Calming a Storm

Interestingly enough, this may be an actual storm or one of an emotional nature. If the later, you may wish to change the wording somewhat, but the outcome is no less effective.

Begin by sprinkling lavender and violet into the wind for peacefulness. Then, stand with your arms raised, a silver bell in your strong hand, and a clear vision of your purpose in mind. Chant the following three times, softly first, then with growing conviction, "Thunder, lighting, winds and rain, calm ye now, bring peace again. Let drops fall gentle and fires quell, when thrice rings this silver bell."

Ring the bell slowly three times, releasing the energy of your magic in the direction of the storm.

To Disperse a Wind

Take a feather you have found
Plant it firmly in the ground
Legend has it, so they say
That those winds will fade away!

To Bring Wind

Take a fluff of dandelion and blow it towards the East, visualizing the winds bringing it back to you.

To Bring Rain

Each time I do rain magic, I am reminded of the old children's rhyme, "Rain, rain go away," although these days it is more common to wish for rain to come. An adaptation of this rhyme may be used in weather spells very effectively. How you change it depends directly on the need, but use it as a chant, adding a drum or other rhythmic sound to help the effect.

An example of this came from my husband. To ask for rain, he took a handful of water, and tossed it into the sky and chanted three times, "Rain, rain, come our way. Fill our skies, refresh the land. I give you water from my hand." When the water is tossed into the sky, it releases the energy to begin working.

Another rain chant given me by my friend Morgana is "Tiamat, Osiris, Mari, Neptune, Poseidon, Isis, bring the rain soon!" This chant lends itself very well to some kind of dance or movement as it grows naturally in energy until you release it. Traditional herbs which may be burnt during any of these spells to increase their effectiveness include fern, heather, and rice. In the instance of the latter, you may also want to soak the rice in water, allowing it to draw the rain towards you.

It is interesting to note that creating the sound of rain is one of the more popular methods of working weather magic in various cultures. To do this, people sometimes take a stick and slap it against the water of a river or pond, or wet a broom and shake it outside. This type of sympathetic magic is very old, growing out of legends and tales.

To Bring Favorable Weather

An old sailor's superstition says that if you find a coin on deck and toss it into the winds before sailing, it will bring favorable weather. At home, you may wish to save pennies found for this, and toss them toward the wind before venturing out for the day.

OTHER OUTDOOR MAGICS

Safe Travel Spells

Softly chant this spell over your vehicle before going on a trip: "Lady light, be our guide, where 'er we are, stand by our side. Keep us safe by will and might, keep us always in your sight." Another version of this spell entails taking a leaf or paper airplane and allowing it to float in the general direction of your destination, using the same chant as it moves gently to the ground.

Manifestation

This spell can be done in your own driveway. Mark a symbol of what you wish manifested in your life in the dust resting in the drive. Then, using a hose, wash the wish out to find its way, and perhaps scrub the car at the same time!

There are many other applications the natural world gives us for our magic. All we need do is look around us with the appreciative eyes of our Victorian ancestors, and take advantage of what we have been given with a touch of inventiveness, respect and lots of love.

I take thee, herb, to cure my ills
Or perhaps while dancing 'pon the hill.
I'll dip you in the cauldron fine
Then asperge a circle in the pines.
I'll make you into teas and brews
When picked from 'neath the morning dews,
Or hide you in a pillow seam
To guard me close, come night and dreams.
— Marian Loresinger

CHAPTER FIVE

The Victorian Herbalist

Be careful of reading health books, you may die of a misprint.
— Mark Twain

The Victorian lady knew her plants and herbs out of necessity. The women were taught from the time they were very young not to buy anything that they could produce themselves at home, especially things grown easily in the garden. So, the kitchen garden was stuffed full and tended well; its contents were used year round to flavor food, scent baths, and cure all manner of ills.

Folk medicine and herbalism flourished during Victorian days because most doctors were far too expensive to consult on a regular basis. So, it was the wife who managed the care of the family's health. Many "age-old" remedies we still quote today come from this time. The kitchen was the place where the domestic and healing arts flowered along side of other daily activities, such as homework, sewing, and ironing.

Magical formulas and ancient practices were still held in high regard by these people. They often made pilgrimages to see herbalists and bonesetters, visit magic fountains, etc. Hawkers and barkers sold medicine which borrowed so much from real medical knowledge that this may have well been the beginning of medicalization. Other healers, whose talents were being limited by law, may have also had an effect on our modern professions of surgery and orthopedics.

Today we have begun to rediscover the merits of herbalism. Not only do many of the herbal remedies work remarkably well, but they are natural and are not harmful to the environment. Before we start, though, we must reclaim some of the basic knowledge our Victorian ladies learned at the feet of their mothers. First, an understanding of the technical terms traditionally used by herbalists is very helpful to this art. A brief list of these terms and remedies, as well as descriptions of how to make them, follows for your reference. When preparing herbal remedies, always use stoneware or enamel pans if possible for best results.

HERBAL TERMINOLOGY

Decoction

Place 1 ounce of herb in 1 pint of water. Make certain that the roots are put in to boil before the leaves. Once the water has come to a boil, simmer for about 30 minutes, *covered*. Then let it cool completely. Strain and use as directed.

Gem Elixir

This is a potion of sorts, which uses the natural energy of a crystal combined with the sun or moon to create a specific magical effect. To make an elixir, select a stone for its magical properties and place it in distilled water. Next, place it either in the light of the sun or moon (depending on the energy you want manifested) for 2 weeks. I recommend keeping the top of your container covered with cloth if you plan to drink the elixir, to keep out dust and bugs. These elixirs can also be well-employed in the tub.

Infusion

The original form of a potion, an infusion is not unlike a tea in quality. To make an infusion, pour boiling water over your herb in the proportions of 1 ounce of the herb to 1 pint of water (although you may need much less of the herb for herbs that infuse quickly in water). Steep for 15 to 30 minutes until a tea is formed. Use as directed.

Macerate

Macerate means to extract and soften through the use of a liquid, usually an oil. For our purposes, it will generally refer to the process of steeping an herb in fat, as is done with salve and ointments. The best oils to use are almond and sesame. Warm 1 cup of oil over low flame. Wrap 1/2 ounce of the herbs in cheese cloth and place them in the oil to soak. Continue until the herbs have lost their color and the oil is rich with their scent.

Ointment

An ointment is a fatty substance, such as lard, to which herbs are added. Choose herbs according to the effect you desire to create. For healing ointments, choose the herbs that correspond to the physical ailment. Here is the recipe: Steep 3 teaspoons of herb in 1 cup of fat; heat and steep it several times and it should prove very nice. If you desire, you may leave the herb in the ointment for a stronger effect. (There is a recipe which allows you to preserve it later in this chapter.)

For those of you who do not want to use animal fat, vegetable shortening will work very well, especially almond and saffron. All ointments should be kept cool and in airtight containers for best results. For magic, ointments work best when applied to pulse points or chakras.

Poultice

A poultice is made from finely ground, moistened herbs. Here is the basic recipe: Add 1/2 ounce of the herb to 1/2 ounce boiling water; steep. Once the herbs have been fully dampened, strain the water and place herbs in gauze or cheese cloth and apply it directly to the affected area. This can be a little messy, so have a towel handy, but it does work fairly well, especially for rashes and other mild skin disorders.

Tincture

A tincture is a solution of herbs and alcohol. Here is the basic recipe: 4 ounces of herb steeped in 8 ounces of alcohol for about 2 weeks will give you a reasonable tincture. The bottle containing the mixture should be sealed and left in a dark area. I have also had reasonable success with combining fresh and infused herbs, adding alcohol, and then leaving them in the sunlight. Take care, as alcohol should not be allowed to get too warm . . . it can evaporate or internal pressure can explode a bottle.

Wash

A tea or infusion meant only for external use. A mild form of a wash would be 1/4 ounce herb to 1 pint of boiling water, steeped until lukewarm and then applied.

Other Notes

A tea ball works very well for steeping herbs, as does cheese cloth or gauze. Most herbs can be measured out with common measuring spoons. If you plan on making and storing various oils and concoctions, go to Goodwill or other second hand stores and get bottles with *secure caps* for storage. These should be cleaned with boiling water before use. Various sized funnels, a mortar and pestle, eye droppers, a small sharp knife, labels and perhaps even a reference file for your recipes and sources all are good things to have on hand.

I cannot emphasize enough the importance of a *clean working area and tools*. Fresh herbs should always be rinsed before use, and all tools washed in warm, soapy water. This is your personal health and well being of your family we are talking about, so don't skimp on this step.

THE WHO'S WHO OF KITCHEN HERBS

This delightful herb whose garden green,
Fledges the river's lip on which we lean.
—Edward Fitzgerald

Second to understanding the jargon of our ancestors is knowing what herbs were used and how. There have been many wonderful books written on folk medicine and magical herbalism in recent years. In the interest of not beating a "dead horse," the only herbs and plants (including trees and garden flowers) listed herein are those most common to the average household. Should you desire a more detailed account of herbs and their uses, I highly recommend any herbal books by Cunningham, Beyerl, Culpeper, Gerald and others who have spent a lifetime researching that subject.

It should also be noted that although certain magical effects have been attributed to various herbs over the ages, this doesn't mean you can't use the herb in a different spell because of its significance to you. For example, although the bay leaf is not directly associated with love magic, perhaps you bit into one the night your husband proposed. For you, this little leaf brings romance and joy into mind, so you may wish to use it for those ends in your magic.

This is why I cannot stress enough the importance of using your own creativity and life experience for Victorian enchantments. The end result is to have a spell, ritual or whatever that is far more meaningful and powerful to use and to share with friends.

In employing herbalism for remedial purposes, I issue a bit of caution. Herbal "cures" were applied for many years when medical knowledge was not available. While medical science still finds many herbal recipes have very real healing qualities, under no circumstances should this become a substitute for proper treatment by professionals, especially regarding life-threatening illnesses.

ALLSPICE

Magic — Love and healing.
Medicinal — Tea for cramps or gas.
Other — Aromatic for oils, potpourri.

APPLE

Magic — Love, health, peace.
Medicinal — For intestinal infections (raw or as a tea); for stress (apple juice in the morning); for hoarseness (baked apple with butter and honey).
Other — Dried as decoration and used in foods.

BASIL

Magic — Purification, protection, love, initiation.
Medicinal — For minor wounds (boil fresh leaves in salt water and apply to the wound); for gas, tense stomach (use in a tea or steeped in wine).
Other — Aromatic, good with herb vinegars, excellent in a rinse for hair luster.
Lore — Sacred herb of Vishnu and Krishna. If a man gives a sprig to a lady, she will fall in love and never leave him.

BAY LEAF

Magic — Protection, purification, good wishes, victory.
Medicinal — Bruises (ointment or poultice made from leaves or berries and applied).
Other — Aromatic, good for stew and soups. Often used in branches for herb wreaths; a mild insect repellent.

BIRCH

    Magic — Excellent for connecting with the forest spirits.
    Medicinal — For headaches (tea); for burns and bruises (poultice from bark).
    Other — Make birch beer from branches; make skin lotion from branches/leaves boiled.

CARAWAY

    Magic — Luck, passion.
    Medicinal — Digestive aid for children (tea mixed with milk).
    Other — Increase milk flow for nursing mothers. Leaves can be added to salads and roots and be cooked like parsnips.

CARROT

    Magic — Sex.
    Medicinal — For liver ailments; as a juice to ward off flu and colds; as a cream soup for children with diarrhea.
    Other — Snack food for nervous eaters.

CATNIP

    Magic — Love, cat familiars, animal friendship.
    Medicinal — Colds, headache, sedative (tea).
    Other — As a digestive aid and a treat, dip fresh leaves in egg white and lemon, then dust with sugar. Let dry. Store in refrigerator.

CAYENNE

    Magic — Purification, motivation.
    Medicinal — Purgative. Also can be used in a liniment: To prepare this liniment, add 1 tablespoon cayenne to 1 pint cider vinegar and warm the liquid. For sore throat, mix with water and gargle.
    Other — From the Greek word meaning "to bite."

CELERY

    Magic — Sex, weight loss. Seeds are used in divination.
    Medicinal — Insomnia, swollen glands. Use the seeds in a tea.

CHAMOMILE

    Magic — Protection, success.
    Medicinal — For insomnia (a concentrated infusion); for fevers (a light tea); for pain (oil applied to affected area); for eczema (compress applied).
    Other — Chamomile flowers in a medium wash make an excellent deodorant and shampoo.

CHIVES

Magic — Protection.
Medicinal — As an antiseptic (oil); for faintness (oil).
Other — Flowers may be used in salads.

CINNAMON

Magic — Purification, money, love.
Medicinal — Tea to calm the stomach.
Other — Aromatic; good for potpourri. As an air freshener—take a few sticks of cinnamon, adding fresh ginger root and nutmeg to an open pot of hot water.

CLOVES

Magic — Stop gossip, protection for children, kinship.
Medicinal — For toothache (oil); for stomach trouble (tea).
Other — Aromatic; principle ingredient in pomanders.

CORIANDER

Magic — Protection, love.
Medicinal — For digestion (crushed seeds in tea).
Other — Roots and leaves are edible.
Lore — A bunch of fresh coriander tied with a ribbon and hung in the kitchen is said to bring harmony to the home.

CUCUMBER

Magic — Healing, fertility.
Medicinal — For headache (place fresh peels on your forehead); for dandruff (leaf and root in tincture); for puffy eyes (place raw slices over each eye to sooth the discomfort).
Other — Often used in facial creams for moisturizing effects.

DAISY

Magic — To attract the Fairy Folk; love divination.
Medicinal — For canker sores (chew the fresh leaves).
Other — Leaves may be used in salads or cooked as a vegetable.

DANDELION

Magic — Wishes, welcoming.
Medicinal — Laxative (mild infusion of leaf and root).
Other — May be used in salads, or as a base for wine. The tops can be chopped and added to butter. Yellow dye for wool is made from the flowers. For a face rinse, boil fresh flowers for 60 minutes and strain.

DILL

Magic — Mental strength; blessing.
Medicinal — To aid in sleeping (warm dill water); to relieve colic (tea).
Other — From the Norse word meaning "to lull."

ELM

Magic — Grounding, protection, divination.
Medicinal — As an astringent (bark boiled in water, flowers steeped for tea).
Other — The water in elm leaves, if removed by mortar and pestle, makes
a wonderful skin cleanser.

FENNEL

Magic — Strength, weight loss.
Medicinal — For hiccups (tea); for flu (spoonful in warm milk).
Other — Used as a breath freshener (tea). For a facial, make an infusion of
ground seeds. Also used to make brown dye.
Lore — Take a fresh sprig of fennel, dip it in water and sprinkle that water
around your home for protection.

GARLIC

Magic — Protection, purification, health.
Medicinal — For hoarseness (mix garlic, honey and warm milk); for infection
(put a mild concentration of the juice on gauze, apply to skin);
for worms in dogs (one clove, eaten).
Other — "There is no such thing as too much garlic."

GINGER

Magic — Health.
Medicinal — Indigestion or motion sickness (crystallized or in a tea).
Other — Ginger beer made from the whole root.

GRAPEFRUIT

Magic — Weight loss, purification, health.
Medicinal — Good any time you need vitamin C.
Other — Rinds may be dried and used in potpourri, or any time
citric acid is required in a recipe.

LEMON

Magic — Love, joy, banishing bad habits.
Medicinal — For your liver (infusion of 1 tablespoon honey, sliced lemon);
for cold/chills (lemon tea in very hot coffee); for sore throat (gargle with
lemon juice and honey); headache (place 1/2 lemon on each temple and wrap
a cloth around around your head to secure them. Leave on for 15 minutes.)

Other — Dry peels hung in closets will ward off moths. Lemon juice may be used to clean silver jewelry.

LETTUCE

Magic — Tranquility, money.
Medicinal — For insomnia (decoction of leaves); for bronchitis (about 1/2 cup decoction, 3 times daily).
Other — Lotion for acne and boils (use seeds).

MARIGOLD

Magic — Consecration, blessing.
Medicinal — For burns (flowers in compress or lotion); for dandruff (infusion applied to scalp); for warts (fresh crushed leaves applied to skin).
Other — Add to butter for coloring; use in a rinse to lighten hair.

MARJORAM

Magic — Marriage and love.
Medicinal — For colds, migraines, sleeplessness (infusion); for muscle pain, toothache (oil); for hay fever (gargle with tea).
Other — Tops yield a green dye.
Lore — Put sprigs in your hope chest or around house to freshen air and bring love.

MINTS

Magic — Success, motivation.
Medicinal — For hiccoughs, mild stimulant (infusion); for coughs (use in vaporizer); for pain (in balm or lotion); to ease stomach (mint in warm milk); for toothache (oil).
Other — Put crushed leaves on insect bites to relieve sting; mint water makes refreshing drink or facial.

MUSTARD SEED

Magic — Courage, faith.
Medicinal — For muscle pain and increased blood flow (use seed paste).
Other — Leaves may be used in salads.

OAK

Magic — Luck, fertility.
Medicinal — For hemorrhoids (mashed compresses of outer bark); for vaginal infection (boiled tincture of inner bark); for gargle (tea of inner bark).

ONION

Magic — Protection, endurance.

Medicinal — For infected wounds (paste of boiled onions and their juice);
for baldness (rub on head and lie in the sun); for weight loss
(eat an onion a day).

Lore — It is said that Alexander the Great fed onions to his troops before battle
to give them strength.

ORANGE

Magic — Prosperity, joy and love.

Medicinal — For stomach distress (orange flower-water and sugar mixed in
a light tea, or a tea of fresh leaves).

Other — To make a nice wine, put 6 oranges in a quart of brandy and let them
sit for 2 weeks. Then add 1 quart of wine, strain and let the mixture age
for at least 2 weeks or more. This gets better with time.

OREGANO

Magic — Joy, energy.

Medicinal — For swelling (poultice applied to muscles); for
coughs/headaches/menstrual aid (mild tea); for stiff joints (herbal bath).

PARSLEY

Magic — Prosperity, luck, energy.

Medicinal — For insect bites (apply crushed fresh leaves); for cramps
(infusion of fresh leaves); as a laxative (mild tea made from the root).

Other — Parsley acts as a natural breath freshener.

Lore — It is said that the Greeks placed wreaths of parsley on their horses
to give them stamina.

POPLAR

Magic — Relief from grief.

Medicinal — A tea made from poplar buds is much like aspirin and is good
for any ailment which calls for it.

Lore — It is believed that the fabled Willows of Babylon were poplars.

PINE

Magic — Repels negative energy, cleansing.

Medicinal — For sinus (decoction of buds); as a douche (decoction of buds);
for pain (decoction of needles in a bath); for boils/acne (paste of inner bark);
for anemia (mild tea of needles).

RADISH

Magic — Strength, protection.
Medicinal — For jaundice (eat 2 radishes in the morning); for cough
    (slice radishes thin, sugar them and let sit for 24 hours. Strain and
    take 1 teaspoon every hour).

ROSE

Magic — Red for passion, pink for simplicity, white for innocence or protection,
    yellow for jealousy.
Medicinal — For boils (poultice of inner root bark); for sore throat (rose petal tea).
Other — Jams, jellies, rose water, wines, etc. Chew on petals to freshen the breath.
Lore — The Greeks believed the red rose got its color from from the Goddess
    Aphrodite, whose foot got stuck on a thorn when giving aid to Adonis.

ROSEMARY

Magic — Memory (wear a sprig in your hair); protection against bad dreams
    (place on pillow).
Medicinal — For rheumatism/bruises (mild oil in liniment); for sickness
    in the home (burn sage in the house—it has an antibacterial effect);
    for an antiseptic (strong tea).
Other — Put it among your stored clothes or books to keep moths away.

SAFFRON

Magic — Prosperity, love.
Medicinal — Aphrodisiac, appetite aid (a pinch in tea).
Other — To bring out red highlights in your hair, make a saffron tea
    and rinse with it twice a week.

SAGE

Magic — Safety (for children); longevity.
Medicinal — For digestion (2 to 3 leaves as a tea); for stress (2 to 3 capfuls a day,
    as infusion); as a gargle (decoction); for diarrhea (infusion in warm milk).
Other — Crush some sage leaves and add them to baking soda to use
    as a deodorant.
Lore — From the Latin word for salvation.

SAVORY

Magic — Sexual magic of any kind.
Medicinal — Sore throat (make a tea by mixing 2 teaspoons of herb in
    1 cup of water, taken once a day).
Lore — From the roman word meaning Satyr.

TARRAGON

Magic — Fatigue (put a sprig in your shoes).

Medicinal — For fungus (place some powdered tarragon in your shoes); for sore throat (mild tea).

Lore — From the French word meaning "little dragon," because of its serpent-like roots.

THYME

Magic — Shyness, honor.

Medicinal — As an antiseptic (poultice of leaves); for digestion (tea); for toothache (raw leaf crushed and applied).

Other — Insects (burn thyme to get insects out of the house).

Lore — A bed of thyme is believed to be a home to the Fey.

VIOLET

Magic — Jealousy, creativity, comfort.

Medicinal — Expectorant (tea of fresh petals and leaves).

Other — Violet petals are good candied, and also make a lovely water for cooking or creams.

WILLOW

Magic — Moon magic, healing, love.

Medicinal — The bark is an aspirin substitute. Use 1 teaspoon of bark boiled in 1-1/2 pints of water for 30 minutes.

Other — Traditionally binds the witch's broom and makes good wands.

WINTERGREEN

Magic — Refreshing.

Medicinal — For aches (a cloth soaked in water and wintergreen oil); for fever/ulcers (mild tea).

Other — Chew for a few moments to freshen the breath.

Science is the housewife's hand maiden,
invention a servant following her to light the path
where she has not yet discovered the need for light.
— Lillian W. Betts

COLLECTING, DRYING, AND STORING HERBS

In every copse and shelter'd dell,
Unveil'd to the observant eye,
Are faithful monitors which tell
How pass the hours and seasons by.
—Charlotte Smith

Now that you have the information on how various herbs were used, you can begin to take the precious plants from the gardens into your home. Because of the harsh winters, the Victorian people were very aware of the advantages of canning vegetables, drying their herbs, and preserving flowers for use throughout the cold season. This was especially important for them considering sickness was more prevalent during these months, and the kitchen garden would long be buried under the veils of snow.

Many of the techniques we use today have been handed down to us from this era, and the generations which preceded them. For the Victorian lady, pressing all kinds of leaves and plants was very popular as a "gentle" pursuit. There is a certain charm about opening a book and finding a small bloom lying there silently, ready to bring a smile to your face.

Aside from the obvious practical and artistic advantages, having dried herbs year round is very handy for magical work. While many of your magical herbs are picked at Litha, you may harvest them at other points of the year's wheel for the different effects which coincide with the symbolism of different seasons.

Information on canning can be found in almost any good cook book, so I have not presented it here. Instead, I have dedicated space to helpful hints on gathering and preparing your herbs for use any time of the year. Once you have your herbs dried, they can be employed for everything from herb wreaths to healing.

Seeds

Plants such as caraway, dill and fennel are best picked when ripe and fragrant before they fall to the ground. When the pod develops, you can tie paper or cheesecloth bags to the stem, and let the seeds ripen and then catch them neatly as they fall. An alternative to this is to cut the plant while still green, tying no more than eight stems together, and place them upside down in a paper bag to dry. This method is very effective, but be sure to label all of your bags. A third technique is to gather just the pods and string them over a cheesecloth net. Which ever method you choose, be certain to keep your seeds in a well-aired place for best results.

Roots

Roots (such as comfrey) are best when you pull the entire plant from the ground late in the fall. Wash your roots carefully, breaking them up into small pieces. Lay them to dry on flat screens. Make sure they are spread out, and turn them once or twice a week to ensure even drying. They can then be ground in a coffee filter or good blender for use any time.

Gathering Seeds

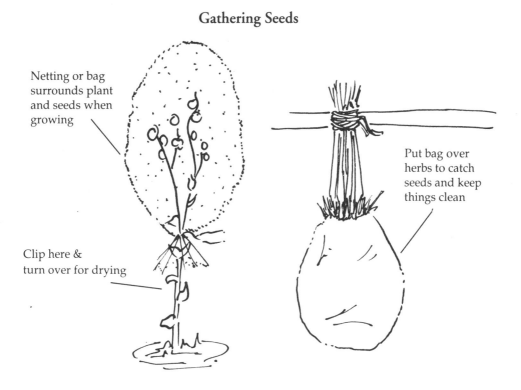

Netting or bag surrounds plant and seeds when growing

Clip here & turn over for drying

Put bag over herbs to catch seeds and keep things clean

Barks

Barks should be gathered in vertical strips during the late fall or early spring. Although hanging them on a clothes line is an effective means of drying, all too often the rain comes to delay your efforts. Instead, use a dry spot in your house where you can hang them in a similar manner, then grind them as you would roots.

Flowers

Flowers are best picked first thing in the morning before the sun gets hot. Half open blooms are excellent because they hold together better, while fully opened ones tend to loose petals easily. You can then place them on screens until they are dry. An even better approach is to buy a length of cheese cloth and hang it about 1 foot from the ceiling in an airy room, laying the flowers inside the hammock to dry. The extra advantage to this is the wonderful aroma the room has as the fall breeze moves through!

The Victorians had many methods for drying flowers. A favorite way was to take some well-cleaned, white, fine sand and fill a stone flower pot with it. Gather the flowers and set them in the sand carefully and cover them completely. This vessel is then placed in the sun or (in a room where the fire is kept) until the flowers are dry. Remove them with care and dust them with a feather to remove the last of the sand. About 1 week seems to be the timing on this method, but it varies according to the plant being dried. To alleviate this uncertainty, leave 1 "sample" piece close to the surface to check periodically.

Herbs

When harvesting herbs for drying, cut the stalk about half way from the top of the plant. Clean off all dirts and molds with a soft toothbrush. The herbs can be placed on a cookie sheet in a warm oven for quick drying as long as you take care to stir frequently. With the wonders of modern conveniences, herbs can also be dried in a microwave. Place them between a layer of paper towels, set the microwave for 3 minutes, and stop every 30 seconds to turn them.

If you plan to hang-dry your herbs, and dust is a problem, you can cover them with a paper bag, open-end down. Parsley, coriander and rosemary can be dried very well in the refrigerator by simply placing them in a sealed paper bag and waiting for 30 days. This process allows the herb to dry but still retain its color and shape. In this form they are excellent for use in herb wreaths.

Once your herbs and plants are dry, keep them in a cool area so that their fragrance and flavor are not dispersed.

Herb Wreaths

*Let thy graceful wreath for one moment be lightly flung
round the mirror of beauty to show Her beneath.*
— Rebecca Hey

Herb wreaths were among the many creative Victorian methods for storing herbs. They were practical and made excellent decorations for the home. It was not uncommon to see a circle of myrtle with well-made muslin flowers, pine cones, leaves, and dried flowers adorning almost any room of the house. When they didn't have the flowers, they used substitutes such as shells, leather, hair, and seaweed to create a floral effect.

The culinary gardener might design a wreath out of rosemary, parsley, bay leaves, dill, and garlic so that they could walk to the wreath and pick off their supper herbs. The magical gardener can also be creative and make wreath arrangements designed to encourage good fortune, love, blessing, health and any number of other enchanted compositions for their home, friends, family and rituals.

To make a wreath, take some heavy wire and lash some straw or Spanish moss to it with lighter, florist's wire. This will create your base for the wreath. (Sometimes you can get prefabricated bases at hobby and craft shops, but it is fun to make your own and bend them into interesting shapes.)

Once the base is affixed, decide on your background or predominant color and fill in with the appropriate herb or flower. Insert these until the whole wreath is covered. A little glue may be added to the end of each sprig to give extra security. If you wish to periodically place fresh flowers in your arrangement, you can tuck in a few water tubes from the florist beneath the greenery. Finally, place accent flowers or herbs all around the wreath (taking into consideration their symbolic relationship to the whole piece), then add a few ribbons or lace and whatever else pleases your eye to finish your creation.

One note of caution. I do not suggest making a medicinal herb wreath, unless it is only used for decoration. This is because dust which collects from displaying it is not conducive to healthy remedies. Also, generally speaking, the rule "the fresher, the better" tends to be true with most remedial care.

Making Herbal Wreaths

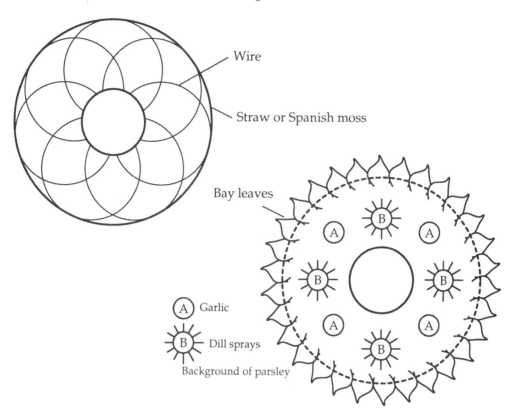

Wire

Straw or Spanish moss

Bay leaves

(A) Garlic

(B) Dill sprays

Background of parsley

DYEING WITH HERBS

*True economy of housekeeping is simply the art
of gathering up all the fragments so that nothing
be lost — I mean time as well as materials.*
— Mrs. Ellet, 1857
The Practical Housekeeper

Our Victorian ancestors discovered that a wide variety of leaves, barks, flowers, and roots could create permanent dyes. The natural substances usually needed fixing agents, such as chromic acid, iron, tin crystals, potash or copper sulfate. I mention herbal dyes here because I know many people are leery of using commercially produced ones. Also, the colors produced from natural ingredients are far brighter than those provided by artificial dyes.

To reproduce this process for home or magical use, you will need: a large iron pot, a fixing agent (alum, chrome, tin or copper), a large stirring utensil; the cloth you want to dye, and spring water. Begin by preparing what is basically an herbal bath for the fabric. Steep blossoms for 30 minutes; barks and roots should be soaked overnight then boiled for 1 hour; and berries are best crushed and cooked for 30 minutes. This mixture is strained and then left sitting.

Next, mix water with your fixative to dissolve it. Use the following proportions to create the fixative. For 1 gallon of water you need:

1-3/4 teaspoons alum and 1-1/2 teaspoons cream of tartar
1/2 teaspoon chrome
1 teaspoon tin and 1-1/2 teaspoons cream of tartar
2 teaspoons copper

Add your cloth to this solution and simmer for about 30 minutes. Squeeze out the fixative liquid and move your cloth into the herbal bath. How long the fabric remains in the herbal bath is personal preference. Begin with 30 minutes, then remove to check the color. If it is not dark enough, put it back in the pot to continue soaking. Once the color desired is reached, rinse your cloth in very hot water and allow to air dry.

Here are some of the dye colors you can achieve using plants:

Black — Boil the material with sorrel leaves, then boil again with
    longwood and copperas.
Blue — Elderberry, also wode.
Brown — Hop stalks.
Crimson — Pokeberry boiled with alum.
Gold — Chamomile and chrome.
Green — Pressed goldenrod mixed with indigo and alum, parsley,
    bay and alum, lily of the valley and alum.
Ocher — Red clover and chrome.
Orange/Yellow — Sassafras bark or balsam flowers, bloodroot.
Pink — Pink zinnias and chrome.
Purple — Iris petals, marjoram flowers and alum.
Red — Madder, dogwood.
Yellow/Brown — Hickory or red oak bark, catnip and alum,
    marigold and alum.

Along much the same lines it is possible to make natural dyes for your Eostre eggs without the fixative. Bring the herb to boil, then simmer 30 minutes. Add 1 teaspoon of vinegar in an enamel pan and then dip your eggs. For best results use the following:

Blues or Purple — Red cabbage, blueberry, blackberry.
Brown — Coffee grounds, walnut shells, maple bark.
Green/Yellow — Carrots, calendula, onion skins.
Reds — Cooked beets, cranberry, raspberry.

You may want to experiment with combinations for various shades and effects.

THE SONG OF SIMPLES

Oh, who can tell the hidden powre of
herbes and might of magic spell.
— Edmund Spenser

Simples, as discussed before, were herbs used medicinally by the Victorian people. This word was also used to describe many of the home remedies. Perhaps this was because of their obviously "simple" and pragmatic approach to discomfort. Many of these recipes and ideas have been handed down to us with little change—thanks to increased literacy, people who kept diaries, and the technology of improved printing equipment.

Since the study of simples is worthy of a book itself, I have given but a brief list here to aid you in your home. In applying them, realize that most simples were not created to be mystical cures, but useful ones. In some instances, folk medicines grew out of superstition or magical charms, but those more commonly used were employed because their abilities had been time-proven through the centuries. The magic was not supernatural, but very natural, because it came from the herb itself. Most folk medicine has a magical side which lends itself very well to our modern practices.

I have included some mystically based remedies here to show the historical nature of symbolic magic and a little of the charm of folk remedies. Some will strike you as humorous, others as absurd, but in many we can still see the glimmers of country magic shining through. Should you decide to try any, I suggest using them imaginatively, as your inspiration and wisdom dictate.

To make a simple more magical is no more difficult than any other form of cooking magic. A little bit of white-light energy and love blended in for good measure never hurt anyone. I repeat however, that herbals, simples and magical "cures" may not be enough for more serious problems. If symptoms persist, please use common sense and seek the help of a professional. Herbalism is a wonderful way to help your family live healthier as long as it is kept in perspective. Seeing a doctor when other methods fail is not a lack of faith, it is wisdom.

Abracadabra

While this particular charm has been around since the second century as a ward against disease and disaster, the following poem can still be found in an 1864 copy of *The Gnostics and Their Remains*, by C. W. King:

> *Each under each in even order place,*
> *but the last letter in each line efface.*
> *As by degrees the elements grow few*
> *Still take away, but fix the residue,*
> *Till at last, one letter stands alone*
> *And the whole dwindles to a tapering cone.*

Tie about the neck with a flaxen string
Might the good 'twill to the patient bring,
Its wondrous potency shall guard his head
And drive disease and death far from his bed.

Acne

Wash 3 times daily with tincture of dandelion and chamomile.

Another method is to take 1 teaspoon each borage flower tips, chicory, ash leaves, mugwort, wild pansy, and sage and boil them for 45 minutes in a quart of water. Place this liquid in a bowl and steam your face for at least 5 minutes, then dry it off with cotton. Repeat this once a day for 3 weeks, take 1 week off, and repeat again in this manner for the next 2 months.

Amulet

Any ring made of 3 strands of braided mistletoe gathered on June 22nd by the light of the moon and worn was believed to be a powerful form of protection.

Backache

Next time you have a backache, bake a towel! Take a bath towel and dampen it thoroughly, then place it in the oven or microwave to warm. Apply to the area that hurts. If you find that heat does not relieve your troubles, try an ice pack. One or the other should ease your discomfort.

Bee Stings

Several old methods for easing this discomfort have been handed down in my family. One is simply to make a paste of baking soda or salt and apply it directly to the wound. Two other methods, less familiar to me, are to slice either a clove of garlic or onion bulb, placing it on the sting with some tape until the discomfort eases.

Birth Pains

Raspberry leaf tea is supposed to ease the pain, along with a knife placed under the bed to slice discomfort away.

Boils

Make a poultice of flour and bruised ginger to apply to the boil. Leave in place for at least 1 hour to help draw it out.

Bug Repellent

Men should stop fighting themselves and start fighting insects.
—Luther Burbank

This recipe is especially good for children who are afraid of (or dislike) the commercial aerosol repellents.

Take 1 cup of almond or coconut oil and warm it with pennyroyal and citronella (oils can be obtained from many herb shops). Add to this approximately 1/2 of a 9-inch taper candle (any color is fine) and begin beating with a fork. Continue until a creamy texture is achieved, then pour into a container with a good seal for the lid. Store and use as needed. For the magical flair here, add herbs of protection.

Burns

If you are burned in the kitchen and can get to your refrigerator, yogurt and/or butter help relieve the pain of a burn very well. A fresh slice of potato or aloe gel applied directly to the burn, or a tea leaf poultice will also ease the soreness.

Burn, Bruise and Scratch Cream

You can easily make this ointment at home. The basic process of this can be adapted for literally hundreds of lotions depending upon your need. If you want, you can make a scented skin lotion for moisturizing by simply deleting the healing herbs and substituting flower petals and other aromatic herbs.

Measure 1/2 teaspoon each of yarrow, marshmallow root, comfrey, roses, sage, mint, rosemary and pine. Steep these in 1 cup of mineral oil over a low flame, until the oil smells strongly of the herbs. Strain through cheese cloth and beat in approximately 2 tablespoons of honey until smooth. Add some wax (equal to about 1/2 of a 9-inch taper). Allow to melt and then begin beating. When the ointment begins to get creamy and semi-solid, pour it into a container with a lid. Seal and use as needed.

This ointment has a very long shelf life (well over a year). I carry mine with me camping, to picnics, or any place else people are likely to have sunburn, scratches, or bumps to attend to. For a base which will have a stronger moisturizing ability, add cocoa butter, lanolin and/or aloe to the wax.

Cold Brew

Make a tea of eucalyptus leaves, marshmallow flowers, lavender, mint, marjoram, rosemary and thyme. Steep herbs for 5 minutes in 3 cups of hot water, then strain. Drink this hot 3 times a day, with honey and 1 teaspoon of lemon.

Another method from a recipe appearing in *Our Own Book of Every Day Wants* (1888 edition) is to boil a common sized turnip and put it in a sauce, adding about 1/2 cup molasses. Let this stand for 15 minutes. Pour off the syrup while squeezing the turnip to express the juice. This mixture may be taken warm before going to bed.

Cold and Sore Muscle Rub

This is a cream much like the fabled "Tiger Balm." You can make it at home and use it on sore muscles or to help congestion. Take 1 cup of oil (your choice) and simmer the following ingredients (1 tablespoon each) for about 1 hour: Eucalyptus leaves (oil sometimes available at the pharmacy), yarrow, bayberry, mint, camphor, rosemary, cayenne. Next, beat in 1/4 blue candle (a healing color) until you have a lotion. Store in air-tight container and use as needed. An equal portion of tea tree oil may also be added to this mixture to aid people who have joint problems.

The decongestant effect of this cream will be improved if you leave a eucalyptus leaf right in the jar and use with an humidifier.

Corns

Make a tincture of tea and apply it (together with a fresh slice of lemon) each night. In the morning, cut off the loose skin and let dry. Reapply until gone.

Cough

Find a stream that runs south. Prepare a fire on a griddle over the stream. Cook porridge on that griddle and eat it.

Another method entails roasting an onion under hot embers and eating it with honey, pepper, and butter twice a day.

Cough Syrup

Take 1 teaspoon of ginger, comfrey, cloves, and fennel and place them in a container with 1 cup of honey. Add to this 2 drops each of spearmint, pennyroyal and anise essence. Pour in 1 pint of water. Simmer all of the ingredients gently for 30 minutes, then strain. May be used by anyone age 12 and older. The dosage should be 1 teaspoon 3 times daily.

Caution: Please be certain you are using pure plant essences or extracts. Do not use perfume fragrances! Check with your local pharmacy on this.

Cramps

Combining equal proportions of wintergreen, chamomile, clover, valerian, and mint to create a tea works well. This mixture may also be made into in warm compresses and applied directly onto the area which hurts.

Dandruff

Make a rinse by combining equal parts of camphor, lavender, bay, sage, and rosemary. Add 1 capful of alcohol and steep in water for 2 hours. Bottle this and use it each time you shampoo.

Diarrhea

Chamomile and ginger tea is especially effective for children. For an adult, add 2 or 3 grape leaves, mint, and balm. Drink 1 cup at night.

Disease Transference

There are literally hundreds of examples of what is called disease transference in the folk medicine of the late 1800s. For example, to cure the whooping cough, a hair would be taken from the afflicted person, placed on bread and butter, and then fed to a dog. If the dog coughed, the patient was believed to be free of the sickness. Likewise with laryngitis, a frog might be kissed then asked to "hop away" with the sore throat. This may have well been where the expression "frog in your throat" came from.

Animals were not the only ones employed in this type of folk remedy. Inanimate objects were cited as well. To relive pain, an amulet made from a poultice of red coral and ash leaves would be placed on the affected area, then buried under an oak tree. Similar methods were used to rid the body of warts—by placing a potato on the wart, then burying it.

Symbolic magic, whether called by that name or not, is very evident in these examples as well as others found in W. G. Black's *Folk Medicine*. Here, the patient would attach a string to the affected area and the healer would place the other end in his mouth to "suck" out the sickness. Or, if someone had been bitten by a dog, it was believed necessary to get a hair from that dog to cure any infection. To break curses or mark transitions from the sickness to health, sometimes the patient would be moved through a fire or wreath. In all instances, the patient is given a strong image of their problems leaving them and new life beginning. How effective these cures were is difficult to trace, but their importance to our magical traditions remains.

Eye Disease

At sundown, take some club moss and kneel in the light of the moon. Show your knife to the moon saying, "Do thou cut, what thou cuttest, for good," then slice the club moss, wrap it in white cloth. Boil it in water from a nearby spring.

Fatigue

To refresh yourself, sip a cool tincture made from fennel.

Fever

Sip catnip tea, or (if available) elder flower and tansy tea.

ʒ white and beat it until stiff. Continue beating and add 1 cup of water, the juice ι, and 1/3 ounce powdered sugar. Apply this mixture to your freckles before bed, rinsing it off each morning.

Gargle

Simmer some sage and mint (also eucalyptus, if handy) and make a strong tincture to which 1 cup of brandy is added. Store and use as you would any mouth wash.

Glandular Swelling

Green's forsaken, yellow's foresworn,
And blue's a color that must be worn.
—Old Scottish saying

Wear a flannel fabric that has been dyed 9 times in blue. Blue was a color sacred to Druids, and 9 was a multiple of 3, a number believed to have many mystical powers.

Gum Bleeding

Brush with baking soda twice a day. It will help ease the tenderness, and decrease the bleeding in time. I suggest using this on a regular basis if you often have gum trouble. The aforementioned gargle should also help.

A rinse made of marshmallow leaves, red wine, agrimony, oak bark, comfrey, sage, chamomile, and a pinch of salt may also be used daily. Place 1 tablespoon of all the herbs in 3 cups of red wine over a low heat for 45 minutes. Strain and use as a mouth rinse (do not swallow).

Hay Fever

A tea made of orange, eucalyptus, dandelion root, dried fig and yarrow, seasoned with honey should relieve it somewhat.

Headache

Cucumber peel applied to the forehead is an old remedy. Or try drinking basil, catnip, rosemary, and raspberry teas.

Another Victorian method was to wear a ring made of lead and quicksilver.

Healing Amulet

Take peeled cloves of garlic, some cinnamon stick pieces and some sage and saffron. Put them together and sew them up in a pieces of blue or green cloth. These can be carried with you until the sickness is gone. Make sure to do affirmative visualizations while you sew. Rosemary and carnation petals may also be added.

The process is essentially the same for any small amulet that you might wish to make, just change the colors and herbs to suit the magical working.

Indigestion

To 1 liter of boiling water add a tablespoon of fennel, chamomile, mint, thyme, verbena, sage, and 1/2 tablespoon of dandelion root. Steep. Take 1 cup of this after your meal.

Itching

I have a simple philosophy, fill what is empty,
empty what is full and scratch where it itches.
—A.R. Longworth

Oatmeal and baking soda make a wonderful paste for itchy skin. Add just enough water to make the ingredients spreadable. If the scratching is caused by a bug bite, denting it with your fingernail crosswise will also help. My mother used to do this for me as a child and it almost always stopped the irritation. Another simple aid is to place cool, clay earth on the wound.

Liniment

To make an herbal liniment, take eucalyptus, cayenne, chamomile, peppermint, sage, camphor and bayberry and place them in oil to warm. Repeat this until you have a very strong solution, reddish in color, then store and apply to joints and muscles. For external use only.

Nausea

Drink chamomile, basil and clove tea.

Nose Bleed

Take a skein of scarlet thread. Have someone of the opposite sex tie 9 knots in it. Wear this around your neck. This particular remedy probably stems from a longtime belief that red was a protective color, sacred to many earlier traditions.

Oily Skin Treatment

Take a cup of violets and steep them in warm, fresh milk over night. Next soak a wash cloth in hot water, ring out, and soak it in the milk solution applying same to face and neck (or other areas of your skin which are oily).

Pain (especially in joints)

Take some burdock leaves and soak them for 24 hours in apple cider vinegar. Heat these leaves until they are as warm as the skin can tolerate and place on the irritated areas.

These leaves can be returned to the vinegar mixture and reapplied as long as no infection is present.

Protection before Surgery

Take 3 spoonfuls of fresh milk, plus 3 hairs from the back of an animal and its belly, let stand 3 hours and drink in 3 doses over 3 days. This cure illustrates the mystical nature of the number 3 and its multiples. For example, to cure epilepsy it was believed that 9 pieces of elder tied with 9 knots was necessary.

Sickness: General

Collect 12 pennies from 12 maidens and exchange them for a shilling collected on Sunday. Then wear this shilling on your neck. This is an example of how coins and metals played a role in the superstitions of the times, as well as how the folk healer often worked hand-in-hand with the church.

Sleeplessness

Drink tea made from anise, chamomile, parsley, valerian, clover, lavender, woodruff, dill and/or a verbena. Valerian is probably the best to use, but the others can be combined for a relaxing and tasty drink before bed.

Spider Bite

Take 1 cup vinegar and dissolve as much salt in it as you can. Dip some cotton in this mixture and apply this directly to the bite.

Sty

Pluck 1 hair from the tail of a black cat. On the first night of a New Moon, rub the hair over the sty 3 times, then throw it over your left shoulder.

Sunstroke

Apply salt directly to the head. Then, fill a glass with water and dissolve a handful of salt in the water. Place this glass against the salt, tilting your head slightly backwards. According to superstition, if the water starts to boil, the sunstroke is cured.

Toothache

Repeat this phrase 3 times over 9 bramble leaves immersed in water, as you pass each leaf over the diseased tooth: "An angel came from the North and he brought cold and frost, an angel came from the South and he brought heat and fire, an angel came from the North, and put out the fire."

For a more effective approach, try a little oil of clove to ease the pain.

Vapor Baths

Thought to cure many ills—from circulation difficulties to fevers and skin conditions—the vapor bath was employed frequently in the Victorian age. To make one for yourself, take a red hot brick and put it in a can, standing on end. Place this can under a chair with a flannel covering on the seat. Drink a large cup of ginger and yarrow tea, then pour boiling water over the brick until the can is half full. Sit down and wrap yourself in a heavy blanket until you begin to perspire on your face. Next, wash down with a vinegar and water rinse, dry off completely and go straight to bed.

Interestingly enough, a review of this method shows a similarity to our modern saunas, which are helpful to sinus problems and colds, and also helps to cleanse the skin of impurities.

Warts

Apply a slice of onion or garlic at night with some dandelion sap, keeping it on the wart with tape and cotton. Repeat this each night for a month.

Worms

According to folk medicine, you should rub garlic on your neck then string 15 cloves as a collar to wear at night.

Wounds

Marshmallow ointment is especially good for all kinds of inflammation and sores. Take some green marshmallow leaves and elder flowers, bruise them and add them to lard. Simmer in the oven until the herbs are crisp. Strain this through a cloth before it gets cold. If you want it to be stronger, simply repeat the process before adding beeswax (1 ounce of beeswax to each pound of ointment). After adding the beeswax, beat until cool. Marshmallow root may be substituted for the leaves. Another, simpler approach is to take 2 ounces of fir balsam and place it in a pint of alcohol. This may be placed on the wound as a wash.

Medical science, like everything else,
is the reward of long seeking after the light.
—W.G. Black

As a final note of interest, herbs have been so important to our civilization that there is a National Herb Garden to honor their contributions. It can be visited at the U.S. National Arboretum, 3501 New York Avenue, Washington, D.C. Colonial knot gardens, Victorian roses, and specialty herb collections can be seen there, including many that were popular during the Victorian period. If you ever travel that way, it is well worth the time to stop and walk those paths.

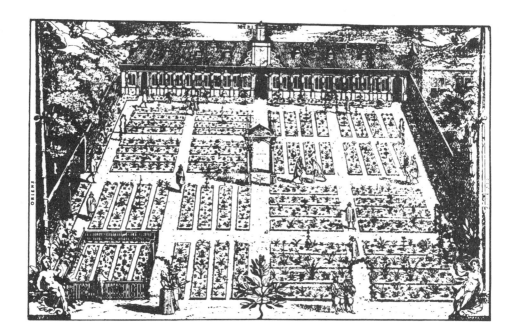

A HOUSEHOLD ABC

As soon as you are up, shake blankets and sheet;
Better be without shoes than sit with wet feet;
Children, if healthy, are active, not still;
Damp sheets and damp clothes will both make you ill;
Eat slowly, and always chew your food well;
Freshen the air in the house where you dwell;
Garments must never be made to be tight;
Homes will be healthy if airy and light;
If you wish to be well, as you do, I've no doubt,
Just open the windows before you go out;
Keep your rooms always neat, and tidy and clean,
Let dust on furniture never be seen;
Much illness is caused by the want of pure air,
Now to open your windows be ever your care;
Old rags and old rubbish should never be kept;
People should see that their floors are well swept;
Quick movements in children are healthy and right;
Remember the young cannot thrive without light;
See that the cistern is clean to the brim;
Take care that your dress is all tidy and trim;
Use your nose to find out if there be a bad drain,
Very sad are the fevers that come in its train;
Walk as much as you can without feeling fatigue—
Xerxes could walk full many a league;
Your health is your wealth, which your wisdom must keep,
Zeal will help a good cause, and the good you will reap.

—Peterson's Magazine, June 1888

CHAPTER SIX

A Kitchen Dance: Cooking Magic

Wake! For the sun behind yon eastern height
Has chased the session of stars from night.
　　　　　　　　　　—Edward Fitzgerald

From the garden outside to every room inside, morning in the Victorian home was filled with wonderful smells floating full-bodied from the kitchen. The scent of fresh breads, teas, sausage, and biscuits all hung lightly on the air, tempting expectant stomachs and waking people from their sleep.

In addition to the culinary delights, much more was happening in the Victorian kitchen dance. This was one area of the home where mother and children had time to communicate. Lessons were recited at the breakfast table, conversations about friends and family took place over a sturdy meal, and a few pennies might be given out for candy after school. On weekends or during the early evening, the recipes of the family would be taught to the next generation by the best possible means—hands on experience. As each item was prepared, the story behind it was imparted, and in this manner the family traditions were kept and became even more treasured memories.

Even with today's technology, the kitchen has tremendous potential for magic. Whether you are at the stove preparing family meals or making an herbal tea for a cold, adding magical flair to your kitchen and pantry creations is easy, and definitely gives a whole new meaning to the idea of "whipping something up!"

To move your culinary skills into the realms of magic is not as difficult as it might first appear. To begin, you follow your recipe as you usually would, but then add a specifically blessed and charged herb, designed to bring about the magical effect you desire. As you mix, keep that goal firmly in your mind. Since kitchen magic depends on your ability to remain comfortable with the process, make sure your combinations feel right and make sense. One word of caution, though. Certain powerful herbs for magic may not be ingested because of their toxicity or abrasiveness. Please check the effects of any unusual herbs you are thinking of employing.

Visualization is also very helpful when doing almost any type of magic. It requires nothing more than concentration to help get forces moving in the direction of your desire. Take care in this, however. Visualization tends to distract you from the actual product and focus your attention in the mystical realms. Because of this, I do not recommend having sharp implements in your hands when doing any type of conceptual magic.

The next step is to blend in a chant or incantation. It was not uncommon in the Victorian era to have people sing a verse or repeat a rhyme over and over again while making a product. A timely example came to us from Laura Ingalls Wilder when writing about the churning of butter. While the butter was prepared a familiar verse could be heard. It went, "Come butter come, come butter come. Peter's standing at the gate, waiting for a butter cake, Come, butter come!" The effect this has is two-fold. Rhythm is something people naturally respond to, and it helps almost any work along. The second effect, however, is very magical by nature, that of reaffirmation.

Say, for example, you are making bread for a gathering. You might add a bit of cinnamon, nutmeg, clove or vanilla bean and say, "Bread, bread, rise for me. Fill this space with prosperity!" As you knead the dough and repeat the chant, focus your mind firmly on the goal. Once the loaf rises and is baked, it is a visible and symbolic confirmation of the magical work taking hold. The final step here would be to eat the bread, allowing the magic to grow within you.

COOKING FOR RITUALS

Since cooking itself has a ceremonial nature (we follow the same procedure each time), it is easy to move mundane recipes and skills into an enchanted realm. Obviously, taking a different approach, (and especially a different attitude) is necessary when cooking for ritual. For example, you may wish to create a sacred space for your cooking, or do the baking during a specific time of day to enhance the desired result. Again, change your herbs and spices in subtle ways (not so drastically that they make your foods inedible). Share their significance and power with your gathering.

The recipes here are for the cakes and wines recommended in Chapter Three, so that the wheel of the year is filled with tasty and meaningful edibles. I have not included recipes for the herbal teas here because general preparation methods are included in the medicinal section later on in this chapter. Wherever possible, I have used the original spelling as found in the Victorian cookbooks.

Ritual Cakes

Apple Goodie (For Mabon)

8 medium sized apples, peeled
1/2 teaspoon nutmeg
1/4 teaspoon salt
1 tablespoon lemon juice
One 9-inch pie shell, baked

1 cup sugar
1/4 cup butter
1/2 teaspoon cinnamon
1/2 teaspoon ginger

In a saucepan, combine sugar, apples, nutmeg, ginger, cinnamon, butter, salt and lemon juice. Cover and cook until apples are soft. Pour this mixture into the pie shell.

Apple Goodie Topping — Take 1/2 stick of pie crust mix it, 1 cup brown sugar and 1/2 stick of butter (melted). Break the pie crust mix up and mix thoroughly with the brown sugar, then stir in the melted butter. Dot this mixture on top of the apples and bake briefly in a 300 degree oven until crispy (about 10 minutes).

Biscuits (For Imbolc)

It is interesting to note that until 1855, baking powder was made at home, and even after it was marketed, it took another 20 years to catch on!

2 cups flour	3 teaspoons baking powder
1/2 teaspoon salt	3 tablespoons butter
1 cup milk	

Mix dry ingredients together thoroughly. Cut in butter with a knife and add milk. Mix lightly with a large spoon. Turn dough on to a floured bread board and roll it out to the thickness of 1/2 inch. Cut with a biscuit cutter. Place these about 1 inch apart on a greased cookie sheet and bake at 450 degrees for 15 minutes or until golden brown.

Candied Violets (For Beltane)

1 egg white	Violets
Granulated sugar	

Whip your egg white until it is frothy, but does not peak. Gather the violets, washing them quickly in cool water and allowing them to drip dry. Then, dip each violet in the egg white and roll the flowers in the sugar to coat them evenly. Be careful not to put the sugar on too thick. Finally, leave the petals on waxed paper to dry for 1 day. These may be stored for several months in an airtight container (waxed paper between each layer) without loosing fragrance or flavor.

Corn Bread (For Mabon)

1 cup corn meal	1 cup flour
1/2 cup white sugar	1 cup cream
1 egg	2 teaspoons cream of tartar
1 saltspoonful salt	

Sift dry ingredients together first, then add the egg and the cream. Bake in 2 loaves or several small tins. A nice touch is to glaze the top with honey and butter just before the loaf is finished baking. Loaf should spring back to the touch when done. My best estimation of a saltspoonful is: approximately 1/2 teaspoon.

Ginger Bread (For Yule)

3 cups flour
2 tablespoons ground ginger
1/2 cup brown sugar, packed
1/2 cup light molasses
1/2 cup butter
2 teaspoons baking soda

1/4 teaspoon salt
2 teaspoons ground cinnamon
4 tablespoons milk
2 tablespoons dark molasses
3 eggs

Mix all your dry ingredients (except for the baking soda) together in a large bowl. Place 3 tablespoons milk into a small pan with the molasses and butter and melt all over a low flame. To this add your eggs, (well beaten) and the flour mixture. Mix well. Dissolve baking soda in 1 tablespoon of milk, then fold this into the rest of the batter. Pour into a 10-inch baking pan which is well-oiled and place in preheated 375 degree oven for about 50 minutes.

Graham Bread (For Lammas)

This was invented by Sylvester Graham, a Presbyterian minister who believed in proper eating as the way to improve the morals and health of the nation. Central to his diet were crackers and a bread made from unsifted whole wheat flour. This tradition stays with us even today, with Graham crackers available at your market.

2 cups graham flour
1 teaspoon baking soda
1 teaspoon salt
1/4 cup molasses
1-3/4 cups buttermilk

1 teaspoon baking powder
2 tablespoons sugar
3 tablespoons melted butter
1 egg, beaten

Mix all dry ingredients together in 1 bowl, and all the liquid in another. Stir the liquid into the dry, mixing quickly and well. Bake at 350 degrees until the edges pull away from the pan and it is golden brown (approximately 30 minutes).

Mint Tea Cakes (For Spring Equinox)

1 quart flour
6 eggs, beaten
Dry mint or mint flavoring

1 quart milk
2/3 cup softened butter

Flour and milk should be rubbed smoothly together. Stir in 6 eggs, beaten very light, and butter till mixed. Pour into greased pan (or muffin tin) and bake. Serve with a sprig of fresh mint, or garnish with violet petals. Bake at 350 degrees for about 10 minutes.

Oatmeal Bread (For Lammas)

1 cup wheat flour	3 medium apples, chopped
1/2 teaspoon baking soda	1 cup raisins
2 teaspoons salt	1 teaspoon cinnamon
1 teaspoon nutmeg	1 teaspoon ginger
1/2 cup brown sugar	1-1/2 cups rolled oats
1 cup butter	1 egg, beaten
1/2 cup nuts	1-1/2 teaspoons vanilla or orange

Mix above ingredients together completely, then place in a greased 9-inch cake pan. Bake at 350 degrees for 30 minutes, until it begins to move away from the sides of the pan. When cooled, this bread may be shaped for ritual. Also, the fruits and nuts may be changed for different seasons.

Plum Pudding with Sauce (For Yule)

1-1/2 cups flour	3/4 cup sugar
1 teaspoon salt	3/4 teaspoon cinnamon
1/4 teaspoon allspice	1/4 teaspoon powdered clove
1/4 teaspoon nutmeg	3 eggs, beaten
1-1/4 cups ground beef suet	1/2 cup brandy
1 cup raisins	3/4 cup currants
1/2 cup dates, chopped	1 cup candied lemon peel, orange peel and citron, diced

In a bowl, mix flour, sugar, salt and spices. Fold in eggs, suet and brandy, mixing well. Next, add your fruits, stirring until well incorporated. Pour into a greased 2 quart pudding dish. Cover tightly. Place the pudding dish mold on a rack in a kettle. Pour boiling water into the kettle until half way up. Cover and let steam on low for at least 5 hours, adding water as needed.

Plum Pudding Sauce

2 cups confectioner's sugar	1 cup butter, softened
4 egg yolks, beaten	2 tablespoons sherry

Cream sugar and butter together. Whip in beaten egg yolks and cook in double boiler over lightly boiling water. Stir constantly until this is thick enough to coat a wooden spoon. Add the brandy last and serve warm over the pudding (or other desserts such as ice cream).

Popovers (For Beltane)

2 eggs	1 cup milk
1 cup flour	1/4 teaspoon salt

Recipes for popovers began to appear in the 1870s. For the best results, beat eggs slightly then add milk, flour and salt. Whisk quickly until smooth (2 minutes), so the batter has the consistency of heavy cream. *I do not recommend an electric beater.*

Divide batter into a muffin pan which is well greased, baking in a preheated oven of 425 degrees for 40 minutes. Serve at once, filled with any type of fruit, cream, etc.

Pumpkin Pie (For Samhain)

1 unbaked 8-inch pastry shell	1 cup cooked pumpkin
1/2 teaspoon cinnamon	1/4 teaspoons ginger
1/4 teaspoon nutmeg	dash of ground cloves
1 cup half cream, half milk	1/2 cup sugar
1 slightly beaten egg	1/2 teaspoon salt

If you would like to make your pumpkin pie directly from the pumpkin, as our Victorian ancestors did, it is not as difficult as it might seem. Begin by cutting the pumpkin into small squares, and taking off the outer skin. The meat of the pumpkin then can be broken up into small pieces for cooking. If you have a blender, it helps to almost mash the pumpkin for the best cooking results.

Take the meat (the pumpkin mash) and add a healthy amount of water (to cover) and bring to a low boil. Continue to add water and boil until the meat turns a medium brown color and has a smoother texture. At this point, you may add your milk, egg, and spices to the mix and freeze it in pie-size portions for use later. When defrosted, simply put into a pie shell and bake at 400 degrees for about 50 minutes, or until a knife comes out clean from the center.

If you buy canned pumpkin, simply blend it with all the other ingredients and follow as above.

Rose Water and Angelica Wafers (For Imbolc)

1 pound flour	2 tablespoons butter
1/2 teaspoon salt	Sweet milk
2 capfuls rosewater	Pinch of angelica

Mix dry ingredients thoroughly, adding sweet milk until a stiff dough forms. Roll out the dough very thin and cut this into round cakes, rolling yet again. They should be thin as paper, as they swell in baking. Dredge them in flour. Put in a well-greased baking pan and bake in a quick oven (about 425 degrees) till lightly brown. Serve with sweet, beaten cream.

Samhain Cake

4 cups flour	1-1/2 cups raisins
1/2 teaspoon salt	1 cup dried apricots
1/2 teaspoon nutmeg	1/4 cup candied orange peel
1/4 cup butter	1 tablespoon granulated yeast
1-1/4 cups milk	2 eggs beaten

Mix flour, salt and nutmeg in bowl. Cut in butter, then add sugar and yeast. Warm milk until lukewarm, stir in eggs and add this to the dry mix, stirring until dough is stiff but workable. Fold in fruits and form dough into a ball. Place in greased 9-inch round baking pan (at least 3 inches deep) and press down so that dough is evenly spread and fills about half of the pan.

Place your tokens evenly around the dough, enough for 1 per person, making sure none of them will melt in the oven. Bake at 425 degrees for about 20 minutes, then reduce your setting to 350 and finish baking for 1 hour. Remove immediately and turn onto a rack. Brush with honey and butter while warm.

Sugar Cookies with Anise Frosting (For Yule)

2 cups flour	1-1/2 teaspoons baking powder
1/2 teaspoon salt	1/2 cup butter
1 cup sugar	1 egg
1 teaspoon vanilla	1 tablespoon cream
1 teaspoon orange extract (optional)	

Sift together all dry ingredients except the sugar. Cream your butter until soft, then beat in egg, sugar, extracts and cream. Stir in the flour mixture until your dough becomes stiff enough to roll. Place this in the refrigerator overnight.

The next day, roll out your dough on a lightly floured board to about 1/8" thickness and cut into desired shapes. Bake on ungreased cookie sheets for 8 to 10 minutes in a 375 degree oven.

The anise frosting can be made simply by mixing a little confectionery sugar, anise flavoring and milk until a thick glaze is formed. Add a little food coloring or sprinkles for a special flair. Be sure the cookies are completely cool before applying the frosting.

Happiness Cake (Year Round)

Another type of cake, while not edible, is a charming reminder of the way people viewed life in the Victorian era. It was something called a happiness cake. Recipes like this could be found tucked in drawers, in diaries, or on sheets of paper to read, and re-read. To make this unusual confection, you take a cup of good deeds, a measure of thoughtfulness, a heaping tablespoon of consideration, a sizable portion of forgiveness, and mix thoroughly with tears of joy, and the seeds of faith. Blend daily into your life, baked with the warmth of love, served with a blessing and a smile to make a life full of peace and happiness.

Ritual Wines

> *Religions change, beer and wine remain.*
> —Harvey Allen

Apple Ginger Beer (For Samhain)

1 gallon apple juice	4 cups sugar
1 sliced lemon	1 sliced orange
2 ounces ginger root, bruised	1-1/2 ounces cream of tartar
1/2 package active yeast	

Boil all the ingredients together, except the yeast, until well mixed. Allow to cool to lukewarm and add the yeast (dissolved in tepid water). Stir it only enough to mix in yeast, then cover pot with a thick towel and let it sit. This mixture usually begins to bubble within 3 hours. Strain off the orange and lemon the next day (retaining the fruit portion for conserves). Allow to sit for another 24 hours before straining and bottling. Screw top bottles are best because they allow you to bleed off excess pressure from fermentation periodically (once a day is good for the first week).

Ginger beer may be drunk immediately, but is best served within 2 weeks to a month of making or it tends to get bitter.

Dandelion Wine (For Litha)

16 cups dandelion blossoms	1/2 teaspoon wine yeast
1/2 gallon water	2-1/2 pounds sugar
Juice from 2 lemons	1 used tea bag

Rinse your blossoms in cool water, but do not allow them to soak. Make sure all the green is removed and only the blossoms remain to put in your kettle. Next, in a separate container, heat 1/2 gallon of the water and pour it over the blossoms. Let mixture steep until cool. Drain these petals off, squeezing as much liquid out as possible, and discard the flowers.

Take the remaining liquid and add 1/2 the sugar, lemon juice, tea bag and yeast. Cover with a clean dish towel to let the mixture ferment at room temperature, adding 1 cup of sugar every 3 days until used up. After 2 weeks, pour off into a gallon jug corked with cheese cloth ball. This should sit for 30 days, then may be put in freshly scrubbed bottles, corked and labeled. Serve after 1 week; keeps for about 1 year.

Egg Nog (For Yule)

In the Victorian era, this drink was often served as a dessert with cantaloupe and ice cream, using the liqueur as a garnish. The version given here was more popular on the Eastern Shore.

8 egg yolks	1 cup sugar
4 cups milk	3/4 cup heavy cream
1/4 cup brandy	1/3 cup rum
Nutmeg to taste	

In a bowl, beat the egg yolks, adding sugar a little at a time. Slowly add milk which has been warmed to just under the boiling point. Return the entire mixture to a saucepan and continue to cook until it reaches 175 degrees on a candy thermometer. Pour into a bowl and chill.

Whip your heavy cream until it peaks. Fold this into the cool milk mixture until it is well incorporated, then put it into the freezer until it just begins to harden. Finally add the brandy and rum, stirring well, and whip for another 30 seconds. Top with nutmeg.

If you prefer a non-alcoholic drink, you may substitute 1/2 cup of fruit juice for the rum and brandy. Pineapple is very refreshing, as is apple and orange. If you prefer a more classic warm egg nog, simply beat the eggs with the rest of the ingredients and warm them together over low flame. Serve with a cinnamon stick garnish.

Honey Mead/Horilka (For Lammas)

1 gallon of water	2 teaspoons ginger
2 teaspoons cinnamon	5 whole cloves
A sprig of saffron	2 capfuls rosewater
2-1/2 pounds of honey	12 ounces fruit or juice
1/2 cake yeast	

Bring water to a slow boil with all of the herbs so that a tea is formed. Add honey until dissolved, then add fruit or juice. Cover tightly and boil for about 15 minutes. Cool to lukewarm and add yeast dissolved in warm water. Cover with towel for 2 days before straining and bottling.

Just as was the case with your ginger beer, this may need to be aired periodically to prevent pressure build-up. A fermentation lock may be purchased from a distributor of home brewing supplies for about 50¢ to eliminate the need for airing, or a balloon may be fastened over the bottle neck to allow excess pressure to be released.

To make Horilka, a Polish vodka mead, decrease your water to 2 cups, delete the yeast, and decrease your honey to 1 pound. You will also need to add the vodka after the fruit juice and simmer for about 30 minutes, covered tightly. Let cool completely and bottle. Horilka will not ferment as quickly as mead, and does not need to be aired. It may also be drunk immediately, but is excellent after 6 months of aging. As with your ginger beer, retain your fruits to make fruit conserves or jams.

Rose Petal Liquor (For Litha)

In the early 1800s, a Londoner by the name of John Farley wrote a recipe for rose petal liquor: "Put into that vessel sufficient quantity of rose leaves and rose water, and set it for an hour in a kettle of hot water. Repeat this until the liquor has the full strength of roses. To every gallon of liquor put 3 pounds of sugar and put into a cask or other convenient vessel to ferment." While we may not make rose wine in that vast a quantity, Mr. Farley's recipe is essentially the same one given here.

1 pound of rose petals	2-1/2 pounds of sugar
1 lemon	1 gallon of water
1 teaspoon of wine yeast	

Begin by picking your roses first thing in the morning before the sun gets hot. Take only the petals and place them in a clean, 2 gallon crock. Add 1 gallon of water and bring slowly to a simmer. Stir your roses frequently until they have lost all color and appear almost transparent. Drain off all liquid and discard your petals (unless you wish to use them in potpourri).

To the warm flower mixture add your sugar, juice of the lemon, and wine yeast dissolved in lukewarm water. Cover with a towel and let sit for 2 weeks before bottling.

Rose Water (For Mabon)

The making of rose water is very simple, but I suggest you make it in small quantities, as the shelf life is only about 2 weeks. Then it begins to ferment.

Just as with the wines, your flowers should be freshly picked. Use only the petals. Place these in a bottle with a screw top, and pour boiling water into the bottle. Shake well and leave it sitting overnight. Drain off the petals the next day, setting aside the liquid. Use as desired in cooking, or even use it for an after-bath splash. Keep in the refrigerator for extra longevity.

Wine Punch (For Spring Equinox)

The original name for this brew, Claret Punch, name comes from an English term for table wine, Claret, so the punch incorporates that as the major base.

3/4 cup sugar	1/4 cup lemon juice
1/4 cup orange liqueur	Fresh mint leaves
2 bottles dry red wine	1 bottle soda
Ice	

In a punch bowl, mix the sugar, lemon and orange liqueur with the fresh mint leaves (to taste). Let this stand for about 1 hour, then remove the mint and add the wine and soda (or ginger ale). Stir and chill, adding ice just before serving.

Woodruff Wine (For Beltane)

10 cups Woodruff blossoms	1/2 teaspoon wine yeast
1/2 gallon water	2-1/2 pounds sugar
Juice from 1 lemon	1 used tea bag
Juice from 1 orange	

Rinse your blossoms in cool water, but do not allow them to soak. Make sure all the green is removed and only the blossoms remain to put in your kettle. Next, in a separate container heat 1/2 gallon of the water, and pour it over the blossoms. Let mixture steep until cool. Drain these petals off, squeezing as much liquid out as possible, and discard the flowers.

Take the remaining liquid and add 1/2 the sugar, lemon juice, tea bag and yeast. Cover with a clean dish towel to let the mixture ferment at room temperature, adding 1 cup of sugar every 3 days until used up. After 2 weeks, pour off into a gallon jug corked with cheese cloth ball. This should sit for 30 days, then may be put in freshly scrubbed bottles, corked and labeled. Serve after 1 week, keeps for about 1 year.

If you plan on doing a lot of brewing yourself, there are many good books available at your local bookstore. *Brewing Mead* by R. Gayre and *Wine, Beer and Soft Drinks* by Phyllis Hobson are two which are very useful.

Fruit Conserves

While these are not directly related to cooking for ritual, they are made from the left-overs of your brewing efforts, and may be used as a garnish for your ritual cakes. As a side note, it is also a very creative way to recycle.

When you strain off your brews, keep the fruit in an air-tight container in the freezer. When you have enough (about 6 cups worth) add some fresh chopped apple, raisins, and a little coconut along with 6 cups of sugar and 1 to 2 cups of water. Bring this mixture to a boil until it becomes candy-like. Let cool, and then can the mixture, using as desired on toast, over ice cream, with crackers or whatever.

For those worried about what little alcohol content may be left, it is boiled off in the conserving process, so that all which remains is a sweet, lightly spiced jam.

OTHER MAGICAL RECIPES

Candles

Candles were a staple in the Victorian home. If you would like to dip your own for home or ritual use, be prepared for a time-consuming task. Using molds is much easier, but makes bulkier candles.

The Victorian Recipe for Candle Making

Take 2 pounds of alum dissolved in water and 10 pounds of tallow. Melt the tallow in water with frequent stirring. Use loosely spun cotton or hemp for wick, adding your bayberry after the tallow is incorporated. Take your wick, dip it in until covered and let cool. Dip again. Repeat until the candles are of a goodly thickness. Store in a cool room.

Today, we can get already prepared wax and wick at a hobby shop, or use our own wax ends and pieces to make candles. To scent them, simply add a few drops of essential oil or a handful of dry herbs to the liquid before dipping or molding.

Easy Essential Oils

There are a wide variety of oils you can make at home. For cooking, you can make herbal oils by simply placing some fresh herb in the bottle of oil (garlic works especially well) and letting it sit in there for as long as you use the oil.

Oils designed to be used for magical, anointing, massage, bath and/or potpourri purposes demand a slightly different process. Begin by deciding what effect you want the oil to have and choose your herbs accordingly. If you are looking for a certain smell, remember that dried herbs do not always incorporate their smells into oil as you might expect. For example, roses make wonderful oils, but if any of the leaves or other green parts get into the solution, the end result will be have a plant-like smell and be very unpleasant.

The next step is to decide what type of base oil you prefer to use. Olive, almond, safflower, mineral, and many other oils work perfectly well for steeping herbs, but some are heavier in consistency than others. Find one that has a texture you enjoy. You may also discover that certain oils work better with specific herbs and plants. Just like any new recipe, keep cooking till you get the product just right.

Pick your buds (or plants if using fresh) early in the morning before the sun gets to them. This is when their smells are strongest. Steep them in warm (not boiling) oil until the petals become translucent or until the oil has the strong scent of the herbs. Remove from heat, strain, and repeat this process until you have the intensity you were looking for. Remember that trial and error are great teachers, so be patient with yourself.

The alternative method (which I prefer to use in the summer) is to let the herbs steep for several months in a dark bottle. (Make sure you place the bottle in sunlight). Keep a close eye on this process so that you don't get "fuzzy" results. This is a more time consuming process, but well worth the wait if you have the time. In the winter I switch to a sun lamp.

There are certain things to keep in mind when making oils. If making an anointing oil, make sure the herbs are not skin irritants. Be certain you know what you are working with, always remembering the herbal rede, "if one can cure, two can kill." In your research process look to see what herbs are paired together magically for a more powerful effect.

You may wish to store your oils in bottles that do not leak, such as cough syrup bottles. This way you will not ruin clothing or robes if one opens up accidentally in travel. Many druggists will sell these bottles to you for as little as 25 cents each (2 ounce size).

Two other methods for extracting oils from flowers just recently came to my attention. The first is to hang the flowers, stem and all, in a dark bottle with secured lid. After

about a week the solution in the bottom will be the essential oil of the flower. Another method (specifically for roses) is to warm them in water until they become translucent, strain off the petals, then refrigerate the water. Small patches of oil will form on top which can be taken off like butter, then used in various preparations as needed. With this type of essence, a very small amount goes a long way.

In the process of my personal experimentation, I have found a couple of blends which I really like, not only for their magical significance but also for the lovely scent they produce. You should also explore your imagination for combinations. Bear in mind that each plant should be harmonious in body, scent, and desired effect. I also suggest that you limit your combinations to four herbs, flowers and/or fruits at most. Remember, the more ingredients you use, the harder it becomes to create a successful oil. Herbs are touchy, and each reacts differently to heat, light and the base oil.

Here are a couple of tried and true blends for you to try:

Prosperity Oil

Blend 2 ounces of base oil, 1 teaspoon each of cinnamon, ginger, vanilla (bean or extract) and orange (rind or extract). This oil is especially nice because the scent is created and "set" almost immediately upon warming. Touch a little of it to any prosperity sachet, dress your candles with it during spells for abundance, and wear it regularly to help bring the vibration of success into your life.

Romance Oil

This is a special blend which I call Enchantment. Warm 1 cup of almond oil and place it in a dark bottle. Add 1/4 cup of lilac, rose, and lily of the valley petals plus 2 teaspoons of french lavender. Shake the bottle daily and leave in a sunny window, checking regularly for any signs of decay. When the flower petals have turned translucent, replace them with fresh ones and repeat until you get a strong enough scent to please you. This oil is wonderful for any magical work pertaining to love relationships, especially the tender and fanciful facets.

At first, I produced this oil specifically to help me write this book, but now I like it so much that I often use it as personal perfume.

Anointing Oil

Warm 1 cup of saffron or olive oil. Add 1/8 cup each: lilac petals for harmony and peace of mind, jasmine for love, a piece of vanilla bean for power, and 2 to 3 drops of sandalwood oil for increased psychic awareness. Anoint all of your energy centers during meditation, use it for the ritual of self blessing (see Chapter Nine), or as an aid to healing techniques (such as touch therapy).

Incense

Incense has been part of humankind's religious life as far back as the time of the Egyptian temples of Ra, when an incense known as Kyphi was burned to honor the God. The belief then was that the powders not only manifested the God(s) but also gratified them. Babylonians used it extensively while offering prayers or divining oracles. By the 5th century B.C., it had been imported to Israel, where altars were set apart for incense offerings. In Greece, from the 4th century B.C., woods and resins were burned for protection against demons. It was not until the 4th century A.D. that the Church began to use it in a ceremonial fashion and it came to symbolize the prayers of the faithful ascending. Although it was mostly used in the religious realm, some herbs were burned in the home for protection, to keep away evil spirits, to heal ailments, etc. Also, on a more pragmatic level, for a people who did not bathe regularly this would make the home more pleasant smelling.

Today, Hindus use incense for ritual and domestic offerings, as do Buddhists. Shinto festivals use it for processions or to honor ancestors. The Catholic Church still employs it for certain high masses, and of course it is used widely for magic. The enterprising Pagan or Witch can easily make his/her own incense at a reasonable cost with relatively few tools.

Having a mortar and pestle is nice, but if you don't have one handy, a wooden or ceramic bowl and sturdy spoon will do. Start by obtaining some aromatic wood powder (cedar, pine, and sandalwood are the most common). These powders are usually available through any good herbal shop, but if not, just ask a friend with a fire place! Next, you need to collect dried herbs (the fresher, the better). I recommend looking at various health food stores, co-ops, crystal shops and Magikal Outlets (see Appendix C).

The incense "recipe" I use is fairly simple: 1 cup of shavings, 2 or 3 tablespoons of each herb, and a fixative (I use benzoin, as it is readily available at most pharmacies). Remember that not all herbs smell the same when burned, so begin simply, adding 1 or 2 herbs to the wood powder, then testing on the fire. Kitchen herbs which almost always give off a nice aroma are cinnamon, fennel, thyme, mints, ginger, orange rind, rose petals, lemon powder, and vanilla.

You may also add essential oils, orange and rose water, or other liquid scents if you have adequate space to dry the mixture properly. I suggest using a large, wooden cutting board which can be kept far away from pets or little hands, and covered with a light cloth to inhibit dust.

It should be noted that you can add or delete any herbs you like to make the mixture more personally significant. Also, take care not to add an ingredient to which some member

of your group or household is allergic. Do not add too many ingredients or your incense will be overpowering, especially if used in a confined space. Usually 3 or 4 herbs added to the base is best. Most of all, there should be an appropriate magical space created for your work. You should keep a strong vision of your purpose for the incense in your mind until the final product is done. Bless and consecrate it for its intended use, then enjoy!

Incense of Cleansing

Begin with a base of 1/2 cup of sandalwood powder. Blend in 1 tablespoon each cinnamon, clove, and frankincense for purification. To this add 1/2 teaspoon of patchouli leaf or flower and rosemary for protection. Burn before rituals or any time your home needs relief from negative energy.

God Incense

During the summer months, especially when I go camping, I make this incense to honor the Sun God and help bring good weather. Start with a base of 2/3 cup sandalwood powder to which 1 teaspoon each fennel, thyme, cinnamon and chamomile have been added. Blend in 2 teaspoons of frankincense and myrrh and spread the entire mixture out on a dry surface. Sprinkle in rose water and 2 to 3 drops Pennyroyal and let dry. Store in air-tight container.

Goddess Incense

For connecting with the Divine Feminine aspects. Also excellent for use in Moon magic (see Chapter Three). If you can find ground or powdered cedar, it makes a much better base for this incense. Again, you will need 2/3 cup of the wood, adding 2 teaspoons dried apple rind, and 1 teaspoon each French lavender, pine needles, crushed rose petals, and dried Jasmine. Lay this on a wooden board and sprinkle in a few drops of lotus oil. Allow to dry before storing.

Soap

During the late fall and early winter, when hogs were butchered for meat and preserved, their fat did not just get tossed into a garbage pile. Instead, the Victorian lady collected it (along with wood ash) to make her family's soap. Even after lye became available on the market, most continued making their own from the ash gathered in a large wooden barrel over winter, having been taught not to buy anything they could make by hand.

You, too, can make soap for any occasion, not to mention regular use in your family shower. It is inexpensive, fairly easy, and often fun for the children as well. Thanks to attempting this process, as of this writing I have not needed to purchase soap for my family for well over 2 years now, and often have friends drop over to buy a bar or two for themselves!

Begin with 6 cups of lard (this must be clarified lard, tallow, vegetable or olive oil, but lard is best). Melt this over a low flame. In another ceramic or stoneware bowl, mix 3/4 cup of lye with 2-1/4 cups of water. Take care, as this mixture is very caustic and hot. Both the lye and lard must be cooled to body temperature (in other words you can touch the containers comfortably) before mixing the two together.

Once they cool to body temperature, slowly pour the lye solution (make sure to use lye—*not* Draino®. Draino® has other chemicals which will ruin your soap) into the lard. You will notice the mixture becoming milky in color. Stir slowly until you get a lotion-like texture. This is the point where you can add powdered herbs, crushed flowers, oils, lanolin, aloe and/or cocoa butter for various physical and magical effects. I have found that rose, frankincense, pine, lavender, citrus, and most baking herbs make lovely smelling soaps. Should you desire an abrasive soap, you may also add sandalwood powder, oatmeal or pumice at this time. If you want to add a natural dye to your soap, carrot and spinach juice or beet root work for yellow, light green and red, respectively.

You will now need a 9" x 6" x 2" wooden box. Old wine crates which have the wooden pieces fitting closely together work fine. Soak the box in water. Inside of this box you need to place a piece of damp linen, big enough to cover the entire interior. For even better scent, place a few drops of essential oil on this cloth. It will soak into the soap during the setting process.

Next, pour the soap into the box. Cut a piece of cardboard which will fit snugly to the edges of the box, lay it gently on top of the soap, then cover with a heavy cloth to sit over night. Try not to peak! Each time you let some heat out it damages the consistency of your soap. By morning you can remove the cardboard to discover the soap solidified and ready to cut into pieces. These pieces then need to be left in open air for 2 weeks before wrapping.

It should be noted that if you want a more finished appearance for your soap, you can steam the edges and rub it with alcohol and wool cloth for a nice shine.

You know your soap is of a good quality if it curls when sliced. It should not crack apart (too much lye) nor should it separate out (poured at wrong temperature). If any of these things happen, have no fear! Your work is not lost. Simply cut up what you have, pour it all back in your pot including the lye (I use a huge iron cauldron) and bring to a boil with water. If you did not use enough lye, (your soap was soft and greasy) you may dissolve some in water and add a little more now. Likewise with the lard. As the mixture boils it will become ropey in consistency. This means it is ready to pour again.

The boiling process creates a harder soap which lasts a very long time in the shower. Your yield should be about 24 bars of good quality soap, which aging only improves. It will not bubble like commercial brands because of the lack of chemical enhancers, but instead surrender a small, clean foam.

A FEW KITCHEN TIDBITS

Let all housekeepers remember that there is no possibility of
producing nice dishes without liberal allowances of good ingredients.
—Miss Leslie's New Cookery, 1888

The kitchen deserves some extra attention because of the amount of time spent there. This was probably the most "common" room of the house (for household hints concerning other parts of the house, refer to Chapter Seven). There were literally hundreds of little pamphlets available for the wife to choose from in making her kitchen even more functional and welcoming. I would like to share a few tidbits here for your enjoyment and also to give you an idea of how creative the Victorian mind was:

❧ In *Practical Housekeeping*, (1883) it was reported that the taste of fish may be removed from silverware by rubbing the items with fresh orange or lemon peel.

To make meats tender, adding a spoonful of vinegar into the water before boiling will improve the texture.

❧ Miss Ellet, *The Practical Housekeeper* (1857) tells us that if you cut lemon and orange peel when fresh, place it in a bottle of brandy, then use this brandy to flavor pies and cakes, your finished product will be much more savory.

She also mentions that rose leaves may be preserved in brandy. I have only recently learned they may likewise be frozen for future use.

❧ In 1886, Mrs Rorer gave us advice on how to keep eggs fresh. She recommends varnishing them, dipping in melted suet or packing them in salt with the small end down.

❧ In *Household* (1877), we are given a list of many practical applications for eggs other than eating. According to this amazing study, we discover eggs will stamp or seal letters, sooth burns, keep plaster from blistering, and dislodge fishbone from your throat!

METAPHOR MAGIC FROM YOUR PANTRY

That men may live in health and joy, and all their
varied power employ, and die by weight of years.
— William Fox, M.D.

Between 1850 and the early 1900s, some of the foods that have become American traditions were born. Corn flakes, catsup, hot dogs, white bread, potato chips, chewing gum and even Coca Cola® had their beginnings in the Victorian era. Now we think nothing of turning to our kitchen cupboards and finding them well stocked with any number of these items, but for the Victorian lady this was a wonder and a pleasure. In many instances some of these things were even considered a delicacy until they became more firmly incorporated into daily life!

In considering the novelty these "new foods" must have presented, I began to consider how central edibles are to our lives. Because of our need to eat, we really don't think of dining or food preparation as being a magical pastime, but it can be. It is also one which requires little extra time out of your busy day! The Victorians knew that it was often necessary to do more than one thing at a time to keep up with their many tasks. Taking this idea one step further, we can begin to approach our time in the kitchen from a magical construct.

Here are some magical ways of treating food to try yourself. They include not only food, but some common kitchen items which lend themselves to sympathetic magic. This is by no means a complete list, and I am sure if you take a moment to look you will come up with at least a dozen more ideas yourself. The thought here is to give you the opportunity to perceive your kitchen through new eyes and see it as a place where real, functional magic can take place at the same time as supper.

Alphabet Soup

This can be used for divination. As you eat a bowl of alphabet soup, concentrate on a specific question. When you get to the point of having about 6 spoonfuls left, close your eyes and scoop up 3 of the remaining spoonfuls, still thinking on your question. Now examine the letters left in your bowl. Do they spell anything? Perhaps the number of letters left is significant to your question. I have tried this and you would be surprised at how well it works.

Black-Eyed Peas

This is an exercise for centering. After you eat your peas, feel the fullness of your stomach. Try to visualize one of the pea's "eyes" in the center of your belly, and allow warm energy to flow to that place. That is the center of your gravity and should help bring you back into balance.

Bread

Bread has fostered fellowship for a long time. For thousands of years, bread has been a staple of the home and a symbol of hospitality and trust. Whenever I have friends over, I often make a rye bread with poppy/dill dip on a bed of lettuce. The lettuce symbolizes peace and comfort; the poppy, fertile ideas and friendships; and the dill is protection and love.

Brooms

The broom was such an integral part of Victorian life, it had hundreds of superstitions surrounding it, as well as many traditions. For example, it was bad luck to take an old broom into a new home. If you found a broom in your new place of residence it was considered good fortune, and you should use it to sweep out any bad luck as soon as you move in. Newlyweds would jump over a broomstick to ensure longevity and happiness for their marriage.

The history of the broom in the Craft is long, and reasonably well known. Broomstick jumping and riding is still used in some older forms of ritual. Today, a broom may be used instead of a wand to cast a circle, or used as a symbolic means of cleansing and purifying a circle. This is done by sweeping the outer edges sunward while calling the quarters). It can be a focus for any magic involving luck or love.

A broom decorated with dry flowers and herbs is an elegant accessory for any altar or home. Choose your herbs according to what you want the broom to symbolize, and change them with the seasons. Thus your broom can become a standing reminder of the cycles and of the simple beauties of your magic.

Butter

Use butter to get on better terms with someone. You know the old expression, "butter someone up?" Well, why not use the strong association it has to help a stressed relationship? Take a piece of bread and write the name of the person on it with a tooth pick. As you place it in the toaster, envision that the heating energy from the toaster is "warming up" the individual to being more receptive to a calm discussion. Next, apply the butter as if it were a healing salve between you and that person. By the way, in Victorian days, toasters were made for the open fires, and bread had to be turned by hand.

Another use for butter may be in the area of patience. Churning butter was a very arduous task for the Victorian lady. It took time and care to make it turn out just right. So, perhaps when you apply butter to your toast, apply some patience to your heart as well.

Cheerios®

If there is a situation in your life which you want to rise above, Cheerios® (or anything that floats) are a great help in the visualization effort.

As you pour in the milk, see the difficulty lifting. As you scoop up the cereal, see the problem leaving your life. You may want to try a chant something like "As I eat, so flees my strife, as I eat I control my life!"

Cookies

The Victorian family loved their sweets. Children would rush home from school in the hopes that mother had made a special treat to bring a smile to their day.

Here's a magical way to help sweeten a sour disposition. Prepare the cookies with the needy person in mind, then eat some of them to help open the lines of pleasant conversation between the two of you.

Corn Meal

For blessing any plans, as you bake your corn bread chant this three times, "grain of corn, gold like the morn, bless my plans, let joy be born!"

Corn on the Cob

Some people take the whole stem and gnaw out with their teeth . . .
—Fredrika Breme, 1850

Corn has been a staple in America since the earliest settlers came. It was from the heart of our country, and often defined the difference between feast and famine for farmers. We can use corn today to represent plenty in fertility magic. Before eating the cob say, "As I eat you give to me, a womb full of fertility. Bless my womb, this seed of Earth, grant to me a healthy birth."

Crystal Glasses

Victorians adored crystal, especially glassware that depicted flowery scenes. If you have any real crystal glasses or bowls in your house, they can be used like Tibetan meditation bowls. Simply take the glass and fill it with a little water. Put a touch of the water on the index finger of your power hand and begin moving it around the rim in a clockwise fashion. The sound the crystal gives off will remain consistent as long as you keep the movement slow and steady. Listen to the sound, it is very wave-like and brings inner harmony and centering. If you find the pitch too high, add water.

Dish Towel

Don't have a smudge stick handy? Try using a damp dish towel to asperge your kitchen. The proper Victorian kitchen would have clean dish towels readily available over the sink.

To use yours in a creative way, sprinkle a little extra water on your towel and begin moving around the kitchen clockwise. As you go, allow drops of water to be shaken off, and visualize the towel being like your wand or athame in a magical circle. Pour white light energy through it into your kitchen until it is filled with freshness.

Dough

Dough, like mashed potatoes, can work for almost any spell, but I personally like it for "smoothing out" tense situations or bad feelings. You can write anything in the dough, then use your personal energy (and a rolling pin) to smooth it over. The repetition of this process until the dough is ready to cook also helps.

Flour

Flour can help reveal a secret. Have you ever noticed how traces of flour make you aware of what areas in your kitchen are clean? If you feel something is being hidden from you, dampen a surface while thinking about the things that have happened to make you concerned. Next, sprinkle the flour over that surface and see if patterns form. For this divination, it is best if you unfocus your eyes, not looking directly for a specific pattern, but allowing your senses to lead you. The pattern which develops (if any) will be something you alone can recognize as an answer.

Fruit

This is for sharing. When you feel the lines of communication between you and someone else are not as open as they should be, take a piece of fruit and slice it into equal portions. Put one part across from you, symbolically for the intended individual. Say, "As I give to you, you give to me, soon our words will all be freed." Then, eat your half, thus opening things on your end. I suggest drying the remainder of the fruit which you put aside and use it in the garden, where the energy can grow.

Gravy

Gravy is good for bringing consistency and congruity to a situation, or to calm confusion. Keep the situation in mind as you stir in your flour paste. If your gravy becomes lumpy, it probably means you have a few "bumps" ahead before things settle down.

Ice

An old folk spell tells us to write the name of a person who is acting against us and place it in water to freeze, thus leaving them unable to do more harm. To cool a "hot temper," write the name of the person on paper placed on a saucer, then put an ice cube on top of it. Allow it to melt slowly and completely over the name so the anger is diffused.

Juice

To revitalize your energy, fill a glass completely full with juice and set it in sunlight for a few minutes. See the energy of the sun permeating the juice, then drink the whole glass to drink fully of that blessing. Lemon juice may be added to any spell for cleansing and purification.

Mashed Potatoes

Mashed potatoes are great for 101 different kinds of spells because you can draw in them. Next time you have a plateful, carve a rune or symbol into the center to show your intention, fill it with gravy (to fill it with energy), then enjoy (internalizing the magic)!

Peanut Butter

This is good for stick-to-itiveness, and follow through. Any time you have a peanut butter sandwich, think of an area in your life where you have been a little lax or lazy, apply the sticky substance to it, then go ahead and eat.

Pickles

Someone being a sour-puss? Take a pickle from the refrigerator and sprinkle it with sugar, visualizing the sweetness being sent to the individual in need. Then, allow the sugared pickle to sit in the warm sun, allowing that fire to burn out whatever is making the individual angry.

Pie Crust

This is a nice spell for manifestation. As you shape your pie crust, visualize your desires also taking shape. When you put the filling in, bless it, allowing what you have shaped with your hands and through visualization to be filled with positive energy.

Rice

For patience, make a batch of rice and practice the oriental art of picking up one grain with chop sticks. Remember here that the process of learning is more important than actually being able to accomplish this feat. At first this exercise is very frustrating, but the means of learning patience is often likewise so.

Rolled Roast

Rolled roasts come with a twine around them. Name this twine according to something you want to cut away from your life. The heat of the oven helps to burn away the habit or problem (ever notice how the string often falls off after cooking?) Finally, as you remove the cord from the roast declare, "As I say, I'm free today, my problem must be cut away!"

Soup

Any time things seem to be stagnant, try making some soup to "stir up" a little action. Stir clockwise to bring movement, counterclockwise to slow things down when progressing too quickly.

Spaghetti Noodles

To untangle a sticky situation, make a small handful of spaghetti noodles, cooked as you usually would, but toss in a handful of chamomile into the water for mediation. Then, when the noodles are cooked, pour them into a bowl and untangle them one at a time, keeping in mind the situation to which you are giving this energy.

Spinach

Spinach symbolizes strength. When feeling very weary, visualize the strength of Popeye pouring into the spinach, then eat 1 cup.

Tea Kettle

Even tea kettles can be good divination tools. Pour water into your kettle, concentrating on a yes or no type question. When the water comes to a boil, a slow steady whistle means yes, a broken up whistle means no.

Vegetables

Use vegetables for grounding. Anything which comes to us fresh from the earth is great to help us bring our feet back down out of the clouds. The noise of chewing doesn't hurt either.

Wooden Spoons

The Victorian kitchen was filled with wooden implements of all kinds, but perhaps the most versatile was the wooden spoon. From stirring the soup, measuring and serving, to spanking a naughty child, the wooden spoon became a symbol of domestic ability, prudence, discipline and adaptability. And so should it remain in our magic.

There is no reason why a trusty wooden spoon could not become the Kitchen Witch's faithful companion. She can use it to call the quarters instead of using a wand or athame; she can sprinkle water with it to asperge the sacred space; it can be decorated with flowers to adorn the altar; it can measure out precious herbs for medicinal and magical use; and it may even be used to mix the cakes and wines in preparation for ritual.

In this way, this tool takes on great personal energy and significance. It is also interesting to see how emotionally attached one can become to their spoon. When one that I had used for years finally fell almost literally to shreds, I felt a sadness which is difficult to express. I placed the shards of wood in my garden, and allowed the energy of those years to bring life to my plants. Then I went quickly to the store to get a new one to hang back in the distinctly hollow place on my work-room wall. It was some months before the new spoon started taking on character (as the old one had throughout the rituals of my life). But even so, the useful nature of this tool never ceases to amaze me, which is probably why it also had a place of honor with the Victorian lady as well.

Yeast

Use yeast to help activate any spell or to speed up a legal matter. For spell activation, simply add a little active yeast to your other components. For a legal matter, place a container of yeast soaked in warm water and a teaspoon of sugar on top of your legal documents and allow the energy of the growing yeast to pour into the papers (and/or related people) to motivate action in the court.

    No matter what kitchen implements you decide to use in your magic, remember that nothing is silly if it is meaningful to you. In the same respect, don't be afraid to look at your entire living environment as the perfect place and opportunity for fresh, inventive magics to be born from your heart.

A room where the family may come together
and savor the sweetness of being a family . . .
— W. D. Howells

So we'll go no more a roving
So late into the night
Though the heart be still as loving
And the moon be still as bright.

For the sword outwears its sheath
And the soul wears out the breast
And the heart must pause to breathe
And love itself have rest.

Though the night was made for loving
And the day returns too soon
Yet we'll no more go a roving
By the light of the moon.

                    —Lord Byron

CHAPTER SEVEN

The Grand Tour:
Magic Through the House

We believe, above all things under heaven,
in the power and virtue of the individual home.
—A. J. Downing, 1850

To give you a better feel for the Victorian home, I would like for a moment to take you on a tour from one end of the house to the other. Bear in mind that to the Victorian, a proper house was a reflection of a proper spiritual life. Back-to-nature themes, the idea of being part of God's tapestry—these values were exhibited in all areas of the home. Even flower arranging became part of housekeeping. These feelings may have been inspired partially because the individual's right to a home was highly prized. (It is interesting to note that even conservation had its first roots in the Victorian age, again giving us the image of a pragmatic people with a love for beauty unrivaled by any time period since.)

We begin our tour on the front porch, overlooking a well-tended garden and yard. Here the scents of freshly blooming flowers fill the air, as if to smile sweetly on the young couples who would hold hands, steal a kiss, and say goodnight. The porch became the out-door living room around the 1890s with the addition of swings, hammocks, and tables. Throughout the fine weather, these would be filled with friends or family sharing music and tea. From here, you would be welcomed into a hallway containing a hat and/or umbrella rack, a shelf and a stool for your comfort.

As a guest, you might next be guided into the dining area. The first thing to strike you once inside is a sense of stateliness in the home. Victorians were flamboyant and ornate, using tapestries and all kinds of art to decorate their homes. The dining room was the most ritualistic room of the house. Candles were usually found in here, and specific codes of behavior worthy of acolytes were required at the table.

Once it was time to eat, you would saunter to the table, which would be set with fresh flowers, crystal, matching china, finger bowls with flower petals, candles, and usually some type of favor for the guest. Depending on the season, the meal might vary, but the hospi-tality was always warm and gracious.

Another area you might visit for light conversation and some entertainment is the drawing room or parlor. This area was the housekeeper's pride and joy, retaining the symbols of civilized living for the guests to view. The family's musical instruments were there and perhaps a phonograph alongside some comfortable chairs, a fireplace, pomanders, rose potpourri, and again more art. Music was very important in Victorian life because it was one area where emotions could be expressed more openly, yet in a socially acceptable manner.

There were some areas of the home you might not see unless considered a dear friend. The snuggery was a library of sorts where the man of the house could retreat for a while. This room was furnished with book shelves, a writing table, a chair for him and one for a welcome associate. Likewise, some women were very protective of the kitchen until it was properly cleaned up after the meal. Then, you would spy many different dressers for cookery and china, pie safes to protect baked foods from bugs and heat, corner cupboards, a wood burning stove, baskets full of a myriad of things, kegs, a table, and all sorts of wooden tools.

The last room, the bedroom, was a place only for the family to see. This was a personal realm, where memoirs were kept and treasured almost as much as the family Bible. It was common to make notes of family events and to write down private history in such a way that we could only guess what they were saying without someone from that family and time interpreting it. The bedroom required three to four chairs, a wardrobe, a wash bowl, a bureau of drawers, a little chest to house gloves, and dressing screens, as it was improper to undress in front of someone.

As you leave your tour, you are left with a feeling of warmth, a sense of propriety, and a new perspective of how valued these walls were. Many hours of the family drama were played out in the home, a drama which helped to create the people we have become in the 20th century. So what happened to that feeling of home? That sense of stability and security which kept people warm, even in the coldest of winters?

Part of what happened has to do with mobilization, population, cities, and apartments. Over time and miles, the extended family has been separated. Not everyone has a permanent place to hang their hat anymore; not everyone wants one. Also, even those of us who do own homes are so busy that often we spiritually neglect the very place where we spend many hours of our free time.

Victorian magics behoove us to take a close look at our priorities, and focus again on the home. We need to find ways to reclaim the warmth, comfort, sweetness, and beauty the Victorian age knew in association with the word "home" and transport it to the place we live, be it an apartment, rented room, or actual house. This chapter explores some of the ways we can do just that. It also examines various ways to use our home and its contents as part of our daily magical practices.

Home to an ear refined is the sweetest of spoken words.
　　　　　　　　　　　—A. W. Mills, 1882

DECORATIONS

It is well to know how to enter a room, but it is
much better to know when and how to leave it.
—The Ladies Indispensable Assistant

The stately Victorian home was filled to overflowing (both inside and out) with all kinds of art. Inside, there were many paintings reflecting myths, magic, and especially the Fey (fairies). While these artworks were narrative, sentimental, and morally instructive, there was also a certain wildness beneath, reflecting the mysticism of nature. Using classical motifs, the Victorian artists were able to blend wondrous tales, a glorification of the elements, and moral values of the time into a new, powerful pattern.

Hexagrams

 Good luck, protection from evil eye

Abundance, goodwill & faith

 A barn sign to protect cattle & keep lightning at bay

Another interesting art form evidenced in decorations of the Victorian era was developed by the Pennsylvania Dutch. The Pennsylvania Dutch emigrated to America in the 18th century, bringing with them a wealth of traditions, including the tradition of placing of a yew branch or an upright horseshoe in the apex of a barn for protection. They also brought their "hex signs" with them. Hex signs are symbols designed to give good luck or protection. They found their way onto the sides of barns or on stones placed near the boundaries of land. Inside the home, they also appeared on trivets, tinware, quilts, pottery, cedar chests, and much more. These big, beautiful geometric designs were produced with the faith that they would ward off ill fortune, help maintain peace in the home, and protect the very precious land.

Every empty space in the Victorian home was filled with something considered pleasing to the eye and uplifting to the soul. From the ornamentation of hexagrams, to intricate flower arrangements, paintings, fans by the hearth, lace doilies, fanciful china and vases, ferneries and statues, their environment was filled to the brim with this effort. This was also the era when the home began to be a place where the outward expression of inner individuality that was starting to develop in America. This desire to make one's living space into something unique and indicative of one's personality has not changed, and indeed, has grown even more over the last century.

Today, we have many ways to buy or create decorations for our homes that reflect our mundane and spiritual personalities. Thankfully, the New Age movement has made many "magical" items more commonplace in the home once again, allowing us to have our faith present in the form of crystals or other objects, without declaring to the world our Witchhood. I am not an advocate of remaining in the broom closet, but there are circumstances that require us to keep a low profile, either out of respect for those we love, or out of necessity, to protect our livelihood. So, instead of blatant pentagrams painted on the walls, or strange sigils around our doors, we can allow the New and Victorian ages to give us some of their art and symbols, thereby beautifying our homes with a reflection of our spirituality.

ALTARS AND SACRED SPACE

You could place your altar in a room no one sees, tucked away for your eyes only, but most magical people I know really don't want to do that. They have a strong emotional attachment to their tools, as well they should, and want them nearby. So how do we make our homes into an altar that doesn't declare to the universe walking through your door, "Hi, I'm a witch!?"

One solution is through a bookshelf. I have a rather tall one. The top of it is filled with my tools, crystals, and what might be considered pretty knick-knacks to an untrained eye. The shelves below neatly hold all my magical books. This type of set up can be kept in a room where you spend a lot of your personal time, but which is private enough that guests do not have to walk through it unless you wish. The added advantage to the parent or pet owner is that bookshelves are usually high enough to keep tools away from little hands and paws.

But you say that your mother is a staunch Catholic, and your neighbor is a fundamentalist, and any type of outward expression just won't do? O.K., let's try it the Victorian way! If you have a dining room table, allow the center piece to reflect the seasons. Change the flowers so that they correspond to the holidays you are observing, adding a colored candle which is also symbolic to you. To anyone else, this just looks like a very well thought out centerpiece.

Also, it is perfectly acceptable to have crystals around the house for decorations since they are being sold even in shopping mall's interior design shops! If you just happen to place appropriate ones at the four elemental points of your home, modifying them periodically to symbolize the wheel of the year, all the better. Dry and fresh flowers can also be employed in much the same way, except you would probably have smaller arrangements placed in various rooms.

The plants you pick can carry their meanings from the Victorian flower language, or from your favorite magical herb book. The end results in either case are decorations which have deep meaning to the occupants of the house, but which do not attract the wrong kind of attention. Add to these ideas the marvelous number of different cultural symbols available (thanks to what Pauline Campanelli, author of *Ancient Ways*, calls "the melting pot of magic") and you begin to see what a wide variety of choices we have for metaphysical decorating.

The Victorians felt that their homes should be a proper reflection of solid spiritual lives. By changing your spiritual focus from the altar to the whole home, you are making your entire living space a sanctuary, instead of just one specific area. To me, there is nothing more wonderful to give yourself or your family than a spiritual haven in which to share time.

Other examples of decorating ideas include putting a feathered wall hanging in the eastern portion of your house to mark the watchtower of Air, placing a potted plant in the North for Earth, a crystal vase filled with water and flowers in the West for Water, and a red candle in the South for Fire. You can also decorate your house with any number of "mythic" pieces of art representing the God/dess in its in many aspects—from the beautiful maidens and the brave knights of fantasy books to the strong warrior women, aliens and tender males of science fiction. Even among these books, posters and paintings, true images of magic appear again and again. By placing them outside of the magical realm. we make them "safe" to the uninformed or fearful individual, yet still allow the powerful impressions of the Divine to surround us, fill us and make us whole.

The truly illustrious are they who do not court the praise of men, but perform the actions which deserve it.

— Tilton

SACHETS, SWEETBAGS, AND POMANDERS

The Victorians loved rich smells. They would place potpourri around the house as part of the entire decorating scheme. Roses were favored by far, their petals filling sachets, sweetbags, herb pillows, and pomanders to give each room a light, fresh flavor reflective of the setting.

For magic, these items have applications as rich and varied as your imagination will allow—just consult your magical herb guide and vary the ingredients as the situation dictates. Although the Victorian recipes were designed to ward off insects, protect from the plague, and freshen linens, they also made everything around them smell absolutely wonderful.

What was true for your flowers and other decorations is true for herbs: they can be changed according to the time of year, in keeping with your magical observances. You can also use the herbs to create sachets, sweetbags, and pomanders for protection, cleansing, and refreshment.

Sachets

Making a sachet is a very simple matter. Collect the aromatic or magic herbs you desire, place them in cloth, and tie it tightly at the top with a ribbon. If the herbs are large enough, you can use netting to hold them, which will allow the scent to be released better. If you like to sew, take a square of fabric, sewn together on 3 sides. Turn it right side out and stuff it with the herbs, finishing off the last side. The best thing about sachets is that they fit anywhere, including your pet's bed, dresser drawers, and laundry baskets.

For your pet's bed, you can make a sachet filled with pennyroyal to inhibit fleas. If you own a cat, you can add a little valerian root and catnip to the mixture to make a toy.

To make a sachet which you can hold during meditation, fill it with nutmeg and myrrh to help settle your mind and focus your concentration. Or, if you are feeling weary, make one with rosemary and vanilla to carry with you for revitalized energy.

Sweetbags

Here again the multiplicity of recipes I found for sweetbags was amazing, and definitely reflective of Victorian personal tastes. A recipe designed to protect items in storage against the ravages of moths was made from orris, cloves, dried roses, lavender, cedar powder, rose oil, and vetiver. Other recipes recommended for keeping linen were made from roses, cloves and mace; another variation on this was to add white loaf sugar, orris, coriander, cinnamon, musk powder, and calamus to the rosey clove and mace mixture.

Truth be known, I believe that sweet bags were really an older name for sachets, or just a slightly different version of them. I could not find direct references to their size or placement other than one author instructing the powder to be added to small silk bags. For the most part, there is really no reason why many of these recipes could not have been used as body powder too. Perhaps that is why most instructions were given in rather large proportions, resulting in a finished product that averaged from 5 cups to 5 pounds!

Sweet bags that I personally like to make are: rose and clove for love; bayberry, mint, and pine for prosperity; and sandalwood, lotus, and allspice for enhancing spiritual energies.

Herb Pillows

The variety and unique nature of herb pillows make them a perfect gift item, let alone decorating idea. Many herb pillows were simply 2 pieces of fabric stuffed with crushed, fallen pine needles, (they were commonly made of fir needles, which hold their scent for a long time). These pillows were then placed in chairs, on sofas and in the bedroom.

Other versions were not so simple. One recipe calls for layers of herbs such as clove, cinnamon, allspice, cardamom, lavender, lemon mint, rosemary, marjoram and spearmint to be mixed with orris root, benzoin and bergamot oil until all the ingredients are used. This mixture gets stored in a tightly covered box for 6 to 8 weeks before being placed into a pillow. The resulting smell is incredible, but patience is definitely required.

Another example comes to us through folk magic, in the form of a dream pillow which is supposed to assure that the bearer will have sweet dreams. This particular version of an herb pillow is a wonderful gift item. It is easy to make and usually becomes a cherished item in any home.

To make a dream pillow, cut 2 squares of fabric (9" x 9" is a good size). Sew right sides together, leaving 1/2 of one side open for stuffing. Next, mix together in equal proportions some aromatic herbs. The selection of herbs should be very individual, according to the recipient's needs or according to the wishes you are trying to extend to them. I have found that pine, frankincense, myrrh, jasmine, rose, lavender, mints, cinnamon sticks, ginger root and many other easily obtained herbs work very well together. Mugwort is almost universally employed as well.

Be sure the final scent obtained is not overwhelming, and that the recipient isn't allergic to any part of your mixture. Lavender, rosemary, apple, pine, mugwort and cinnamon is one blend that I personally like, because they are the herbs commonly chosen for restful sleep, healing, harmony and a little bit of luck!

Now that you have selected the herbs, take a muslin bag and stuff it with these herbs and tye it closed. Wrap the muslin bag in cotton bunting and then put it in the center of your pillow, filling the rest with more cotton. The advantage to this step is that the recipient may remove the little herb cache and refresh it whenever it begins losing its potency.

Sew and finish the final edge, adding lace, applique, embroidery or other personal touches. Then, write up a small gift card detailing your ingredients and why you selected them. The thoughtfulness of a gift like this is perhaps more important than the magic itself.

Whatever form of herb pillow you make, place it where people can enjoy your handiwork, and benefit from the herbs.

Pomanders

Pomanders were originally made with an ambergris base, to which herbs and/or perfumes were added. Pomanders were carried to ward off the stench of a people who did not bath as regularly as we do. They were worn on a chain around the neck or hung off the belt and considered a safeguard against disease, so they can easily be adapted for magical work, especially that which pertains to safety or protection.

There are three basic methods of making pomanders today, and two of them were done in the Victorian era. The first is to take any citrus fruit (oranges being the best) and

Making a Dream Pillow

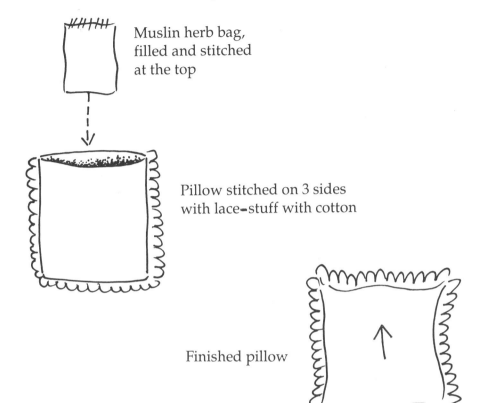

Muslin herb bag, filled and stitched at the top

Pillow stitched on 3 sides with lace-stuff with cotton

Finished pillow

about 2 ounces of whole cloves. Put the cloves all over the fruit until it is completely covered. Next, dust the fruit with ginger, cinnamon and nutmeg for a more spicy scent (please note that for magic, frankincense and myrrh work very well). Lastly sprinkle orris root or benzoin powder (most pharmacies carry it) over the whole fruit. Leave this in a dark airy spot for approximately 4 weeks during which time the fruit will shrink. You can then decorate it with a ribbon for hanging, place it in a drawer, use it as a Yule ornament, or give it as a gift.

My first experiment with this method was a total failure, so don't be discouraged if you end up with mold. That just means the area was too damp or warm for the process to work right.

An alternative to this method is to take equal portions of rose petals, cinnamon, ginger, lavender, rose water, powdered clove, nutmeg, myrrh and benzoin and crush them together with mortar and pestle. This mixture will be pasty, but to help it hold together better, add a few drops of white wax before forming into a ball. Let this ball dry completely before placing into a decorative container.

I have found that small lace doilies (decorated with ribbons) can be sewed or pasted together to contain these scented balls. They are quite lovely and you could hang them in any room of the house. Or simply put the ball in your drawer, in an open potpourri, under your sink, or any place where nasty odors hide. I have also discovered recently that other dry flower petals and herbs can be used instead of roses to create a variety of scents and for many magical purposes. In this instance I combined lavender and violets for harmony in my home and lily, rose and willow for love.

The third method, which is one I devised myself, is to use wax as a base for your scent. Begin by finding a mold whose top and bottom are equal in size. If the top is smaller, you will not be able to get the wax out once it sets. Ideally, if the top is a little wider, this process will be easier. Grease the mold with a little cooking oil.

Pick out 2 or more candles (depending on the size of your mold) of a pleasant color and slowly melt them down. Add some herbs, or herbal oils, until the scent is a little stronger than you might normally like. You will find that the scent decreases with cooling. Pour your scented wax into the mold, and as it begins to cool, place a "wick" (even a thick piece of string will work) at the center.

Once the pomander is solid, you can run hot water over the bottom to get it loose from the mold. If you would like to decorate the wax, a little lace can be glued around the side, and shells or crystals placed at the center. Use the "wick" to hang the pomander in a sunny place where the heat will slowly release the scent into the room. When you find the pomander has lost its fragrance, don't throw it away. You can now re-use it as a candle.

Herbal Beads

The most common herbal beads are made of roses. However, I have also had some limited success with lavender and mint. Here's how to make them: Gather fresh flowers or leaves early in the morning. Crush them thoroughly with your mortar and pestle. Simmer for 1 hour in an iron pot, with just enough water to cover them. Let cool. Repeat this process every day for 1 week with the same rose petals until you get an ebony-colored, pasty substance. Roll your beads into balls that are about twice the size you want them to be because they will shrink while they dry. You may want to add a touch of scented oil here for better, longer lasting scent. Before they finish contracting, you can take a large needle and make a holes in their centers to enable you to string them.

Polish the beads with a soft cloth and wear them, use them in drawers, for baths, potpourri, and incense. String herbal beads made of lilac, violet and clover, and hang them in windows to relieve negative energy and mobilize your magic, as their scent fills your home.

CHORES

*The best way to clean a house is to keep it clean
by daily attention to small things.*
— Robert B. Thomas, 1855

Between 1850 and 1900, the gentility bug bit America deeply. The virtues of housekeeping and all "feminine" arts were extolled as the protectors of the country's moral backbone. Even though the home was already the center of the Victorian woman's attention, now it was even more so. This became so much the case that an actual schedule of chores became commonplace. Washing was done on Monday, ironing on Tuesday, baking on Wednesday, brewing on Thursday, churning on Friday, mending on Saturday and church on Sunday. Brewing on Thursday came from the need to have safe drinkables for the family (many people made apple cider). When this need diminished, Thursday became market day. Similarily when cheese was sold by merchants and more readily available, a woman's attention on Friday turned to household cleaning. This tradition was passed on not only through books, but by word of mouth from mother to daughter.

The writers at that time began to take a more romantic view of chores, feeling that each daily duty, if approached properly, could be poetic; that it was possible to surround their existence with loveliness.

I am the first person to admit that there appears to be nothing less poetic or spiritual in life than scrubbing floors. However, since the busy nature of our lives does not often allow for complex rituals, we are left to discover ways of expressing magical principles through more mundane processes. When we apply a little creative elbow grease, almost any daily activity can become a ritual, and thus a celebration of the divine nature in all things. In the exercises that follow, I encourage you to add a little of your own talent and vision to make them uniquely yours, and therefore more effective for your home.

Dishes

One of the fun things about teaching magic is finding uncommon ways of getting a point across. One night I was doing readings for a couple of my students, and the energy in the room was unusually high. One of the young men, Terry, absorbs energy like a sponge and found it difficult to relax, to the point that he was becoming almost hyper. So, I calmly picked up a few stray dishes and told him, "Take these to the kitchen and rinse them off. As the water pours over the cups and washes away the food particles, let the excess energy go with it . . . get the picture?" He nodded politely, not really thinking much would change, but when Terry returned he was much more grounded, and somewhat amazed. This is a very functional example of how the magic of the mundane can work for an individual or group.

Any time you are doing dishes it represents the opportunity to get in touch with the element of water on a tactile and spiritual level. Water is a very powerful force. It is a creative well, the place of our birth, a cleanser, a refresher, and a healer. So, why not take advantage of the time you spend sink side? Again I recommend some music, if for no other reason than it helps me get jobs I hate doing done quicker, and I dislike dishes a lot. As you rinse each dish, rinse away a worry, burden, tension or other specific problem, allowing them to flow down the drain and away from you. Don't look down the sink to see where the worries are going, simply turn your attention to the next dish. It may take time and repetition (especially for old habits) to see solid results, so don't become discouraged if change isn't instantaneous. Remember that magic takes honest effort on your part as well.

Continue doing your dishes until complete, then take some time for you. Pat yourself on the back for a job well done and find pleasure in being free of the tensions which usually plague you. *Resting is important.* If you go right from this visualization to another chore, you will probably become tense again and undo the good your magic just accomplished. You must also remember that anything you want to do will get done more effectively if you approach it rested and refreshed.

Another method for doing dishes is with sing-a-longs. No matter how terrible you may think your voice is, making chores fun mean they get done. The joy and silly nature of sing-along music tends to be very contagious. The dishes will get done and you will have a good laugh or two in the process. Try throwing some fresh herbs in the hot water to scent the kitchen, or, if it is warm enough, open the windows to let the winds of change revitalize your home.

If you have children, let them get involved too. I play a game with my five year old called "wash your worries away." We sing those words to no particular tune while he helps rinse the dishes with a plastic cup. He feels more a part of home life this way, and I enjoy the time with him tremendously. The repetition of the words acts like a mantra or a chant, which actually makes both of us feel better!

If you find you are really enjoying yourself, don't be afraid to let go. Do a jig with a wooden spoon as a pretend microphone, jump around and sing or do whatever feels good at that moment. These types of activities serve to release a lot of pent-up tensions and aid in relaxation. It is the simple magic of happiness at its best.

Laundry

In the Victorian era, a version of the clothes dryer was invented and considered to be quite a convenience. It consisted of a main center pole with arms radiating out and upwards from it. Ropes were strewn in between the arms. In those days, doing the laundry was no simple task. It began with building a fire to heat a kettle of rainwater, adding lye soap, sorting, making starch as needed, rinsing, hanging and then using leftover water for cleaning the privy.

Today we have much better methods of washing clothes, but we can still do some things the old-fashioned way. When you have the advantage of warm weather, hang your laundry outside to give it a fresh scent and save on electricity. If you happen to have had problems recently with gossip, this activity can ease the tongues of those trying to "air your dirty laundry." As you hang up each item, visualize the clothes hanger binding the lips of the gossiper saying, "truth, truth, be my guide. Truth, truth, stand by my side!" Continue chanting softly until you are done hanging things, then allow the winds of change to do their work.

Also, whenever you have been experiencing sickness in your home, it is a good idea to wash and air the bedding. From a purely medical standpoint, you are getting rid of the germs you have been sleeping in. Magically, this allows for a new freshness to enter the home when you bring the spreads back in. Should you desire, you can also take your smudge stick and wave it near each item while it hangs outside, and cleanse it psychically.

Ironing

The most common place for the iron in the Victorian home was probably the kitchen. Here the housewife would keep a different iron for almost every chore, including ones for varying weights of fabrics. In other words, there were irons to meet every need. For magic we can extend this symbolism and use an iron to press out problems in our lives. As we work with our clothing, we can maintain a strong image of whatever difficulty burdens us and cast that image onto the clothes. Allow the warmth, water and pressure of the iron to literally, "iron it out"!

Sewing

The first American patent for a sewing machine was taken out in 1851, the first electric one becoming available in 1889. Even so, widespread use did not occur until around the 1920s, meaning that most Victorian women did their mending by hand. Darning socks, quilting, and making clothing for their ever growing children were part of the common responsibilities for a Victorian wife.

General sewing approaches have changed very little on the home front since that time, except for the much wider use of the electric models. If you have access to a sewing machine, or are willing to take the extra time to sew by hand, stitching techniques offer a wide range of opportunities for magical applications. In making things by hand, we can endow them with special personal energy, attention to detail, and a quality not commonly found with mass produced items.

Like most things in my life, I approach sewing from a very pragmatic angle. How can I make the best item, using the least amount of fabric, in the shortest span of time? These are things even the Victorians considered. Fabric was a valued commodity, not to be squandered.

I also find that some people are discouraged from sewing because of the sometimes complex patterns. If this applies to you, you will be happy to know that you can sew without patterns, using your own clothing as a model and starting point. I have been sewing for seven years now and have never used a store-bought pattern.

When making things for magical applications, there are other things besides patterns and time to consider. First, what type and color of material best suits the item's application. If you are making a summer robe, you probably won't want to use wool or dark colors. Next, do you want to sew during a special season or moon phase? This isn't necessary, but it can add a wonderful dimension to the finished product.

The Tarot or Rune Pouch

This pouch may be used to house any magical tool, but is especially designed for Tarot decks and Rune sets. I found I didn't like keeping mine in their boxes, and wanted something pleasant to carry or store them in. For this pouch, I suggest using a sturdy outer fabric such as a heavy woven cotton, which is also washable. This way your pouch will be able to handle wear and tear without falling to shreds in the first year. For linings, silk, satin, or a white cotton are advised. White is used because it is the color of protection, and silk/satin have been traditional wraps for Tarot decks for many generations. On the other hand, if you have a deck or set of runes with a unique character to them, you may wish to change the lining color to match that vibration more closely. For example, if you have rose quartz runes, you may want a pink lining.

Tarot/Rune Pouch

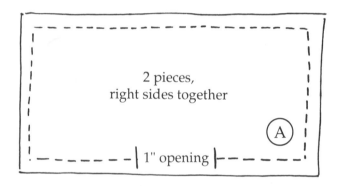

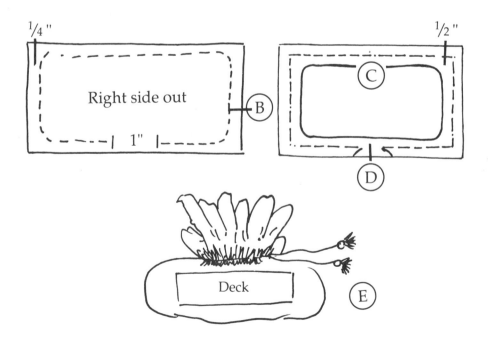

have been traditional wraps for Tarot decks for many generations. On the other hand, if you have a deck or set of runes with a unique character to them, you may wish to change the lining color to match that vibration more closely. For example, if you have rose quartz runes, you may want a pink lining.

Cut one 9-1/2 inch square out of each piece of fabric and put them right sides together. (See the diagram to understand these directions.) Sew all the way around the outside, leaving a small hole through which to reverse the material (A).

Turn the whole piece right side out and sew another seam all the way around; sew it approximately 1/4 inch in from the edge, again leaving the 1 inch opening in the same place (B). Repeat this once more, sewing a seam without an opening 1/2 inch in from B, or your original seam. (This new seam is illustrated by C).

Next, by hand, stitch under the opening where your ties will come out so it doesn't ravel (D). To pull the draw string through the canal you have made for it, attach a safety pin to one end and thread it around. Place your deck or runes in the center, and draw the tie tight (E).

This particular design on a pouch can be used to house crystal balls, change, and a myriad of other items by simply changing your dimensions to suit the need. In the case of crystals, however, I suggest adding a 1/4 inch of bunting between the two layers of cloth (you can purchase this in 1 inch squares at most fabric shops) to help keep the stones from being damaged.

Altar Cloths

I have received a number of letters asking me for ideas on patterns for altar cloths. The Victorian lady would have been content to use a lace or linen covering, probably inherited from her family. Actually, my altar cloth is a Victorian gauze scarf with a white on white pattern. Be that as it may, I have considered several ideas for altar cloths made by hand.

The easiest method by far is to take a good piece of fabric that you like, cut it to the right size and shape, and simply finish the edges by turning them under twice and sewing along the edge. You may want to make several in different colors or textures to reflect the seasons.

For something a little more elaborate, take strips of fabric in the colors of the rainbow and connect them so they form a rectangle. Now just sew the edges down as before.

Rainbow Altar Cloth

RED
ORANGE
YELLOW
GREEN
BLUE
INDIGO
VIOLET

Finshed edge,
turned under twice

If you have a talent for applique or embroidery, you can stitch on various sigils, runes, or personal symbols when you are finished to make the cloth even more reflective of your magic. Another suggestion along these lines is to make one cloth for Solstice celebrations (with a sun appliqued in the middle) and another for celebrations of the moon (decorated with moon phases).

The Ritual Robe

If you decide you would like a ritual robe and can't afford to buy one, consider making one yourself. First check your local yellow pages for wholesale fabric outlets. We have one locally where I can obtain fabric for as little as 50 cents a yard! For the average sized individual (5'7"), I recommend getting 3-1/2 yards of 45 to 60-inch wide material. This will give you have a little room for error, for matching colored thread and using several needles. Check the shrinkage on your fabric before purchasing with the clerk. If it is going to shrink a lot, buy more! Prewash your fabric in lukewarm water so you can be certain you won't have a t-shirt instead of a robe after cleaning it.

Begin by folding your fabric in half, leaving 2-1/2 feet at the bottom, which you can cut off for sleeves (A). (See the diagram "Sewing a Ritual Robe").

Next, find a shirt which fits you very well and lay it out at the top of the fabric with arms folded in (B).

Take a water soluble marker and make small dots to use as guidelines, extending the line of the bottom of the shirt out toward the two corners of the fabric (C).

Cut along those lines, leaving 2 inches extra at each side to allow for seams and room for you to slide the robe over your head.

Take the 2-1/2 foot piece that you cut off and fold it in half length-wise (1) and cut.

These 2 pieces will now be your sleeves, which should be pinned into the arm holes, right-sides together and attached (2).

Remove your pins.

Turn the robe over now, turning the sleeve edges under twice and sewing them before refolding the robe with right sides together. (3)

Sew the main seams 1/2 inch in from the edge along (D). You may want to do this twice to be sure the seams are very secure.

At the bottom hem, turn under the fabric twice and then sew all the way around (E).

If need be, you can trim down the bottom so that the garment is 1 inch longer than floor length when worn, then turn under the hem (1/2 inch twice).

At this point you can try on the robe to be sure you are comfortable, and adjust the neckline before putting a finished edge on it the same way you did the hem (F).

If you find the fabric was not wide enough to allow free movement in the robe you can leave a side seam open (G) and simply fold down the fabric and sew it for a finished look.

Sewing a Ritual Robe

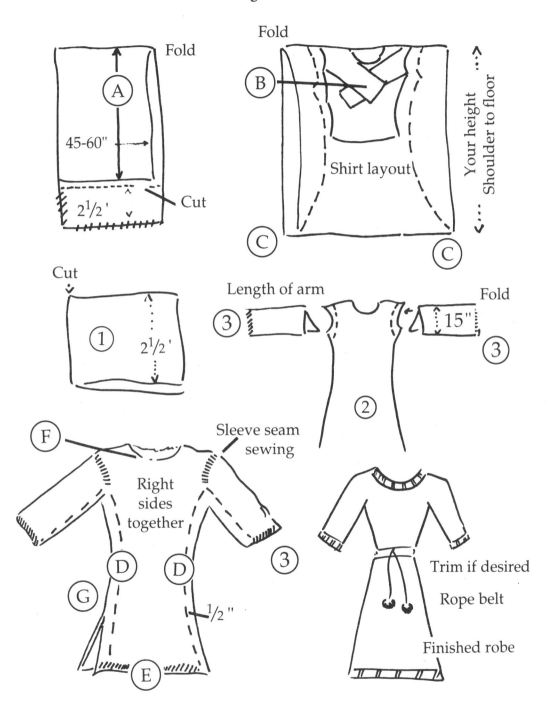

Fold

(A)

45-60"

2¹/₂'

Cut

Fold

(B)

Shirt layout

Your height
Shoulder to floor

(C) (C)

Cut

(1)

2¹/₂'

Length of arm

(3)

(3) 15" Fold

(2)

(F)

Sleeve seam
sewing

Right
sides
together

(D) (D)

(G)

(3)

¹/₂"

(E)

Trim if desired

Rope belt

Finished robe

SPIRITUAL HOUSE CLEANING

Much of the character of a man may be read in his house.
                              —A. J. Downing, 1850

It's time to sweep, dust and wash your home again, but how long has it been since you spiritually cleansed the area where you spend much of your time? Houses, like people, need spiritual attention on a consistent basis.

Even though most of us might not be as concerned with the visual presentation of our home as the Victorian people were, we should be concerned about the spiritual atmosphere created there. The value of the sanctity of your home can not be underestimated. It is because of this that, while many other types of magic can be performed in the home, the most important magics for the home are those of protection and cleansing.

How frequently you perform rituals or spells for your home is a personal matter, but for anyone living in a city environment I suggest reinforcing your protections on a weekly basis. The vast amounts of negative energy created in any heavily populated area wears down magical shields more quickly. In the country, less frequent fortification is necessary.

Remember, your home is a sanctuary for you, your family and/or your friends. When they enter it, they should immediately feel a peacefulness fall over them like a warm blanket, no matter where you live. I call this, for lack of a better term, the "Ah..." effect of protective magic. I have seen it over and over again in my house, and visitors even comment on it! They walk in, sit down, and suddenly their shoulders relax, and they let out a long sigh of relief. They feel and know they have come into a safe harbor.

The following are but a few examples of how to begin to create this very special, and very important ambience in your own home. Add to them things from your personal tradition, vision or inspiration to create a sacred space that is always present not only to give protection, but also a sense of warmth and comfort.

I remember when I was a child, my mother going through the house singing while she cleaned. It was terribly out of tune, as my mother is tone deaf. Even so, when she was done the house not only looked better, it felt better too. Unconsciously, I believe my mother was putting the joy of her music into the house as she cleaned away tensions (and dirt) from the previous week.

It is not difficult to accomplish this in your own home. My approach is pretty
I begin by putting on some music that helps me feel energized. Then, I get out all my
"tools" adding to my wash water a little lavender, cinnamon and lemon.

Go through the house as you usually would, but as you go, visualize white, protective light pouring from your hands into everything you touch. We use our hands so much on a daily basis; they are excellent conductors of energy.

When you are finished with each room, take all evidence of cleaning supplies out of the rooms and light a stick of incense from your altar there. For a fresh scent that continues, place a few dried herbs under cushions or under rugs. Replace them each week. (The added bonus here for pet owners is that many aromatic herbs inhibit fleas.) Continue this routine until the whole house is done, then sit and have a cup of tea with which to bless yourself, enjoying the peaceful atmosphere you have created. I know from experience that the average home only looks really picture perfect for about one day after cleaning, so savor it while you can!

In this process, make sure to use herbs which have subtle scents—you don't want it to be overwhelming. Also, consider your household members' allergies and avoid herbs which might trigger them. If you happen to have an allergy to smoke, instead of lighting incense in each room you may substitute a white candle, or you could draw a rune of protection with your hand, saying a little blessing as you leave.

If your home has been particularly tense, you may wish to walk through it with some burning sage to help disperse any negative energy remnants. Change your herbs and incense to meet the needs of your family. Remember, the more aware and sensitive you are, the more you can improve the atmosphere of your home every day.

Cleansing (General)

Burning basil, mint, sage, cedar and/or lavender works to alleviate much negative energy in the home. You may also add these herbs to your vacuum bags, wash water, or potpourri to continue the effect. Remember to add visualizations while you clean. One which works very well for me (thanks to modern commercials) is that of little white-light "scrubbing bubbles" collecting up all the tensions and bad feelings and washing them swiftly away.

A more Victorian method might be to use a broom to sweep the out any residue stress left laying around, right out the front door. As the fresh air moves inward, see it as a refreshing influence, bringing new perspectives and positive attitudes. If you do not have a broom, use your vacuum, visualizing all dark energies being drawn into the bag, then thrown away.

Protection

Tie dill, nettle, yarrow, and ivy together by a string and hang it somewhere in your house to ward off evil intentions. Protection sachets may be made by assembling the following things: a silver coin, some basil, bay, fennel, tarragon, dill, and rosemary. Bind them with white thread and hide them somewhere in the house where they will not be disturbed.

Another bit of folk magic says that if you take four bells of silver, consecrate them for protection and hang them in four windows, (one for each direction) that they will sound to warn you of danger coming from that direction.

To make a protective wreath for your home, gather several branches of rosemary and tie them together with green yarn (or any color which symbolizes protection to you). Fill out the wreath with additional pieces of rosemary as needed, and place a decorative bow at top or bottom. If you wish, you can add other protective herbs to the wreath, then hang it on your front door saying, "Bonds of power, bonds of light, grow strong, protect, defend against all who would rend."

There are literally hundreds of other methods for protecting and cleansing your home. Some of them include: scattering salt all around the perimeter, planting protective crystals at the four corners of the building, putting a witches bottle (a bottle full of sharp objects meant to trap negative energy inside) on the grounds, anointing the door frames with protective oils, placing sigils discreetly in the wood by carving or visualization, burning herbs of protection with incense, charging various items in the home to act as watchtowers, and many more.

The best advice I can give on this matter is to consider your living space and what makes the most sense to you. Like all other forms of magic, the amount of effectiveness will depend greatly on your perception of the method as productive. If one way doesn't seem to work for you, try others until you can feel the difference it makes. Like any good recipe, change it until it bakes up "just right," making your home a place where both you and your magic can dwell in harmony.

Airing out the House

Perhaps one of the easiest methods of clearing sickness and negativity out of your house is to open the windows and doors wide, allowing a fresh wind to move in. Now, if you happen to live in the north and it's the middle of winter, this may be a little difficult, so perhaps one window can suffice—if aided by a visualization of the cool air carrying white, cleansing light to every corner of your house. You may want to hang a sprig of rosemary and mint in front of the open window to help the wind convey a healing essence into your home.

And though they sweep their hearts no less, than maids were wont to do,
yet who of late for cleanliness finds sixpence in her shoe.

—Bishop of Oxford and Norwhich

HOUSEHOLD HELPFUL HINTS

The Victorian Lady was infamous for having 101 ways to take care of any number of little problems around the home. It was her job to take care of everything from maintenance and cleaning to stains and pest control. For the 20th century Witch, even with our newer technology, it is still nice to have natural or simple ways to tackle some of these situations. Here are a few for you to try:

Air Freshener

Cinnamon, ginger and allspice may be placed in boiling water on the stove to freshen the air in your home. Stringing lemon and orange rinds together and hanging them in an open window is also effective.

Antibacterial/Antiseptic Herb Wash

Before cleaning, make a tincture of 1 part basil, bay cinnamon, comfrey, and rosemary, with 2 parts lavender and lemon balm to add to your wash water. This will help keep the house free of germs.

Ants

Place tansy and/or strips of cucumber around the area where ants come into the house.

Candle Drippings

If you have wax stuck on a table cloth or other item, try taking some newspaper, laying it over the wax, and applying an iron on low heat. Repeat until the newspaper has absorbed all the wax. Another Victorian means was to soak the wax with cider vinegar for one hour, then rub vigorously until all the wax was dissolved.

Be sure to retain your candle ends and pieces for future use. You can make new candles with them simply by melting them down into a mold and adding a new wick.

Cockroach Cure

Place black hellebore root in the areas they frequent, or capture them by putting water and molasses in a glazed china bowl with an old piece of carpeting on one side. This captures the creatures inside like the modern roach motels. Borax and cucumber parings also tend to deter them.

Copper Cleanser

Plain sorrel leaves and water will scrub the shine back into copper pots.

Corn Shuck Mop

Wonderful for cleaning pine floors, the corn shuck mop was one way the Victorian lady made use of left over corn shucks. To make one, use an 8-inch piece of wood with holes drilled into it all around. Twist the shucks in tightly until each hole is filled. Attach a handle to this and use it with lye soap. When the shucks wear out, just replace them.

Cleansers

If you are looking for natural cleansers, salt and baking soda both work very well. Salt may be used on any surface that is not delicate and baking soda is excellent for most things, especially silver jewelry. In this case, apply with a soft toothbrush and rinse.

Creaking Doors

Apply a little soap on the hinges and they will quiet considerably.

Fly Control

A major problem in the Victorian home (due to the lack of good screening) was flies. One recipe I found suggested taking 1/2 teaspoon pepper in powder form, adding 1 teaspoon sugar and 1 teaspoon cream, then placing this on a plate in the worst room (probably the kitchen). Another method was to soak leeks in water for 24 hours, then use this liquid to dab on furniture to keep the flies from landing.

To make homemade fly paper the Victorian way, take resin with sweet oil, lard, and lamp oil, and mix them together until they take on a honey-like consistency. This substance is then painted on strips of paper and hung.

Glue

One Victorian recipe recommended using quick lime and old cheese (beaten together) for a strong household glue. Another advocated taking sap gum balls from fruit bearing trees, powdering them, and dissolving them in vinegar. For a slightly simpler method, I suggest using tree sap mixed with powdered myrrh and orris root. This is an effective glue which also has a lovely scent. It is especially useful in setting stones into magical wands.

Grab Bags

Keep a bag for odd pieces of tape and string, along with a box of old buttons so you know where they are when you need them. This hint comes to us from *The American Frugal Housewife*, 1844.

Herbal Tea Bags

When you are done with these, do not throw them away. They can be dried on screens and reused for incense, potpourri, sachets, to scent oils, or to enrich your soil.

Ink and Grease Spots

According to Victorian cookbooks, to remove ink or grease spots, make a sand soap and add a good portion of coarse sand to the cooling mixture. This soap is also excellent for cleaning tin. (The basic soap recipe is found in Chapter Five.)

Another method was to mix carbonate of ammonia with rain water and dab this on the spot.

Laundry Freshener

Make a tincture of lemon rind, orange rind or other aromatics and add this with 1 teaspoon of baking soda to your rinse water.

Moths

Bind rosemary and wormwood together and hang it with your clothes.

Rug Deodorizer

Put a full box of baking soda in a bowl and add 1/8 cup lavender, 4 teaspoons fennel, 5 crushed eucalyptus leaves, a dash of cinnamon, 4 teaspoons lemon balm and any other aromatic herb you enjoy. Dust your rugs with this before vacuuming.

Wine Stains

Pour salt immediately on the area where wine has spilled and brush it off. Repeat until all the stain is removed.

Wood Polish

Lemon balm leaves make an excellent wood polish; the oil in them helps protect the wood and their scent leaves everything lemon-fresh.

Anything green or that grew out of mould
Was an excellent herbe to our fathers of olde.
—Rudyard Kipling

SPELLS ENGAGING COMMON HOUSEHOLD ITEMS

Yes, let the rich deride, the proud disdain,
The simple pleasures of the lowly train;
To me more dear, congenial to my heart,
Our native charm, than all the gloss of art.
—Oliver Goldsmith

Despite the intricate nature of the Victorian home, there was little which could be considered frivolous about it. Everything had a specific function, be it aesthetic or serviceable. In some instances I think we have overlooked a wealth of tools which could be used for magic and could be found right in our own homes. Stop for a moment to look around the area in which you live. Do not see conventional chairs or tables, examine items instead for their magical potential. The following is a list I came up with for my home. You may use this if you choose, add to it, or make a whole new one specifically for your home and hearth.

Drawer

Drawers may be used in sympathetic magic when you wish to close yourself off from something. For example, you can visualize yourself placed in a white-light drawer for protection.

An interesting application of a drawer, though, is for saving money. For this exercise, take an amount which, to you, is enough to really splurge with. Fold the money three times and wrap it with a piece of green cloth and a piece of paper which has the word "restraint" or "discipline" written on it in bold lettering. Now place this in a drawer where you will see it once a day. Keep telling yourself, "no" until the weather is really stormy. Then, remove the money from the drawer, tear off the paper and let imaginary winds carry the energy of restraint into your being. Take half of the money and treat yourself, the other half should get re-wrapped with a similar paper for another rainy day. By the time the funds are completely expended you should have incorporated this ability into your life.

Fireplace

Fire is an element of purification and healing. If you have bad feelings towards someone or want to rid yourself of a nasty habit, try writing down what you want to clear away on paper. Tear it up while pouring the energy of those feelings into the document, then toss it in the fire, allowing the purifying flames to begin their work.

Heater

To help warm the "cold shoulder" in your life, try this. Write the name of the person who is being distant on something they gave you in the past, or on a piece of paper. Tape the item/paper to a heater duct (or a sunny window). While pouring love into the paper, repeat these words three times: "I bring you warmth, from my heart to yours, let your anger be free. I bring you warmth, I open the door . . . so mote it be."

Lamps

Any time you need to shed light on a situation, anoint one of your lamp bulbs with oil of manifestation (blessed thistle or cinquefoil work well). Then turn the light on, allowing the fragrance of truth and reason fill your home and mind.

Mail

When one collects as I do, real post cards (or more correctly 'postal' cards) one does not like being confused or confounded with picture gatherers.
— 1903 *Stamp Collectors Fortnightly*

During the Victorian era, the advent of mail service was still new and fun. The Swiss and British post offices introduced post cards in 1870 along with the half-penny postage stamp. Thematic cards and all manner of dispensers lined many shop walls, the most predominant motifs being humorous, political, and art nouveau. More important than style, however, was the fact that mail delivery kept the extended family in touch with each other when circumstances drew them to different areas of the country.

I think we all still enjoy receiving a letter or post card today. If you have been feeling sad, try placing a cup of water on top of letters or cards from friends. Allow their love and concern to flow out of the writings and into the water, which you may drink to internalize the magic.

Also, if you are having nightmares, try sleeping with a few of these tucked into your pillowcase, along with their good wishes.

Mirrors

Folk legends say that if you place a mirror in a window facing outward it will reflect negative energy aimed your way. Also, if you have a mirror in your home, never turn its back to you. This is believed to be an invitation to not-so-pleasant spiritual company.

Stairs

When going up the stairs, repeat phrases about things you want to accomplish or bring into your life. While going downwards, speak of things you wish to release. This is not unlike working with the waxing and waning phases of the Moon.

Telephone

The telephone, for all its annoyance, offers us the opportunity to heighten our awareness. Each person you know has a very specific vibration, which you can learn to recognize even through the phone. This exercise will help you to develop your intuition and foresight.

Each time the telephone rings, make a note of who you think it is. Try this at first on a simple guess level. Next time, try waiting a minute, closing your eyes, taking a breath and responding to the first name that comes to mind. Continue doing this exercise and keep track of your progress. In most instances, the more you practice, the more you should see an increase in correct predictions, meaning your general awareness is also improving.

Television

A television which has been turned off makes an excellent scrying instrument. Simply stare at the blank screen as you might a crystal ball. Allow your mind to be calm and see if any images form. Also, I predict the longer it stays off the more likely you are to read a good book.

Toilet

Known in the Victorian era as the Privy or water closet, what better place to flush out a trouble maker or to flush away a problem. I suggest writing these items on toilet paper (which won't clog your pipes) and following the same process of visualization as with other spells given here.

Vacuum

Believe it or not, even the Victorians had a type of floor cleaner where the operator would squeeze a bag to produce a "vacuum" like action, and pull up the dirt. To spiritually vacuum something away, write your specifics on paper and tear it to shreds. As you pull apart the energy of that situation say, "Fly away from me, my burdens, with the light of day take wing, that I might fly from our this night, and with the stars may sing!" Now take the scraps of paper and toss them to the winds (on an easily vacuumed floor) and vacuum them away! A broom will also work for this spell.

Windows

Earlier in this book we talked a little about letting good luck in and back luck out of a house through the windows. An open window can be used as a symbol whenever you need a new perspective. The fresh wind which blows through the open window symbolizes beginnings and creativity. Closed windows can be used in visualizations for protection, security, completion and fulfillment. Like the stairs, this may also relate somewhat to the conscious and unconscious mind or waxing and waning moon.

The home was not only a living space for the family, it was also the center of recreation and a source of pride for Victorians. Any opportunity to invite guests for gracious and delicate conversation was not overlooked. During these visits they often played party games, many of which were Olde Ways, cleverly disguised as simple fun. Thus it was that tea time and divination became linked with entertainment in the Victorian home.

For I dipt into the future,
        far as human eye could see,
Saw the vision of the world,
        and all the wonder that would be
Saw the heavens fill with commerce,
        argosies of magic sails,
Pilots of the purple twilight,
        dropping down with costly bales;
Heard the heavens fill with shouting,
        and there rained a ghastly dew
From the nations' airy navies
        grappling in the central blue;
Far along the world-wide whisper
        of the south-wind rushing warm,
With the standards of the peoples
        plunging through the thunderstorm;
Till the war-drum throbbed no longer,
        and the battle-flags were furled
In the Parliament of man,
        the Federation of the world.
There the common sense of most
        shall hold a fearful realm in awe,
And the kindly earth shall slumber,
        lapt in universal law.
                    —Alfred, Lord Tennyson

CHAPTER EIGHT

Parlour Divination

The window into the unseen is opened in waking hours . . .
sitting in solitude, [is he] who closes the channels of the
senses and opens the eye and ear of the spirit, and places
his heart in relation to the Divine World.
— Al-Ghazali, an Islam Sufi

During the early 1900s there was a persistent, growing interest in the mystical, to the point where such experiences were even believed to somehow enhance mental health. This, combined with honest curiosity and the natural desire to know one's fate, may be why parlour divinations became so much a part of the Victorian social life and home.

In reviewing the era it is interesting to notice that mystics of the time were very much like those of other times, seemingly detached from the turbulence which surrounded them. As defined by visionaries of the period, the art of the mystic is one that defies expression because of insights transcending normal intellectual processes.

One of the most popular mystics, Swami Vivekananda, who came to the United States in the 1890s from the Ramakrishna order, had a magnetic disposition, the peacefulness of a thoughtful man, and yet enough drive to launch three lecture tours through the nation. For many Americans he may have well represented the enigmatic Oriental thought which, until now, they had only read about in books. The presence of this man, and the fact that several Ramakrishna orders were eventually established in America, illustrates on a small scale the spiritually-hungry atmosphere of the era.

With this in mind, it is understandable that divination techniques disguised as "party games" were so successful. There were many means of discovering your future love—it could be done at teas, by the fire side, and sometimes just when walking down a country path. Perhaps you would meet a strange man who had a mole on his forehead; this would tell you that your future mate would someday own many great possessions. If you met a woman with a mole on her right ear, it was a sign of honor. A mole on the private parts, however, was a sure indication of debauchery.

Augury (divination by signs and omens), palm reading, and dream interpretation were among the more common techniques used. The lines cutting through your life line on your palm could foretell how many children you would have, and a sister line to the life line near the thumb might warn of a woman who would kiss in a corner! If you dreamed of birds singing it meant joy; making pies and tarts was a sign of happiness and profit; bells signaled an alarm; and gloves on your hands in a dream symbolized true honor. By way of augury, if a lass happened to hear the first dove of spring coo, the next man she saw go by in a carriage would be her future husband!

The sheer number of divination techniques found at the turn of the century is almost overwhelming. There was even a method devised of divining by dust. Hmm . . . I wonder what my coffee table is trying to tell me? There is simply not space to share all of them here, but I have detailed those which I feel were most interesting and popular then. I have also noted if they are still used today.

ASTROLOGY

At the start of the 19th century, the study of astrology had almost died under the scrutiny of the "Age of Reason." In England, however, it received a bit of new life when in 1819 James Wilson published *A Complete Dictionary of Astrology*. This revived interest in astrology as a science, and was followed in 1827 by Robert C. Smith's periodical known as the "Prophetic Messenger," which is still in publication today. Mr. Smith wrote under the pseudonym Raphael, and is considered the father of modern astrology. Later, near the turn of the century, Dr. Alan Leo began work with the Psychical Research Society to help bring astrology into new public awareness as a symbolic system for understanding humankind's nature.

Despite this new kindling added to astrology's formerly glorious fires, real interest on both sides of the Atlantic did not begin to blaze again until the late 1920s and early 1930s, when newspapers began to publish astrological columns. Because of this, I will not go into a detailed account of this divination technique in this book. Yet, it is important to note it from the aspect of seeing how the seeds which were planted during this era bore fruit in our life times.

CHARMS

The use of charms, either worn or carried, has been popular in many time periods throughout our history. This was certainly no less so during the Victorian era, especially considering their love of jewelry. The following is a short list of some symbols which were made from various materials—from wood to fine gold. They were used for charm bracelets, to adorn art work, carried in pockets, or left innocently around the house as a decorative item. You may notice that some of them still figure predominantly in modern charm bracelets and ornamental items.

> **Acorn** — For youth and true love.
> **Arrowhead** — Protection from the "evil eye."
> **Badger tooth** — For luck with cards.
> **Coral beads** — To protect children from disease.

Bee jewelry — Energy, success in business.
Four leaf clover — Health, wealth, love, and fame.
Coal — If found, it promised a year of prosperity.
Fish — Wealth.
Hearts — Fidelity and devotion.
Horseshoe — Good fortune, protection.
Key — Opening doors.
Knot — Unity and harmony.
Lyre — Accentuation of good qualities.
Penny — Good luck.
Ring — Eternity.

DIVINING RODS

I think that in most of the cases in hand, in which
the wand is held by an honest man whose faith is in it,
the movement is the consequence of an act of mind.
— Michel Eugene Chevreul,
Academy of Science member, 1854

The origin of the divining rod is lost in antiquity. Our version of this art probably comes from the Greek practice of forecasting known as rhabdomancy. Divination of this nature appears in every culture, and includes j180
the rods of Mercury, Circes and Moses. In Europe, it was believed to guide the pixies to ore. In America, rods were used for everything from mineral detection, discovery of treasure, weeding out criminals, and even finding landmarks to establishing property lines!

In 1876, Charles Latimer read an essay before the Civil Engineer's Club which stated that the rod worked on a number of principles, but chiefly on an electrical current which was transferred from the ground to the stick. While most people scoffed at this, someone must have taken notice, so much so in fact, that the U.S. Department of the Interior was compelled to do a study of "Water Witching" in 1917.

When the rod was used as a fetish, it was believed to protect against disease, ill fortune and even give evidence of having positive personal characteristics. More frequently, though, the rod was used to find things, especially water. This process of finding things through the use of the divining rod is known as dowsing.

The basic methods of dowsing rarely changed, and continue to be employed today. A forked twig slightly larger in width than a pencil, which still exhibits some pliability, would be chosen. The favorite woods to use for divination were peach, willow and witch hazel. To use the divining rod, the operator would grasp each end of the fork, one in each hand. The butt end of the rod would be pointing slightly upward in the air. The operator concentrated on the goal while moving slowly over the ground. If water or the object of focus was reached, the branch would swing down (with much more force than can be attributed to gravity) toward the ground and bob up and down. The number of times it bounced was thought to indicate how deep the object was, in anything from inches to miles.

While this was not the most precise method ever devised for divination, the phenomenon so interested Albert Einstein that he formulated a theory that electromagnetism would eventually be discovered as the source of this curiosity.

Modern dowsers continue to use twigs to find water and lost objects. I know some people who use the rods to try and find natural energy currents on their land (lay lines). Once found, they use this knowledge in planting gardens, building greenhouses, placing additions on their home, and to help channel the power source for positive effects on their living space.

DREAM DIVINATION

With men such as Freud and Jung on the scene at the turn of the century, it is easy to see why dream interpretation became a favored pastime. Jung felt that dreams were a storehouse for memories, reflections and impressions. He did not give his patients a rigid system of analysis, but instead encouraged them to discover personal meanings by asking them specific questions which prompted introspection. Even so, dream dictionaries which purported to give meanings on all manner of night visions were very popular, so much so that even these scientists consulted them because they were the only current literature available on the subject. Titles such as *What's in a Dream*, published in 1901, were seen everywhere. Other larger texts on the occult, such as *The Great Book of Magical Art*, simply included chapters on the subject.

It is interesting to note that some of our classic horror stories (Dr. Jekyll and Mr. Hyde, Frankenstein, and Dracula) were inspired by dreams from the Victorian novelists Stevenson, Shelley and Stoker. The belief then, as seems to be the case now, was that somehow during our sleeping hours our mind becomes more open to psychic impressions, let alone our subconscious needs, desires and feelings. Thus, as night visitors, dreams can be helpful in understanding who we are, as well as being creative forces and perhaps even divinatory tools.

Dreams are subjective, so I meet the aspect of divination by dreams as an "iffy" prospect. True prophetic dreams do occur, as was the case for President Lincoln in 1865 when he viewed his own death. Unfortunately, even when dealing with imminent danger to self or a loved one, prophetic dreams often loose their meaning in our waking hours. President Lincoln was disturbed enough by his dream to communicate it to his wife, yet as far as history can tell, nothing further was thought of it.

There are many modern manuals of dream interpretation, but for the following list I have returned to sources from the turn of the century. It is interesting to note that things commonly used in other "languages," such as flowers, fans, and umbrellas, also figure into the symbolism of dreams, and their interpretations are frequently similar.

When interpreting your own dreams, I suggest refraining from trying to over-spiritualize the double cheese pizza or too many horror films from the night before. Keep a dream diary and watch for recurring themes, lessons, or new perspectives on currently pressing matters. As you discover common threads running through your sleep, you can then refer to these or other dream guides to see if there is a hidden intrepretation. It is good to remember that dreams can also be straight forward in their meanings, so if they appear obvious, you may wish to accept them at face value.

Anchor — A disappointment, something holding you back.

Apples — Long life with many children.

Arrow — You have written a letter which you may regret.

Bath — Health, long life, early marriage.

Blooms — Fruitfulness.

Bracelet — Good luck and fortune soon to come.

Cakes — Positive omen.

Canary — A charming home.

Cherries — Good news, pleasure and enjoyment.

Clock — Missed opportunity, lack of imagination.

Cornfield — Wealth, security.

Daffodils — Pleasure and amusement in abundance.

Doves — Success, especially in love.

Drinking — Celebration.

Fairy — Success, riches, flights of fancy.

Fan — Rivals in love, a quarrel.

Feathers — (black): Loss and failure.

Flying without wings — Attainment of goals.

Fountain — Laughter, abundance, flowing good feelings.

Gypsy — Profitless travel.

Gloves on the hands — Honor and safety.

Hammer — Triumph over difficulty.

Hearing Hymns — Consolation during trials.

Iron — A good bargain.

Jug (drink from) — Vigorous health and virtuous pleasures.

Kettle (copper) — Luck soon to come.

Kitchen — Success and advancement.

Leaf — Present problems are only temporary, impending change.

Meadow — Comfort, peacefulness.

Milk — Peace in the family, possibly a child to come.

Needle — Family quarrels.

Nightingale (singing) —Joyfulness, success, faithfulness.

Oak —Steady growth.

Sage — Wisdom and carefulness.

Snow —Hidden matters.

Thread — Perplexity, troubles, tangled situations.

Tied hands — Difficulty in getting out of trouble.

Wall — Obstacles in achieving future plans.

FLOWER/HERB DIVINATION (FLOROMANCY)

The pink, by Knight to Ladye given,
Prays her to be his bride —
The proud Carnation answering tells
That fervent prayer's denied.
                    —Louisa Twamley

We all know the childhood pastime of gathering up a daisy and saying "S/he loves me, s/he loves me not," or gaily running up to a friend and placing a butter cup under their chin to see if they like butter. Our Victorian ancestors enjoyed these activities tremendously. Add to that the fact that flowers had a language all their own ascribed to them, it is not surprising that I came across other methods of "divination" by flowers in my research.

The first says to go to your garden and gather a nosegay for yourself. While you pick, think about your question, much as you would do in a Tarot reading. Return to the house with your flowers in hand and refer to the list of flower symbolism given in Chapter Four or to a magical field guide to plants. Pull out one flower at a time, look up its implied meanings, and write them down. When finished, you can review the "reading" and see what the flowers were telling you.

Another more complicated version of this was invented in 1847 by Thomas Miller. For this you would take your question to the garden and randomly pick a petal off a pansy (without looking—no cheating, now). When you examine your petal the following information may be divined:

- If the petal has four lines in it, it is a sign of hope.
- Five lines coming from a center branch is hope founded in fear.
- Thick lines bent to the right mean prosperity.
- Thick lines bent to the left mean trouble ahead.
- Seven streaks is consistent love.
- Eight streaks means fickleness in either you or those around you.
- Nine, a changing heart.
- Eleven, an early grave (note: this may also mean the death of an idea or habit).

It is said that in the spring, if you happen to find the first flower of the season on a Monday, it is good fortune for the season. If on a Tuesday, your greatest attempts will be successful. On Wednesday it denotes a marriage; Thursday, a warning of small profits; Friday, wealth; Saturday, misfortune; and Sunday is excellent luck for many weeks to come.

If, on the other hand, the first flower you discover is wild, see what type it is. If it is a daisy, buttercup or lily, watch for someone with the initials D, B, or L to become interested in you. If someone presents you with a yellow flower unexpectedly, watch for a gift to follow.

It was also believed that it was exceptionally good luck to wear the blossom associated with your birth month. The similarities in this system to the flower calendar spoken of in Chapter Three are impossible to overlook. January is snowdrop, a symbol of purity. February is the violet, for kindness and faith. March is the daffodil, an emblem of sincerity. April is the primrose, for the new love springing up in the world. May is the white lily, for strength; June the wild rose, for healing; and July is the carnation, for protection. Come August, white heather appears for good luck through the rest of the year. September is the Michaelmas daisy, for happiness; October is rosemary, for kind thoughts; November is chrysanthemum, for truth; and finally December ivy is worn for fidelity and faithfulness.

Flowers were not the only garden items used for divination. Another method, known as daphnomancy, uses fresh laurel leaves. Place them in your incense burner (or an open fire) while concentrating on a question. It is said that if the leaves crack loudly and burn brightly that the time is favorable. If they smoulder and die out, it is not. Throw a handful in your fireplace all at once and watch the flame. If the flames rise up together, this is also a positive sign. Three flame points means that things are coming together to a harmonious conclusion, one point is single-mindedness and two flame points mean you may need the aid of a friend to accomplish your goal. Bay leaves may also be used for this technique, and are easier to obtain.

Another way to use herbs for divination is by making a pendulum out of them. Take some yarn the length of your hand (plus a little extra to allow you to tie the herbs into the yarn with three knots). Select your herb according to what subject matter your question reflects. In this instance, your bay leaf could be used for a question regarding the *outcome* of a situation. Attach the herb securely to the yarn. Then place your elbow on a table with the end of the thread in your dominant hand. Continue to concentrate on the question. Circular movement is considered a yes, back and forth, no. If there is no movement it means that the fates are too tangled right now, and no certain answer can be given at this time.

One of the most popular fancies has been given to us by the four leaf clover. An old legend says that three sisters, Faith, Hope and Charity, came over the seas and wherever they walked, clover bloomed beneath their feet. During their travels another being, Love, joined them and in honor of this certain clovers added a fourth petal. In time, this legend inspired love-sick maidens to wear the leaf as a means of protecting or inspiring love. It is also regarded as a symbol of good luck.

GRAPHOLOGY

During the 19th century, handwriting analysis never became as popular as other parlour games. However, it captured the interest of Edgar Allen Poe enough for him to write a series of articles published in "Graham's Lady's and Gentleman's Magazine." These pieces discussed the writing of various noted authors by examining their signatures. Poe did not always critique his peers' handwriting with objectivity, but it is certain that his articles increased the interest in this system of divination.

Somehow graphology was more popular in Europe than in the United States. By 1906, a well known psychologist, Alfred Binet, published the results of his studies which seemed to substantiate the link between personality and handwriting. Binet felt this study was a science, and gave much credibility to the art. Binet's stance was critiqued by another man, Raphael Schermann (born 1879) who felt that contrary to these studies, graphology was a psychic phenomena. For his art, however, he took in hand some of an individual's writings, closed his eyes, then proceeded to give a description of the person, their past, and the predominant characteristics of personality. He even used these abilities in collaboration with the N.Y.C. police.

Should you desire to look at your own handwriting to see how accurate the interpretations are, here are a few things to look for. Please remember that this is only a brief overview of a very complex study, meant for your amusement:

Backwriting — Self consciousness.

Downward slope — Laziness.

Upward slope to excess — Carelessness.

Right sloping lines — Person of energy.

Level direction of written lines — Calm demeanor.

Letters in words upright — Inner strength.

Letters slant right — Tenderness.

Letters slant left — Poise and composure.

Signature slanted up — Ambition and success.

Small lettering — Curiosity.

Medium lettering — Outspoken attitudes.

Large lettering — Promptness.

Fine handwriting lines — Diplomacy.

Connecting lines which hook — Tenacity.

Connecting lines which dash — Persistence.

Large, well-formed capitals — Pride.

Printed capitals — Dignity.

Exaggerated capitals — Love of ceremony.

Capital separate from word — Easy going nature.

Capital connected to word — Practicality.

Rounded letters — Affectionate.

Flourishes (many) — Kindness.

Today many companies employ a full time graphologist to reveal things about prospective employees of which they, themselves may not even be aware. Handwriting is also sometimes used in considering promotions. Modern graphologists do not look at graphology as a way to foretell the future, but as a tool to help give clues to the internal characteristics of individuals not normally seen in a simple interview. It is not an exacting art, but like many things, is influenced by the individual. By combining the slant, formation and ornamentation of letters with how fast the person writes, and other external observations, the graphologist makes certain conclusions, which as yet must be considered a good hypothesis. Considering that hand writing analysis has existed since Aristotle, it may well be that we will have to be content with that much.

HAZELNUTS

I have yet do discover the reason why, but the Victorians had a love for hazelnuts when it came to divination. Their use may well have been derived from the pragmatic, creative mind-set of the era; anything that was available was used. No matter the origin, however, these three methods themselves are so full of Victorian charm that I wanted to share them with you.

To discover if a lover was faithful, the young person might place two hazelnuts side by side on the bars of the fire grate. If they burnt as one, true love was assured, but if one nut failed to burn, or the nuts popped apart, her lover was surely untrue.

To discover the name of the person they would marry, they would write the names of all the young men/women they knew, one name per hazelnut, and roast them by an open fire. The first nut to jump or pop was the name of the expected lover. This method of divination was also often applied to any question with multiple answers, the first nut always being the response to the query.

Lastly, a young person would place a handful of nuts in the hot embers of a fire and whisper the name of the one s/he loved. If the nut jumped, the affair would be successful.

MOLES

A good face is a letter of introduction.
—Joseph Addison

Divination by moles was known to the ancient Greeks, but did not become popular until the late 1700s. Even so, the theories of the Greeks acted as the foundation for all interpretations to follow in history. The basics begin with the head, it being the most visible part of the body. A mole on a man's forehead is a sign of happiness, and for a woman it predicts power. Close to the eyebrow of a man or woman, a mole predicts a good marriage. When on the bridge of the nose, it suggests extravagance; on the nose, a sign of travel; and on the lips a mole betrays gluttony. Other representations are as follows:

Round in shape — Good naturedness.
Angular shape — Good and bad characteristics.
Oblong shaped — Material wealth.
Light colored — Luck.
Black coloration — Difficulty before success.
Belly — Self indulgence.
Buttocks — Lack of ambition, poverty.
Chin — Great character and personality, many good qualities.
Finger — Exaggeration and lies.
Ear and Neck — A sign of good fortune.

Shoulders — Unhappiness, restless nature.

Chest — Poverty.

Hands — Fertility, especially in regards to bearing young.

Ankle — On a woman is a sign of courage.

Under right arm — Vigilance.

Back — Beware of hidden matters, get all the facts in deals.

Navel — Desire for children.

Wrist — Frugality and ingenuity.

To these (and even more detailed descriptions which existed), some people added whether the mole appeared on the left or right hand side of the body, the right being favorable in their interpretation. Later, further precision was given by ascribing signs of the zodiac to the positions of moles appearing on the face, the characteristics of which were used in the reading regarding the individual's personality and future.

The art of divining by moles often worked hand in hand with another divinatory system, metoposcopy, an occult science which studies the lines on the forehead. Even so, the Victorians seemed far more enamored of the moles, perhaps because it was an amusing pastime which could be done from "afar."

OMENS AND SIGNS

Omens were probably born from the earliest attempts to understand some of the strange occurrences in life. If one unusual incident was followed shortly by something else remarkable, and if such a combination happened again, a portent was established and handed down through generations.

The Victorians were rather superstitious by nature to begin with, and augury by omens or signs was known well to the farmer. Most omens dealt with things such as general luck, weather, health and in true Victorian manner, love.

If a bat were to fly in your home, or if an apple broke while you ate it, it was an omen of ill fortune. On the other hand, should you see a dove hovering near your home or cut an apple in two without hitting a seed, these things portend good luck and joy. Busy insects or a bat hitting a building predicted rain, while smoke rising straight up was a sign of a fair day ahead. In the romance department, a hopping toad across a bridal path means a happy marriage, cold hands indicate a warm heart, and a knife should never be given a sweetheart lest it cut the relationship.

These types of omens existed side by side with the belief that itching hands were itching for money, and burning ears meant someone was gossiping about you. There's our thanksgiving tradition of wishing before pulling the wishbone apart, wishing before blowing out the birthday candles, wishing on stars, and many other time-honored traditions that we follow with little thought as to their origins. More specific information on superstitions and ways of applying their symbolism to magic can be found in Chapter Thirteen.

OUIJA BOARDS

*Between the conception and the creation, between
the emotion and the response, falls the shadow.*
— T. S. Eliot

A version of our modern Ouija® boards can be traced as far back in written history as 371 A.D. to Emperor Valens. In order to find out who would succeed him, he used a device that consisted of a tripod of laurel wood with a metal plate and the Greek alphabet etched around the edge. Above it there was a linen thread and ring. Incantations to an appropriate god would be added to move the device into action.

Hundreds of versions of the Ouija® board "game" are still in existence, including ones as simple as placing pieces of paper with letters written on them on top of a table and using a glass to spell out the message. The Victorian board would commonly have been round, unlike the oblong one seen today. The board itself is meant to focus spiritual power to answer questions, as its name in French might imply, translating quite literally to "yes, yes." Another interesting difference between modern boards and those from earlier periods was the fact that many older boards employed a suspended object for the reading, instead of the physical contact with the pointer, as is now common.

The Victorian interest in the Ouija® board was a rather natural outgrowth of "table tipping," discussed later on in this chapter. For the most part, their use of this device was for amusement. Serious practitioners who had a board handed down through their family did exist, but more commonly a Ouija® board might appear at a noon day tea, alongside of a tea leaf reading.

The major controversy in use of Ouija® boards is whether the communications are from the spirit world or whether they are due to the psychic talent of the individual using the tool. There seems to be more sentiment towards the former in magical circles. Also, there is some question as to whether a Ouija® can be used safely in anyone's hands, especially those less knowledgeable or trained, because of the belief that the board acts like an open door for a spiritual entity. Within this school of thought, each board would carry one specific spirit with it, who would use it as a channel.

There is no doubt, even among Christian authorities, that the Ouija® board should be viewed as a device which sometimes yields magical information, because so many documented messages go beyond the normal range of human knowing ability. There was quite a bit of research being dedicated to this aspect, even at the turn of the century. In 1914, Sir William Barrett of the American Society for Psychical Research reported that after "reviewing the results as a whole, I am convinced of their supernormal character, and that we have here some intelligent, disincarnate agency."

Because of these observations, and due to the uncertain nature of the spirits you may encounter, I do not recommend Ouija® boards as a party game, let alone a magical tool for the neophyte. Even in the hands of an experienced practitioner, certain simple rules should be followed to help ensure positive results. Take the time to set up protection in your home, cleanse and bless the board before use, keep it stored as carefully as you would any magical tool, NEVER use a board which has been handed down through inheritance unless you are a member of that family, and finally, if you ever get the indication that you are dealing with a malevolent entity, stop immediately and seriously consider destroying the board. Unless you have the ability to send that spirit away, the board will be of no constructive use, and could even prove detrimental to a novice if explored without proper caution.

PALMISTRY

Palmistry over tea was a very familiar sight during the Victorian era. In 1889, the English Chirological Society was founded to bring the study of the hand to a scientific level, to promote palmistry, and to safeguard the public against fraudulent mediums.

With this group's formation, basic information on this art became common knowledge, and it was more frequently applied. Ladies and gentlemen alike might be speaking of a young person's future, encouraging a relationship, and then asking, "Let's see what your hand says about it!" In these instances the lines on the hand were examined for certain standard interpretations. There were also nonverbal clues of hair style, clothing, nervous habits, and skin texture that an adept palmist could use. These additional indicators were not be taken as impressions themselves, but used in conjunction with other confirming signs to aid the reader.

Here are some common interpretations of the hand: Smooth skin denoted a refined nature, elasticity, virility, flexibility, energy, and adaptation. Next, the reader examines the shape of hand and the fingers. Broad hands tend to be people of strength rather than culture. Pointed finger tips seem to occur on artists, tapering fingers indicate extremes, and round/flat fingers are the outdoors types. Other things to look for when doing palmistry include:

Knotted or swollen hands — Strong mind for philosophy.
Smooth fingers and hands — Inspiration, intuition, artistic person.
Long center bone in the thumb — Great reasoning power.
Short top bone in thumb — Little will power.
Square hands — Practicality.
Long tapering fingers — Artistic.
Long hands and fingers — Gentle, idealistic.
Life line high on the hand — Ambition.
Life line circling into palm — Generosity.
Broken head line — Ill health.
Head and heart line join — Impulsiveness.
Heart line crossing palm entirely — Extreme sentimentality.
Short heart line — Short lived relationships.
Full fate line — Success, charisma.
Fate line stopped at head line — Obstacles to overcome.

In answer to the question of which hand should be read, the best response is both. This way a more balanced indication of "fate" can be formed. Many modern palmists believe their abilities have less to do with the lines in the hand and more to do with a minor telepathic link established with the querier during a reading, which is enhanced by contact with the hands, thus a calm mind and centered energies are important to the success of your attempts.

Reading Your Hand

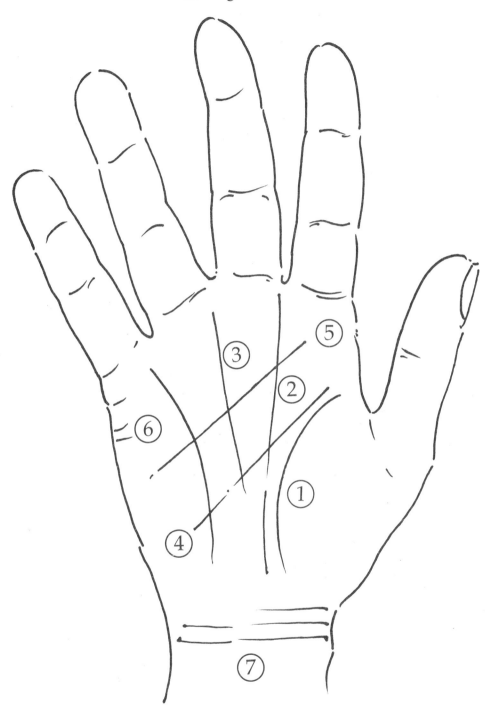

1. Life line
2. Fate line
3. Health line
4. Head line
5. Heart line
6. Marriage lines
7. Bracelets

PHRENOLOGY

She is going to offer her hand and brow to the diviner's scrutiny.

—Juvenal

In 1832, a young student of the Amherst College became enthralled with the new "science" of Phrenology. His name was Orson Fowler. After graduating, he and his brother Lorenzo took their studies to any place where people could gather to explain the principles and render examinations. It seems their zeal and talent for sales would quickly make phrenology a contagious American novelty. By 1936 the Fowlers opened a New York office where they also operated a museum and monthly "American Phrenological Journal." While this magazine centered mostly on phrenology, it also focused on psychology, science, home education and agriculture. In other words, with the written word, it represented the Victorian mind very well, to the point where it had a circulation of 50,000!

The Fowlers' business flourished, and their lectures gave birth to many books and charts on the subject. By 1842, they had begun to educate hopeful phrenologists at their institute. They used the phrenologist's chart (developed partially by the Fowlers) to teach prospective phrenologists. It was also sold to traveling practitioners to help with their readings. It identified over forty "organs of the brain" and helped the practitioner to identify areas of the human cranium structure which were said to be indicative of certain mental functions. More involved charts even included information on nutrition and bathing. The illustration "A Phrenololgy Chart" is highly simplified to give you an idea of where the phrenologist begins.

True to the American vision and amazing progress of the times, the Fowler family seemed to typify, in miniature, what was happening throughout Victorian society. Lorenzo's wife, Lydia, was the second woman in the nation to become an accredited physician, while the rest of the family became avid speakers on a variety of subjects—from vegetarianism, women's rights, and slavery to the need for educational reform. There was no part of Victorian life which phrenology would not touch on. They felt it was a science that met face to face with human reality to the point where Lorenzo even advocated sex education; something which was not met with positive reviews.

It would have been difficult to find a town or city in America that was unaffected by their studies and teachings. Certain companies even required phrenological examinations as a preliminary to employment. Worried in-laws-to-be would send in a chart on the prospective young person for analysis.

Phrenology reflected the desire within all of us to simplify the way we relate to the rest of the world through a unified system, and perhaps in the process find hints about the future. While today phrenology is regarded with some amusement as an interesting pastime, its place in Victorian history shows how the idea developed of the body somehow reflecting clues to the inner person. Modern body language studies are somewhat different in scope, yet strong similarities in ideology are impossible to overlook. It may well be that in one hundred years our body language "science" will be likewise regarded by our children as a parlour game.

A Phrenology Chart

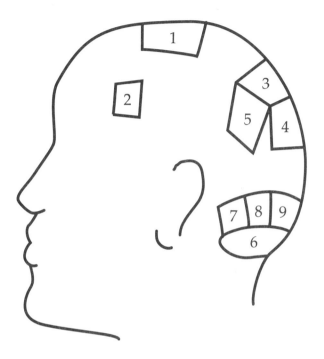

1. If this area is well developed, it indicates generosity, kindness, and benevolence. If over-developed, it warns that these traits might be so exorbitant as to cause the person to overlook his or her own well-being.

2. Happiness and good wit are shown here. This is a pleasant individual who will often smile on adversity. If the area is too developed, this individual will never be taken seriously, is the "class clown," and pokes fun at everything. If underdeveloped, it is a person who does not have a sense of humor, and rarely smiles.

3. Strength of mind, good judgements. If over-developed, it is a sign of stubbornness. If underdeveloped, the area indicates one who is wishy-washy on every decision and is easily swayed by peer pressure.

4. Self esteem, dignity, and pride. If over-developed, it portends egotism to the extreme, and probably selfishness. Underdeveloped, it divulges a person with poor self-image and uncertainty.

5. Duty and accountability. To the excess, duty always comes first. Under-developed, it may indicate a person who is unreliable and unwilling to take responsibility for his or her mistakes.

6. Love which is balanced and healthy. Over-developed indicates a terminal romantic who sees hearts and flowers everywhere. Under developed, it may warn of a person who finds giving or receiving love difficult, someone with a more defensive nature.

7. Courage. To its furthest ends, it is courage without thought of self or others. Where this area is lacking, it is a fearful nature, undesirous of adventure or anything which threatens security.

8. Desire for marriage. In the extreme, this becomes a quest for a mate, where all else in life takes a back seat, and jealousy may occur. Under developed, it indicates a person who is content to be alone or who is flirtatious.

9. Love of children. An over-development in this area may indicate a person with a whole brood of spoiled children, while the under developed may remain childless due to lack of patience.

SCRYING

In the late 1800s, a renowned English psychic investigator, Mr. Frederic Myers, estimated that one in twenty people had scrying abilities. His declaration, along with the comment by Lord Lytton (author of the *Last Days of Pompeii*) that there was a crystal ball in his familial home, inspired many amateurs. A number of books and articles were published soon thereafter to describe some rather lengthy and "proper" techniques for those who wanted to try crystal gazing.

In 1896, a small paper called "Crystal Gazing and Clairvoyance" was put out by John Melville. This treatise included not only instructions, but descriptions of tools which were typically Victorian in their flamboyance. An ivory or ebony stand, inlaid with gilded magical words, was where the ball should rest while the scryer incanted a long Christian prayer. Mr. Melville gave strict admonitions that no one should have ill intentions because, "when he or she uses the crystal it will react upon the seer sooner or later with terrible effect."

For the scryer of today, the tools are usually less fanciful, and the techniques not so formal. Generally speaking, the crystal should be round or oval, and as close to clear as possible while still being made of natural stones. Most people recommend keeping the ball in the same place when stored. Before use, it should be purified by washing in warm spring water and dried with a clean, natural fiber cloth.

A candle-lit room, or one with dim lighting seems to work best as a setting for scrying. A dark velvet cloth, or other heavy material, should be put underneath the crystal (this cuts down on reflections). Settle your mind with a few deep cleansing breaths, and look towards the crystal while not actually staring at it. Allow your mind to be completely set on the question at hand. Within about 10 minutes, veils or clouds begin to appear within the sphere, sometimes forming pictures, sometimes becoming an entire three dimensional vision for the scryer.

Miss Angus, a turn-of-the-century psychic, explained that at these moments it almost seems as if the ball itself disappears. The solid pictures which appear are sometimes difficult to interpret, because they tend to be personal in nature, often having meaning only to the querier. On the other hand, according to Melville, the colors of these clouds may have certain meaning. These color representations are still accepted among many scryers. White traditionally was a positive response and portended good things, while black was just the opposite. Bright colors tended to mean bothersome surprises were on their way, while quieter tones of green and blue were interpreted as joy and good fortune.

It is important to note that scrying was not always done with a crystal. Any smooth surface, such as a bowl of water or a mirror, would do. Wax drippings, blobs of ink and/or the fires of a hearth were also sometimes used. The latter was an important part of the Victorian home; it was where people would spend many hours socializing. When a group of them wanted to know the answer to a question, they would wait until the fires burned low, then toss a little salt on the wood. Then, sitting quietly, they would watch for images to form in the ember's glow. If steps were seen, the number of them usually indicated the amount of time before a good event occurred. If pillars appeared, it meant a love affair. Trees symbolized business success; an unfamiliar face meant a new friend; flowers meant disappointment; and a hand reaching towards them was a cry for help from someone known to them.

This method of scrying is quite functional, and indeed many modern magicians still turn to flames for their visions. More information on techniques for pyromancy can be found in Chapter Two.

TABLE TIPPING

Table tipping was, for much of the Victorian era, an evening diversion wherever there was a gathering of people. As portrayed in the "Illustrated Magazine of Art," 1854, the world became very interested in this "newly developed force." The picture shown implied that even several children's weight upon a table would not keep it from moving if the divination system was properly done.

To accomplish this unique occurrence, the people would gather in what was called a "spirit circle" around a circular, lightweight table and rest the tips of their fingers upon it. Usually, the hand was spread out, with the pinky of each person touching the adjoining person's hand, so that an unbroken circle was formed. The group would also agree in advance which directions meant "yes" in answer to their queries, and which meant "no." Next, silence would fill the room, each person making a concerted effort not to influence the table.

If the process was done correctly, the table would begin to move in such a manner as to cause the people to have to follow it. Sometimes, instead of a positive or negative answer, the group would try to get the spirit helper to spell out a message. Once the table began to move, they would start reciting letters of the alphabet, allowing slight pauses between each letter to see if the table stilled. If the movement stopped, that was the first letter of the message. This continued until some type of understandable missive was received.

Since that time, many investigations have been done, showing that often the tables were moved by unconscious muscular pressure. In this scenario, since everyone in the room is concentrating on the same thing, usually the person who has the strongest will unwittingly determines the direction. Even so, it might be fun to try some night when you have a group of magical friends over. As with all things, I urge caution in taking proper protective measures before inviting "spirits" to respond. If you get any interesting results, I would love to hear about them!

TEA LEAF READING

Like plants, most men have hidden properties that chance alone reveals.
— Maxims La Rochefoucauld

Since tea-time and the art of preparing a proper tea were fashionable (see also Chapter Three) it is not startling to discover people turning to the bottoms of their own cups to see the future. As a matter of fact, from what I can ascertain, this was probably the most widely used form of divination, other than the simple augury known to the Victorians.

How much was discerned during a tea reading certainly depended on the abilities of the reader, since the pictures formed by the leaves were somewhat subjective. To do a reading of this nature, tea would be prepared without an infuser, allowing the leaves to settle in the cup. The cup was unornamented, so as to not distract from the reading. While drinking the beverage, the individual should think on their question. Leaving just enough tea to cover the leaves, the questioner takes the cup in their left hand, swirling it three times. Then the questioner turns the cup upside down on a saucer, allowing the water and leaves to come out. This drains the cup, then it is ready for interpretation.

The cup itself figures into the interpretation, the handle representing the querier and home. Symbols farthest from the handle are also those most distant from the individual. Those near the rim are closest to the future, while the leaves forming pictures at the bottom of the cup are probably visions of things years away. As with the Tarot, more than one symbol can complicate the matter of the reading because they affect each other.

Most commonly items such as stars, leaves, anchors, trees, floral bouquets, crowns, triangles, and bridges are markers of good fortune, while crosses, snakes, swords, ravens, and churches portend bad luck. If a negative sign is combined with a positive, it usually means some type of delay or difficulty before success. The following is a list of other symbols, which are remarkably like other icons of the Victorian era in their interpretation:

Acorn — Good health.

Anchor — Voyage.

Balloon — Troubles lifting.

Basket — Congratulations due.

Bells — Good news.

Book — Awareness, learning.

Bridge — An offer.

Cat — Treachery.

Chain — Success with effort.

Chair — Unexpected guest.

Clouds — Doubt.

Cow — Prosperity.

Cross — Suffering.

Dice — Loss of money.

Dog — Faithful friends.

Dots — Wealth.

Dustpan — Strange news.

Egg — Fertility, increase.

Fish — News from abroad.

Flowers — Love, honor, esteem.

Fly — Petty annoyances.

Garden — Prosperity.

Glove — Luck and honor.

Goat — Misfortune.

Hammer — Triumph over adversity.

Heart — Love.

Hen — A new child.

Horse — A lover.

Key — Unveiling of mystery.

Lace — Fragile matters.

Ladder — Advancement.
Letters — Initials of people.
Locket — Loyalty and friendship.
Mouse — Financial insecurity.
Pendulum — Indecision.
Question mark — Uncertainty.
Ring — Marriage, partnership.
Snake — Temptation.
Thistle — High ambitions.
Umbrella — Annoyances.
Weathercock — Unreliable.

Ladder — Movement.
Lock of Hair — Devotion.
Mirror — False facades.
Owl — Scandal.
Penny — Attention to detail.
Rat — Danger.
Scissors — A fight.
Spider — Luck.
Tree — Success, fruitfulness.
Walking stick — Need support.
Well — Dig for knowledge.

If you want to try and do tea leaf readings yourself, look at the remnant leaves as you might an open sky with clouds to see the pictures. Do not focus on any one point, but allow your mind to wander until a strong impression comes. Begin at that impression and move outward. Like any visionary tool, you will get better with practice.

There is a great deal of poetry and fine sentiment in a chest of tea.
—Ralph Waldo Emerson

One lesson, Nature, let me learn of thee
One lesson which in every wind is blown,
One lesson of two duties kept at one
Though the loud world proclaim their enmity—
Of toil unsever'd from tranquility;
Of labor, that in lasting fruits outgrows
Far noisier schemes, accomplish'd in repose,
Too great for haste, too high for rivalry.
— Matthew Arnold

CHAPTER NINE

The Solo: Personal Care for the Body and Spirit

To love oneself is the beginning of a life long romance.
—Oscar Wilde

From table side divination and conversation to changes in law and opinions, Victorian ideas were transforming as quickly as Victorian technology. The new emphasis on individual expression and ever growing self-sufficient attitudes manifested itself in new ways of thinking about the human body.

With medicalization, a growing understanding of how diseases were transmitted extended itself to more of the public, and cleanliness became more important. The bathtub and shower were first introduced during these years. Even so, factors of sex, age, and profession tended to govern the frequency of washing. These new devices did not completely ease the folk tales about bathing being injurious to health and women's fertility cycles, let alone the fact that frequent washing was thought to damage linen. Needless to say, it took many years before the bathtub was commonplace among the general populace, although the wealthy grew quickly fond of them.

When cleansing rituals became acceptable, things such as elder flower water rinses, chamomile tincture to open pores, rain water and almond oil to refresh the hands after gardening, and astringents of cider vinegar and roses became much more prominent in the Victorian home. Period cookbooks began to include simples, cold cream, ink, smelling salts, and perfumes so that each homemaker could continue to meet her personal and family needs with prudence.

With the rise of personal ambition, a new modesty was introduced, including layers of lingerie for the impatient male hand to deal with. A new appreciation of curve and line appeared in fashion. Despite this, certain traditional Victorian mind-sets continued. An appreciation for more leisurely pursuits, balanced by self discipline, rounded out the care of the individual. In this way they, like us, were doing their best to incorporate the wisdom of their upbringing with the new world being presented to them. Amidst this confusion, it is not surprising that families began attaching more importance to religion in order to provide a little stability in changing times.

ATTENDING MIND AND SPIRIT

*Divine, am I, inside and out and I make holy
whatever I touch or am touched from.*
— Walt Whitman

There was a deep belief in Victorian days that religion improved the dignity of humankind and provided for the betterment of the race itself. The writers of the day seemed to reflect a belief that religion should conform to rational ideals and the advancement of science. Henry David Thoreau (author of *On Walden Pond*) was one of the greatest examples of this. He, along with Ghandi, was one of the first people to support the idea of nonviolent civil disobedience as a means of bringing attention to a cause. Yet he, himself, choose to move to the country and live simply with the land, applying all the knowledge he had available to him, then communicating these lessons in written word.

In considering Victorian views for modern application, we have to look at the individual on all levels. From creating an atmosphere around yourself through decorations, sounds, light, and action—to working within your spirit via meditation, each corner of your reality should be an attempt to reflect the beauty of the God/dess.

Education

How frugal is the chariot that bears the human soul.
— Emily Dickinson

As the desire for individual expression grew, the need for solid educational systems also grew. People wanted to learn, to make a niche for themselves in this world, enrich their lives, and by so doing, enrich the lives of their children to come. As a reflection of this, a succession of books was published called "The Mental Efficiency Series." These books included titles such as *Poise and How to Attain it* (1916), *Speech and How to Use it Effectively*, *Practicality: How to Acquire it*, and *Opportunities: How to Make the Most of Them*. Other subjects in the series included timidity, character, common sense, influence and personality. These treatises not only included theory, but exercises to help the reader bring each virtue into full blossom for themselves.

At first, such books are amusing to our 20th century eyes, but on closer inspection there is much wisdom to be found in the pages. The authors present perseverance and practice as being the most faithful of aids, emphasize the need for self confidence, and illustrate how powerful the mind and will can be for powerful and positive living on a non-magical level.

When we are discussing the subject of spiritual training, many comparisons can readily be made between the Victorian era and our time. Here are just a couple of the ideas found in the books of that time that are similar to ideas found in best-sellers today: Life itself becomes the teacher, our bodies the classroom, and nature provides some of the best books. There is no such thing as being too informed about your faith. An important differentiation, though, is separating what you know by fact, and what you believe. The head and the heart often fight over this point, but we need to be aware of it nonetheless.

This is also true when we are reading books or listening to a metaphysical teacher. Truth is a very subjective thing, tainted by hundreds of factors, not the least of which is personal perceptions. The Victorians became aware that their lives and emotions were not ruled by externals, but that they had some control over what was once considered the whims of fate. Our spiritual education is a major part of what allows us to determine what will be truth for our lives. So, as you study and listen, do so with a discerning ear, wise eyes, an open mind, and carry a healthy portion of skepticism in your back pocket.

We do not have to swallow all the garbage the world tries to feed us under the guise of it being good for us. There are just as many "money changers" looking to make a quick buck on the New Age bandwagon as anywhere else. Despite the many wonderful teachers this century has given, the flimflam artists are the people of whom we must be careful. If our education is going to be a positive one, we need to develop the sensitivity to know the true psychics, healers, and teachers from those who are using gifts for the wrong reasons.

Always remember that if what you read or hear is truth, it will return to you through another source. It will ring in your heart like a lovely song that you know you can sing. Truth challenges us to be and do our best, to take responsibility, and to accentuate the positive. These are generally good guidelines to use during your study. Even for the experienced practitioner, questions arise which require the council of others who are also experienced. Don't forget the valuable resource you have in your magical community.

Meditation/Visualization

> *Life is real, life is earnest, and the grave is not its goal.*
> *'Dust thou art, to dust returnest,' was not spoken of the soul.*
> — Henry Wadsworth Longfellow

Meditation techniques come to us from many countries and many time periods. Some call it prayer, others call it communing, but whatever the words, taking time to bring our spirits back into center and focus our minds is perhaps one of the most important disciplines we can bring to our lives, let alone our magical training.

A dictionary from the 1920s defined meditation as exercising the mind in contemplation, or to plan mentally. From this definition, we can assume that each of us meditates in some form, even unknowingly. The Victorian focus on the mystical as a means to enrich the mind teaches that the key to unlocking psychic gifts and deeper meditative states already exists in our mental code. All that remains are those two nagging words, patience and practice.

Some traditions do not seek to focus on anything in particular, but I think most people find it more productive to center in on one issue or thought, and to combine that with visualization for best results. Techniques vary, but almost all begin with a slowed, rhythmic method of breathing, combined with a focus on an object (such as a candle).

A common problem which occurs in meditation, especially for beginners, is that of distraction. Either you will find your foot is falling asleep, your nose itches, the phone rings, a car will honk its horn and these things will divert you from your goal. This is common because you are trying to train your mind, which is usually busy doing many things at once, to concentrate on one defined item for specific results. Try not to get frustrated. Instead, get past that point. It will ease with practice, and your meditative states will deepen.

Other important points to remember in meditation are to take your time. Don't try to quickly get up and run around afterwards. You're likely to get a headache and undo all the good your restful time accomplished. You may want to take notes on any unusual feelings or visions you had in a journal, together with your impressions of how productive each exercise was for you. Finally, set aside a specific time and place each day for meditation and stick to it. Like any good habit, nothing can be gained or lost if you never try.

I have listed several guided meditation/visualization techniques which I have found very useful for myself alone and in a group setting. If you are doing them alone, either have a friend talk you through them, or tape them (with music) for yourself. In a group setting, one person can read the material and guide the whole group.

Crystal Body Meditation

Inner world, of caverns and candles, I come to you.
Between yesterday and forever, I float.
Between the waves of dawn and darkness, I float.
Here, with the light of morning dancing to the rhythm of my heart
And the winds of day singing with each breath,
I am touched by the waters of a universe,
Until nothing exists but the soul in flight,
And the simple peace of knowing I am.

— Marian Loresinger

This is an excellent meditation for rejuvenation, relaxation and especially healing work. Start by lying down in a comfortable position. As you close your eyes, visualize your body exactly as it is right now, only it is made out of crystal. Begin breathing in a slow, all-connected manner, one which is easy and relaxing. Feel yourself calming down. There is no need to hurry or rush. Listen to the sound of your breath moving through you like a wind of inner cleansing. Hear your heart beating steadily, like a far off drum. This is all that exists right now. You as body; you as mind; you as spirit.

Once your mind is soothed, begin to observe the crystal of your body in your mind's eye. Notice especially any spots which seem to have a strange texture or color. These indicate tensions, injury, imbalance or sickness of some kind. Now, from above you picture a healing light flowing down over you like a silent river. Begin to breath in the light as if it were air itself. See it filling each muscle, bone, and cell, until it is exhaled as a muddy brown color, returning it to the Mother. This is an indication that the light-energy is collecting your tensions and cleaning them out, and allowing for the body's natural healing process to work.

Continue this process until the color and quality of the light which you exhale is the same as that inhaled, until your entire being has become the clearest crystal from which light can shine. Don't worry if you fall asleep during this, as it is a natural side effect of the meditation. If you are still awake at the end, move from your pelvis to get up, taking care not to change your center of gravity so that you can bring this fresh wholeness of being with you into the conscious state. Take notes on your experience. This meditation can be repeated whenever you like.

Tree of Life Meditation

For the purpose of this meditation, I suggest choosing to visualize a tree which thrives in a four-season climate. You may wish to put on some soothing music, or go outside away from the phone and other disturbing influences. This particular meditation is good for grounding, connection with the land, and enables us to have a broader understanding of cycles within ourselves and Earth. Since this is rather long, if you have trouble remembering the meditation, try taping it or having a friend tape it so that you can just concentrate on the words.

To begin, sit erect. As your spine straightens, feel the energy rising from the floor into you. Count backwards slowly from five, breathing in through your nose and out through your mouth fully, in an all-connected manner. Close your eyes, and as you do begin to see yourself as a great tree. Your stomach becomes part of the trunk, your feet are roots, and your head and arms form branches. What kind of tree are you? What colors fill your leaves and bark? Take the crayons of your imagination and create your tree and surroundings.

It is fall, and your boughs are full of color. You share this color with the ground beneath you. Right now, your sap is slower, you feel a restfulness, an almost-sleep falling over your branches like a warm cloak. Allow yourself to put aside the busy day, the rushing, and slow-down, like that sap. Allow the fall breezes to move freely through your leaves, taking all tensions, sickness, anger, and frustration with them. Continue to visualize this breeze until you feel peaceful, rested and relaxed.

Now the winds grow colder. You find you are all but still. The winter snows move in with a fury, bringing to the entire Earth a much needed sleep. This is not death, there is no fear, but instead a repose before transformation. Allow this cold to freeze any bad habits or negative feelings and drop them in the snow so that you can change and grow.

When the spring Sun comes you start to awaken to a new sense of being. The time for sleep is past and your roots are bringing you new life and vitality. Take a moment to feel how secure your bark is, how strong the wood of your spine is. Smell the wonderful scent of leaves and of flowers just blooming.

Once you can see yourself clearly, look downward where your feet once were. See how your roots stretch and reach for water, moving ever deeper into the vibrant moisture of Mother Earth. Sense the fresh, clean water filling your roots . . . moving through your veins in waves that refresh and heal with each breath. Taste how crisp and thirst-quenching it is, and let your roots drink their fill.

Move deeper still, allowing your roots to grow, search, and stretch till they find the womb of the Earth itself. Here are the creative fires of your birth. These fires do not burn, but cleanse and heal, purify and revitalize. Your roots wrap firmly around the center of the Earth . . . feel how connected you are at this moment, how grounded and centered. The fire will begin to move through your roots, warming the water they have absorbed, until your whole body is alive and tingling with warm energy. The fire continues to move upwards into your branches and leaves, until these too are warm and relaxed. As the light of the fire and water reach the outer leaves, they are freed—exploding to create the stars above your head. The sky above you glitters with them, like a flower in bloom. Enjoy this fullness and energy . . . let it meet whatever needs you may have.

Now stand back and look at the beautiful, strong tree of self. With each breath you become more alive. The crown of your head now blossoms with stars, your branches sweep upward with rich leaves and then bend back down to Earth. As you move from spring into summer, feel how you also move with the winds, grow towards the sun and how you are wholly connected with the land in a circle of power that dances through your veins as sap might. Enjoy this connectedness, the fullness of life that summer brings. Gain what energy you need to fill your empty cup. Allow your tensions, problems, and struggles to flow away until nothing remains but the peace of knowing self as a part of the Mother and the universe.

When you are ready, count forwards one to ten, slowly bringing yourself back to normal breathing and awareness. Do not move too quickly. Take your time. Get up and write down your impressions in a magical diary and see how they change as the tree of self grows into light!

Energy Sensitivity and Charging an Object

This is an excellent way to help attune yourself to the energy of objects, as well as attuning to your own personal magic. It will help you to charge various objects as well. Make sure you have a crystal or item that you're fond of before you begin.

Again, make yourself as comfortable and as free of distraction as possible. Relax your body, working out all the tensions until you are at ease where you sit. Remember that each meditation is like a voyage. Begin moving outward on your voyage with a backward count of five, until you reach the center of your being, the place of thoughtful contemplation and of energy. This is your personal magic center.

Focus your attention on the crystal you are holding. Feel how it has texture, temperature, and a very specific vibration. Allow yourself to sense all aspects of it, and begin to understand its function for your life. Is it for healing? Centering? Balance? What colors does it radiate as you activate its energy? Are they pure and bright? If not, take the time now to cleanse the crystal. Fill it with a pure light until it has no more blemishes to mar its beauty.

Once you have finished cleansing the crystal, stop to sense its energy again. Can you feel the change in the object? Is it warmer, richer somehow than before? Remember that crystals can act as a focus for your magical energy and this one is now ready to be used because you have prepared it.

Deep within you is a flame of power, an energy source from which you draw. The flame is the essence of your magic and the core of your being. Allow this flame to fill your body until you tingle with power. This is the energy of the universe itself, and it is part of you! You are the center, the control, you now open the door to gifts that have been hidden within. Let those energies escape their seclusion. As this energy wells up within you, you may feel rather odd, as if static electricity were surrounding you. Try not to be afraid, but breathe through this part until you become accustomed to the magic you are creating.

Pour this energy into the crystal. Keep in mind the specific purpose that you felt it was meant to have. Visualize light of an appropriate color to that purpose filling every corner of the stone, shining ever brighter until it can hold no more. Then, bring the excess energy you released back into the well of self to fortify your foundations. Feel whole, peaceful, balanced. Finally, prepare your mind to return to its normal level of awareness. Breathe normally. Stretch. Put your crystal somewhere safe and take it out as needed.

Meditation for the Senses

For this meditation you will need one person who is especially sensitive to group ene
act as a guide. They begin by ringing a bell or sounding a gong to signal the moment for
centering and focus. After this, one of the sentences listed here is spoken and meditated
upon by the group for several minutes. Once the guide feels everyone has reached a state of
understanding of the first sentence, they then repeat this procedure with the next thought.
You may add or subtract from this list as inspiration dictates. The idea here is to heighten
spiritual awareness through the normal sensual range.

- See forever in your closed eyes.
- See the light of day, and the dark of night within you.
- See the burning of your soul with the fires of the universe.
- See yourself with the eyes of a child.
- See the breath which fills your body.
- Listen to the silence of your breathing.
- Listen to the blood rushing with life through your body.
- Listen to the sounds of the living world around you.
- Feel the rhythm of your heartbeat.
- Feel the quiet air about you as it touches the skin.
- Feel the movement of a living earth beneath your feet.
- Taste the worth of your words.
- Taste the sea in the air.
- Taste the fruits of your labor.
- Smell the strength of earth in your body.
- Smell the balance of elements in the air around you.
- Smell the colors of the rainbow.

The Sand Man

This meditation is designed specifically for those who have difficulty getting to sleep or
staying asleep at night. If you find you are tossing and turning, begin by laying in the most
comfortable position you can. In your mind's eye, see yourself exactly as you are now, only
your body is filled like a balloon with sand, and where your two big toes should be, there
are two large corks.

In your visualization, move down and pull the out the corks, watching as the sand
slowly leaks out of your toes. As the sand leaves each part of your body, feel your tensions,
and all the heaviness you have been carrying flowing out with it. Allow your muscles and
every bone to relax until you are almost weightless on the bed. Continue in this manner
until your entire body is empty of sand and the tension which often afflicts it. Most people
fall asleep long before this point.

REST, REPOSE AND RAILLERY

I celebrate myself, and sing myself.
— Walt Whitman

People underestimate the need for what is commonly called "down time" today. Our bodies and minds need proper rest, times when there are no pressures, and a good laugh on a regular basis in order for our spirits to be healthy. There are many ways to take a little extra time for yourself, but one method which you can work into your daily routine is especially useful. Every night when you come home, try removing your troubles along with your clothes. Let your troubles fall to the floor with each item you take off. Don't look where they land, and don't pick them up immediately. Instead, get into something comfortable and put your feet up for a few minutes. You can straighten up later.

By doing this regularly you are helping re-train the ever-busy self to leave the day's rushing behind. This is even more important for those who are workaholics and over-achievers like me. After about two weeks of this you should notice that you are less short-tempered at home, and able to cope with things that might otherwise annoy you. Your relationships with your family will also improve because there will be more of you to share, instead of giving them your tensions.

Ritual of Self Blessing

This is another excellent habit to get into at least once a year. While we often share the special energy of a blessing with other people or objects, sometimes we forget about the Temple of Self. I like to perform this on my birthday as a way of giving thanks for the good things in my life, and ask Divine guidance for the year ahead. Begin by preparing your magical space, as usual.

Invocation

> *I see the mystic morning*
> *Rising out of the heart of the Mother.*
> *I see the light of learning*
> *Touching the minds and the hearts of my brothers.*
>
> *I see the magic moments,*
> *Reaching out from a soul full of sharing.*
> *I see the waves of warmth sent*
> *Washing fresh with the waters of healing.*
>
> *I see the Lady laughing,*
> *High above with the moon on an autumn night,*
> *While in my circle dancing*
> *To the songs of all ages, by fire's light.*

I see all people gathered
Hand-in-hand round the altar and singing.
I see earth grow and blossom
with new life from the music they're bringing.

This new age can be now and forever;
Let it teach me a new way of reason.
This new day can break through my darkness,
Let it bring, now, a new harvest season.

Activities

Cast a circle and approach your altar with anise oil. As you speak the following words, anoint a point on the body which corresponds to that verse. Add or delete things as are appropriate to your situation. For example, if you have had trouble recently with understanding another person's views, ask that your mind be blessed for perspective.

"Bless my mind that I might think clearly.
Bless my ears that I might always hear truth and wisdom;
Bless my lips that I might speak with kindness;
Bless my arms that they may give and receive love;
Bless my hands for healing;
Bless my legs that they may stand strong for my faith;
Bless my body that it might be healthy;
Bless my spirit and give it solid foundations;
Bless my thoughts that they might reflect the light;
Bless my perception so I may see without judgement."

Tools and Ritual Components

Ritual Soap — Apple for wisdom and internal change.

Anointing Oil — Anise for fulfillment and continued joy.

Ritual Cup — Lemon verbena tea to protect and purify.

Altar Decorations — Ferns, which symbolize your future potential, and flax to bring blessings and health.

Cakes — Your favorite birthday cake!

Note: After you have finished your ritual, you may not want to close the sacred space immediately. Curl up with a favorite book, write in your diary, and listen to some inspirational music. From a strictly spiritual perspective, the way you pass your day of birth can be powerful and transformational if you don't rush it. Allow the energy of the moment to fill and refresh you. It is your birthday, after all, and you deserve a little pampering.

The outward shows of sky and earth,
Of hill and valley, he has viewed;
And impulses of deeper birth
Have come to him in solitude.
— William Wordsworth

Ritual of Self Dedication

In the past, initiation was most often done in a coven setting. A person wishing to join a group would study with them for a specific length of time, commonly a year and a day, then be welcomed among them in whatever fashion was appropriate to the coven.

Now there is a growing number of people who choose, for whatever reasons, to practice as solitaries. I am sure the private practitioner existed in our history, perhaps best evidenced by the wise person in the woods, or a hermit who was sought for council. The difference today is that most solitaries do not retreat, and may indeed live next door to you!

In the instance when an individual has studied alone, and is desirous of initiation, the ritual of self-dedication becomes the means to declare their chosen path to the universe in the privacy of their own home. In many ways, this ritual is one of accepting all the responsibility that goes with magical power, so it should not be done in haste. Be sure your heart and mind are prepared, and that you really understand the step you are taking. Initiation marks the end of a mundane existence and the beginning of a new level of awareness, one in which we accept ourselves and our gifts, and pledge to do all we can with them for the betterment of Earth and humankind. This does not mean casting aside our "normal lives," but working within the reality we have been given with new understanding and intuition.

Initiation is a recognition of a magical path that has long been deep within a person, only waiting for expression and a name. It is a moment when time and space are suspended, and the Divinity within can ignite to find expression outwardly. Before this ritual, be sure to spend some time considering the spiritual step you are about to take, then prepare your sacred space.

This invocation is a celebration of your newly declared Path. It may be sung, chanted or spoken while candles are lit at the altar points indicated. The candles symbolize the light awakening within you!

Invocation

(Altar candle)
Oh healing waves and love and light,
Awake in chambers of my soul;
Bring from its edge a vision bright
Of seas where time began to flow.

(East candle)
Oh serving hands and breath of night,
Be blessed by powers of the Air
Bring from the winds my inner sight
Of gifts of Earth and Sky I bear.

(West candle)
Oh cleansing tears and pen and rhyme,
Be blessed by waters of the land,
Bring from the seas of spiral time
Words to rouse my sleeping sands.

(North candle)
Oh vibrant joy and life grown long
Be blessed by soils of the Earth
Bring from the ground the Mother's song
To sing her child's way to birth.

(South candle)
Oh sacred space and fire's glare
Be blessed by powers of the flame.
Bring from the hearth the will to dare
Be born anew, the old man tamed.

(Center candle)
By Earth and Air, Fire and Sea
I speak of things that I shall be.
To Seas, Air, Fire and Land,
I give my life into your hands.

Activities

Very often it is good to preface this ritual with a day of fasting, retreat, and meditation to consider what initiation means to you and why you wish to make this passage.

Tools and Ritual Components

Ritual Soap — Basil for courage.

Anointing Oil — Heather for a deeper understanding of the nature of the soul.

Altar Decorations — Elder flowers for protection and increasing awareness of the energies present in the world today.

Ritual Cup — Mint water for rebirth and consecration.

Cakes — I suggest making a full meal for yourself with your favorite foods. After a day of fasting you will be hungry, and ready to eat. Eat slowly at first.

PERSONAL CARE PRODUCTS

To maintain oneself on this earth
is not a hardship but a pastime.
—Henry David Thoreau

Since the body is the temple of the soul, it is important to maintain it in a fashion that is becoming of such a grand instrument of learning. The Victorians made everything they could for their family at home. They also knew how to turn almost anything into a useful item. With the changing times and a different Earth, we need to go back to this mode of thinking, which is healthier for both our bodies and this planet. Chemicals have had their reign and ravaged both skin and soil. Let us reclaim the land and ourselves by finding or making personal care products which are useable, natural and non-harmful to our world.

To do this, our knowledge of Victorian herbal practices comes in very handy. The creative Victorian housewife would be certain that the herbs she purchased or grew could be used in two or more recipes to maintain the economy of the home. I think that in the recipes which follow you will find this is no less the case.

As a reminder, while these recipes are very practical, you can change them into magical recipes simply by altering an herb or two to add special significance. I also feel strongly that there is nothing more "spiritual" than living a life which reflects a deep respect for nature.

After-shave

Men have feelings;
this is perhaps the best way
of considering them.
                    —Richter

Mix 2 tablespoons warm apple cider vinegar with 2 cups of witch hazel tincture (available at your drug store). To this add 1 ounce of sage, peppermint and/or wintergreen, then mix the solution with about 3 ounces of rubbing alcohol. Let your herbs steep in a sunny window for 2 weeks, strain and use as desired.

For the Bath

*I am inclined to think bathing
almost one of the necessaries of life.*
—Henry David Thoreau

The bathroom is one of the few places in this world where almost everyone can be insured of privacy. So, keep a few books you have been meaning to get to on the back of the toilet. Or, use your bathtub as a place to meditate by adding some herbs to your water, lighting a candle, burning a bit of incense, and playing some music.

The Ritual Bath

The use of water in religious ceremony is very ancient, but the most widely known application is that of baptism. In old days, a person would be totally immersed to mark the death of the "old wo/man," and when s/he surfaced, it marked a resurrection, a new life. This symbolism need not be lost to the modern magical practitioner. Along these lines, I think the ritual bath is something which has been somewhat neglected in modern magic. It is a wonderful means of washing away the old and making yourself fresh for whatever is to come. The ritual bath is recommended for any special rituals such as coming of age, investing a new priest/ess, initiation etc. to help give that same freshness to your rite.

For this, I suggest employing all the same techniques as you would for meditating in the tub, but in this instance add the dimension of a special herb soap (see the section in Chapter Three on annual observances). Begin by washing each part of the body with the soap and rinsing with the water. As you do, allow all your tensions and angers to be moved away and dispersed into the water below. As you wash, keep a strong vision in your mind of the ritual work you are going to do so that when finished, you are relaxed and mentally prepared for any type of magic.

Aromatherapy Bath

While our ancestors may not have considered tossing a handful of herbs into their wash water therapeutic, they definitely knew the value of fresh scents. When preparing your water, consider what type of bath you would like. To relax, add lavender, sage, chamomile, tangerine rind, sandalwood, rose, thyme, or vanilla. To energize yourself try rosemary, rosewood, patchouli, peppermint, juniper, lemon, lime, bay and yarrow. To uplift your spirits, add geranium, orange peel, jasmine or rosemary.

Seventeenth Century Aromatic Bath Tincture

For people with dry skin, an alternative to the bath salts is to make a tincture, which may be added in any proportion to the bath. Take a quart of spring water and add to it one handful each of bay, rosemary, thyme, marjoram, lavender, mint, lemon and pine needles. Let this boil over a low flame for about 15 minutes, then cool completely. Strain off the liquid, adding 1 cup of brandy (or other alcohol). The mixture retains its scent for at least a year, and brings a wonderful aroma to your bath water.

Scented Bath Salts

These can be made by taking 3 cups sea salt or Epsom salt (readily available at your druggist's) and adding 3 tablespoons each french lavender, dried rose petals, lemon rind and orange peel. Mix thoroughly and store in an air-tight container. Age it one month. Change your herbs to suit your mood and taste, remembering that the hot water will release the smell rather potently into your bathroom. You may also add essential oils to strengthen the scent. The proportion is about 1/4 cup per bath.

Oatmeal Baths

The soothing nature of oatmeal has long been known to the herbalist. To condition your skin, and for deep cleansing, take some well-ground oatmeal and place a cupful in a cheesecloth bag. Sew the bag closed. Use this in the bath like a sponge. It will remain usable for approximately three baths.

Deodorants

For people with sensitive skin, baking soda and corn starch make perfectly useful powder deodorants. For improved scent you can add any of the following herbs in powdered form: orange peel, lemon peel, orris root, chamomile, marigold, comfrey, lavender and sage. This powder may also be sprinkled in shoes, the bottom of drawers, in hampers, or placed in an open box in the refrigerator. Put it any place where difficult odors hide.

To make a spray deodorant, add 5 drops of any essential oil to 1/2 cup of spring water and place this in a pump spray container. Shake well before using. Best scents for longevity seem to be sage, lemon, basil and lavender.

Eye Care

To make a refreshing rinse for your eyes, take 2 ounces of rose water and add it directly to 8 ounces of distilled or spring water. Bottle this and apply whenever needed, using an eye-cup or hollow palm. It will not spoil, so you can even keep it in your medicine chest.

Hair

Conditioning Oil

Take 1 ounce of oil of rosemary and add to it approximately 10 drops (1/8 ounce) lavender oil. If you are a blond, lemon oil can also be added; a redhead should add saffron, and a dark haired person, vanilla. Simply dab a little bit of this mixture on your brush daily. Bend over and allow your hair to fall freely from your head, brushing it 75 to 100 times.

Dandruff

To make an herbal dandruff tincture, try taking 1/2 cup each of pansy, violet, red clover, peppermint, rosemary, marshmallow root, marigold and nettle. Add the fresh or dried herbs to 4 cups of boiling water and let steep. It is best to leave these for a few days until the petals are translucent and the water smells heavily of them. Strain, placing in an air-tight bottle and apply about 2 cups per washing. If you have excessively oily hair, 2 capfuls of lemon juice may also be added.

Another effective rinse can be made by employing the same method with rosemary, witch hazel, lavender, lemon grass and comfrey. In either of these rinses, add chamomile to bring out highlights of light hair, witch hazel for oily hair, sage for dark hair, or marigold for dry hair.

To Clean Hair Brushes

Fill a quart pan full of water and add 1 tablespoon of ammonia. Dip the brush and allow it to soak for a few minutes until the dirt is removed. Rinse thoroughly and dry. A version of this technique appeared in the *Ladies' Home Cook Book,* 1890.

Lip Care

A old folk remedy for chapped or cracking lips was to make an ointment of red clovers. Boil 1 cup of flowers in 3 cups of water over a low heat for about 45 minutes. Strain off the liquid and repeat this process twice more. Now allow the remaining juice to cook down until a syrup forms. Keep this in a container and apply to lips as needed. Violet petals and sage are also effective.

Another lip balm is made with 1 cup almond oil, 1 ounce of bees wax, 2 teaspoons of honey and 1 teaspoon of rose or vanilla extract for flavor. Mix all of these ingredients over a low heat until well incorporated, then store in an air-tight container for use.

Perfumes and Scented Waters

> *The deep recesses of her odorous dwelling*
> *Were stored with magic treasures:*
> *Sounds of air which had the power of all spirits compelling,*
> *Folded in cells of crystal silence there.*
>
> —Percy Bysshe Shelley

Many of the Victorian methods of making perfumes were rather painstaking. The traditional method was to put fresh flower petals in layers of fat between sheets of glass for twenty-four hours. These petals were changed daily until the desired concentration of scent was achieved. The fat was then washed in alcohol to separate out the precious oils. These oils were to be used very sparingly in preparations. For simpler methods of making scented oils, see Chapter Six, the section concerning Easy Essential Oils.

While there are many ways to make a sweet water, this is the one I like best. Take a gallon of spring water, a handful of lavender, peelings from 6 oranges, 3 handfuls of rose petals, a handful marjoram, 12 cloves, and 1 ounce of orris powder. All herbs should be bruised, then added to the water. Warm the water until it has incorporated the scent, then draw off just the liquid. Add a bit of musk and juniper (sliced thin) and use in a basin for rinsing the face, for finger bowls, or refreshing the skin. Note: this is best kept refrigerated until used.

Skin Care

> *Soft as the bloom on the cheeks of morning,*
> *Frail as the foam on a wind-driven sea;*
> *Faint as a sail in the dim distance dawning,*
> *Like to a fairy flotilla set free.*
>
> —E. M. Holden

Astringent

To 1 quart warm vinegar add 1/2 cup of orange peel, leaf and flowers. Leave it for 3 weeks, then strain and use as needed. Or, take 5 to 6 chopped marigolds and warm them in a jar of Vaseline® for 1 to 2 hours. Strain this mixture and place back in the jar. Apply to minor scratches—especially good for pimples.

Cleansing and Opening the Pores

Hazel water followed by cucumber juice to soften and moisturize your skin.

Complexion

Take 1/4 pound of almonds (blanched and skinned)and mash them. Rub these with white soap for 15 minutes then add 1 quart of rose water until the solution looks much like milk. Strain. Apply after washing with a soft cloth. A version of this recipe appeared in the *Ladies Home Cook Book* of 1886.

Facial Mask

Apply honey in an even coating. Then soak it off with warm water. Honey may also be mixed with your favorite lotion to condition the skin and is an excellent remedy for athlete's foot.

Facial or Body Steams

Steaming is very good for the skin in that it cleanses impurities and is very refreshing. To steam just your face, add the recommended herbs to a bowl of hot water and lean over it with a thick towel. Do not get too close to the steam, as it can burn. For the whole body, run your shower at a comfortable body temperature into a plugged tub. As the bathtub fills, add herbs. Then stand or sit only partially immersed in the water.

Any or all of the following may be used in the preparation, proportioned to your personal taste: yarrow, fennel, lavender, marigold, elder, basil, chamomile, peppermint, pine needles, lemon rind, and sage. The end effect is not unlike a sauna, but it is not recommended for people with dry skin or asthma.

Vinegars for Cleansing

For dry skin, prepare a tincture of warm vinegar with mint, orange leaf, parsley, and clover. For oily skin, lemon, rose, sage and lavender are best. If you are having trouble with wrinkles, fennel and lemon balm added to the vinegar should help tighten the skin.

If you find the vinegars are drying your skin too much, simply make a tincture of the herbs in warm water and apply as a rinse. As an aside, herbal vinegar blends are also wonderful for marinating meats, or other flavorful cooking!

Freckles and Blotches

Parsley juice mixed with buttermilk makes an excellent bleach for facial blotches.

Moisturizer

Take two tablespoons of the appropriate herb water as listed in vinegars above and mix it with a teaspoon of honey. Apply this as needed to dry spots.

Powders

The best homemade powders are made from two different bases. The first is made by using 1/2 cup baking soda, 1/4 cup orris root, and 1 cup cornstarch, with a handful of powdered roses. This may be used on the body or in shoes to keep cool and fight odor. The longer it ages the better the scent will become. For a less sweet scent, substitute well-ground lemon rind, cinnamon, orange rind and ginger root for the rose petals. Adjust your proportions for a texture and scent you like.

The second base is that of soapstone. I get mine through a mineral dealer or local geologist (check any neighboring colleges for the later). Take the stone and file it with a rasp until it is very fine. A rasp is a metal tool with rough sides (kind of like metal sand-paper) which can be found at most hardware stores. Collect all this powder and sift it, putting it on a wooden board. Add drops of scented oil to the powder and let it dry completely. Sift it again. This makes a very soft powder of a much better quality than store brands.

ms

method for making skin cream has been around for a very long time. Take 1 part bees wax, 3 parts almond oil, plus generally 1/2 portion of whatever herbs are needed for the skin (some specifics to follow). You may also use various colors of candle wax to prepare your creams, thus color-coding your end product!

Warm your oil with the herbs in it until it smells heavily of them. In some instances I even choose to leave the herbs in the mixture to continue their work. Stir in the wax until melted. Turn off your heat and keep beating until a creamy texture forms. This is the original way cold cream was produced. The cream has a very long shelf life and should be stored in an air-tight container.

For dry skin, add powdered chamomile petals and marshmallow root during your initial steeping process. Marigolds help tone up the skin and relieve pimples. Sage cream with aloe eases the pain of sunburn and helps put moisture back into the skin. Lime, lemon, parsley and rosemary are said to help ease blotches and freckles.

Teeth

Baking soda is perhaps the easiest form of homemade toothpaste, and it is also excellent for your gums. If you want to get a little fancier take 3 to 4 eucalyptus leaves and 2 teaspoons lavender and steep them in a cup of water. To this water add 1 teaspoon salt, 1 teaspoon baking soda, and 2 drops of anise oil or licorice. Once all ingredients are incorporated, add extra baking soda until a pasty substance is made. Keep in air-tight container, using twice a day.

In MacKenzie's *Five Thousand Recipes* (1848) we find yet another recipe, "A mixture of honey with the purest charcoal will prove an admirable cleanser."

I sing of the body electric,
The armies of those I love engirth me,
I engirth them . . . and charge them full
With the charge of the soul.
—Walt Whitman

SPELLS

In the economy of well being of a family, personal and
individual improvement should be sedulously kept in view.
—Sara J. Hale, 1853

Abundance

Place some patchouli oil at the base of a green candle to bring abundance to any situation, be it love or creativity. Let the candle burn during a ritual or any time when you are thinking heavily about this situation.

Back Trouble

Try standing upright with your backbone against a strong, healthy tree. Visualize your back being that tree trunk, its strength revitalizing you. Release your pain to the ground beneath your feet.

Fear

To free yourself from fear, write your fear on a strip of paper. Attach a cord to it. Tie this loosely to a favorite tree, and watch as the winds of change free the fear and blow it away from you.

Grounding a Sickness or Problem

Go to a place where you know the soil is rich and healthy. Sit down and allow the illness or problem to be drawn into the dirt. You may wish to plant a seed there so something positive can grow in its place. Walk away, and do not look back.

Headache

Go outside and watch clouds or birds which are moving away from you. Allow your headache to be carried away with them.

Money

Pick up some kelp in your local food cooperative and wash your floors with it. Or, a money sachet may be made with lavender, saffron, and a silver coin which is wrapped in a luxurious green cloth and bound in gold. Visualize your burdens lifting as you make the sachet, and carry it with you frequently.

When balancing your check book, light some green candles and burn incense of prosperity (sandalwood, cinnamon, and patchouli leaf works well). Before you begin writing checks say, "Lady/Lord my burdens see, bring to me prosperity" three times, visualizing your needs being met. Then continue to pay bills as usual. With spells like this, it is often good to request a time frame during which you will actively pursue your objective.

Sorrow

Legend says that if you rinse yourself with thyme or marjoram in the spring, you will wash away your woes for the coming season.

Mother of this unfathomable world,
Favor my solemn song,
For I have loved thee ever and thee only.
I have watched thy shadow and the darkness of thy steps
And my heart ever gazed on the depth of thy deep mysteries.
        —Percy Bysshe Shelley

How do I love thee? Let me count the ways.
I love thee to the depth and breadth and height
My soul can reach, when feeling out of sight
For the ends of Being and ideal Grace.
I love thee to the level of everyday's
Most quiet need, by sun and candlelight.
I love thee freely, as men strive for Right,
I love thee purely, as they turn from Praise;
I love thee with the passion put to use
In my old griefs, and with my childhood's faith;
I love thee with a love I seemed to lose
With my lost saints—I love thee with the breath,
Smiles, tears of all my life! And, if God choose,
I shall but love thee better after death.

—Elizabeth Barrett Browning

CHAPTER TEN

The Serenade: Romance, Love and Sex

A lovely lady garmented in light
From her own beauty, deep her eyes as are
Two openings of unfathomable night,
Seen through a tempest's cloven roof;
Her hair dark; the dim brain whirls dizzy with delight,
Picturing her form. Her soft smiles shone afar;
And her low voice was heard like love, and drew
All living things towards this wonder new.

— Percy Bysshe Shelley

At the turn of the century, the issues of morality were wandering through nearly every mind, and were sternly spoken of in each church service, as well as in the home. But, considering the medical knowledge of the day and the fact that tuberculosis and syphilis were two common killers, these warnings were not without foundation. The awakening awareness of personal hygiene made some inroads, but it did not alleviate the situation altogether (as is evidenced even today).

So it was that young women were reminded of the values of virtue, and young men taught to be "gentlemen." It is perhaps because of these strict rituals between men and women that so much romance comes through in Victorian writings and art. Their passion had to be expressed in manners appropriate to their times, and thus the languages of flowers, clothing, ribbons, and lace were all used to move the hearts of those desired.

At this point, love was most often expressed in deeds rather than words, and arranged marriages were still very common. The family had a key role in matters of love, which is probably why so many crimes were ones of passion. On the other hand, the 19th century was not the least bit shy about introducing erotic themes into bedroom ornamentation, to the point where the bedroom might have appeared to be a gilded harem.

Houses in general were also more private than those of today. Each room was capable of being closed off from the others. This segregation had much to do with the fact that nudity was never to be exposed. It would never occur to anyone before 1870 to sleep without a nightcap, let alone proper pajamas. Thus it was that privacy was valued greatly, especially between husband and wife, but often at the expense of intimacy.

219

There was also a deep belief during this era that happiness and stability should be rewarded. The anniversary gifts, and publication of what each anniversary item should be, was a reflection of this. Traditionally the first year anniversary gift is paper, the fifth year is wood, tenth is tin, fifteenth is crystal, twentieth is china, twenty-fifth is silver, and the fiftieth is gold. Likewise, the idea of a honeymoon caught on somewhere around the 1890s, with a gift registry for couples starting in 1901.

Our ancestors would probably shudder to discover our openness with courtship, what to them would appear to be rather free sexual morals and the lack of what might be considered demureness in women, but such is the world of today. The question is, what can the Victorian days share with us with in regards to romance, love and magic?

We begin by building on the foundation of personal care discussed in the last chapter. After all, we cannot hope to really share our lives with another until we, ourselves, are whole. I think that the Victorian mind-set can help us to reestablish the idea of the body as a sacred thing. Much of our self-esteem has been torn away by certain misconceptions prevalent in our society: the need to be outwardly beautiful, the early pressure for sexual activity as a way of proving attractiveness, the still lingering notion that a woman who is sexually active is "loose," while a man who is sexually active is considered virile.

While the Victorian's were not liberal in their assessment of women, they did treat the body with a different reverence, one that accepted it as a God-given gift. Our bodies are ours, and we are the ones who must decide what is healthy for them sexually and socially. This is not a matter for our culture (or even our traditions) to dictate, but our hearts.

Thus, if in some areas this chapter seems prudish, it is not meant to be. Instead, I am urging caution and forethought in all of our physical and emotional encounters. We, like our ancestors, are facing new times with new diseases that cannot easily be dismissed. The rede of "harm none" in magic must also apply to ourselves if it is to have any meaning.

Since love is the most powerful force on earth, our romance and sex can be incredibly magical in nature. It is because of this, and the deep feelings that come into play in the courtship ritual, that I have encouraged prudence. Our bodies are holy, they have been given to us as carriers of our soul, to learn with, grow with, and eventually share. The sharing, however, should be when we are ready, and thus can give so much more of our being to the person we choose.

Familiarity breeds attempt.
—Goodman Ace

LOVE MAGIC

Ah, Love, could you and I with fate conspire,
To grasp the sorry scheme of things entire.
— Edward Fitzgerald

Just after the civil war, a series of Chap Books were produced called *Mother Bunche's Closet*. These books had recommendations on just about everything, not the least of which was how to find a mate. I cannot honestly tell you if her methods are effective, since my husband might object, but here are three which were printed:

1. On Midsummer's even, take a smock and dip it in fair water. Turn this inside out and place it on a chair before the fire. Have a vessel of wine and a little salt before the hearth. Do not speak. In a little time the likeness of the one you will marry will come and turn your smock around, then drink to you. Those who will never marry will hear a bell.

2. Take some hemp seed to a private place, carried in an apron. Then toss the seed nine times with your right hand over the left shoulder saying, "Hemp seed I sew, he that must be my true love come after me and mow." After this, expect to see the figure of your love-to-be or hear a bell as before.

3. Go to a church yard at midnight with a sword. Go around the building nine times saying "Here's the sword, where's the sheath?" The ninth time the person will meet you and steal a kiss, or you will hear a bell as before.

These may seem rather silly to the modern magician, but they are not at all uncommon for the time. Some more practical symbols which we can use for modern magic are found in the flower language we spoke of in Chapter Two. These petaled messengers allowed for whole conversations between lovers to ensue. So, using them for opening the lines of communication, or applying their emblems for love magic, seems logical. Add them to incense, decorate your altar with fresh blooms, or give them to someone you care about, allowing their language to silently impart your heart's desire. Other symbols come to us in the forms of lockets. Two birds meant love, an anchor symbolized hope, a cross, faith; a horseshoe, luck; and ivy meant fidelity. These items can be used in symbolic magic for the same purposes. You can make them part of a visualization, add small versions to sachets, and paint them on magical tools for a wide variety of applications.

While I issue caution in using things such as love potions and spells because of the possible interference with another's will, love magics have long been employed to help bring companionship. If used with the proper attitude, they can be very successful in assisting your search for the right person with which to share a season or a life.

Modern Romantic Enchantments

It is not surprising that heaven comes down to touch us when we find ourselves safe in another's heart. Human love is like the shine of gold in the prospector's pan, so different from its surroundings that it seems we must have found it in a better world.

—A. Whitman

With the Victorian ideal of romance and love as a foundation, and a pure desire on our part to find the right person, or strengthen our present relationships, we can approach modern love magics in a new way. Beginning with a healthy respect for ourselves and the lives of those around us, we can send out a non-manipulative energy for love, trusting Divine powers to guide it gently along its way.

Here are several examples for you to try:

1. Three nights before the full moon, light two candles, one which represents you, and one which represents your perfect mate. To choose the color of your candles, consider the predominant characteristics of each individual. Then, look over this list and see which color you feel best suits your magical intentions.

    Red — For strength, courage, fire and vitality.

    Pink — Loving, friendship, relaxation.

    Orange — A color of energy, the sun at morning.

    Yellow — Power of the mind, divination, movement, Air.

    Green — Prosperity, growth, faith.

    Blue — Water, peace, healing, joy.

    Purple — Spirituality, devotion, sensitivity.

    White — Protection, purification.

    Black — Banishing, the night, the void.

    Brown — To increase the effect of any other color, also for use with pets or natural magic. Earth.

    You may wish to place the candles on a red colored cloth or a heart-shaped piece of paper to symbolize love and union. Next, center yourself and meditate for about 15 minutes on all the attributes you desire in a help-mate. Focus that energy strongly into the candle that represents your mate. Do this each night until the Moon waxes full. The evening of the Full Moon, place a third white candle of purity in the center of the other two. Light the pair again, but this time visualize the two of you coming closer, symbolically doing so by moving the two candles towards the white one until they meet, and light the flame of love. Allow this candle to burn until it goes out by itself, thus releasing the magic.

    One note here. What we envision as a "perfect" mate is not always what the Fates send our way. No one is "perfect," and everyone will have faults that get on your nerves. The idea behind this kind of spell is to send out energy of a like mind to help bring to you a person with many of the attributes you desire. Sometimes, though, we will be given something completely different because the real needs we have outweigh our desires, and it is to the need that magic responds.

For those who are already joined, this spell can act as a part of a reaffirmation of your love and unity during times of trial and stress. Take time out to focus on your union, and the strength which can be found there. Light the candles and bring them together, then hold each other close in peacefulness. As you watch the central candle burn, allow yourselves to relax, be refreshed, and gain new perspective. I suggest doing this on a night when you can simply allow the candle to burn out while you sit with only each other and stillness for companions.

2. On the night of a waxing moon, take a silver bell which has been blessed and a red or purple candle. Again, center yourself and visualize your desired love. Next, take the bell in your hand and ring it thrice, each time saying, "I ring once to bring him/her with a love that is pure. I ring twice, him/her to find and our two hearts to bind. Come the ring of three, I set this spell free!" Allow the candle to burn for three hours undisturbed, then blow it out, allowing the residual smoke to carry your wishes to the winds.

3. Stand before a slightly foggy mirror. Take a deep cleansing breath, focus your eyes, and speak these words: "Mirror , mirror on the wall, my wish be heard, in faith I call; Mirror, Mirror, close I look, open now your magic book. Mirror, mirror on counts of three, my true love will come to me. Mirror, mirror, before my eyes, show me now where true love lies."

   Count to three, then watch and see if a place or visage is forming in the fog of the mirror. If the fog only swirls, it means there is too much happening in your life right now for a definitive answer. One word of warning: divining the future is a chancy proposition at best. The future is always changing with your every action. Because of this, what you see in divinations is actually the most possible of predictions at that moment. Consider what you learn with that in mind.

4. Take a handful of blessed, fresh rose petals, and concentrate on your wish to find or strengthen love. Then, scatter them to the four winds, allowing the breeze to carry them to their destination.

5. A love sachet may be made with any combination of pink, purple or red flowers, bay leaf, marjoram, one whole rose bud, a heart cut out of red fabric, and all bound with a white cord. This is to draw a romantic type of love, or as an aid to marriage. Keep it near the items given to you by those you love.

6. For two people who wish to deepen their love, a potion can be made with clove and rose water to encourage an increasing sense of kinship and the desire to nurture and cultivate romance.

7. An incense good for any ritual or spell involving love can be made with one part each rose petals, apple blossoms, lavender, orris root and patchouli. This is for tender love.

COURTSHIP

I am not one who believes in love at first sight,
But I do believe in taking a second look.
—H. Vincent

While courtship may seem like an outmoded concept to our mind, it served an important function in the Victorian home. It was a season to get to know your future mate and their family, and it carried with it definite rituals which must needs be followed to make a proper impression. At first, the man would send flowers to a girl before their initial date, and then thereafter they would always be chaperoned. Too much open affection was frowned upon, but other things, such as gifts, were acceptable as a sign of warmth.

The ultimate expression of the Victorian courtship ritual came at Valentine's Day. This was the time when pretty story books, glove boxes, jewelry, roses twined together, perfume vials and lacy cards with scented inks would appear by the dozens, all handmade with loving care. On this day, love's message was clear, full of appreciation, and delivered to waiting hands with gentle, eloquent words.

When finally the ritual ran its due course, the two young people agreed to wed, with permission of the family. A gift basket would be given to the bride by the groom, full of trinkets, and her family would provide a trousseau. Snippets of hair might be placed in a locket or ring as a forget-me-not, and the two would then move towards wedded life with reverence and acceptance.

Today's courtships, now known as dating or engagements, are far less structured. Personal inspiration has taken hold, along with conflicting signals of how to approach the whole affair. Even so, I think creating courtship or betrothal rituals among magical participants could be quite lovely and empowering. It would act as a personal means of expressing interest or proclaiming love openly among friends.

More beautiful than the ceremony itself, though, is the magical binding taking place by mutual consent. Because of this, be the truss temporary or permanent, neither the participants or guests are likely to forget it quickly. The other advantage to this type of ritual is that, should the bond need to be broken, it may be done in the same respectful atmosphere. The ritual would be reversed, emphasizing the positive lessons learned and the benefits of parting friends, instead of the negative arguments often seen at such times.

The personal nature of such things does not really allow me to write word-for-word instructions on courtship. I can, however, impart the story of my own betrothal as an example. First, my partner and I had to consider where and when the ritual would take place. We agreed upon a camp site in Pennsylvania where we have gone every year since then to celebrate. Next, each of us chose a token to exchange and discussed with whom to share the sacred space.

Instead of actually setting up an altar and candles, as might be the case in a more formalized atmosphere, we decided to hold the ritual just before sunset. This way, our final words to each other would be spoken as the night fires were lit, along with our love. Our "robes" were actually medieval costumes sewn by hand because we both love historical lore. A tiki torch was ignited, and in proper gentlemanly manner, Paul got down on one knee to propose. I accepted, taking the ring presented in a satin lined box, and replacing it with a needlework favor as ladies of olde might. Our words were not fancy, and there was periodic laughter during and afterwards, but we and our friends have never forgotten that evening. Just under one year later, as is proper, we were married, and our son came into this world ten days before our first anniversary.

All in all, it is a terribly romantic scene filled with individual preference and vision, as well it should be. If you and your partner decide you would like to do something of this nature to give a little magic to your relationship, talk it over first. Then, find a couple of friends in your spiritual community from which to get advice and suggestions. Most of all, realize that magical bindings are very powerful and special. It is a way of saying that you want to learn and grow with another person, if only for a season; that together you want to work a magic that will make you both better people, and hopefully build from the two of you a new oneness of mind, heart and soul.

There be none of Beauty's daughters with a magic like thee,
And like music on the waters is thy sweet voice to me.
— Lord Byron

UNIONS

My luve's like a melodie that's sweetly play'd in tune.
— Robert Burns

I separate betrothal and courtship from unions for the obvious reason that the first does not always guarantee the second. In many ways, courtship and betrothal are a testing ground where certainty (or lack thereof) about your partner can grow. The final step of marriage or handfasting is more powerful and a deeper commitment than anything the couple has embarked on before.

In the Victorian home, a marriage was met with great joy. It marked the true adulthood of children, the continuance of the family line, and in some respects, the success of the parents in raising their young ones correctly. Marriage was also a sacred vow, divorce being heard of only rarely. If there was infidelity in a union, it would not be spoken of openly for the shame it brought to a home.

Marriage and Handfasting

*Could a greater miracle take place than for us to
Look through each other's eyes for one minute?*
    —Henry David Thoreau

The Victorian era held a terribly romantic view of love and marriage. In 1857, Thomas Bridgeman, a writer of the time, wrote about "the matrimonial garden" with a true Victorian flowery flair. Some of his advice is still well worth heading today. One section says, "If you are desirous that this garden shall yield you all the bliss of which it is capable, you must take with you that excellent flower called good humor, which of all the flowers of nature is the most delicious and delicate; do not drop it or lose it, as many do, soon after they enter the garden; it is a treasure the loss of which nothing can supply." He also speaks of the weed called Indifference, the deadly flower of Jealousy, crooked paths of Perverseness, thorns of anger and bees of Avarice growing alongside more beneficial plants of Regularity, Economy, Simplicity, and most importantly Charity.

By comparison, handfasting is basically the magical version of marriage except that it may or may not be legally recognized depending on the couple's choice in the matter. It is the recognition and enactment of a true partnership and oneness of love where the couple embark on learning the lessons of flexibility and patience. This ritual is most commonly performed on a Waxing to Full Moon with the understanding that the vows we make in

Magical Circles, whether witnessed by friends or the Watchtowers, are just as binding, if not more so, than any made in churches.

Invocation

This invocation should be recited by the Priest and Priestess, the woman taking the West and North, the man speaking for the South and East. When they come to the center point, the invocation should be done in unison. The couple can be seated somewhere in a meditative state in order to open all their senses to the event about to take place.

> *Lord of the Spirit, Ruler of the Tempest, call our breath to your service. Let us inhale your violet winds from the East, smelling the airs of knowledge and intuition as they move with our blood until we are full. Sense of the eagle, sense of the hawk, sense of the owl, be of a like mind. Let us fly on your winds, enjoying the breath of Earth, and be free.*

> *Lord of Fires, Master of Strength, call our eyes to your service. Open their windows wide to see things both veiled and revealed. Let naught be hidden here. Let us see with the innocence of a child, the love of all parents, and the wisdom of elders as we look on the world which is ours. Eyes of the golden lion, eyes of the red dragon, be our eyes. Let your vision set our hearts aflame with energy, spirit and life.*

> *Lady of Spheres, Ruler of the Deep, call our mouths to your service. Bring full our emotions and bless our tongue, we pray. Let us taste of your healing waves as they fill our souls. Tongue like a sea rush, tongue of the dolphin, let us know you as we swim at your side in this well of creativity.*

> *Speaker of Mysteries, Mother of Earth, call our hands to your service. Awaken these tools to touch all the wonders you grant. Let them caress both mountain and shore, cave and grove, feeling texture in each. Hoof of the stag, paw of the kitten, hands of the healer, be ours. Let us touch you full as we grow in rich moist soil, together.*

> *Lord of Darkness, Lady of Stars, call our ears to your service. Transform the way we listen until truth and beauty are known. Open our ears to all the sounds within and without, above and below. Let the sphinx ask her riddle, and our answer be love. Ears of a dog, ears of the rabbit, be our ears. One step beyond time shall we listen to both sounds and silences, finding unity.*

Activities

The bride and groom are crowned in flowers, and elder flowers are scattered to the winds for blessing. The couple might be taken to the four cardinal points to be reminded of life's journey. After vows, their shoulders or wrists are bound together with floral wreaths as a sign of union. After this it is a traditional activity to jump over a *small* fire, sword or broomstick at the end of the ceremony to mark the new life together.

Tools and Ritual Components

Incense — Rosemary for fond remembrance. This may also be woven into the bridal wreath.

Ritual Soap — Dried red and white rose petals added to the base for love and purity.

Anointing oil — Lavender for stability, awareness, and inner peace. This may also be braided into the wreaths for the couple's heads.

Ritual Cup — Wine with a touch of basil to embrace a new life, coriander to bring peace to the home, and marjoram for romantic fulfillment.

Altar decorations — Flowers and horseshoes may adorn the altar, while daisy, lemon, and violet are scattered for the outer circle. Rock crystal may be brought into the sacred space to channel energy and keep the couple protected.

Clothing —This is whatever the participants decide to wear.

Cakes — Anything with anise, for a gentle happiness that does not consume one as a fast fire would, but endures.

I have you fast in my fortress,
And I will not let you depart
But put you down into the dungeon
In the round tower of my heart.
—Henry Wadsworth Longfellow

THE GREAT RITE

For the rose, the rose is the eye of the flowers,
It is the blush of the meadows that feel themselves fair,
It is the lightning of beauty that strikes thro' the bowers
On Pale lovers who sit in the glow, unaware.

—Sappho

Sometimes a couple will choose to continue the ritual of handfasting with the Great Rite. Here they become the archetype of God and Goddess incarnate in order to bring to union the most sacred and powerful living communion known—where man, woman, Earth and Sky become part of one great dance. This is the holy unifying of the visible and invisible, sounds and silences, with the recognition that sex is the vehicle for continuance of life and learning of the soul in this world.

Certain Victorian people would have practiced this if their family practiced the "Olde Ways." Usually, the Great Rite was performed to insure harvest and good weather. At this time, however, it may have carried the less pretentious title of the Rite of Joining. Most young couples, however, would wait nervously for their wedding night to discover the magic of union. While few couples today enter marriage/handfasting without some knowledge of procreative customs, there are still times of great need when a man and woman may choose to invoke this Rite as part of their lovemaking. Under no circumstances should it be done without forethought and the proper attitude. The Great Rite is not simply sex for sex's sake, but a means to raise pure magical power which can be directed for the happiness of the couple or other urgent situations.

Because magical binding is so transformational, and at the risk of being considered a conservative prude, I do not recommend the use of this Rite without just cause or serious consideration. I also recommend that the parties involved either be married to each other or unattached, so that other, more difficult emotional situations do not arise to impede the workings of the magic later. If done in the correct spirit between two loving, magically trained adults, this can be one of the most powerful experiences for them and/or the coven.

It should be noted that the Great Rite can be enacted symbolically via the use of athame, wand, or sword combined with the cup, horn, or cauldron, should a physical Rite be inappropriate. Even so, it should be done with no less reverence, understanding that tokens are recognized in magic as being able to become what they symbolize in the spiritual sense.

Invocation

I recommend this invocation be done by the two people planning to participate in the Great Rite to help bring them into a more focused state of awareness. The ingredients for each altar point may be changed according to inspiration and/or availability as long as the nature of the meanings is not varied.

Lord of the Spirit, Wind of Understanding, we call and charge you. Smell the sandalwood upon our hearth, as yellow flames dance with the wind. Come to us. Surround us with your essence. Empower our very breath this night.

Lord of Strength, Spark of our Will, we call and charge you. See the thistle and holly upon our fire as the red candle greets the sky. Come to us. Grant us your strength and purity of purpose, pray, burn within us this night.

Lady of Spheres, Water of Creation, we call and charge you. Savor the heather and ivy which billows in praise, as blue wax drips towards your sea. Come to us. Let waves of healing and unity meet the shores to fill our souls this night.

Lady of Stars, Speaker of Mysteries, we call and charge you. Feel the jasmine and sage burn ever upward as the green taper lights the dark and come to us. Let our seeds of magic grow without, and Ye within, this night.

Activities

The use of drums, cymbals and anything with a low, energetic beat make the perfect atmosphere for the Rite. A private space should be prepared for the participants to go to enact the Rite, so they are uninhibited by onlookers. Natural surroundings are best.

Tools and Ritual Components

Incense — Orchid, lemon and rose for blessing, sexuality and ritual love making.

Ritual Soap — Sandalwood for increased spiritual focus.

Anointing Oil — Rose and jasmine for the woman, to symbolize beauty and to invoke the Goddess. Patchouli and cinnamon for men, to increase their focus and invoke the God. For both, the chakra points should all be anointed.

Ritual Cup — Tea of fennel and cloves for strength, virility, and to increase psychic focus.

Altar — It may be decorated in a manner similar to a handfasting, but the addition of something that represents the God and Goddess is appropriate. Also, onyx may be brought into the space for sealing, obsidian for concentration, and pearl as a pledge of honor, purity and wisdom.

Clothing — The Great Rite is most frequently done sky clad, but if the participants wish to stay clothed earlier, that is perfectly fine.

Cakes — Anything with cinnamon for manifestation of the magical working/spell.

Love is the only priest,
Ignorance is the only slave.
Happiness is the only good.
The time to be happy is now,
The place to be happy is here . . .
— R.G. Ingersoll

❦

OTHER FAMILY MINI-RITUALS

There are many occasions in our every day lives which may inspire us to work a ritual. The idea behind these rituals is to bring the family closer together, and reclaim the value Victorians placed on the family unit. The home should be a place of peaceful sanctity, a shelter in the storm . . . not the storm itself. By considering mini-rituals for various occasions, we help to maintain this almost "sacred" ambiance, where our hearts and homes are in accord, reflecting Victorian flavored tranquility for our spirits to grow in.

Anniversary Ritual

Find someone to take care of the kids for a full day, and go to a special spot. Even if you have been angry with each other lately, put those feelings aside and take time for an outing for just the two of you. Pack some photo albums and a picnic basket full of favorite goodies.

When you go, take a little wild ivy to decorate the area and honor the celebration, then set up a little make-shift altar with two pieces of bloodstone in the center for long-lasting love. Burn lemon in your incense for stability, and ginger for health. Wear each other's preferred outfit and cologne, and spend the day reminiscing. Rediscover the reasons you fell in love and thank the powers for the strength to stay together. When you return home, cuddle up with a terribly sentimental movie, dance with each other, and tuck your bloodstones in a special place. Perhaps have them mounted in a shared ritual cup or medallion which can go with you each year as you celebrate your union.

Forgiveness Ritual

There was a naughty boy,
A naughty boy was he,
He would not stop at home,
He would not quiet be.
— John Keats

In any group or family situation, there are going to be times when we say things we don't mean, get angry or hurt, and need forgiveness. Magical Circles give us very powerful symbols to use in aiding the emotional healing process. For this forgiveness ritual, I suggest bathing the altar with candlelight from white candles and a draping it with a white cloth to represent peace. A branch of olive or another herb which represents peace should also adorn it somehow. The incense can be comprised of lavender, tansy, passion flower and verbena to bring about a release of sadness and negative energy, replacing them with peacefulness, and most importantly, understanding. A verse which I wrote can be used at some point in the ritual. It should be chanted by the participants:

> *Fly away from me, my fears with the light of truth be gone,*
> *That I might walk upon my path with spirit, whole and strong.*
>
> *Fly away from me, my pride with the light of mind be tame*
> *That I might learn of what I am and whence I truly came.*
>
> *Fly away from me, my guilt with the light of thought be free*
> *That I might dance the dance of life, in time with destiny.*

In this way, all people involved are setting aside the pride, fears, and guilt that often accompany stressful situations, and are looking together to find a solution.

When those taking part join the Magic Circle, they should bring with them a symbol of their negative feelings. This symbol can be anything from a rock to a poppet, and is set in front of the participants during the ritual. Next, everyone should sit around a table (also the altar) and take the symbolic object in their hands. Each person then takes his or her turn to verbally pour into that item all their guilt, anger, and fear regarding this specific situation. For example, if the problem has been between a husband and wife, where communication has been all but lost, the husband might take his symbol in hand saying, "I place my anger towards you in here. This is my guilt for not always being responsive to you. This is my confusion and my inability to see your perspective." The wife should respond in kind, honestly stating all the things she wants to get rid of, and allowing all the negativity to be channeled into the icon. I should note at this point that you will want to choose a tool which can either be burned or buried, thus quite literally putting the pain away from you.

When you have finished pouring your bad feelings into the symbolic item, put it aside, away from both of you. Next, have a small bowl of edibles (M & Ms® work exceptionally well) on the altar. Each person in turn takes one to eat saying, "I take peace with you into my life, I take new joy at our new beginning, I take fresh love for you." Each time you think of something else you want to bring to your relationship, pick up one of the M & Ms®, speak that desire, and eat it, internalizing that magic. The candy in this magical atmosphere becomes like a seed which can grow in your heart.

The casting of the circle and prayers can be done in a manner appropriate to the situation. Once the people involved have finished, they should give their apologies, embrace, then leave their symbols on the altar, turning away from their anger when leaving. Someone else can take the items later to burn or bury them under a flowering tree so that instead of resentment, beauty can be grown.

It should be noted that this is not a ritual which can be forced on anyone. It must be born of an honest desire in all parties to put their bad feelings on the altar and leave them there. Once this ritual is done, the situation should not be brought up again by any of the participants. If anyone outside of the circumstances should bring up the past, all participants must be willing to state with conviction that it is a matter now forgotten, and ask that it not be spoken of. It is now dead and buried; forgiveness has been sown like a seed to bring a new, loving harvest among friends and family.

Healing and Support Ritual

Drastic times often require the supportive help and friendship of others to get us through. When someone in our family or circle has a need, it should be seen and responded to with as little commotion as possible. Sickness and other apprehensive situations create enough confusion in an individual's life without us adding to it.

Instead, a quiet call should be placed to a few close friends in the magical community. A special circle may be cast with frankincense and myrrh for protection and cleansing. Dances and chants can be done, with the individual in need in the center of the circle so that the energy raised can be directed to them. If the seriousness of the situation (or proximity of the individual) does not allow them to attend, use a poppet or other item to symbolize them and channel your energy towards it. When health is the problem, you may wish to add flax, ginger and juniper to your incense, along with one herb to represent the person so that they are surrounded with the essence of healing. Your herbs, invocations, chants, etc. should be changed to best represent the situation at hand.

One of the greatest gifts our magical training can offer to those around us does not come from the mystical movement of energy, but the simplicity of the outstretched hand and Divine love.

RITUAL FOR THE DEAD

Our birth is but a sleep and a forgetting:
The Soul that rises with us, our life's Star,
Hath had elsewhere its setting,
And cometh from afar.

— William Wordsworth

At first glance, this section may seem terribly out of place in this chapter, but in actuality it is not. Death was a far more prevalent occurrence during the Victorian era. Life spans were shorter, disease more prevalent, and medical science was just finding its place. The death of a husband or father was considered especially tragic because of his role as financial supporter and general leader within the family unit. While medicine has obviously taken great strides, and our lives have become much longer, that does not lessen the terrible loss felt when someone we love dies. No matter our faith, we find ourselves questioning all that we believe about life, death and the immortal soul. Sometimes in the shadow of death's reality, all our words and ideals seem shallow, at least for a brief instant. As we grapple with the inner questions, there are many different emotions playing in our minds, ranging from guilt to relief, especially if the individual has been ill for a long time. All in all, it is a very confusing experience.

Having weathered the death of my father only six months ago at the time of this writing, I struggled greatly with this section. At first, I avoided it, not wanting to face that pain again, but then I realized that in order to help others release themselves and the spirit of their loved one, I had to contend with my own feelings.

Looking back, I realize now how shocking it was to see the body without a soul. It truly is a hollow shell with no remnants of that personality left. Paganism and Wicca teach us that the wheel of life never really stops moving. Just as in nature, energy is never destroyed, it simply changes shape. When we are faced with death, we must eventually recognize that change, and allow ourselves to let go. From experience, I know that this personal release comes after buckets of tears, a period of numbness, a lot of talking, and through the support of family and friends. That is why funerals are important for the psychological well-being of those left behind.

On another level, the funeral rite is meant to help the soul's transition into its new state. Like those who loved this person, I think the soul sometimes goes through a period of shock and a time of mourning the loss of the body. People who have had near death experiences speak of looking at themselves, and feeling confused as to why their body won't work. I believe that the soul becomes accustomed to having its housing. Because of this, certain spirits may have trouble letting go of this framework, especially those who die tragically in sudden accidents or through acts of malice.

So we perform the Ritual of the Dead for the benefit of both the living and those who have passed over, in order that both can be free to move forward on their journey. If the individual was not of a magical persuasion, you can perform this rite privately to honor them, and give your heart rest.

> *Death is the mother of beauty, mystical within,*
> *Whose burning bosom we desire.*
>
> —W. Stevens

Invocation

> *Brother, hearth of burning might*
> *Torch the fires, fill the night,*
> *Warm all homes across the land*
> *While midst the ancient stones*
> *We stand.*
>
> *Father, wind of dancing rites*
> *Waltz the flames, grant them flight.*
> *Carry safe the hearth's first spark*
> *Throughout the land*
> *Ignite the dark.*

Sister, sea of welling souls
Cleanse the Grail, complete this bowl,
Caress your shores with golden dawn
Till magick flows
Upon the lawn.

Mother, Earth of singing ken,
Chant the wards, protect this glen
Hum low your song with drum and fife
Bring the White Hart back
To life.

Cousin, time of healing power
Calm the moment, shape peace this hour.
Wrap all that lives in soothing balm,
While shining ones take heed
Our psalm.

Family, heirs of binding ties
Join your hands as fires die,
Let your love breath from out this cairn
As spirit, whose light keeps all
From harm.

Prayer

Goddess, to you I open a door, and bring the spirit of _____. Let him/her join with the Lion! Join with the Druids! Know the Grail and the Loom. Teach him/her the magick of being by the light of a harvest moon. Teach him/her the music of bards. We draw now the sacred runes.

Goddess, to you comes this child of light walking in the path of ancients. Join him/her with Taliesin. Join him/her with the Old Ones; teach of the Pipe and Braid. Show the magic of unicorns, the dance of lord with maid. Give us a star to wish on that our hearts might be stayed . . .

Activities

If the individual practiced magic, now is the time to dispose of their tools in whatever manner they request. Some may be given away, others buried with them, etc.

The spirit of the individual should at some point be welcomed to the circle for the last time to partake of that fellowship before moving to their next existence. This may be done symbolically by the priest/ess by bringing something of that individual's to help adorn the altar. The song "We All Come From the Goddess," by Starhawk makes an excellent piece for this ceremony.

Tools and Ritual Components

Incense — Basil for protection and communion with spirits, bluebells for peace of mind and to herald the soul's journey, and lotus to allow the sweet scents to rise with the spirit, and bring them tranquility.

Ritual Soap — Borage to fortify the inner-self and bring joy, even during times of sorrow.

Anointing Oil — Cypress to help us understand all aspects of death.

Ritual Cup — Anise and thyme may be added for communion with sacred energies.

Altar Decorations — I suggest using willow and violets, often traditional on such occasions, along with items the beloved may have favored for their personal altar or for the coven. Jet was the stone used in the Victorian era for mourning.

Clothing — This is the choice of the participants.

Cakes — Foods are best prepared by friends. Often, favorite edibles of the beloved are featured, along with finger foods and other simple snacks which require little fuss.

Possibilities exist in even
The smallest grains of sand:
It is the eye of faith which
Discovers hidden promise,
The heart of hope which
Sustains the dream,
And the hand of perseverance
Which creates magick
From seeming nothingness.
    —Marian Loresinger

RITUAL FOR CONCEPTION

I would pray to the Mother, to loose her ban,
The holy Goddess to whom, and to Pan
Before my gate, all night long
The maids do worship with dance and song.
— Pinder

In the Victorian era, children were not only a blessing but also a necessity. During a time when life spans were much shorter, children became the way to ensure a family, and their legacy to the future would continue when the parents were gone. During pregnancy, the woman would sew, crochet and knit all manner of items to prepare for the arrival. A bassinet would be chosen and placed in a warm section of the house (often the kitchen or near the hearth), ready for use. An appropriate midwife or traveling doctor would be contacted for periodic examinations.

The first two years of childhood were not too different from what is experienced now, except that far more books were read, and toys were not as plentiful. As they grew older, children learned much from their parents about the responsibilities they would have. A boy of three might begin to tend the fields with his father, while a girl would start to help darn socks. Even so, their presence in the Victorian home lent new life and vitality to the environment; a special freshness which brought smiles and laughter to friends and family alike.

This fresh vitality is not lost to magicians. For us, a new child symbolizes the wheel coming round again from death to life, and a new beginning. A baby represents an opportunity to help another soul along its path, and to learn much ourselves in the process. While we have many more choices today than our forefathers regarding when or if we have children, when two people do decide they want a baby, I can think of no lovelier setting to begin the process than that of a private magic circle.

The ritual chamber should be prepared with yellow sheets, the color of creative energy. Above the bed can be hung a bundle of yarrow, mistletoe, parsley, myrtle and St. John's wort which was picked on Midsummer's Eve, all of which are believed to help in conception. A small altar should be placed in the room, with the image of a pregnant Goddess in the center.

Before the ritual, the couple should prepare themselves according to magical and medical standards. We know from our doctors that a man should not have sex for about a week, and that a woman should be in her fertile period. They should both eat well, get plenty of rest, and try not to get nervous about the whole matter. It is, after all, the most natural thing in the world.

On a magical level, they may wish to consume things such as basil, poppy, cucumber and pomegranate to increase fertility. To symbolize the union of the God and Goddess, you can create an incense. Mix acorns and hazel nuts with two herbs—One to represent the masculine and one to represent the feminine. Somewhere near the bed, a small container of mandrake and jasmine, well mixed, can be placed to help insure sexual prowess. To bring a sense of peacefulness, it is also appropriate to have a bath, massage, or an anointing with lemon.

The couple should spend some time together meditating and attuning themselves to each other's physical rhythms. In order to best accomplish this, the phone should be turned off and friends asked not to stop by. Take away anything that might distract you from your desire.

When love making is finished, and the couple is well rested, they should go to a special place with their clay Goddess. This area should be one where the image can remain undisturbed. Bury her there with a braid of your hair, and allow nature to take her course.

Should a pregnancy occur, there is a Victorian way to tell if it will be a boy or a girl. According to an old tale, if you go to your garden with your eyes closed and spin around to pick a flower, if it is a dark color (deep red, a brown leaf etc.) the baby will be a boy. A light hue, such as pink, indicates a girl. This is a terribly exciting and educational time in any family. Once a child is growing within the mother, a couple begins to discover a whole new dimension of their relationship. This new young spirit begins to share their lives, helping them to learn much about themselves, and indeed, their magical perspectives.

Monday's child is fair of face
Tuesday's child is full of grace
Wednesday's child is full of woe
Thursday's child has far to go
Friday's child is loving and giving
Saturday's child works hard for a living
But the child that is born on the Sabbath Day
Is bonny and blithe and good and gay.

Anonymous

CHAPTER ELEVEN

The Lullaby: Spiritual Activities for Children

The Lady up in the skies turns the trees green.
— Karl Anthony at 3-1/2 years old

There were interesting changes in the attitude of parents towards children during the Victorian era. For the first time, young ones were recognized as individuals and as investments for the family's future. Because of this feeling, discipline, manners, and proper appearance were sternly taught. Responsibilities were given to each child depending on age, social status, and sex. Even so, childhood was considered a very special time, full of magic, which adults reminisced about, remembering that time joyfully, but also believing it to be the foundation for the building of character.

The Victorian child might have marionettes, go carts, doll houses and moving picture contraptions as toys. They would also have the simpler daisy chains and butter cup games still played by children today. Miniature kitchen tools might be given to a little girl to teach her how to become a "proper" house wife. Young men would learn the trade of their fathers.

Despite the rather rigid standards for roles in the community, the family of the Victorian era believed strongly that a home surrounded by love and beauty would mean that their children would grow up to be generous and compassionate, or so was the hope. Today, bringing up children is still no easy matter. Parents still desire the best for their children, and can only hope that the lessons they have taught them were heeded well. The children of today face a more complicated world with very few guidelines to help them create a picture of themselves and what they should be. This makes Pagan patenting a challenge, to say the least.

There is great controversy within Circles as to whether they are the proper place for young ones, and if we even have the "right" to teach our children about our faith as other religions do. This is not an easy question for any family, and it is a deeply private one. I personally feel that the basic lessons of any religion are things we can give our children without compromising their opportunity to choose a path to God for themselves. It is important, however, to make your decisions on how you will handle this early in their lives so that you know what to say or do the first time a Christian family member has them pray, or talks to them about "baby Jesus." In our house, it is now well known that Jesus is not the only one who tells us to be nice to each other, as my sisters have taught, but so does the Goddess and Buddha (my husband is Shinto)! In this manner, the main lesson coming across to the child is not a name or an image, but one of kindness.

In talking with other Magical parents on this subject, there is a concern over finding projects to help teach important foundational principles to children in the spirit of fun instead of lecturing. This chapter is meant to help in that area. These are things I have done with my own son, with a fair margin of success, so they come to you "kid tested and mother approved." Actually, the end result of these types of activities, and the atmosphere of our home was to have my son, Karl, approach me while I was teaching someone how to focus using a candle. He placed his hands gently near the flames, making them dance, then looked at me very seriously and said, "Mommy, I'm a witch." Karl is not even five yet, and I have said nothing directly to him about magic, so I know it was his decision. Now, I feel I can continue his training, employing the activities in this chapter with more direction. I have kept them rather simple, but almost all projects, except those related to birth, can be adapted for any age just by improving vocabulary and jazzing them up a bit.

In working with the children in your life, it is best to remember that they have a rich imagination, which should never be discouraged. The magic of childhood is a wondrous gift for people young and old!

While standing near a river bed,
A three year old boy was asked,
"What would your special name for God be?"
To which, he responded, "Bigger waters!"
— Shared by Dawn

BIRTH

Hope is the thing with feathers that perches in the soul.
—Emily Dickinson

The birth of a child, in almost any culture or time, is a reason to celebrate. It marks new life, new blood and especially, a hope for a better tomorrow.

In recent years we have learned the necessity of bonding, and in magical realms know the importance and power of a name (see also Chapter Thirteen). Thus the spiritual bonding of parent to child, and the welcoming of a soul to this Earth are some of the most beautifully refreshing and life-affirming ceremonies in all faiths.

Bonding with a Newborn

Soon after the child is born, snip a few strands of it's hair and your own (if the baby is bald, your's and your mate's will do). From this, fashion together a braided anklet. As you work the hair together, repeat this phrase: "Lady of Motherhood and Light, bind this child and me together in joy and love. Keep him/her always in your sight, blessed by Thy hand above," until it is long enough to tie onto the baby's ankle.

Tie the anklet on, kissing the child's third eye and allowing the braid to stay on the child as long as safety and health will permit. Then, remove it and store it with your other treasures. Give it to them when they reach the age of maturity, as a symbol of release.

Baby Blessing Ritual

The timing of this ritual is up to the parents, but waiting for a waxing to Full Moon is probably best for positive growth energies. If done at the home, the crib can be decorated with daisy, lavender, and parsley for protection and bounty. If performed elsewhere, the parents may wish to carry sprigs of fresh herbs which have significant symbolism and keep these with the child during the ritual. Afterwards, dry them as a keepsake. This ritual, sometimes called Wiccaning, often marks the naming of the child and welcomes a new soul to this world.

Invocation

A canopy of eventide spreads dark from out the glen,
With ravens wings, a rising moon, and blessings that we send.
To you, our friends, we build a bridge to span the air and sea,
With beams of light and lavender that magic might move free.
To touch the hearts of those we love,
This child whom now, we bless
With songs of hope and harmony, sealed with a holy kiss
We call upon the Goddess Minne, to hold _____ in Her hands
With arms of warmth and comforting,
And keep you ever safe from harm.

Activities

Friends and family often bring gifts. Having a pot luck supper is so that the family doesn't have to fuss is especially thoughtful. Use a sprig of parsley to asperge the circle. Present the child to the four Watchtowers and to your group; give a small libation to the Earth in thankfulness. Plant a tree; it is the traditional Victorian way to insure growth and joy to the child.

Tools and Ritual Components

Incense — Cedar and rosemary to bring consecration, purification and protection to all participants.

Ritual Soap — Elder, which may also be used in bath water for safety and protection.

Anointing Oil — Milkweed juice to bless the child with growing imagination, inspiration, and creativity.

Ritual Cup — A mild cup of chamomile tea for soothing. A bit of the tea may be placed on the baby's lips.

Altar Decorations — The daisy is traditional. Iris may be added for joy. A small moonstone can be placed center table to bring happiness and health for the future, representing the phases of life as represented by the cycles of the moon. This stone should be set into a ritual tool. This tool should be given to the child at their Rite of Passage (Graduation).

Cakes — While the child may be too young to enjoy them yet, Zwieback cookies would be a nice touch to remember the child's part in the ceremony. A recipe for them can be found under Snacks in the next section.

The finest qualities of our nature, like the blooms on fruits,
can only be preserved by most delicate handling.
—Henry David Thoreau

ACTIVITIES FOR CHILDREN

Let us then, be up and doing,
With a heart for any fate
Still achieving, still pursuing,
Yet learn to labor and to wait.
— Henry Wadsworth Longfellow

Afraid of the Dark?

Most children dislike the dark. It is the place where their fears wait, lurking in each shadow. A Victorian mother might have allowed a candle to burn in her child's room until they fell asleep. For my son Karl, I handle this fear in a couple of different ways. First, I gave him a "magic" blanket. Whenever he was scared, I told him to hold this blanket tight, and know that I was not far away and that I could take care of him. All I actually did was a little protection/blessing spell for the well-loved cloth, but it made him feel much better.

Another thing that helps is to let children know that they have some amount of control. Children believe that dreams and some of their imaginings are real. They will not begin to believe otherwise until about 7 years old. So, you need to teach them that while dreaming or imagining, they can take over and be victorious. In desperation one night to get Karl in bed, I told him to punch the monsters in the nose or tell them to go away because mommy says so. The change was not immediate, but now Karl is more interactive with his imagination. He tells me how he "got rid of the monsters." This is a small thing on the surface, but making sure that children know they have the power to change the things that frighten them the most is an important step forward in magical training. Fear and hatred are two of the most powerful emotions; they even hold adults back from progressing in their spiritual growth.

When your children get old enough, teach them about simple protection visualizations, spells and/or amulets. Let them choose which they would like to try, and then take them through the process, step-by-step, allowing them to do as much of the work as possible. Examples might include a simple white-light "bubble" (see Appendix B), a blessed object which can be easily worn or carried (such as a ring or necklace), or protective incense (such as frankincense.) Again, this is a means of teaching them how to take a problem in hand and change it for the better. It also shows that you don't regard their feelings as unimportant or silly and are willing to take the time to help.

Dreams

Children often remember their dreams, and we can learn much from listening to the accounts. At first the temptation might be to dismiss the child's dream as so much youthful rambling, but the Victorians placed a great deal of stock in the importance of dreams. I find I spend a fair amount of time talking to Karl about his, learning about his fears, joys and even mistakes I had made with him. In the course of discussion I have also discovered misconceptions about magic which I quickly tried to correct.

One night he had a dream about an "ugly old witch who cooked him." I assume this came from the story of Hansel and Gretel at school, but either way, I wanted him to know that very few witches are old or ugly and mean. I reminded him about Glinda in the Wizard of Oz (not the best example, but it worked) and myself. Not long after that, in the next dream he had about the old Hag, it turns out that a "nice lady helped me beat her up."

On another occasion, after nearly a week of nightmares, I tried a different approach. Before bed I asked him what he would like to dream about, to which he gleefully responded, "Flying!" So, I took each one of his favorite stuffed animals and showed him how they could fly different ways. I also told him he could take anyone he wanted with him. As we talked, I traced an invoking pentagram on his forehead saying, "you're going to dream about flying with friends," three times in almost a sing-song and fun manner. I really was uncertain if the result would be positive, but much to my delight he slept through a full night and told me all about his winged adventures the next day.

You can quickly see from these stories how much we can help ease our children's fears with a little creativity and teach them important things at the same time. Attend carefully to what your children say about their dreams. You will rarely need to look for "deep symbols" as is the case with adult dream interpretation, since children's minds work on very honest, forthright levels. You will discover with good listening skills that your children's dreams can teach you much about what is happening at school, with their friends, and even how strong a self-image they are building.

Apple Doll God/dess Image

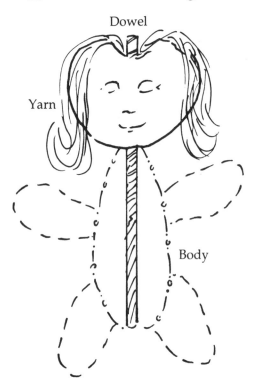

A favorite Victorian pastime was making these little dolls for decorations around the home. For the magical home, it is a way to allow the children to participate in an upcoming ritual especially fall celebrations) by adding their decoration to the altar. To make this doll, peel a large apple and place a dowel (available at hardware stores) in the center where the stem would be. This dowel becomes the framework for the body. Cut deep holes for the eyes and mouth—make sure they are proportioned to the size of the apple.

Let the apple sit out in a dry place so it can begin to shrink. As it gets smaller, you can insert crystals or stones into the eye holes. When the apple is completely dry, add a wig made of yarn, which may be attached with glue or toothpicks. For the doll's body, place an old stocking open-end-up over the dowel and stuff it with dried aromatic herbs. For arms, you can on stitch smaller pieces of stuffed stocking just below the "neck." Allow your children to make felt dresses or aprons for the doll in various colors, corresponding to the different seasons.

An alternative to this method is using things like paper-mache, clay or salt dough to create a figurine. These mediums also work well for many other projects listed in this chapter. The only advice I have is to encourage the children to work outside, away from rugs. Provide plenty of newspaper and paper towels, and have the clean up tools handy.

Candle Making

> *Beautiful hands are they that do,*
> *Deeds that are noble, good and true.*
> — W. McGuffey

In the chapter on cooking magic, we spoke a little of how central candles were to a Victorian home. Since the common Pagan or Wiccan is using candles on a regular basis, why not save the ends and pieces for your children, and allow them to make a special candle of their own.

Begin by gathering together a fair amount of old wax, a milk carton, and a wick. Melt the drippings down and ask the child what is it that they want the candle to help them with (like homework, being nicer to other children, etc). Then, add a few herbs or herbal oils to represent the child's request, (such as rosemary to help them remember their chores) explaining what you are doing as you do it. Children are much more sophisticated than we give them credit for, even at a early age, and will remember a great deal of what you tell them.

Pour the wax into the milk carton to let harden. When completely cool, just cut away the carton. Then, the next time your child is having trouble with that portion of their lives, light the candle for them, saying that the flame is a reminder of what they need to do/learn. When it is time to blow it out (when you feel the lesson is understood), let the child perform this final function. You may even wish for him/her to dismiss the quarters (or guardians of the magical circle) with a simple, "Goodbye and thanks for coming, blessed be," so they start to understand the basics of ritual.

Obviously, children's rituals need to be simple and use words they understand. Every time I do a little home ritual now, it is Karl's job to dismiss the quarters and blow out the candles in that manner. He loves it, feels more a part of what I am doing, and I think it makes our rituals even more special.

Crystal Balls

There are several things that make good scrying balls for children. One is the old pieces of hand blown glass which sometimes wash on shore from fishermen's nets. These pieces of smooth glass are supposed to trap bad feelings inside of them. If you are fortunate enough to find one at the beach, keep it and allow your child to daydream with it or hold it when they are sad.

An alternative to this are the small tumbled stones available at most New Age stores and certain science museums. They are very reasonably priced and children love their texture. Let the children pick one out for themselves. They have a natural aptitude for knowing what they need with out actually "knowing" it. Other scrying devices that may be used include the sea at night (especially if the water is calm and flat, like a mirror), any smokey glass you have in the home, a foggy mirror, an Etch-A-Sketch®, marbles, etc.

A good time to begin teaching scrying is when your child loses a favored object. You can show them how to use the crystals to find it. Sit them down and let them stare at the crystal. They may find their eyes cross the first few tries, but encourage them to keep trying. Tell them to think about what was lost and when, watching the surface of the object for a picture, like on a television set. Have them think back over the steps they have taken that day, and see what happens. Until they know how to guard themselves, you will want to put up some protection for your child before working on this aspect of magic with them (white light is good). This is a good imaginative exercise that also teaches concentration and creative interaction.

Dancing, Singing, Music

> *But when thou joinest with the Nine,*
> *And all the powers of song combine,*
> *We listen here on earth:*
> *The dying tones that fill the air,*
> *They charm the ear of evening fair,*
> *From thee, Great God of Bards,*
> *Receive their heavenly birth.*
>
> —John Keats

Kids of every age and era relate well to music and movement. Sufi dancing, simple Circle dances and Native American dances seem to be the most fun for them, teaching them the elementary movements that help them to experience the rhythm of magic and of the universe first-hand.

The same principle applies to singing. There are hundreds of easy, repetitive Pagan songs that children can learn. By all means teach them! I think I would much rather hear Karl singing about corn and grain than ring around the rosie (which is a reference to a plague) any day. Sing the songs during car trips, chores, or just when you have quiet time together.

In the music department, look for tapes from Sesame Street and other non-sectarian, non-prejudicial companies so that they can enjoy playing them on their tape recorders. Some even offer personalized tapes with the names of friends and family included. Some, such as Kid Trax®, have music about how special each person is. Others have folk music and you will both enjoy singing with these tunes. With regard to instruments, the easiest type for anyone to learn is the mountain dulcimer, which just happened to have its origins in America around the turn of the century, thus making it perfect for this book. This is a long-bodied string instrument that is played in the lap by strumming, but is far simpler to master than a guitar, for example.

There is a wonderful company in Pennsylvania who not only reproduces the mountain dulcimer at reasonable prices, but also provides numbered music so that children and adults alike can enjoy playing familiar songs with little, if any, musical training! I purchased mine there, and have found they are durable, have a warm sound, and are also fairly child proof. Should you desire a catalogue or further information on this type of instrument, write to: Rocky Mountain Enterprises, 364 W. 13th Avenue, Homestead, PA 15120.

If you are feeling creative and would like to try a musical project with your child, here are some very simple methods to make musical instruments. Once they are completed, teach the children a song to practice with their new toy.

Guitar

To make this instrument, you will need a sturdy shoe box, the cardboard tube from paper towels, four big rubber bands, a pencil, scissors, and strong tape. Cut a large hole in the center of the shoe box's lid. This might be more easily achieved for the child if the parent uses a knife or gets the hole started.

Next, stretch your rubber bands around the box (A), about 1/2 inch apart. Place the pencil (unsharpened) under the rubber bands as shown at (B). Tape the tube to one end of the box (C) and it's ready to strum! A more complicated version of this may be made by cutting a long, flat piece of cardboard and using toothpicks for frets. In this instance, the rubber bands would go to the top of the cardboard as shown in (D).

Drum

To make a drum, you will need to have an empty oatmeal box or coffee can with a plastic lid. I prefer the oatmeal boxes because they have no sharp edges. Get a long piece of string (tied in a loop), some tape, paper, crayons and two spoons or chop sticks. Lay the loop of string over the open top of the box (A), then tape the top on tightly. Cut the paper to fit around the container (B). Have your child decorate this paper with drawings, then tape it in place. Spoons or chop sticks become your beaters!

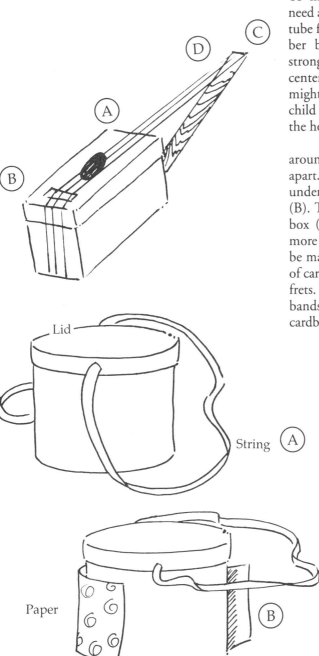

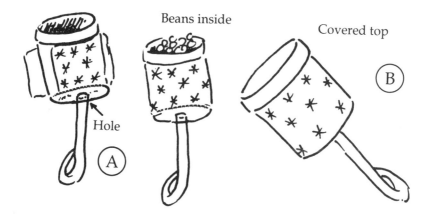

Beans inside

Covered top

Hole

Maracas

The simplest form of maraca is probably a dried gourd. In this instance, it is nice to have your child help plant and tend the gourds from spring until fall, so when it is ready to use, it will be something they have really helped create.

In winter months, however, when this is not practical, you can make maracas from two plastic spoons, two small containers with tops (such as from margarine or yogurt), dried beans, small pebbles and/or macaroni, glue, paper, and crayons. Begin by covering your containers with decorated paper and gluing that paper in place. Next place a small hole in the bottom of each container and place the spoon in them for a handle as shown in (A). Fill your container with whatever you have found to sound like a rattle and put the cover on (B). Tape or glue this in place and your maracas are finished.

Egg Potpourri

During the winter months, many of your child's friends will come down with the flu or other malady. You can help them make gifts for their sick friends. This fun project begins with the empty plastic "eggs" in which certain pantyhose are sold. Start by poking holes all over both parts of the "egg" with a warm needle or nail. Then get your child to cover both sides of the egg with cloth or paper, gluing it securely in place.

Next, help them pick out a stuffing for the egg, explaining the significance of

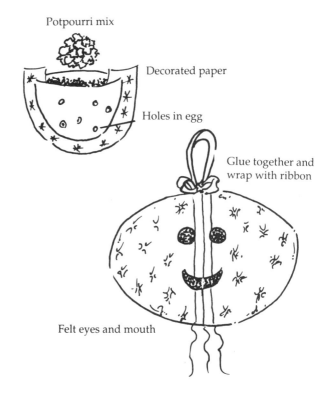

Potpourri mix

Decorated paper

Holes in egg

Glue together and wrap with ribbon

Felt eyes and mouth

certain herbs. For example, things like cedar and calendula for health, lavender for protection, lemon for cleansing and zest, and pine for hope are excellent choices. Place these herbs in the center of the egg and glue it shut. Then the child can cut out bits of ribbon, felt, and other creative decorations to finish the outside, including a loop at the top to hang it in their friend's room! From an adult standpoint, this little gift serves two functions; it cheers up the child and it also helps alleviate that "sick" smell in the room where they're resting. For the child making and giving the gift, it has the added satisfaction of feeling as if they have helped a friend.

Imaginary Friends

Don't dismiss those imaginary friends so quickly! Your child may be telling you many things. For one thing, this friend may or may not be imaginary; children are far more psychically open than adults. Also, what an imaginary friend says will often mirror what your child feels and is afraid to tell you directly. Imaginary or real, dreams or friends, these times of communication are terribly important between you and your child. Allow them to weave their stories, and watch their minds and imaginations grow. Show them that their words are important to you, and respond to those words. Magic can often begin in our dreams and our ability to go one step beyond reality, so let them begin now!

Graduation (Rite of Passage)

> *God offers to every mind the choice between truth and*
> *repose. Take which you please, you can never have both.*
> —R. E. Emerson

Every culture has a different way of marking a child's passage into adulthood. Today, for the most part, graduation from high school is the best time to have a ritual for the Rite of Passage.

The child should be as involved as possible in the planning process so that it is more personal and meaningful to them. Pictures marking various transitions in the child's life should be hung around the room, and incense of anise, apple, gardenia, and lotus burnt to bring joy, luck, psychic growth and positive spirituality to the graduate.

Since symbolically the individual will be entering the circle as a child and leaving as an adult participating member of the group, it is good if they can come in by one path and exit by another. During the ritual, they should be taken to each of the four cardinal points where an appropriately colored candle will be lit, and a lesson of that element imparted. These lessons should come from other members of the family or group whom they are close to. This movement around the Circle also marks their passage through time to the present.

The child should be allowed to choose or make their own robe for the occasion, and if they have decided to continue their magical training, magical tools might be blessed and given by the group/family at this time. If this is the case, it is also an appropriate time to share with the gathering their selected magical name and the story behind it.

Finally, the person graduating should be allowed to dismiss the quarters as their first act as an adult member of the group. This is a very important change for most young people. They have looked forward all their lives to adulthood, and now find that it awaits them with certain fears and responsibilities. Helping them to greet this new challenge among friends gets their new life off on the right foot.

Horsetail Flute

If you have a child who loves music, and I know few who don't, this is a wonderful project that will get them outside and leave them with a special toy at the end of the day.

Go to a place where you know beforehand that there are some horsetails and make a game of seeking them out. The treasure hunt idea works very well. Once your child has found one of a good size and length, help him/her cut it off. The stem will need to be cut with holes (like a flute) and then dried. Legend has it that once the flute has dried, its music can charm snakes. The tops of horsetails can also be used as a scrub brush when camping.

Nature Walks

Walks and reveries in natural settings were beloved by Victorians. Family and friends often joined each other in these excursions, and a picnic might be added in for good measure. Following their example, take your children to different natural settings to look for feathers, holy stones, to identify herbs, find old robin's eggs, or whatever. This is a good opportunity to teach them how to listen to the elements: the gentle whispers of the wind and the song of the waves are the easiest for children to notice quickly. Eventually, this listening exercise will give them a better feel for weather patterns and a stronger connection to Earth.

While you are out wandering around, watch for animals and insects which can teach a lesson. Ants, for example, show determination and strength. A humming bird teaches us that what we think is impossible, often isn't. Trees exhibit the need for strong foundations. In other words, there is a whole world around us waiting to share valuable lessons if we but open our eyes long enough to see.

Nursery Rhyme Chants

Children love nursery rhymes. They are easy to remember and can be used during play time for any number of games. Nursery rhymes offer us the opportunity to teach our children little chants to help them in their daily living too.

For example, we all know the saying, "See a penny, pick it up, all the day you'll have good luck." This can be employed just as it is to create a magical effect, but you can also change it to say, "Put a penny in your shoe, surely luck (peace, joy) will come to you!"

A perfect opportunity came to test this idea after Karl caught the chicken pox from me. He was having a terrible day with them and I finally convinced him to take an herb bath to make him feel better. While I washed him off, I began to say, "dots, dots go away, don't come back another day." I did this in a rhythmic manner touching each of the sores with oatmeal soap as I went. Karl thought this was great fun, and laughed for the first time in days. More importantly though, was the fact that I heard him repeating the phrase to himself later that day when he began to itch again. Obviously, the rhyme left an impression with him because it used his own words. Since that time I have heard him make his own revisions to the chant substituting things like "cold" for "dots."

Your chants do not have to be award-winning. Actually, keep them generic in nature so you don't get notes from the teacher about your child's religious beliefs. Also make them short, easy to remember with words that are natural to your child's age group.

Other adaptations of nursery rhymes include:

1. Sadness, sadness go away; joy, joy, come today!

2. _____ (insert child's name) be nimble, _____ be quick,_____ no longer wants to be sick!

3. _____ had a little cold that stuffed up his nose, I'll speak three times and try to rhyme, and the sickness, out it goes!

4. See a coin upon the ground, soon the sun will come around.

5. When I go to bed and sleep, I count my toys instead of sheep, so when I close my eyes in bed, only good things fill my head!

The possibilities here are endless. You can adapt almost any nursery rhyme to fit your child's situation. Once learned, they can sing it, repeat it while skipping rope or playing hop scotch, and all the while bring a little spark of enchantment to their day. By the way, these rhymes work equally well for us older kids too!

Participatory Stories

I have never found, in anything outside the four walls of my study,
An enjoyment equal to sitting at my writing desk with a clean page,
a new theme and a mind awake.

—Washington Irving

One way I have tried to encourage the growth of my son's creativity and teach him important lessons at the same time, is through participatory stories. This activity is usually done in bed, just before sleep. It begins by inventing a magical companion for the child, one who can change shape to be anything it wants. Then, you ask the child where they want to go and what they want to do in the story. A typical evening at my house might go like this:

Karl: "Blob and Karl go to Kathy's house to swim!"

Mom: "OK, Karl and mommy get in the car to go to Kathy's house."

Karl: "No! Kathy picks us up in the truck."

Mom: "OK, Kathy picks you, the blob and mommy up in the truck to go to her house and play. The blob needs feet to get in the truck, can he have some?"

Karl: "I gave him feet last night!" He was quite correct, I'd forgotten the blob grew feet in our last story.

Mom: "OK, what do you want to do at Kathy's?"

Karl: "Play hide and seek and swim in the pool."

Mom: "Hum . . . blob will need hands for swimming, can he have hands?"

Karl: "Yup." He motions to magically give the blob hands.

Mom: "Karl and the blob play all day then come home to go to sleep. Blob reminds Karl to brush his teeth before bed. Did you remember?"

Karl: "No . . . I do it now!"

This little scenario illustrates a very mundane lesson. I happen to be having some trouble getting Karl to remember to brush his teeth. By having the instruction come from his magical story companion, it was far better received and much more effective. These stories can work in the same way for nail biting, closing doors, and other little lessons that we get tired of yelling about. Teaching in this fashion becomes fun, and helps build the interaction between you, your child, and their imagination in a positive manner.

Rituals (General)

No man manages his affairs as well as a tree does.
—George Bernard Shaw

How can a child help with rituals? Many ways. Perhaps they can assist with set up, making decorations, blowing out candles, sharing their talents with music or words, or whatever. I firmly believe that our children need to feel welcome in our circles as active participants instead of pests. Obviously, more serious moments may not allow for the youth to always be present, so in this instance I suggest that members of the group take turns caring for the kids, not unlike Sunday School.

If, for whatever reason, your group never allows children at rituals, I propose considering separate rituals that the kids can help design. One such ritual I helped create for The Aquarian Church in Texas was a variation of a druidic tradition of sharing your soul with a tree for a year. To open the ritual, the children would stand hand-in-hand in the woods. Four children who are among the oldest can wait in their respective directions outside the circle. The oldest child should be in the center to direct the ceremony.

To begin, have the children close their eyes, take a deep breath and listen to the words being spoken. Tell them to feel the energy of the Watchtowers as they are called. The child in the East will start walking the circle clockwise with stick incense saying, "Greetings to you, Guardian of the Air. We thank you for joining us on this special day. Let your refreshing winds blow over us and free our spirit. Protect us from all dangers coming from the East. So mote it be." The child should douse the incense in the ground and join the circle.

The child at the Southern point follows next (with a smudge stick) and walks the circle as before, drawing a pentagram over each child as they go saying, "Greetings to you Guardian of the Fires. Thank you for coming to our circle. Cleanse and heal us that our magic can be pure and filled with light. Protect us from all danger approaching from the South. So mote it be." The smudge stick should be extinguished and the child now joins the circle.

The Western point should have a shell full of water. As he or she walks, the water is sprinkled on each person in the circle saying, "Greetings to you, Lady of Water. Thank you for pouring from your cup today. Let us be touched by your warm, soft waves as you protect us from all danger approaching from the West. I now give back to the Earth the bounty you give us. So mote it be." The child then pours the remaining water on the ground before joining the circle.

The child at the Northern point has a clay pot full of rich soil (mixed with salt) that is sprinkled on the ground as these words are spoken, "Greetings to you Earth Mother. Thank you for giving us a place to grow and learn. As we bring our spirits to the trees you have grown with care, we ask your blessing and protection from any danger approaching from the North. So mote it be." The pot is then set back on the Northern point and the child joins the circle.

The priest/ess should have a staff of some kind, but any fallen branch will do. She or he should raise it high saying, "Children of this circle, join with me one-by-one, till the golden flower blooms that brings the light of suns. Let us join our hands and bring our circle round, to share our magic with the land, all evil being bound. We call the Guardians of the Winds to wrap us in their arms. Keeping all within the circle, safe from any harm. So mote it be."

All the children can now be called to sit or kneel for a brief guided meditation done by a parent. "Imagine in your mind that you are a great, strong tree with branches stretching for sunlight like a cat in a sun puddle. Feel your leaves move with the wind, your roots growing into rich soil. Feel the water move to your roots, cool and fresh. Feel the warm sun pouring over your leaves. Your body is that tree. It is strong, growing, and firmly rooted in rich soil. Within this tree, your spirit moves free like the winds. Now go into the garden of the woods, and find your tree. Feel the earth as you move, listen to the trees and their voices. Find the one that sings a song you know. That is where you plant your spirit to grow with the Earth."

Next, the children can move into the woods, the younger ones guided by an adult to help them. A rune or other personal item should be planted underneath the tree they choose. The older children might like to sit and commune with their tree, then return to share the experience. The younger children should be allowed to play during this time so they don't get restless. The circle is then dismissed in whatever manner the priest/ess feels appropriate and a family picnic can begin, provided by all participating members. This entire day then becomes a way of guiding children through magic and self discovery.

There are many other ways to help youngsters to understand the meaning of services. In fall, let them say good by to the sun and welcome the snow or rain. In the winter, teach them about hibernation, the need for rest and how things continue to grow in the Earth even when they look dead. Come spring, get them outside to watch flowers diligently pushing their blossoms through the soil. The cycles of magic do not need to be fancy. For the young, life itself is an adventure and all you need do is help them experience it.

Runes and Tarot Cards

If your child wants to have a set of runes, they can be made from many different items. Find a recipe for salt dough, or go out and pick up similar size pebbles at the beach or in the woods, or even use modeling clay. Once there are enough made or collected, you can give the child paints and show them pictures of the runes. I suggest doing one or two a day so you can take the time to explain the symbolism of each rune (stories work much better). If you are making the rune which symbolizes "flow," tell them about a nearby creek and how the water is always moving, slowly breaking apart large stones and carrying them elsewhere. Make your stories strongly visual and full of action. Often kids will remember part of the stories and ask for more at bedtime.

As for Tarot cards, you can either make a set from cardboard scraps, or 3 x 5 cards, or even buy a blank set at a New Age store. I suggest that these not be attempted with a child under 10 years of age. If they are 10 years old, they are beginning to really understand how symbolism works, so the process of teaching the cards is easier. Allow them to choose the color of the suits, then discuss one card at a time while they create it. It helps to have a couple of different decks to show them, and to explain the symbols in each card. Geometrical designs, flowers, animals, trees and other themes which they are familiar with work very well for the base structure of the cards.

Remember not to assume anything. Begin with the four suits of the Tarot and their meaning, then ask what they would like to use to portray these things. Once you have that to work with, you can help them build in the other emblems (numbers, people, runes etc.) into each card until their vision is literally transformed from mind to paper. GO SLOWLY, do not rush them and try not to push the creative process. Children will often think about things for some time before acting on them, sorting out the details so they make sense to their own mind.

Like other things in this chapter, the process is really more important here than having an artistically "perfect" deck when the child is done. First and foremost, this helps improve communication and understanding between you and your child. Secondly, it helps them to think about many different types of human experiences and how they relate to them personally. Lastly, they have the opportunity to originate symbols to reflect their feelings on these matters. I think you will find you learn as much, if not more, than they do from the experience.

Seasonal Decorations/Observations

Don't overlook the learning opportunity that holidays present. The Victorians loved their holidays, and much of the traditions regarding holidays centered around their children (see also Chapter Three). In this manner they (and we) could use the seasons to help children become more aware of time and its passing, and also the significance of holidays in various other traditions.

For the modern child, it becomes especially important for them to understand both the Christian and Pagan holidays because the two are closely intertwined, and because children are growing up in a predominantly Christian atmosphere in the United States. They are going to have to grapple with playmates who do not understand why "Jonny's" and "Jane's" family don't have mangers in the house at Christmas time, nor do they attend a local church. You need to begin to furnish them with answers and belay their concerns early in life. It's not easy being different.

To help, let your children collect or make seasonal decorations such as the Yule log, Eostre eggs, and corn dolls. Or perhaps they can cook a special meal or dessert, and work on seasonal projects that can be used in the family rituals. All the while, let them ask questions to their heart's content about what you are celebrating and why. In this regard, do your best to instill tolerance spiced with knowledge into your children. They are our future, and if religious wars are to ever end, it will begin with understanding in them. Teach love, respect, and common sense and let them come to their own conclusions about different faiths later. Right now it's most important that they learn about being "good people."

Smudge Sticks

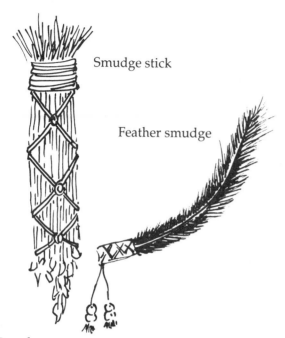

Smudge stick

Feather smudge

It is an easy project to make a smudge stick or feather for magical use. If you have access to freshly dried sage or lavender, you can help the children bind them together decoratively as gifts for other Pagan/Wiccan friends and relatives. Make sure the sage is squeezed together tightly and then kept that way by binding it with string that is knotted and criss-crossed all the way up the stick. This allows it to burn more evenly.

Likewise, if they find a good size fallen feather, a little cloth wrap can be added to the base, along with a leather thong and a few beads to make a perfect smudge feather for the child to add to their tool collection.

Snacks

Every parent in the world looks for snacks that are fairly good for their children. Much to my amusement, my son likes pickles, radishes, carrots, and little white onions fresh from the garden as treats. Since all parents are not that fortunate, how about trying carrot cake, zucchini muffins, pumpkin cookies, potato pancakes that have been formed into various letters of the alphabet, fruit in season, etc. I have also listed below four Victorian recipes which are fun for the children to experience and a little more healthy than chocolate bars.

Rose Petal Candy

Dissolve 2 ounces of gum arabic in 1/2 pint of water. Place the petals of fresh roses on a cookie sheet and sprinkle them with this water and a little sugar. They should be allowed to dry for 24 hours, then be placed on a plate that can withstand heat. Boil 1 pound of sugar in 1/2 pint of water until it threads off a spoon. Keep this mixture well skimmed. Tint it with a little red food coloring and pour it over the petals. This should sit for another day, then be placed in a warm oven until dry.

Rose Tobacco

This is a favorite Victorian edible for children in the summer. Take June roses and pack them in stone jars, layering the petals with brown or maple sugar. This confection could then be cut off a bit at a time and eaten in tiny quantities for months to come.

Citrus Rind Candy

This candy can be made with grapefruit, lemon, lime, oranges, and tangerines. The larger the fruit, the easier they are to peel and cook. Make length-wise cuts in the rinds and remove them from the fruit. Put them in cold water and bring to a slow boil. Reduce heat and simmer until the peel becomes soft. Drain off your water, and remove the whitish lining from the pieces, then cut them into narrow strips.

These pieces are returned to the pan with 1 cup of sugar, 1/2 cup water (proportions are for 4 large oranges) and 2 tablespoons of corn syrup. All of this is cooked over a low flame until it reaches 240 degrees. Remove the peels one by one, and place them to cool on plates. When they are touchable, roll them in granulated sugar and store them in layers of waxed paper.

Zwieback Toast

Zwieback toast became popular for infants in the late 19th century and was also recommended for breakfast. It is low in sugar, can be frozen, and has a very long shelf life.

1/2 cup sugar	3/4 cup butter
3 eggs	1/2 teaspoon vanilla
3 cups flour	1 tablespoon baking powder
1/2 teaspoon salt	2 tablespoons lemon rind
1 tablespoon orange rind	1 teaspoon mace

Cream together the butter and sugar until fluffy, then add 1 egg at a time and the vanilla. Mix all the dry ingredients together slowly, stirring this into the butter mixture. Form this dough into a ball and chill for about 45 minutes.

Divide the dough four times and shape into 1-inch thick logs. Place these well apart on a greased cookie sheet and flatten them to less than one inch thick. Bake at 350 degrees for 10 to 15 minutes, remove and cool. Cut the loaves crosswise into slices and arrange these slices cut side down on the greased sheet. Bake again for about 20 minutes until golden and dry.

Spirit Bags

This is a fun project which can be easily adjusted for almost any age child. For younger ones, use felt, glue, and yarn to make a little bag to be worn at the neck or connected to a belt. The child can decorate the felt in any manner. For older children, who are able to handle a needle, allow them to sew fabric together with leather thonging.

A spirit bag would traditionally carry a carving of a totem in it, but for children it can hold anything that is really special to them. A pebble, piece of egg, a leaf, or other items found on family trips become their treasures, the things that make them feel good.

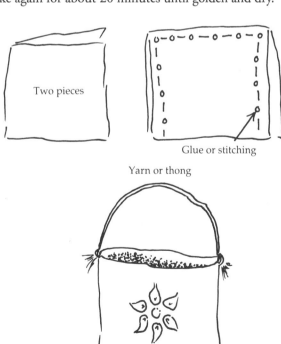

Two pieces

Glue or stitching

Yarn or thong

Explain a little about the life energy in all things as they make their bags, and how carrying the bags will keep love, peace, and joy close to them, just like the memories of which the objects remind them.

Thistle Walking Stick

True humanity, I believe, is our nearest approach to Divinity.
—Oliver W. Holmes

In England, the wizards of old were said to select the tallest thistle and use it as a magic wand or walking stick. Traditionally the thistle is a symbol of strength or a symbol of hex-breaking. For children, it might stand for not giving in to peer pressure.

When you feel your child needs strength, tell him/her the story of the thistle, then go together to get one for him/her to carry. While you look, discuss the problems and how they are feeling. Your love and interest will do more good than the walking stick, but it will become a long cherished reminder of that special day.

Tools

If your child is ready to begin working with traditional Craft tools, but you want something they can relate to (and which is not overly breakable) how about the following ideas:

Cups

Use seashells, wooden bowls, sake cups, a coconut shell.

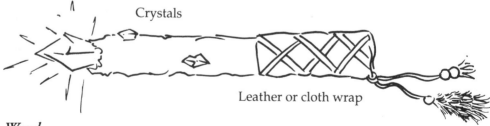

Folded aluminum foil

Wood

Athame

Help them make one from aluminum foil with a branch for a handle.

Crystals

Leather or cloth wrap

Wand

Use wooden dowels, fallen branches, or small copper tubing and decorate them with feathers, beads, crystals, paints, buttons, etc.

Pentagram

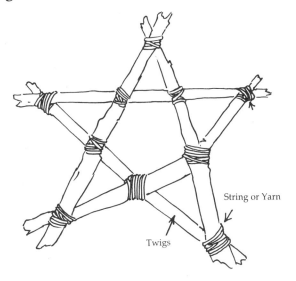

String or Yarn

Twigs

You can draw one, glue one together with Popsicle® sticks, or tie fallen branches together with colorful thread and garnish with seasonal decorations.

Censer

Since you don't want them playing with fire, why not some scented potpourri you can help them make in advance.

Totem Mask

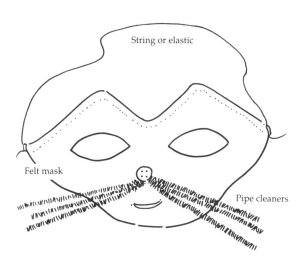

String or elastic

Felt mask

Pipe cleaners

This activity is better for older children who can answer the question, "If you were an animal, what would you be and why?" Once this has been discussed, the youngsters can take cardboard, scraps of fabric, sequins, glitter, glue, and other materials to make a mask of that animal for themselves.

This project is just a simple introduction to the idea of animal friends and helpers and the lessons that they teach, so keep it simple. Tell them a little about how animals sense things differently than humans, and how we can learn from their instincts (more information on animals can be found in the next chapter).

What Makes You?

> *Rather than love, than money, than fame, give me truth.*
> —Henry David Thoreau

A nice verbal game for younger children is one where they have to answer questions. Their answers will often give you a good indication of what you and society has instilled in them already. For example, to the question, "What makes you rich?" most children will promptly answer money. Then, you can explain that money buys things, but it is love that really makes us rich. "What makes you strong?" Well, Karl usually says spinach (which isn't a bad answer) but how about friends?

You can think up lots of questions for this game, and if you are really creative, have a little fable to go with the question to help them see a more positive answer than they get from TV. This game is especially good for long road trips, right along side of count-the-cows game and find-the-letters.

> *Every morning is a cheerful invitation*
> *to make my life of equal simplicity.*
> —Henry David Thoreau

Tyger, Tyger, burning bright
In the forests of the night
What immortal hand or eye
Would frame thy fearful symmetry?
— William Blake

CHAPTER TWELVE

Fur, Feather, and Fin: Animals in Magic and Natural Pet Care

Be still, wild music is abroad.
—Henry Wadsworth Longfellow

Just as the role of a child was changing, so was an animal's place in the Victorian era. The household pet was no longer considered a living doll, but an object of love and sentiment. Through pets, youngsters learned about emotion. At night, prayers for their pet could be heard in almost every home and people often insisted on decent burials when a beloved animal died.

With this change in attitude, the concern over animal welfare increased drastically. The Society for the Prevention of Cruelty to Animals was founded in 1845, feminists being the driving force behind the organization. With expanding humanitarian sentiments, the extension of veterinary medicine was encouraged. Eventually the idea that pets needed man faded to us needing them.

Cats, dogs, and birds—especially nightingales, which were signs of virtue and sensitivity—were favored in the Victorian household. Pets were especially important to the elderly, who adopted them to replace a lost mate, often giving the animal the same name! This nostalgia extended itself into pet broaches, pet portraits, animal charms for bracelets, and hat pins. It was also exhibited in many types of ornamentation around the house.

ANIMALS AT HOME

And feel a kindred spirit to my own,
So that henceforth I worked no more alone.
—Robert Frost

By examining our modes of speech today, we can quickly see how animals have affected our lives as much as those of our ancestors. We talk about people being brave as lions, strong as bears, busy as bees, and spineless as a worm. We also discuss playing possum, being licked into shape, eating like a bird, or giving our swan song! On the home front these expressions often find a place right along side our pets.

Throughout history, and in every culture, we see an adoration of animals. The Mexicans kept hummingbirds, the Japanese had crickets, and in Egypt the cat was venerated as a God. Somehow these creatures satisfy a need in humanity for total, unconditional acceptance. Perhaps it is because of this that pets seem to improve our lives, not only emotionally, but physically. It is now believed that stroking an animal lowers the blood pressure and can actually help prolong life.

First Aid

In return for the love and joy animals give us, we do our best to keep them happy and healthy. There are times, though, when our efforts fail and a pet becomes ill. In the Victorian era, the animal body, like the human one, was also attended to by the wife. In the case of livestock, a nearby vet may have been called in to be certain no disease was present which could spread to other animals. The kind of care these creatures received directly reflected the fact that they were still an important means of getting food and money for the home. While farming and the raising of animals is nowhere near the industry it used to be, the pet commerce today is highly lucrative. Today, pure breeds and other pets that are less common are more popular, but no matter the type of animal, our concern for them and the place they take in our hearts is just as strong as it was for our Victorian fellows.

If an emergency arises with your animal(s) and you cannot immediately get to a vet, it is best to have someone call their office and get verbal instructions over the phone for first aid. When a phone is not available, keep the animal warm and comfortable, applying the following care as applicable. You may also want to invest in a good, illustrated book of pet first aid to help guide you.

Bleeding

In all instances of bleeding, you need to apply pressure to the wounded area. If pressure does not slow the blood flow, you may need to take a scrap of fabric and tie it fairly tightly just above the wound. Should you have to keep this on for more than twenty minutes, loosen it a little to allow the blood to flow to the limb. Continue in this manner until help arrives or is reached.

Breathing

Check to be sure there is nothing visible lodged in the animal's mouth or throat. You can perform artificial respiration by placing your mouth over the animals mouth and nose and exhaling until the animal's chest is seen to be expanding.

Broken Bones

Never attempt to set a bone yourself. Instead, gently splint the limb, wrap it with cloth, and get the animal to professional care as soon as possible. Try to keep them from moving too much to avoid risking further damage.

Burns

Burns should be flushed with cool water to get out any dirt, then wrapped in clean cloth until you take the animal in.

Choking

Wait a minute and watch. Most animals can dislodge foreign objects themselves. If they cannot, see if you can remove the object with your fingers or tweezers. The Heimlich maneuver will work on pets, but you need to take care not to crack a rib.

Constipation

A spoonful of mineral oil, milk of magnesia, or powdered milk will often help, as will adding some graham crackers to their diet.

Cuts

For minor cuts, no treatment is usually necessary. If the cuts are more severe, call the vet to see if any stitches are needed or for other instructions. Clean gauze (wrapped securely) will help protect the injury from infection, but watch so that your pet does not try to chew it off, irritating the cut in the process.

Fits

Roll the animal in a blanket and let it work itself out. While this is going on, try to think over the last few days to see if your pet has exhibited any odd behavior, eaten anything unusual, etc. Your vet will need to know this for further treatment.

Also, realize your pet is not in control when this happens. They are frightened, so a soothing voice will at least let them know they are not alone. Speak in low, calm tones and stroke their head (if possible) until the fit has passed, then take them as soon as possible to your vet for examination.

Heat

In the summer months, heat can exhaust your pet just as it can you. If you notice that they seem to be panting more than usual and are weak, try to get them to a cool spot immediately. Give them water in small amounts, a little at a time, and bathe them with a cool cloth. A reminder here that a consistent supply of fresh water is important to your pet's health.

Poison

If your pet has swallowed a caustic substance, give them milk or egg whites to help absorb the toxin. Do not try to get them to vomit, as this will cause even more damage. Be sure to take the container which held the poison (if you have it) so that your vet can administer more specific care.

If you do not know what your pet has ingested, use of the egg whites is still helpful in absorbing the toxin until help can be reached. If your pet begins to vomit, make sure you keep them well supplied with water in small amounts to keep them from dehydrating.

Porcupine Quills

Pull these out as soon as you can, and quickly. Pliers often work, and you will most likely need the aid of someone else to hold the animal still. You will still want to have your pet examined by the vet afterwards.

Skunk Spray

While this is not always an emergency, it is terribly uncomfortable for both the pet and owner. To help alleviate the stench, bathe the animal in tomato juice and a touch of lemon. Rinse, soap, and repeat as necessary.

Flea Control

In order to make your life, and that of your pet, more comfortable, it is important to do proper preventative maintenance against parasites, such as fleas and ticks. Fortunately, the pet industry is recognizing the need to return to natural forms of control, which are healthier for both the animal and the environment. Here are some hints to try at home:

❧ One popular Victorian method was to take a cord and dab it with lavender and mint, or pennyroyal. The cord was placed around the pet's neck.

❧ Brush their fur twice a week during flea season with a tincture of fennel and pennyroyal.

❧ Sprinkle their food three times a week with brewer's yeast and garlic powder (not salt). This produces a smell in the animal's skin which fleas do not like.

❧ Place aromatic herbs such as mint, eucalyptus leaves, and fennel under rugs or inside cushions, where animals cannot reach them. Fleas do not like strong-smelling herbs, yet these herbs do not create unpleasant odors in the house. You can also make a powdered version of these herbs and sprinkle your rugs with any of them before vacuuming to act as a deodorizer and flea preventative.

❧ Many health food stores, cooperatives, and mail order services now offer chemical-free flea collars and sprays for both dogs and cats. Call your vet or local pet shop to see if they can direct you to these sources.

❧ Pay attention to the flea season in your climate. Begin prevention at least two weeks before it starts, and continue until two weeks after the first good frost. Make sure to wash your pet's sleeping area every week to get any flea and tick eggs out of their mats. Be sure to read directions for whatever forms of prevention you are taking. Some commercial sprays are toxic to the animals, and you will need to close off rooms from them until it dries.

❧ When spraying or placing herbs, do not neglect any portion of your house where your pet spends time, including the box springs and mattresses. Fleas love to nest where it is warm.

Healthful Hints and Miscellaneous Information

During my research for this chapter, I came across some interesting snippets of information on animals, as well as some important facts that are useful to pet owners, especially those new to the wonders of owning an animal. Some are bits of trivia, but others may prove significant in understanding your pet and keeping them healthy:

❧ Go to several veterinarians before choosing one. I had a very negative experience once when I went to a random vet in an emergency situation. Sadly, in this instance the animal died because of an improper, hastily made diagnosis. In all fairness to the veterinary community, I know this was an unusual occurrence, but it made me realize the importance of knowing your animal's doctor. Like any medical service you would need for yourself, your pet should likewise be considered. Find a clinic you know you can trust and one with which you would feel comfortable if you had to board your pet there. Check their records with the Better Business Bureau and shop around until you find a caring, professional facility. If possible, get recommendations from friends who also have pets.

❧ Left-over egg whites placed on your cat's or dog's food periodically will help keep their coat shiny and healthy.

❧ Animals do not see well in perfect darkness. They need some source of light, and when that is not available they use the sense of smell and touch to aid them. Cats' whiskers, for example, grow to the width of their body to tell them if they can get through a specific area.

❧ Allowing your dog or cat to eat a little fresh garlic will often prevent worms and ward off fleas.

❧ Vaseline® or vinegar can often loose ticks from the skin of a pet. These are also useful in ridding the fur of sticky substances. Smear a little on the fur and work it in like a good shampoo, then brush the fur briskly, making sure to remove any parasites as you go.

❧ Sugar is not good for your pet, and in larger quantities can even be lethal. Keep them away from chocolate and other sweets, especially from the hands of children.

❧ Ask your vet about nutritionally balanced foods. They will be able to tell you which commercial foods are considered best for your pet, or offer you specialized products directly through their office. Do not feed an animal table scraps in any great quantity, as it can make them very ill.

❧ There is no reliable test of pets' noses. A perfectly healthy animal may exhibit a dry, warm nose. The key here is watching the pet for other signs of sickness. If their noses are dry and they are lethargic, or showing other symptoms, you should call your vet for advice.

❧ Aristotle believed that animals and people tend to look and act like each other.

❧ Animals have their own ranking system both in the wild and in a home. When introducing a new pet to your household, realize there will be some tension between the animals until the pecking order is established. Do not force the animals to be together, but instead let them find their own way of getting acquainted. Each cat in my home reacts slightly differently to a new animal according to his or her personality.

❧ Generally speaking I have found that young animals are more easily integrated into a home than a full-grown stray. Animals have protective instincts regarding the young, just as people do, which makes it easier to introduce a "baby" than an adult animal who is viewed as a territorial threat.

❧ Play is as important to young animals as it is to children, along with exercise.

❧ Animals do have physical languages which express much to the observant eye. Examples are the tail tucked between the legs in shame, purring in pleasure, large eyes full of desire, etc. Watch these and learn them so you know what your pet is trying to communicate to you.

❧ The desire of your pet to please you is the most powerful tool for training. Remember that animals respond to your voice, facial expressions, and body language, so try to keep them consistent for each command.

❧ During training, correction must be done immediately if it is to be effective. Do not continue to ignore your pet for hours after a mistake. They will not know what they are being punished for.

❧ Check your pet shop carefully to be certain the animals are maintained properly. Once a pet is purchased, take them to the vet for immediate inspection, and advice on healthful care. Many pet stores, at least here in Buffalo, now include free veterinary visits and first shots with the animal's price to insure their health. Ask about this policy in advance, as usually the appointment must take place within 7 days after purchase.

Poisonous Plants

There are many plants in and around the home that may prove harmful to your pet. Just as you might childproof your home, you also need to take care that your house is safe for your animals, both inside and out. Here is a list of some common plants which may make your pet ill if ingested:

Angelica	**Juniper**
Buttercup — Leaves or bark	**Marigold** — Whole plant
Cherry Leaves — Wild	**Morning Glory** — Roots and seeds
Daffodil — Bulbs	**Potato** — Sprouts
Foxglove	**Poinsettia** — Whole plant
Goldenseal	**Tansy**
Holly — Berries and leaves	**Tobacco** — Whole plant
English Ivy — Leaves and berries	**Walnut** — Green shell

Should you catch your pet nibbling on any of these items, call your vet and ask them what, if any, treatment should be given at home.

MAGIC FOR PETS

Really, there is no reason why you cannot do the same types of magic for pets as you do people. Whenever you feel they need something specific, bring a toy of theirs or a snippet of their hair into your sacred space (along with them, if possible), and allow the energy created to begin its work. Some people may laugh at this, thinking it silly to work magic for an animal, but being a pet owner myself, I know that it makes me feel better to have a healing ritual when one of my animal family members is sick. Somehow this, along with a prudent trip to the vet, gives me peace of mind, knowing I have done everything I can on all levels to help them. Also, since most animals respond naturally to magical energy in a positive manner, just being in the circle may be beneficial to their healing process.

A lion of flame, pressed to the point of love,
Yet moves gently among the birds.
—Theodore Roethke

Healing Ritual

Invocation
Call on God/ddess images who themselves have animal companions for their aid.

Prayer
> *Guardian of the animal spirits, we bring before you _____ to entrust to your care.*
> *Allow the natural recuperative powers of their body to be rejuvenated.*
> *Bring the light of warmth and comfort to them, along with waves of healing.*

Activities
Brown candles may be lit, with a picture of the animal at the center altar. Likenesses of other animals of a similar nature could be set at cardinal points for extra protection. If the pet is well enough to be with you in the sacred space, petting is an excellent means of channeling healing energy to the animal. As you move your hands, visualize a white-green light moving from your palm into the creature and smoothing its auric energy, much as you would your own (see *Crystal Body Meditation*.)

Tools and Ritual Components

Incense — Fennel for healing.

Anointing oil — Ginger for increasing health and strength.

Ritual bowl — Milk or water with a twist of lemon for purification.

> *Note:* A bowl has been substituted for the normal ritual cup in this chapter. A bowl is much more suitable to animals, and therefore a more powerful symbolic tool.

Protection Magic

✤ Elder flowers may be placed around your home to protect the animals within. Take freshly fallen sprigs from nearby trees (always thanking the tree for their gift) and attach a little piece of the pet's fur to it. In this manner you are symbolically "joining" the protective energy of the Elder to the animal(s). Then hide the Elder where it will not be disturbed.

✤ In Scotland, it was traditional on Beltane to pass animals through the smoke of their fires to insure their animals' health for another year. You may wish to do this at home with a little specially prepared incense, or a smudge stick fanned by a feather, so as not to frighten the animal. As you fan the smoke in their direction (make sure it is not overly pungent) visualize it carrying away any illness they may have.

✤ Amulets may be made for pets. They can then be hidden in their beds. Here are some suggestions for symbolic decorations for the amulets: draw paws at the four main points, and use the names of Gods and Goddesses who are aligned with the natural world around the outer circle. Runes of protection may decorate this piece of paper as well. Make sure it is placed where they won't chew or tear it up.

✤ You can place little blessed charms (which will not bother the animal) on their collar. To most people looking, it will appear like an ordinary ornament. For my cats, I use small silver bells which are charged with protective energy. They also double as a warning to me when one of them is getting too close to an open door.

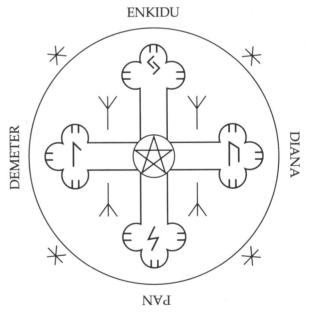

Insert the creature's name where the asterisk appears.

Along with these bells, I have a small heart-shaped tag with their name and phone number on it should they ever get lost. When I purchased these, I held them in my hands and envisioned our home with as many details as possible. As I did, I also chanted "come home," so that should the creature get out, the magic of the tag would help bring the pet back to us.

It's a nice way to live,
Just taking what nature is willing to give.
— Robert Frost

Pet Loss

The loss of a pet can be just as traumatic to an individual or family as the loss of a dear friend. Animals have the endearing ability to love and trust us without expectation. In the Victorian era, pet graves and funerals were not uncommon, especially for the elderly. Even for us more "modern" minded people, when that companionship is gone, there is a very real empty spot inside which we need to cope with in a constructive manner.

From my personal experience, whether the pet has died or wandered off, the nagging vacancy in and around your home is all too apparent. Last summer my son accidentally let my cat Py out of the house. We never found or saw him again. I cried for what seemed an eternity, which in itself is a healing process, but then I considered that no matter where Py was, I really wanted to say goodbye to him. He had been a faithful familiar for three years, and what seemed to bother me most was not seeing him, thanking him . . . before he left us.

I think this emotional state is common to pet owners, and because of this I would like to share with you a visualization that helped me through this difficult time. Begin in the area where you spent most of your time with the creature. Take their toys, a picture and other items which carry your pet's special energy. Get comfortable, close your eyes and begin breathing deeply. Try to settle your mind and heart, as hard as that might be to do.

Next, in your mind's eye, see your pet approach you in this space, just as it normally would have. What you are seeing is the spiritual energy of your animal. Don't be surprised at the reactions you have to this; it is a very emotional experience and should not be stifled. Open your arms and greet the animal. Give it a long, adoring embrace and speak all the feelings you have in your mind and heart. As you do, visualize these warm emotions as a red-purple light flowing from you to your spirit-pet. Continue until you feel relieved and less distressed.

When you are finished, release the spirit-pet and allow it to go it's own way. It may be reluctant to go, as pets hold a special love for their owners too, but encourage the transition. As the animal moves away, you may notice a line of energy connecting the two of you. If so, you must break that cord so you both can be free. I have found this often happens when there is a deep, abiding empathy between pet and owner.

When your spirit-pet is finally out of sight, visualize a white-green light pouring over you to wash away the sorrow. Continue in this manner as long as you wish, returning to normal awareness when you feel your message was received and understood. This visualization won't completely negate the loss you feel, only time can do that, but it will allow you those precious last moments together to share a special connection which time, space, life and death cannot take from you, the connection of love.

ANIMALS IN MAGIC

God had his dwelling in the sea, and was a fish therein.
— Kabbalah

Wild animals are healthier than humankind in general because they adjust to one type of environment and rarely stray from that. They have an uncomplicated way of simply being part of a scheme, moving with the land, and acting on instinct. It is these exact instincts in the wild or at home that we often admire and from which we can learn much.

Many of our Victorian ancestors knew animal behavior well and noted it carefully. For example, when there is an increase in static electricity, animals can be observed exhibiting behaviors that are different from their norm. They become more vocal, active, and often look for shelter from a storm. Even if the Victorians did not understand the scientific reasons for such behavior, it often gave them a clue to weather patterns or other natural occurrences. This kind of information was especially useful for farmers, and helped them to survive. For example, birds starting to sing later than usual in the morning may mean rain because it is the light which wakes them. A cloudy sky will delay this. Swallows will fly lower when conditions aloft force the insects down (rain or wind) and ants exhibit increased movement when the barometer is on the rise. Likewise, almost all animals will become panicked or act strangely just before a natural disaster.

With these abilities in mind, it is not difficult to see why animals and animals as symbols have been intricately woven into magic in many forms, even from the earliest of times.

Animal Symbolism

My soul is as a sacred bird.
— Hafiz, *Ode XIV*

Animals (and many other living things) appear in our dreams, in our speech, they come across our path, or make themselves known in our lives in any number of ways. When this happens repetitively or in a unique manner, we may need to consider if they are carrying a message for us. This message is personal in nature, thus subjective, but even so there seems to be some commonality we can draw on and consider in the symbolism.

Sometimes the theme is subtle, other times blatant, but there are ways of determining what the animal is symbolizing for you. By reviewing and combining Native American lore with Victorian dream analysis, with cliches and your personal inspiration, you can arrive at what could be considered a fairly universal interpretation of what you are experiencing. In some ways, understanding the meaning is not unlike doing a Tarot reading, only the object of your study is the creature which has come to you.

If you wish to explore animal symbolism further, I suggest the getting "The Medicine Card Deck" by David Carson and Jamie Sams. Also, study various resources concerning dream interpretation to discover further correspondences. Those given here should act as working examples, not carved-in-stone truths. Use your own vision and knowledge of the creatures, their habitats, and characteristics to help form a more rounded view.

Bear — Thoughtfulness, need for retreat, rebirth, rest, natural strength. A bear with a fish may indicate a windfall soon to come your way. If being hunted, it is a sign that you feel pressured and may need to "run away" for a while to get perspective. In hibernation, a hermetic stage, needed to refresh the well of self away from interference.

Bird — Movement, attitudes, perhaps the need for grounding. If the bird is moving with the wind, good fortune. Birds flying with you indicate new friends, and companions for a journey. A nesting bird may indicate a new home or family environment.

Cat — Aloofness, balance, wisdom, recuperative power, reincarnation. Catching a mouse may mean success, swift movement, or quick decisions, while a slumbering feline symbolizes a new sense of peacefulness settling into your life. A cat wandering your home nervously may warn you of unexpected guests or trouble. Also, the cat is a time honored symbol of magic. You may find your spiritual energy increasing!

Cow — Vitality, health, prosperity, life of the land. A rather mellow creature who always seems at peace, yet has the ability to vocalize when need be. The cow may teach us how to approach our faith with quiet persistence. A cow laying down is the sign of a storm ahead. In this case, watch for warnings that your health or financial stability may be at risk.

Deer — Gentleness, healing, connection to Earth and the forests. If being hunted—alertness, sure-footing. With young—productivity brought to any endeavor. Sleeping in the forest—assurance that calm will follow the storm.

Dog — Devotion, loyalty and total trust. Carrying a slipper—service and kindness. Running with a pack—social interaction and need for peer support. Playing with a child—a reminder of the need to express the child in all of us.

Dolphin — Life, breath, communion with nature, the purest of joys, protection, psychic awareness. Jumping—power balanced with grace and gentility. Rescuing a person at sea—compassion. In captivity—overcoming difficult circumstances.

Dragon — Ancient powers, intelligence, ferocity, air and fire magic. In a cave or lair—gathering of treasures. Hatching—the birth of new psychic abilities within yourself, growing inner strength. Flying—new perspectives.

Elephant — Memory, strength. With a pack—family ties. In a circus—being on display, lack of freedom, outside influences controlling your movements.

Fish — Fertility, plenty, the sea's bounty, currents and cycles. Swimming against the stream—struggle, determination, fortitude. On a hook—a situation which you feel incapable of escaping. In a tank—a picturesque situation which could ensnare you.

Fox — Camouflage, adaptation, cunning. Knowing the time and place for action. Moving through the woods—stealth, awareness of one's surroundings.

Goose — Luck, innocence. Laying an egg—a pleasant surprise; a golden egg—monetary improvement.

Horse — Strength, movement, grace, dignity. With a rider—a carrier of unexpected news. Lying down—death of an old way, loss of vitality, need for rest.

Lion — Ferocity. With a pride—group interaction or movement. Roaring—focus on verbal skills. Hunting—a search of some kind, usually within self, which takes energy and persistence to reach the end.

Mouse — Shyness, quiet, attention to detail, sneakiness. With a small piece of cheese—prudence. Captured by a cat—feeling as if the odds are overwhelming.

Otter — Playfulness, adventure, the magic of joy, youthful exuberance, zeal. In water—you are in your "element" and have found a real place either personally or professionally.

Owl — Wisdom, the arts, watchfulness, night magics, a messenger of Athena. Hooting—a harbinger, usually a warning to be aware of hidden matters. If the owl flies into your life, you may want to spend some time working moon rituals, especially those related to creative endeavors.

Pelican — Self sacrifice, storage, possibly the need to watch your words.

Phoenix — Overcoming impossible odds, reincarnation, new life/cycles, cleansing energy of fire. Usually an indication of a totally new direction in your life, be it a job, relationship, or attitude.

Rabbit — Releasing fear, overcoming the past, resolution to change. With baby bunnies—fertility, creativity often directly pertaining to conception. If drawn out of a magician's hat—miracles, sudden resolution to a difficult problem.

Squirrel — Conservation, storage. Gathering nuts—a caution to take care with your personal energy or resources. Sometimes an indication that your thought process has been scattered.

Swan — Self transformation, self images, intuition, sensitivity, empathy, moon magics. The swan is the glorious Godself within each "ugly duckling."

Toads — Healing magic, faith, miracles. Turning into a Prince—a surprising love affair.

Turtle — Slow progress, retreat, grounding, chastity, conservation. With head in shell—an indication that you may have withdrawn emotionally from a situation or the need a "hermetic" time alone. Upside down—lack of mobility, stagnation.

Unicorn — Spirit of purity, innocence and childhood. The magic of nature, power of light. If a unicorn approaches you in a dream, hold out your hand and see what wonders come your way!

Whale — Ancient knowledge, sound awareness. Breaching the water—psychic development, sometimes astounding in nature.

Wolf — A pathfinder, psychic energy, inner Divinity, teaching, and careful study.

But upward strained the swan, towards the sky above
the crab kept stepping back, the pike was for the pond.
— Ivan Krylow

As a reminder, teachers from the natural world do not have to be animals. A stone you trip over might speak to you of grounding. A nearby tree might sing of foundations, gathering water for the well of self and the awareness of seasons. Storms remind us of nature's abundance, her power and our need for change and cleansing. No matter what it is that you discover is trying to share insights with you, try to be open to the lesson. When an object or animal offers itself as a helper, you may accept or deny that assistance, but how this decision affects your spiritual growth can be significant. Enjoy the classroom of Earth!

Elemental Correspondence

If you want to use animal carvings or pictures to aid your magic, and desire to apply their elemental correspondence, (perhaps to decorate your cardinal points or altar), I have provided a brief list of examples. Obviously, if a creature lives in a specific environment, they will be far more attuned to that element. Others, who exist on both land and sea, or who seem to have a combination of fire and water as part of their lives (like the eel), will blend the power of more than one element together. The first element you think of when a specific creature comes to mind will usually be the most powerful of icons to use in your magic.

Earth — Snakes, rabbits, cows, gophers, deer, moles, ferrets, mice, many forest dwelling animals.

Air — Most birds, flying fish, butterflies, dragonflies, ladybugs, bees and other winged creatures.

Fire — Scorpions, lions, lizards, horses, desert creatures, electric eels, and any creatures with fiery stings.

Water — Fish, seahorses, dolphins, seals, walruses, crabs, sea gulls, whales, ducks, and beavers.

Ether/Spirit — Any creature of myth, lore and legend.

Finding Familiars

Old German sorceresses used, on occasion,
to change themselves into cats.
> —Ernest Jones

Finding a familiar is a wonderful experience. Suddenly you have a kinship and a link with a living creature unlike anything you ever expected. While cats and birds are probably the most common familiars due to their natural sensitivity to energy, any living creature can potentially become a magical partner and guide.

Sometimes the familiar will find you. Perhaps a stray cat or dog comes to your home and the two of you have an immediate rapport. Later, the creature is always nearby when you are working magic and you notice that their interest continues to grow. These are positive signs that your familiar has come to you. Sometimes the animal will even mark you as their human by rubbing oil glands against your skin. This is especially true with cats. As time goes on you may even find that you can communicate rudimentary ideas to your familiar (and they to you) by simple projected images, or by learning their language. I know that some people will scoff at  this notion, but I have a cat who responds to his name, calls me to come to bed, and who will also answer if I called him with a specific "meow" that mimics his own.

If you are not fortunate enough to have such a creature in your life, but desire one, there are several things you need to know. Do not have any expectations about what form your familiar will take. An animal will respond to your energy and call, but you may be surprised by which type of animal it turns out to be. Next realize that in no way is a familiar a pet. Do not talk down to it as you would a child, but communicate with it as a trusted friend. Once you feel fairly certain that the animal which has come into your life is becoming a familiar (or magical companion), it is nice to give them a token to mark them as such, like a special collar with magical symbols on it. I also highly recommend a tag with your phone number in case the creature should ever wander off accidentally. On the other hand, if a familiar seems to leave of its own accord, you may have to simply let it go. Familiars have their own path to follow, which must be respected.

Interestingly enough, most familiars will reflect the moods and attitudes of their human counterparts. They will also act as early warning systems of untoward energy coming your way. I have noticed that our cats get nervous and uneasy when something is about to go wrong. Our cats, and especially our dog, are far more aware of people I should not trust easily. When I don't pay attention to their signals, more often than not, I am sorry.

The most powerful force between you and your familiar is love. There is an connection here that goes beyond the normal owner-pet attachments. It is spiritual, warm, and trusting. In some ways, the love of a familiar even rivals that of a human because this animal has no expectations or prejudices, but simply believes in and accepts you as you are. Likewise, when they lend their energy to magic, it makes the experience a delightful blend of humankind and nature working in harmony.

The Call for a Familiar

He purrs in thankfulness when God tells him he's a good cat.
—Christopher Smart

To send out the call for a familiar is not unlike leaving a message on an answering machine. You never know exactly when your call might be responded to, but eventually the energy will find its way to the right recipient.

Activities

Once your sacred space is set, begin by calling upon Divine powers which are most closely linked to the natural world, specifically animals. It is important at this point to state the purpose of your magical working so that the energy of your mental summons will be directed correctly.

Next, center yourself and breathe calmly. A sense of peacefulness is important when calling an animal to you because they are often frightened off or kept at bay by erratic energies. As you meditate, allow your mind to send out images of your home, your face, the trees nearby . . . basically the environment into which you will be bringing the animal. Send out a feeling of warmth, respect, and welcome. Keep the images simple, remembering that animals basically think in terms of instinct and locale. Continue until you sense that something has heard you. I cannot tell you how to sense this, but you will know deep down, like a warm spot in your stomach, that the work is finished.

You may also wish to specify a time period, such as six months to a year, in which you will expect a response. This gives the animal time to find you (or vice versa). If nothing happens in that time frame, this ritual may be repeated.

Tools and Ritual Components

Incense — Celery seed for opening the mind and concentration, chamomile for success.

Ritual Soap — Chickweed, a favorite herb of animals.

Anointing Oil — Cloves for the spirit of kinship.

Ritual Bowl — Birch beer in honor of the Lady of the Woods.

Altar Decorations — You may want to dress your altar in earth tones, placing pictures of creatures around the circle which are appropriate to their elements. As you call the quarters, invoke whatever image(s) of the God/dess you have chosen (see also the Divine Zoo in this chapter), then begin the meditation spoken of earlier.

Once you have finished all that remains is for you to keep your eyes and ears open. You may find your familiar in a pet shop, on your porch or out in the woods. It may take a while, but one will come, and when it does be prepared for a friendship unlike anything you have experienced before. If you are looking for an excellent bonding ritual to do with your familiar, refer to the article by Tara Buckland on page 247 of the Llewellyn *1991 Magical Almanac.*

Totems

The unicorn went up to Meg, the kitchen maid, and bowed his
head in front of her . . . his eyes brimmed with trustfulness.
> —T. H. White

Totems are slightly different from familiars in several ways. First, while a familiar may also be your totem, a totem is not always your familiar. The basic disparity being that a totem is a symbol of something—it is a guide, a power spirit, a teacher—and it does not always have to, and very often does not, evidence itself physically to you. Also, a totem can be anything from trees, stones, and plants to mythical creatures. Because of this, it can be said that a totem is more of an ideal, a representation of your truest nature or those aspects which you most need to incorporate into your life presently.

Throughout history, certain families or groups have acquired totems through their names, such as Boarshead, or by their coat of arms, which depict specific animals. Most of us, though, are left to discover our totems through other means. Sometimes you will discover them through unexpected contact, such as having a creature which is normally shy of humans approach you for food. Another example might be a grizzly bear, which, instead of attacking as they might when startled, leaves when he sees you there, as if the bear recognized you as a kindred spirit.

If you have a particular aspect of the God/dess that you favor, check to see if it is associated with an animal, place, or type of stone. That may give you a starting point or clue to what your power animal/item may be. Or, perhaps a certain creature or item keeps turning up in your life again and again, as if displaying itself to you. This may be an indication that you have found your totem.

Totem Meditation Quest

One method of finding a totem is through a quest of sorts. You begin at home, placing the call as you might for a familiar, but now focusing on your truest reflection of self and allowing that energy to flow out. After working at home, you may want to make several excursions into natural settings, just wandering or sitting until something strikes you.

If this is not possible, find a quiet spot at home and center yourself again. Now, try to visualize natural settings and see if any object or animal stands out in them. Wait patiently until you feel that the time has come to leave this private inner-world. You may have to envision several different types of locations before being successful, so try not to get discouraged. When the time is right, when you are ready and your totem has chosen you, you will know it beyond any doubt. Remember, a totem may not show itself to you directly, but can come through a vision, a dream, or some unique experience which is extremely personal to you.

Once you have found a totem, realize that it has much to share with you. It can teach you about yourself, your path, and things that you need to focus on spiritually. It can give you new perspectives and a stronger connection to the land. Each totem has its own worth, but, like any teacher, sometimes your totem may change to reflect inner transformations. If your totem does change, greet your new companion with as much joy as the last. When we are children, we speak and think as children. Our teachers help us to integrate and grow, then move on to others who need their lessons.

As the hart panteth after the water brooks,
So panteth my soul after Thee, O God.
—Psalm 42

THE DIVINE ZOO

The Victorian superstitions and myths regarding animals have their origins in antiquity. Creatures and natural objects have been woven into the stories of the Gods and Goddesses as intricately as thread through a meticulously made tapestry.

In many cultures, it is believed that the God or Goddess who is strongly associated with a specific animal or symbol also is the protector of that emblem, almost as a means of safeguarding a portion of themselves that they hold dear. These divine aspects and their long-time connections with elements of the natural world create an especially useful power to call upon when working magic with/for animals. While there are many which could be named, an abbreviated list is given here for your reference. To explore the various aspects of the Gods, Goddesses, their history, and their companions in detail, get copies of *The Witches' God* and *The Witches' Goddess* by Janet and Stewart Farrar.

For now, however, you can use the following list as a starting point, should you wish to call upon a specific Divine facet to aid in magic for your familiar, totem, or pet. In creating this list, I have attempted to give you a wide range of countries, animals, and environments to choose from so that you can select a God/dess who best reflects the creature's personality, or is a patron of that animal, or who somehow reflects the habitat in which that creature lives. For example, if you have a white, purebred puppy which you wish to bless, you may want to call on Apollo or Arawan during your ritual. Or, if you find an injured owl in the wild, you may want to seek the aspect of Isis or Blodeuwedd for intervention on the animal's behalf.

Gods, Goddesses, and Their Animal Correspondences

> **Akupera** — Hindu tortoise whose back supports the world.
>
> **Amaterasu** — Japanese sun goddess: the crow.
>
> **Amun** — Egyptian: any hatched creature, cow, unicorn.
>
> **Amemait** — Egyptian: crocodile, lion, hippopotamus.
>
> **Anubis** — Egyptian guide of souls: dolphin, jackal.
>
> **Aphrodite** — Greek goddess of love: dolphin, goat, swan.
>
> **Apollo** — Roman god of light: magpie, horses, pure breeds.
>
> **Arachne** — Greek spider goddess, weaver of fate.
>
> **Arawn** — Welsh king of Otherworld: white animals, especially horses and hounds.
>
> **Ares** — Greek god of war: wolf, shellfish.
>
> **Aristaeus** — Greek beekeeper and protector of flocks.
>
> **Artemis** — Greek moon goddess: bears, fowl, wild beasts.
>
> **Athena** — Greek goddess of arts/war: snow owl, peacock, eagle.
>
> **Atergatis** — Syrian fertility goddess: fish, snakes.
>
> **Avilayoq** — Eskimo: seals, whales and all sea creatures.
>
> **Bast** — Egyptian: cats (both domestic and wild).

Benten — Japanese love goddess: snakes, the dragon.

Blodeuwedd — Welsh: the owl.

Brighid — Irish goddess of fertility/inspiration: oxen, ram.

Bullai-Bullai — Australian aborigine: the parrot.

Chingchinich — American Indian: coyote, birds.

Demeter — Greek goddess of flourishing earth: lion.

Diana — Roman goddess of nature: dog, elephant.

Enkidu — Sumerian hero, especially good for befriending animals of the woods.

Epona — Celtic: horses, goose.

Freya — Teutonic: cat, hawk, swan, lynx, sparrow, dove.

Fukerokuju — Japanese god of wisdom: crane, deer, tortoise.

Ganemede — Greek cup bearer: eagle, peacock.

Gengen Wer — Egyptian goose god.

Hecate — Greek crone and keeper of mysteries: often pictured as having the head of a dog, horse or boar.

Helios — Greek sun god: sparrow hawk.

Hermes — Greek messenger of gods: goat, ape, swallow, any winged, swift or sure-footed creature.

Herne — British horned god, protector of nature.

Inari — Japanese vixen goddess: fox.

Ishtar — Babylonian mother-goddess: lion.

Isis — Egyptian: owl, lion, ram, snake.

Jana — Roman goddess of the year: woodland creatures.

Kehephra — Egyptian scarab beetle god: crab, turtle, wolf, fish, dolphin.

Kundalini — Hindu life force: scorpion, beetle, wolf, lobster, crayfish (or other shelled water creatures).

Lalita — Hindu goddess of passion: sparrow, dove, swan.

Loki — Scandinavian trickster: for any animal considered "crafty" such as fox or cat.

Luonnotar — Finnish goddess of creation: eagle, duck and any egg bearing animal.

Manabozho — American Indian inventor of arts and crafts: raven, otter, muskrat, hare.

Mari — Goddess of the sea and of poets: ram, raven, crow, animals of the water, horse.

Nike — Greek goddess of victory: lynx.

Nukua — Chinese creator: wild beasts, dragon.

Nuit — Egyptian sky goddess: winged creatures, specifically the peacock and eagle. All "air" creatures.

Odin — Scandinavian god of cunning: raven, horse.

Pan — Greek god of the woods: forest creatures, flocks. All "earth" creatures.

Poseidon — Greek god of the sea: dolphin, snake, scorpion, fish, eagle. All "water" creatures."

Rhiannon — Welsh fertility goddess: white horse, birds.

Sadhbh — Irish deer goddess.

Sigu — Guyanese lord of beasts and the forest.

Sopedu — Egyptian Lord of the East: falcon.

Vesta — Roman fire goddess: goat, donkey. All "fire" creatures (see elemental correspondence above).

Zeus — Greek god of gods: eagle, elephant bulls and swans.

This sparrow who comes to sit at my window is a poetic truth.
                                        —William Carlos Williams

Goddess! I have beheld those eyes before
And their eternal calm, and all that face,
Or I have dream'd?"
"Yes," said the supreme shape,
Thou has dream'd of me, and awaking up
Didst find a lyre all golden by thy side
Whose strings touch'd by thy fingers, all the vast
Unwearied ear of the whole universe
Listen'd in and found pleasure at the birth
Of such new tuneful wonder.

—John Keats

CHAPTER THIRTEEN

Potpourri: A Little of This and a Dab of That . . .

In the woods, where the streaming moonlight lit up things in a magical checkered play, and it seemed as if the Gods of all the nature mythologies were holding an indescribable meeting in my breast with the mortal Gods of the inner life . . .
— William James

For any writer, having one chapter which becomes the "catch all" for things which didn't really fit elsewhere is a great blessing. After my research, I realized that this chapter was perhaps the best representation of the Victorian era I could give you because it was, itself, a great collage of many things.

Everywhere you looked in the Victorian home, the American lifestyle was venerated. For example, we see quaint little items becoming favored, like whimsey boxes, as a triumph of pleasantry over practicality. These were lovely little chests used to present gifts on various occasions, and then employed as decorations to hold other dainty treasures. These would be put, quite proudly, side-by-side with more pragmatic items necessary to the home.

If you happen to go to a good hobby shop or fabric store, you might still find some plain, light weight boxes which you can decorate for gifts. Begin by painting or wood-burning a special design in the cover, putting some decorative fabric on the outside, and then lining it with felt. You now have your own whimsey box to use for presenting a gift or in which to keep something special.

A sentimental journey through the Victorian home reveals memoir pins made out of buttons that have been saved from baby gowns, uniforms, or various shirts. On each wall, silhouettes of children and pets would adorn the length of the rooms. Baby shoes might be bronzed, and any number of other family memorabilia would decorate the space of the house, making it truly a "home." It was in this way that the Victorians combined, quite unwittingly, touches of technology, intimations of individuality, musings of myth and a strong sense of family. They had a strong underlying belief that hard work, love, and faith

Making a Whimsey Box

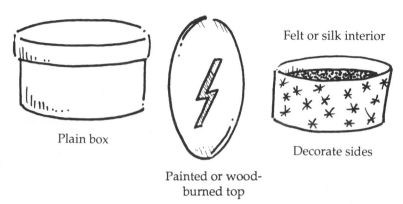

Plain box

Painted or wood-burned top

Felt or silk interior

Decorate sides

could improve not only their own standards of living but also those of their children. These standards were exhibited in many ways. The first, and the most telling for any generation, is that of how children are named.

NAMES

A good name in a man and woman, dear my lord,
Is the immediate jewel of their souls.
— William Shakespeare

The term "name" originally came from a Greek word meaning "to know," almost as if the old saying "I think, therefore I am" had been included in the creation of nomenclature. From earliest of times to the present day, a person's name has remained the single most important thing in their lives, identifying them as a unique individual. If you don't think this is true, just try purposefully misspelling or mispronouncing someone's name several consecutive times and see what happens in their demeanor.

The exercise of exchanging names upon introduction was a very gradual trend in culture. Many early clans believed that names carried power, and if someone knew your true name, they could inflict evil not just on you but your household. Superstitions regarding names have never really been overcome in some cultures. There are Jewish beliefs that say it is bad luck to give a child the name of an old person in your family because the angel of death might mistake the two, taking the child. On the other hand, it was perfectly acceptable to give them the name of someone recently passed over, so that soul could come to live again in the child. These types of superstitions carried over into "medical treatment," when the patient might receive a new name in order that death might be fooled into leaving their side.

Culture is perhaps the strongest influence on an individual's name. Not to have a name in certain countries is to be likened to the dead. To burn a person's name and mix it with medicine is thought to be a way to effect a cure. In many traditions a child is given a new name upon reaching adulthood.

During the Victorian era, there were many popular means of arriving at a child's name. It might be found in the Bible. Or, a child could be named after one of the presidents, flowers, heros, favored characters in books, or relatives. Some popular names included May, Ethel, Thaddius, Ruth, Edna, Olive, Maude, Ben, Samuel and Raymond. These names appeared together with what were considered the English traditional names of John and Thomas. Of course, the name Victoria was popularized by the Queen.

Because of the heavy immigrant population, the number of names in common usage increased, and the changing popularity of names reflected many of the newer attitudes of society. Some careful thought was now being given by parents to the child, who would bear the name they selected for the rest of their lives. Thus, the middle name became more popular, giving a child a choice when they got older of how they would prefer to be addressed, and appeasing certain wealthy relatives at the same time.

It is interesting to note, though, that the use of first names or nicknames in addressing someone did not become popular until well after 1950. Before this, it was considered rude and undignified to address anyone in a fashion other than Miss, Sir, Madam or some other appropriate title. The use of first names by children towards their parents was unthinkable, since the titles "mother" and "father" were considered two of the most beautiful in the English language.

Magical Names

> *There is more force in names than most men dream of.*
> —James R. Lowell

Potent magical names have been produced in many ways, depending on the culture and the individual employing them. A famous example is the name Agla, which is derived from the first letters of a Hebrew phrase which translates to mean, "Thou art mighty forever, O Lord." Other historical methods of name creation include using numerical values or calling on a specific seal, sign, conjuration, or name of the Divine, in the belief that the addition of this name lends power to the prayer or invocation.

In studying the use of magical names, the first thing you realize is that they came into being chiefly for protection. In the earlier days of Christianity, it was far safer to have your coven brother or sister know you only as "Moon," so they could not reveal your true identity, other than by physical description, even if tortured. Later, I believe this also became a method of marking the transition in lifestyle from the mundane to the esoteric. When we enter the circle, we leave behind the conventional self, and allow the arcane abilities to emerge. The magical name helps with that process, creating in essence a new persona, one that is alive with magic!

I have not been able to ascertain, other than by supposition, whether this pseudonym practice was common among rural people at the turn of the century. At that time, it may not have been terribly necessary because their gifts were viewed, for the most part, as natural abilities instead of marks of the Devil. Then too, these wise people were not known publicly for their talents, other than by word of mouth. Mrs. Miller, for example, may have been recommended for her adept tea leaf readings during a ladies luncheon, or old Dame Haggerty trusted for her consultations in matters of pregnancy. The oral tradition played such a strong role in keeping people informed of who in their area had knowledge of the "old ways," that I suspect secret names were not as prevalent.

Today, we employ the magical name partially to ensure privacy from the newcomers to our circles, but also as a way to mark our path and reality. It is, for us, a means to designate the truest and best reflection of self. When we are born, a name is given to us without choice. Later, when we find our spiritual path, we mark this rite of passage with a name. Then, the question remains of how do we choose one?

Well, when the Victorians were naming a child, they might have used a baby book which told of names, their origins and meanings. Actually, that is not a bad place to begin. You would be amazed at the spiritual ramifications of what we perceive as rather ordinary names. The name John means "God is gracious" in Hebrew, Peter translates from the Greek word "petros," meaning rock or foundation, and Victoria is directly derived from the word victory. My given name, Patricia, means noble, and peace maker. Interestingly enough, I am often the one to try and bring harmony to discordant situations. I do not know if this has much to do with my name, but I surmise that just as your diet helps determine your growth, the vibration of the identity you have been given since a baby may, indeed, affect your living in some way, if only on an intuitive level.

Magical names are no different. Each carries a specific energy which should sing the song of your heart and reflect your path and visions in the most positive manner possible. I wouldn't suggest choosing Glinda if you expect anyone to take you seriously. Likewise, if you decide to name yourself after an aspect of the Divine, I would not advise Kali the destroyer as a positive option.

Perhaps there is a myth or legend you love, a character from a book, or even a nickname you have had since a child that triggers a deep emotional resonance for you. But whatever it is, don't expect to find a magical name in your first week of studying the Craft. It took me two years to discover mine. This name is something that will come when the time is right, and you will know beyond any doubt that it is part of your being. To illustrate, my magical name of Marian came to me in a dream, but it really had little significance until many months later. I was reading *The Spiral Dance* by Starhawk, and saw that Mari was the name given for the Goddess of the sea and poets. Since childhood I had always written poetry, and often found peace near the water. After that discovery, I understood why this name was so appropriate for me.

So my advice is to find a name that inspires you to do and be your best, and that others will remember when they see you. Some of the methods of making names are very interesting (such as anagrams of phrases or jumbles of given names) but the end result is frequently all but unpronounceable! Remember that people will often be calling you by this name both in and out of Circle, out of habit. So trust your inner voice on this decision.

As a side note here, I think that drastic life changes can sometimes mean transformations in magical names, power animals, and even personal paths. As we grow, the things which once were common suddenly are not the focus of your thoughts. There may come a day when the name you embraced as a neophyte, like a pair of old shoes, no longer fits, and a new name quest begins. Just like the first one, it will take time and self examination to reach its goal. As you search, you will discover much about yourself in the process, making your magickal name(s) all the more meaningful in years ahead.

I have a passion for the name of Mary,
for once it was a magic sound to me.
— Lord Byron

SUPERSTITIONS

Nature is most lavish in her gifts, and in order to appreciate
them we should listen to her voice and study well her teachings.
—J. Clark

Many old wive's tales have remained with us as part of our heritage. We still cast salt to release negative energy or bad luck, believe that if the ground hog sees his shadow there will be six more weeks of winter, and if it rains by seven it will stop by eleven. I remember as a little girl my mother used sayings like this frequently.

Mind you, not all superstitions have much foundation to them. One said that if you threw a dead snake in the air and it landed on its back there would be rain soon. Somehow I can't imagine the modern magician using divination by deceased snakes to tell the weather. Even so, some of the superstitions have a very magical basis which can be used.

For example, there is a belief that on New Year's you should open your windows to let bad luck out and good fortune in. This symbolism could be used as part of your ritual for Hallows, since it is the Celtic new year! If you find a cricket in your new home, it is said to bring prosperity. In this instance, you might take a moment to stop for a ritual of thanks, giving the cricket an offering of grass to encourage the spirit of luck in your new environment.

At first glance, it may seem odd to combine spells and superstitions, but many spells, both modern and old, have their basis in the beliefs of common folk. To illustrate, people in California today still use window washing as a component of rain magic, based on the old superstition that if you wash your windows, a cloudburst is almost guaranteed.

Along these same lines, there are many charming superstitions that accompany the great outdoors. In the spring, if you see a calico cat it means luck; a blue bird, joy; and a red bird means company is soon to come. In the summer, if a butterfly lights on you, new clothing will be yours within a month, and good health is insured for a whole year. In fall, people would walk to the field of a friend and pick a sheath of wheat to keep in their home for prosperity. This symbol is still used frequently in autumn rituals today. Finally, one other folk spell says if you want to remember something in the winter, write it with your finger on ice and you will never forget.

Other common superstitions from the Victorian era had mostly to do with planting, harvesting, love, and weather. In the spring, root plants such as beets should be planted by the dark of the Moon. In the summer, if the Quarter Moon is tilted, it is a sign of a rainy season. In the fall, if you see a halo around the moon, you had best harvest delicate vegetables because a frost is soon to follow. Thin skinned onions mean that a mild winter is ahead, and the number of days the first snow stays on the ground is supposed to indicate how many snow falls will come for the rest of winter. So it was that country people often wove superstition and magic together to teach themselves the cycles of the Earth and keep themselves aware of these nuances in nature that could literally mean their life or death.

In the modern world, we are not faced with such harshness, and many of our superstitions have fallen by the way side and seen as silly. I agree that, in some instances, these superstitions may seem rather illogical, but underneath is something more powerful, a belief that by being more aware people could take control of their lives for the better. This conviction is very much a part of our modern magics. Each time we weave a spell, it is with the belief that we are making a difference. With this in mind, the following sections contain some examples of interesting superstitions and how to apply them for modern enchantments:

Protection

❧ Carrying cedar chips will ward off evil and disease.

❧ Goat's hair is believed to be a powerful charm against evil.

❧ Aloe prevents household accidents.

❧ Alfalfa kept in the home will prevent poverty and hunger.

❧ Bells drive away evil. It is because of this belief that so many church steeples have them.

If we were to combine these superstitions into a protective sachet or pillow for home or personal use, we would take a healthy portion of cedar shavings, dried aloe, alfalfa, and a little goat's hair (if available) and stuff them into a cloth container. One the piece is sewn closed, you can attach silver bells, which have been blessed specifically to ward against negativity, to the four corners for a pretty finishing touch. As a side note, you can attach a loop to one

Making a Protection Sachet

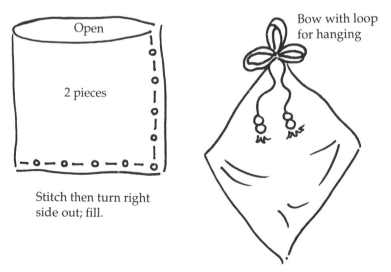

Open

2 pieces

Stitch then turn right side out; fill.

Bow with loop for hanging

corner of a smaller version of this pillow (3-inch square) to create a \
ment. These ornaments can add a touch of beauty to a room and bless
same time (see the illustration "Making a Protection Sachet.")

Divination

> ❧ If a spoon is dropped it means your guest will be a woman, a fork a
> a man and a knife a child.
>
> ❧ Bubbles in your tea mean visitors, bubbles in your coffee mean money is on its way.
>
> ❧ Long pins found in the house indicate a long journey ahead. If the head is facing
> towards you, it will be a pleasant one.

The first two superstitions are just interesting from the aspect of seeing if they come true.
The third, however, is where our magic can come in. Say, for example, you are planning to
take a trip. Since the head of a pin facing towards you is a symbol of an enjoyable journey,
use a pin in whatever protection rituals you do before you depart, making certain the head
is always facing you. Afterwards, I suggest keeping the pin with you, in a safe place, for the
duration of your vacation.

Friendship

> ❧ Wearing sweetpea flowers will attract people to you and promote friendships.

Instead of wearing the sweet pea, why not use the flowers as part of an incense which you
make for a special friend? They would also be an appropriate flower with which to decorate
your altar for the Victorian Tea Ritual (see Chapter Two). Dry some sweetpea petals and
release them to the winds to help bring new friendships your way. Add them to oils for an
increased sense of kinship.

Health

> ❧ A wool string worn around the neck will cure colds.
>
> ❧ Nutmeg or glass beads worn as a necklace will prevent nose bleeds.
>
> ❧ Cuts heal more quickly if you put medicine on the object which cut you.
>
> ❧ You can make headaches disappear by sleeping with scissors under your pillow.

The last two items in this list are not only superstitions, but forms of sympathetic magic in
the most traditional sense. The scissors, a symbol of cutting away, are employed as a component to decrease or cut pain. There is a similar superstition regarding childbirth and
keeping a knife under the bed so that the discomfort of contractions is "cut in two."

In the instance of tending to the instrument which hurt you as a way to help you heal,
in some respects it is like forgiving that tool for the pain it caused. Forgiveness and kindness are great healers, and such actions help our body to do its job better.

To use these concepts in magic, you may wish to have scissors or a knife as part of any
ritual or spell where you are trying to get rid of something, be it pain or a personal habit.

When creating magic that involves healing, you may want to study a superstition regarding the ailment in order to find a symbol to employ. For example, if you have a cold, you may want to bless a wool string, moving it through the vapors of an incense prepared for healing (cedar and pine work well) then wear it to bed, allowing your magic to work while you are getting much needed rest.

Increasing Power

࿊ If a witch shakes her hair loose during a spell it will increase the power two-fold.

Obviously, you can just try out this superstition in your next spell. I have a feeling this idea may have originated with stories like Sampson and Delilah, where long hair was a sign of strength. In the Victorian era, hair was also associated with romance. It was often braided and given as keepsakes. You may wish to use locks of hair, braided together, to help stabilize a relationship. One strand symbolizes you, one strand is your mate, and the third strand is the strength and power to bring a new beginning. You may wish to bless the last bit of hair with water for purification, salt for cleansing, and rose oil for love.

A small braid of hair can also be used as a way of marking your personal wands and staves. I have a small pouch hanging from my wand. This pouch holds a variety of herbs picked especially for their magical significance, a few crystals, a silver coin, and a bit of my hair. In times of great need, when I am gathering with friends, I will toss this pouch on the hearth and release the power, then fill a new pouch come the next waxing moon. A less complicated method, however, is simply saving long strands of your hair, braiding them, then attaching them to the staff or wand with a bit of leather. You could perhaps add a feather or bell at the end of the wand. It will look quite beautiful, and help bring more of your personal power to that tool.

Finding an Item

࿊ Writing the names of suspected thieves on clay balls, dropping them in water, and reciting a prayer will bring the name of the guilty party to the surface.

I hope that you are not looking to find a thief, but if you do happen to lose an item, this superstition (combined with a little visualization) has worked very well in the past to get me looking in the right direction. In this case, instead of names I write on the clay balls the names of various places where I have been since I last saw the item. (Childrens modeling clay works just fine.) Make sure you use waterproof marker or your "suspects" will wash away in the effort!

Next, while your clay is drying, get out an earthenware bowl and some spring water. Sprinkle in a little salt, and bless the water for clarity of sight. While you work, continue to focus on the item for which you are looking. Light two candles, one on each side of the bowl, to help "bring to light" the place where your item lies. Then put the clay balls in the water, keeping a strong image of your lost item in mind, and see what happens. It sometimes helps to close your eyes and hold your hands over the water, allowing your personal energy to mingle with the clay.

If none of the clay balls float, you may be looking in the wrong places, or it may not be lost at all (someone may have borrowed it, or you may have forgotten where you placed it for safe keeping). If more than one bobs to the surface, these areas may hold a clue which will aid you in your search. If only one of the clay pieces floats, go to the spot indicated on that clay ball and sit down. Instead of frantically searching, focus your mind on when you were last there, what you did, and where that item was. Then look around you, continuing to extend your senses. From my experience, three out of five times this will be successful.

Luck

> ❧ For good fortune pick an ash leaf saying, "Leaf of ash, I do thee pluck, hoping thus to meet good luck."

This poem is also a little bit of folk magic which probably originates from the idea that thorn, oak, and ash are the three trees which when grown together create a special unity that the wee folk are fond of. Since faeries are considered good luck, especially if treated well, it follows that leaves from their favored plants would likewise mean good fortune.

To help improve your fate, you may actually recite this poem, add dried ash leaves to incense, or carry a few leaves in a sachet with a found penny, four leaf clover, or any number of other lucky symbols.

Love

> ❧ A man can throw a cockle burr at a girl's skirt; if it sticks, their love will be true, but if it falls away, he should find another.
> ❧ To see your future love, wear goldenrod on the night of a Waxing Moon. You will glimpse him or her on the morrow.
> ❧ Twist off the top of an apple to the alphabet to learn the first letter of your true love's name.
> ❧ If you hear the coo of the first dove in spring, the next person of the opposite sex to ride by will be your mate.
> ❧ Place rosemary on the bride's bed for luck.
> ❧ Valarian tea brings love and harmony to a marriage.

While I have listed quite a number of superstitions here, each one has a particular item which is associated with the love magic. By combining them and making a sachet or charm, you can use these symbols to add to the energy of a spell or ritual. In this instance, I suggest a little valerian root for harmony, rosemary for luck, a fallen dove's feather for manifestation, goldenrod for vision, and a burr from a nearby woods for faithfulness. Obviously, you do not have to have all the symbols as part of your magical working, and for that matter you can add/substitute a few of your own. Again, the concept is simply to add the power of superstition to reinforce the effect of your magic.

Pregnancy

- ❧ Hyacinth amulets will bring safe births.
- ❧ Jade or carnelian worn will ease labor pains.
- ❧ Milkstone will increase mother's milk.

Since all of these apply in one way or another to motherhood, you may want to gather some dried hyacinth, a jade or carnelian stone, and a milkstone. Add any other thoughtful tokens and place them in a decorative container or pouch to give to someone you know who is pregnant. Bless the pouch and present it with a little card explaining the significance of each item.

Freckles

The Victorian superstition was that if you get your hands wet with the morning dew, and rub your freckles saying, "Dew, Dew, do do, take my freckles away with you. Dew, Dew, thank-you," they will go away.

Mother of this unfathomable world, favor my solemn song,
for I have loved thee ever and thee only. I have watched thy
shadow and the darkness of thy steps and my heart ever gazed
on the depth of thy deep mysteries.

—Percy Bysshe Shelley

THE MAGIC OF TECHNOLOGY

Someone once said that today's magic is tomorrow's science. If we were to step, for one moment, into our ancestors' shoes I think we would quickly discover the truth of this aphorism. From our earliest history, humankind has dreamed of flying and been told it was impossible. Yet the unimaginable reality, the first "air machine," got off the ground during this era. With its wings, the world's fancy took flight and technology began to grow. The advent of the telephone broke down communication barriers between people in different locations, then the railroad and automobile made it possible to travel more quickly from place to place. To a people used to horse, carriages, or walking, this and the many other technical advancements of their time must have seemed miraculous, almost like magic.

We still have not seen the end of this enthusiastic technological spirit. If we had told our ancestors that books could be kept on a small square no thicker than a pencil, they

would have thought us quite daft, yet now this marvelous miracle is at our fing
day! While I agree that mechanical objects have caused much damage to our
have also given us many gifts and opportunities which our magical mind shoul
or disdain. For example, the microwave and modern stove allows herbalists to dry their
plants in an effective, quick manner. Freezers allow for year round storage of various products for home and magical use. Computers are a hands-on "Book of Shadow" which can be
sealed by a password to protect your privacy.

These things, and so many more, allow us more flexibility and creativity with our
magic, if they are used responsibly. For example, now you can go to a Circle if it's in
another state via car, but I suggest car-pooling to decrease pollution. When celebrating
outdoors, if your Circle has built a roaring fire, remember the safety-first technology of
having an extinguisher handy. In this manner, you are treating your world with respect,
allowing magical principles and technology to work together, while continuing to have
fellowship and feed your spirit.

There are hundreds of ways you can allow the science of today to reflect your ideals
and augment your magic. The key is a little thoughtfulness. Before you act, consider how
to best do whatever you are planning in an economic, earth-aware manner, and then how
you can use these ideas in your home, Circle or wherever you may be.

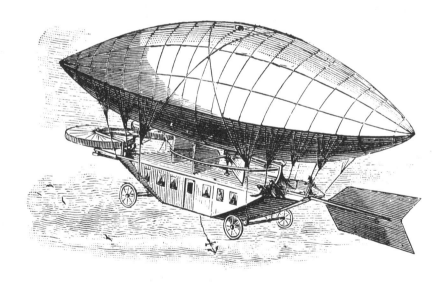

REMINISCING: INTERVIEWS WITH FAMILIAL WITCHES

In most people's lives, there is a grandparent who has somehow influenced their childhood and who remembers well the "way back whens." In my youth, two such people enriched my existence. The first was my father's mother, who was the perfect example of a Victorian lady. She could cook circles around just about everyone I knew and still get everything done. I remember I used to beg her to make huckleberry muffins each time I visited her home in the Adirondack Mountains. She would usually reply that there were too many chores that day, "but perhaps tomorrow." Yet, without fail, the next morning those muffins would be hot on the table, waking me with their fresh scent. This woman's caring and simple ways were a joy to three generations.

The second person of influence was my mother's father. He is now in his late 90s and is still a wily old goat. He brought my mother up on a farm, teaching her about everything from birth to the insects and the stars. (My mother then passed this on to me.) This same man went back to college at age 75 to argue with the professors and keep an eye on my sister. Up until very recently, he went out every Wednesday night to "go dancing with the ladies." In his younger years, he traveled the world and was both scholar and Gypsy, sending his granddaughter books on astronomy inscribed with the phrase, "Reach for the stars."

Knowing these people truly makes for warm and wonderful memories. I do not know, because of distance or death, if there were any magical ways to be found among these people, but the way they lived their lives was lesson enough.

While writing this book, I was fortunate enough to meet two other people who had family members who had been practicing a form of "magic" at the turn of the century, having learned it from their parents. In most cases, the word magic was not used. In fact, many of the talents seemed to be taken for granted. Families who had long used such practices thought them quite natural, but were generally wise enough not to speak of such things with strangers, not knowing how they might react. It seems, from what I have been able to glean through interviews and books, that magic was basically a private affair, something that was mixed with country wisdom and shared when the need arose.

Religion is a way of walking, not a way of talking.
—Dean Inge

Terry

Terry's family had their origins in Germany and Yugoslavia, traveling as Gypsies throughout the European continent. Having been born with a wide range of psychic abilities, Terry was curious about his past and was somewhat relieved to discover the role magic had played in his family's lineage. He also determined that there were many instances of longevity, most of his family living to near 100 years or more even in the eighteenth century!

The strongest sense of magic came from his great grandmother and her father. Through her stories, he has learned of a familial Ouija® board which was used on occasion. It was round, with protective sigils at the edge and a pentagram in the center. His family believed the best woods for such an oracle were oak or yew. This board was probably constructed out of oak. The most unique feature of this board was the fact that instead of the planchette, it employed a bluish crystal hanging from a chain. In this way, there was no real physical contact with the board other than when setting it up. There were the traditional alphabet letters imprinted on it, but it lacked the "yes," "no," and "end" seen on more modern boards. After the reading, the board was stored in a special velvet cloth and left undisturbed. The crystal was left sitting out for ornamentation. Another tool, a two-hundred-year-old, handmade Tarot deck was sadly destroyed when one family member converted to Catholicism. The deck itself was reportedly made of cloth and slightly larger than the decks we use today.

In discussing specific magics, it was interesting to discover that Terry's family not only had a Bible, but employed it in ritual somehow. Terry's great grandfather was talented in exorcising spirits, especially poltergeists, and always wore a silver medallion, the origins of which are unknown to the family today. Terry's grandmother was known as a wise woman and a psychic reader, often employing flower petals for divination in a perfectly Victorian manner, like one would use a Tarot deck. She also had a talent for communicating with spirits, seeing the future, interpreting dreams, and of course, healing a love-sick heart. For pregnant women, she often advised different types of teas for each month, and her commanding demeanor usually kept them listening.

In matters of love, the favorite recipe Terry has been given is for a very distinctive spaghetti sauce. This sauce was (and still is) prepared as if one were arranging a blind date, then given to those who needed it. Most of the herbs employed were for love, sex, and longevity. In this manner, the family could use their cooking magic, share it with star-crossed lovers, and allow the energy to do its work with none being the wiser. Terry was unaware of the significance of the sauce until he began to research the herbs. As he reviewed them, it also sparked some memories of the times when the sauce was specially prepared and given to people they knew. Over generations, this apparently became a tradition. Whether the herbs were ever changed for different circumstances, Terry could not ascertain.

From other members of the family who are still alive, Terry has been able to gather many interesting superstitions and tales. Like the majority of superstitions from the Victorian era, many of them seem to center around birds. There was a strong feeling that these creatures determined your future, and many of his relatives even now seem to have a way of communicating with animals. His grandmother can still feed the birds, in a city environment, by hand!

Of all the stories he had to share, the one which really left an impression on me was about his grandmother's pet bull. She used to guide it through corn fields when no one else could lead him. In fact, one relative tried with rather disastrous results. She also always had unusual animals such as cats with seven toes, porcupines, and skunks. When younger, this woman kept a kitchen garden outside her home, (see Chapter Four) stocked full of herbs. She had shelves filled with jars of all types of spices, and also did her own herb gathering and drying. Usually, the herbs were dried by hanging, but certain herbs had to be dried in the oven at a very low temperature. Unfortunately, since his grandmother's memory is failing, we may never discover which herbs these were.

Certain reflections of the rich magical family history remain in his grandmother's home today. There are candles of every shape and color wherever you look in the living space. Tables throughout the house are adorned with hand crocheted doilies which, if you examine very closely, contain magical symbols. There is also a brass vase which no one is allowed to touch, but it draws children and adults alike to stare at it; energy radiates from the metal like a beacon. If you visit her, she might still warn you of fairies in the nearby fields.

In our discussions, the one thing Terry really wanted me to share in relation to all of this was that if you suddenly discover you have many magical abilities and don't understand them, try looking to your family. Discussions about country sayings, family traditions, and people who may have had uncanny insights, could prove very helpful in understanding your own gifts. Terry believes that magical power is handed down in some form through personal lineage. Of course, other similar family traditions are not unheard of in the Craft. Like Terry, you may be fortunate to discover the memory of a Victorian (or older period) ancestor who has much to share for your modern magics.

Each religion, by the help of more or less myth, which it takes
more or less seriously, proposes some method of fortifying the
human soul and enabling it to make peace with its destiny.
—George Santayana

Lyn

When asked how long she'd been involved in Craft, Lyn's answer was, "Probably all my life, but I only found a name for it about seven years ago. I picked up some books and discovered that what I was thinking and feeling, and what my grandmother had taught me somewhat indirectly, were in those pages."

Lyn's entire family seems to be blessed with inherent magical ability. Her uncle, who is 78, used divining rods with an amazing aptitude, allowing him to find the well for a family home in Atica, New York. Her mother shows evidence of strong perceptions; people often come to her for advice, and her brother has had psychic experiences (specifically with the spirit of their father) most of his life. He is also very intuitive.

The most influential person on Lyn's personal path, however, is undoubtedly her grandmother, nicknamed Bridgit by her husband, who was born in 1893. When Lyn was younger, her grandmother would often give her bits of advice based on common superstitions. For example, if you get out of the house and remember something you need, you were to walk backwards for ten steps before retrieving it. Or, if you happened to put your underwear on inside out it should be left that way. To reverse it was bad luck. When her grandmother was asked why, the usual response was simply, "because." There was never any reference to Wicca directly.

Lyn's grandmother had a typical green thumb and could make any garden grow. She always emphasized proper care for "Mother Earth," accentuating love and respect. She often took Lyn on nature walks, teaching her about how animals thought and felt, and also told her that whenever anything was taken from the ground it should be replaced, so that there was always a reciprocity with nature. Later in life, she ended up spending time with the Seminole tribe in Florida, adopting an owl as an animal under her care.

A certain amount of homecooked healing came along with her love for nature. She was forever preparing teas, especially mint for stomach problems, and had a gift for knowing exactly what was wrong. Lyn remembers her preparing mustard poultices for colds or sore muscles, and seeing her relieving headaches by pressing her palm to the forehead. Interestingly enough, she had always wanted to be a nurse. However, the use of family remedies unfortunately decreased as medical science became more widely accepted and used.

There were other stories and memories which lead to a deeper understanding of this woman's many talents. When Lyn's uncle was young, her grandmother would place him in a separate room while she cleaned, dropping a feather in the doorway of that room. Orvis never crossed that feather. This continued until he was old enough to be reasoned with. She also loved storms, seeing them as Earth's natural means of house cleaning and spoke of how the birds "bring in" the rain with their singing.

Of all her gifts, tea leaf reading was by far the most developed. Lyn said she often got the impression that the tea leaves were only a ruse, that her grandmother just had a way of knowing things, but the leaves made for a convenient excuse. Her accuracy with this was such that it began to attract people from all around to her door, but she never accepted money from them. During the readings, this woman had no fear of stepping in where angels fear to tread, advising people with stern wisdom. Lyn remembers several occasions of her grandmother pulling her aside to do a reading in order to warn her of impending bad situations if she didn't watch her step. Yet such predictions were not overly specific or dooms-dayish. They were trends, always balanced with the emphasis on personal choice and ability to change things by actions. The example she gave was her grandmother warning her in one reading to "avoid triangles." At the time Lyn had no idea what she meant, but learned the hard way many years later that it referred to relationships. The reading often ended with her grandmother suggesting quietly that it might be better to keep this information to themselves, like a special secret they alone would share.

At the heart of all this, though, her grandmother conveyed a strong feeling that everything begins at home and with the self, often saying that "things are exactly as they should be" with a knowing glint in her eye. Lyn would not appreciate that until many years later, when rediscovering her own roots in magic.

FINAL NOTES

This is but a small picture of a large part of our history. The Victorian era challenged the simple manners and modes of country folk with urbanization and technology. This is when people's roles were changing almost as quickly as their clothing, and when I believe the American Dream took on a whole new meaning. It is the very essence of this Dream, the vision of a better future, mixed with a good amount of strong will and backbone, that this book has tried to present.

Take a bold step forward. Leave the negativity of the past behind you, learning from those mistakes. Then you can move toward tomorrow with a vision of the romance, beauty, individuality, and wisdom of those days firmly in mind. Use these ideas for your home, your Circles, or wherever you may be. Allow the richness of your own history to bring new flavor into your magic, so that with our Victorian fellows we can wish on the stars, then make those wishes come true!

So when at times the mob is swayed
To carry blame or praise too far
We may take something like a star
To stay our minds on, and be staid.
— T.S. Eliot

XXI

LE · MONDE

APPENDIX A

Then and Now

Shadows dwelt within its teaming girth,
Of the known and unknown things of Earth . . .
—Dante Rosetti

THEN: 1800 to 1970

The last century has seen many changes, especially in the spiritual arena. In the first chapter, I mentioned a few of these changes and described how they were related specifically to the Victorian era, but there is much more to know about our magical history. To give you a better understanding of the last two hundred years of the Craft, and to help you see how many of its foundations were built in these years, let's begin a brief, scenic excursion to Paris, 1810. A man by the name of Alphonse Louis Constant, better known as Eliphas Levi, was born and trained for the Catholic priesthood. After he discovered that it did not suit him, he learned the old arts of Cabalism and Masonry at the feet of a man who believed deeply in the divine nature of humanity. That man was Josef Wranski, a sage who combined Martinism and Masonry from Polish and Russian traditions in the attempt to reconcile rationalism and religion.

Like many occultists of that time, Levi had a fascination with ancient Egypt, feeling that it was likely the birth place of the Tarot. Even so, Levi believed that the decks available during his life were probably derived from Jewish mystical traditions. Because of this hypothesis, he began to fit the Tarot into the Cabala by connecting the 22 trump cards with Hebrew letters which corresponded to various aspects of God and the universe.

Levi was also strongly influenced by Mesmer in his beliefs, and ended up making his living through writing and teaching about the occult. His book, *Key of the Mysteries,* is an alchemical treatise which reflects this unique combination of ideology very well. Yet I doubt that he was aware while writing that his work would mark a new era for magic as a whole.

Another figure living during Levi's lifetime was Charles Godfrey Leland, a writer, journalist, creator of comic verse and the author of Aradia, The gospel of Witches (written in 1899). This book was the result of a chance meeting with an Italian familial witch, who had learned generations of lore, incantations and medicines at the feet of her mother. According to this tradition, the Goddess Diana gave birth to Aradia, who came to earth specifically to teach humanity the ways of magic. It was mostly a religion of peasants, Christianity being far more partial to feudal lords with money. This Gospel included information on various spells and rituals and the now traditional meal of cakes and wine.

In the late 1800s, Levi died. Around the same time, the Rosicrucian order was established in the United States; Aleister Crowley and Carl Jung were born; and the Theosophical Society was founded by the amazing Russian medium Helena Blavatsky. This society was founded in the attempt to build a bridge between science and religion, and to reconcile Eastern and Western occult traditions. Because of this, Helena herself devoted much time to the study of Hinduism, Buddhism and the Indian faiths. By 1883, the society expanded to have a branch in London with Alan Leo, a British astrologer, adding to their efforts. Leo became a member of the group in 1890 to promote astrology as an ancient symbolic system which could teach humankind about its true nature.

In 1888, The Hermetic Order of the Golden Dawn came into being through the efforts of William Woodman and William Westcott. These two men gave life to a metaphysical system that is still used today. Their efforts were continued by MacGregor Mathers, who spent half of his life studying magical texts in Paris. His studies, combined with his work in the Golden Dawn, produced two books in 1887 and 1889, *The Kabbalah Unveiled,* and *The Key of Solomon,* respectively. Mathers managed to construct a magical style which combined alchemy, divination, Masonry, Tarot, astrology, the Cabala, ritual, and vision. He traced these techniques to their roots in the Rosicrucians, mystical Judaism, and eventually Egypt.

The Golden Dawn emphasized personal development and self responsibility for power, and eventually became like an occult university. It set up degrees, and founded temples in both the United States and Europe. One more notable member of a Golden Dawn faction group was William Yeats. Until the 1920s, he headed the Order of the Morning Star, whose main thrust was that of metaphysical inspiration.

In 1903, A.E. Waite took over the Golden Dawn, bringing with him a strong Masonic background. Mr. Waite began translating Levi's works in 1896, then followed this accomplishment by designing what is now the standard among Tarot decks, The RiderWaite Tarot. In America, Paul Foster Case continued Waite's work by constructing one of the most sacred parts of the Golden Dawn system, known as the Builders of the Adytum (BOTA).

It seems the Order of the Golden Dawn was destined to become a home for many figures of the magical movement. Aleister Crowley, for example, joined in 1896. In 1901, *The Book of the Law* was channeled by Crowley (he heard a voice dictating the book). This book contains the famous phrase "Do what thou wilt shall be the whole of the law." This convinced Crowley of his "mission" on Earth. He formed the Order of the Silver Star in 1907. In 1912, he also got involved in the Ordo Templi Orientis (OTO), a group which then was involved in various types of Tantric practices. While Crowley was not one of the most positive figures in modern magic (due to the darker side of his nature) his *Book of Thoth,* which is a commentary on the Tarot, certainly continues to influence our methodology.

By 1915, branches of the OTO existed in Vancouver and Los Angeles. In the same year, H. Spencer Lewis formed the Ancient and Mystic order of Rosae Cruicis (AMORC) which to this day has a large mail-order business in San Jose. (They concentrate on psychic phenomena, philosophy, and altering perceptions.) While this was happening, anthropologists and writers became increasingly interested in magic as a scholarly pursuit. This pursuit was best illustrated by the fact that Sir James Frazer's *The Golden Bough* was revised and expanded into 12 volumes between 1907 and 1915, having originally been published in 1890.

The 1920s and 1930s saw an increase in the public's fascination with magic, largely due to the depression and the World War I atrocities. In 1930, a London newspaper began printing a regular astrology column. Little did they know how far reaching this journalistic novelty would be. Their lead was followed shortly thereafter by the French and American presses. As of 1969, according to Newsweek magazine, over 10 million people in the United States alone were practicing astrological techniques on a regular basis.

Various mental and spiritual groups sprang up between 1922 and 1949. The root of this may have been the publication in 1921 of Dr. Margaret Murray's book, *The Witch-Cult in Western Europe,* where she discarded the idea of magic as Satanism, and explored Wicca as a Dianic cult, based on historical information dating back to 900 A.D. This book discusses the four Great Sabbats, now celebrated by most Witches, as being seasonal and thematic in nature. Leland did not speak of this, although he did mention meetings which may correspond to Esbats, which mark the phases of the moon throughout the month.

In the United States, experimental research into psychic phenomena began at Duke University in 1927. This was one of the first times this phenomena was studied seriously by the scientific community. In 1938, Gleb Botkin founded one of the early Neo-Pagan organizations, the Church of Aphrodite, located in Long Island. Meanwhile, in France, a self development expert named Emile Coue felt that the human imagination could help control behavior. This was also the period when Dion Fortune wrote *Psychic Self Defense* and *The Mystic Qabalah.* By 1971, the first of these books was in its thirteenth edition and is still considered a classic. Other groups, such as the Druids, were getting attention thanks to the efforts of people like Lewis Spence, who wrote the *Encyclopedia of Occultism* and the *Origins of Druidism* around the same time.

In 1946, *The White Goddess* by Robert Graves, was published. This book talks about the old deity of Europe as a goddess of the moon and poetry, not a god, as portrayed by the Western tradition. Here the themes of life and death, rebirth and the seasons, light and dark, and the triple goddess are illustrated. This book also conveys a feeling that the patriarchal society tended to make humankind more warlike. While Mr. Graves claims no mystical talents, the book was written "under inspiration" in less than three weeks, according to him.

Following closely behind Graves was one of the most popular figures in magic, that of Gerald Gardner. *High Magic's Aid* was written in 1949, followed by *Witchcraft Today* in 1953, the latter being an attempt to expand Murray's theories and focus on a more peaceful, earth-centered religion. While some of Gardner's claims regarding his initiation, background and training are questioned today, there is no questioning his influence on the magical community. He was a flamboyant figure who was fascinated by the occult his entire life. Gardner passionately believed that the Wise Craft should not die, and because of this, he pieced together fragments of research and combined them with his own knowledge to create a functioning system. Thanks to these efforts, there are many long-established Gardinarian covens which still operate under his philosophies today.

In 1951, the Witchcraft Act was repealed, making it no longer illegal to practice the art. Unfortunately, changing the law does not mean that public opinion became any less critical. Even today, people are shot at, fired from jobs, and harassed for practicing magic.

In the year 1968, The Church of all Worlds was established. This group was very diverse, being built on the idea of the church for the future. It embodied Transcendental Meditation techniques alongside a liberal Unitarianism that we could still learn much from today. The Church of all Worlds also based some of its ideas on certain writings by Tim Zell, who taught us that Earth is a living entity, and tried to make us aware of Her needs; a lesson we have only recently begun to heed.

NOW: 1970 to 1991

The only limit to our realization of tomorrow
will be our doubts of today.
— President Roosevelt

In 1970, The Church of the Eternal Source was founded by Don Harison and Sara Cunningham, who were among those who were deeply committed to human diversity. In 1979, Margo Adler published *Drawing Down the Moon,* which highlighted magical traditions through study, interview, and observation. That year also saw the release of *The Spiral Dance* by Starhawk, which is basically a step-by-step explanation of ritual techniques for the entire year, adding the dimension of feminist spirituality. With these types of works being distributed, other magical organizations from Norse to Dianic began to grow around the world. It is difficult, however, to know how many people practice some form of magic, due to the fact that we really have no system of registration. In 1980 it is estimated that there may have been about 10,000, judging from periodical subscriptions and word of mouth, but this is a rough guess at best.

Despite the consistent growth and practice of magic, certain misconceptions about what Wicca is remain deeply embedded in society, and will take time and patience to change. In this respect, the New Age has given us something on which to build. The New Age movement, although somewhat removed from Wiccan philosophically, has done much to help the overall atmosphere for alternative religions. Since Shirley McClaine took a bold step forward, bringing well-deserved attention to the Association which Edgar Cayce founded nearly a century ago (A.R.E.), New Age spirituality has become almost fashionable. This increased general acceptance of more esoteric ways of living has allowed Wicca to slowly take its place among other world faiths. The number of people who openly acknowledge themselves as Witches has grown tremendously, and there are even legally recognized Wiccan Churches in the United States.

With more people practicing magic, there is a new generation of teachers, writers, and artists to share fresh, transformational visions with the world. Individuals such as Marion Weinstein (*Positive Magic* and *Earth Magic*), Isaac Bonewitz (*Real Magic*), Selena Fox ("Circle Network News" and "Sanctuary"), Janet and Stewart Farrar (*The Witch's God*) and Z. Budapest (a leader in feminist magic), just to name a few, began this work in the 1970s. They did everything from public radio shows to the formation of the Council of American Witches in 1974. The Council began producing "The Touchstone Newsletter," feeling that the Craft needed some common ground. In 1975, The Covenant of the Goddess was accepted in California. It tried to build closer bonds for the magical community. Unfortunately, these attempts were dampened by the decentralized nature of magic as a whole. Yet, this covenant did illuminate the meaning of being a Witch in modern America, stressing it as a way of life.

Today we have people such as Raymond Buckland continuing his many years of writing for the Craft; Scott Cunningham focusing on herbalism and Earth magic; Kisma Stepanich bringing a bardic tone to spiritual writing, Robin Wood's art, Kitaro's music, and many other very talented people continuing our education and beautifying our lives.

Because of efforts like theirs, we now see various archetypal images of the Divine portrayed on calendars, posters, and note cards; we hear the music of Native American drums, Buddhist chants, Irish harps; we find books on magic adorning the shelf of our local bookstore, right alongside those of Christianity. This marks a drastic, and long-awaited change for the magical community. Even as little as twenty years ago, these types of things were mostly unheard of. One of the most illuminating comments on the growth of magic came to me through Marion Weinstien. In *Positive Magic*, she stated that a few years ago she would not have expected her book to even be read, but a few hundred years ago she would have died for the attempt. As a point of interest, Llewellyn Publications now distributes over 200 titles on various metaphysical traditions, many of which sell in the area of 500 copies a month. Magic has finally come into its own.

I don't believe this means that various covens will be listed in your Yellow Pages next year, but I do believe it is good reason for hope. We need to continue to educate ourselves and the world about the truth of our faith—its foundations, and its impact on our lives. We also need to step away from quiet complacency and stand up for our right to pursue the religion of our choice. Our forefathers fought for that liberty, and knew the productive power of strong wills motivated by good intentions.

By learning to communicate effectively, and keeping our wits and wisdom about us, I believe we can take magic into the next century with a freedom it has not known before; freedom which will manifest itself not just within the general public, but among our own. I also sincerely believe that by so doing, we play a key role in offering this planet real hope for a better tomorrow: where technology works hand-in-hand with nature . . . where we learn to create instead of destroy. By working together with conviction we can offer our children a future where the family of humankind has learned to live together, love each other and to call the Earth by one name . . . Home.

So what is truth today
may tomorrow only partially be so
to a developing soul.
— Edgar Cayce

APPENDIX B

Modern Enchantments

O! the life within us and abroad
which meets all motion, and becomes its soul!
— Samuel Taylor Coleridge

The last 100 years have brought many wonderful and sometimes confusing changes to our world, let alone the magical community. We have seen the beginnings of a popularized Pagan ideology, especially regarding our planet. It seems we are rediscovering what President Roosevelt knew when he said, "To waste, to destroy our natural resources; to skin and exhaust the land instead of using it so as to increase its usefulness will result in undermining, in the days of our children, the very prosperity which we ought by right hand down to them amplified and developed." The wisdom in these words has returned to us today by way of ecologically minded groups around the world. This new emphasis on the Earth, and indeed much of the ideology of the "New Age" is something which I believe our Victorian forefathers inspired. While some of our magical heritage comes to us from more ancient sources, larger volumes of written material remain from the early 1900s. It is almost as if an awakening spirit, a new spark, was ignited in humanity at the turn of the century. Today that ember has begun to burn more brightly, kindling enhanced interest in magic as a way of life.

The attention being focused on mystical lifestyles is partially due to the fact that many of the fundamental philosophies behind them are in syncronicity with the new Earth-aware culture. Magic teaches first and foremost our responsibility to ourselves, each other, and our world. It also teaches us that one person can, indeed, make a difference. Through this we can see how the strong vision of the Victorian people, especially those who lived on the great frontier, has found a home within magical traditions.

The surge of attention given to "New Age" thinking has also been assisted by a refreshed desire in many people to find a more impartial way of treating each other in hopes of bringing equality and harmony to our world. The "me" generation has been superseded by more unified ways of thinking about ourselves, our environment, the planet, and even beyond our physical boundaries into space. Thus, we are recapturing the essence of dreams which have always been within the human soul: to have adventure, to love, to know peace. No matter how much the world has changed, however, many questions remain for the spiritual seeker just starting a magical path, most of them dealing with the technicalities. What are the basics of Wicca? How do I begin to live in a magical-reality construct? These types of inquiry are where your journey really starts.

In an effort to answer these types of questions, and make this book more useful to those of you who are new to magical traditions, I am including some basic techniques of Wicca in this chapter. This information is not based on any one tradition, but is kept simple and practical, the core of which comes out of my own growing experience within the Craft. Those of you who have been studying for many years may wish to skip this section, or better yet, skim it for some new ideas. If there are terms you find unfamiliar, or ones where you are uncertain of their meanings within magical traditions, I have provided a Glossary for your reference.

As you read, please remember that if anything does not ring true for you, then don't try it. Magic must reflect your conscience if it is to have meaning and effect. Never go against the "still small voice" within . . . more often than not, it is right.

MECHANICS OF MODERN MAGIC

If you have built castles in the air,
your work need not be lost;
that is where they should be —
now put the foundations under them.
— Henry David Thoreau

The most wonderful thing about modern magic is that it is evolving, changing, and growing to meet new times, new ideas and a fresh group of souls who look to the Craft for inspiration. I think that it was the reformational nature of Wicca which really attracted my attention. Suddenly, instead of a religion carved in stone, I found a living, breathing faith that even today leaves me somewhat astounded by its ability to be oriented towards both the individual and group, while still maintaining a decentralized system.

When I first discovered there was a name for what I believed in my heart all along, I also quickly found I had much to learn. Before knowing about magic, there was no way available to me to put the ideas and visions in my mind into a functional system; or so it seemed. Wicca offered all the tools I needed to venture out, but first I had to comprehend exactly what those tools were and what they meant.

During this process, I realized that all my preconceived notions of what constituted "magic" had been inspired by Hollywood movies and Christian theology. The first time I sat and talked to a real Witch, I wasn't sure what to expect. Instead of flashy lights and "eye of newt," I found a calm, understanding woman. She was a Cabalist who learned the Craft at the feet of her mother in Israel.

When I came to her with questions, she smiled gently, explaining that magic in its simplest form is energy to which imagination, visualization and desire are added to help bring about a specific result. She emphasized that magic and psychic phenomena are natural and available to anyone who is willing to dig down deep in themselves, and open their mind to the world just beyond our senses. These two "gifts," if you will, are an example of how we are only beginning to discover the breadth of human mental abilities.

I don't know how long it was before her words really sank in, but I know I left her home a very different young woman than when I arrived (this was nearly 8 years ago). For the first time in my life I began to accept the possibility that there was more to my world than the superficial. My perspective would never be the same again. From a discernment of God/dess to knowing the simple beauties of a magic circle, slowly but surely my religion began to transform my life, within and without.

So, pretend for a moment that I am in your living room, you have brought your questions, and we can begin at the best place I know; the beginning . . .

God and Goddess

The worst moment for an agnostic
is when he is really thankful
and has nobody to thank.
    —Dante Rossetti

Before Christianity, many cultures had images of the Divine which were women, presumably because the female was able to bear new life, therefore it made sense that a woman would birth humanity itself. There are many Goddess names: Brighid, the Irish Goddess of fire, inspiration and healing; Ishtar, the Summerian Goddess of love and benevolence; Hecate, the Greek Goddess of the moon; Ma'at, the Egyptian Goddess of law; and Amaterasu, the Japanese Goddess of the sun; to only name a few. There were also images of a male God, such as Thoth, the Egyptian God of justice; Herne, the Celtic hunter and forest God; Shiva, the Hindu Lord of the Dance; Dagda, the good God of the Irish peoples; and Loki, the Scandinavian trickster who is the embodiment of entropy.

In some traditions, counterparts for either the masculine or feminine are found, such as Mari who was considered the consort to Yahweh, and worshiped in Her own right before the advent of Christianity in Israel. In different cultures, temples were established to a patron God and Goddess, who complimented each other and fit with the people's customs.

Wicca is unique among Western faiths in the fact that the Supreme Being is not "He." Instead, Wicca employs part of these ancient practices, seeing the Divine as androgynous in nature: both male and female, sun and moon, light and darkness, in perfect balance. Thus, all the best qualities of both sexes are embodied in the God/dess for us to tap into, or find within ourselves. The God half is the image of strength, intellect, and our link to nature. Sometimes portrayed as the horned God to remind us of our connection to the Earth, He is the mate of the Goddess, Her companion, a father image, brother, son, the light of day, and fire. The Goddess, by comparison is the maiden, mother and crone; the feminine creative power, a well of intuition, healing, the moon, and the subconscious mind.

This symmetric duality within the God/dess is very important for today's society. It marks the changing attitude towards feminine attributes, and hopefully the dawn of an age when the patriarchy will give way to a more balanced power, liberating not only the sexes, but also races and creeds. This may also be why tolerant, life-affirming attitudes are often found among magical people.

Individuals practicing the Craft choose the names of their pantheon in different ways. Some may choose to call on the patron God/dess image of their coven, if there is one. Others may use different names for God and Goddesses depending on the type of work they do. For example, someone might choose to call on Ea, a Babylonian God of water, insight, and the supernatural for wisdom in their magic. Or, if an individual is drawn to a specific country, they may wish to use only the names of the deities evidenced in that area. Since I love Scotland and the Celtic traditions, I often call on Brighid for inspiration and Cerridwin for knowledge.

At first, this custom may seem more Pagan than Wiccan until it is noted that no matter what name we call the Supreme Being, it is all the same God/dess. If, for a moment, you picture a huge crystal with many facets, each of those facets having a different name, attribute, and image, then you begin to understand the way I perceive the Divine. Since this discernment is purely personal, each person must discover for him or herself which image(s) and allegories of the God/dess make sense, then apply this insight accordingly.

Someone once told me that God/dess was like a huge mirror, who at the beginning of time shattered into thousands of pieces, each lodging in a soul so that part of God/dess would always be within us. This parable is similar to our own rede of "as within, so without." So, in your search for the "right" name for your image of God/dess, remember to also look within your own heart. You might just be surprised at the wisdom found there.

Elements of Ritual

Nature I loved; and next to Nature art,
I warmed my hands before the fire of life.
— Walter Landor

By definition, a ritual is anything where a specific procedure or approach is followed regularly. In more down-to-earth terms, this translates to the "get up and brush your teeth" ritual, "going to work" ritual, "sleeping on Saturday" ritual and the "dinner at mom's" ritual you may experience periodically even now. Humans are creatures of habit. We tend to like a certain amount of order and consistency. In this way, our existence itself becomes a ritual performed by the simple act of living.

In terms of magic, there are both formal and informal rituals available from many traditions, or better yet, you can write your own. At first, this thought may shock or even frighten you a bit, but there are a growing number of Wiccans today practicing what I call creative ritual work. This is done in an effort to continue personalizing the Craft, thus allowing their magic to grow with them and the world around them.

By understanding the basic elements of ritual work, you too can write and perform your own rituals to reflect any need or occasion. The first, best thing to remember is that for something to be considered a ritual all you need do is create a Sacred Space, do something magical in that space (a specific purpose is recommended) and close the Sacred Space.

At first glance this may seem overly simplified, but it can really be that uncomplicated. Magical work can be performed in almost any fashion from the unfettered to the sublime, as long as you remember that no amount of trapping will make the ritual effective if you don't truly believe in what you are doing. Magic is a unique combination of universal energy, will power, imagination, and faith. Rituals, in order to be productive, must contain these ingredients from the start. With those ingredients in mind, writing a ritual is as simply a matter of deciding what you want to say/do, and how you want to say/do it.

One of the most wonderful circles I ever participated in was spontaneous among 70 people all from different magical paths. We didn't know each other's names; we only knew a few of the same songs, but before long, the simplicity of our desire to create a special moment flowed into a wave of warm energy felt by all in attendance. This was real magic, where a group of people could gather with a common goal, putting aside small differences, and bless each other. This experience is why I believe in the creative power of heart-felt ritual, whether it is written by a teacher, a priest/ess, or done completely on impulse. This is also why I encourage everyone to try writing or holding their own spontaneous ritual at least once, if for no other reason than for the educational experience it offers. I guarantee you will understand more about ritual and magic afterwards.

Generally speaking, rituals are held to commemorate the natural cycles: the phases of the moon, the progress of the sun, and the seasons. The customary celebrations of Wicca, and those of the Victorian calendar are discussed in Chapter Three of this book, but those dates should not preclude you from holding a rite any time you feel the need.

Ritual Tools

Before I begin discussing some general tools of ritual, it is important to remember that these are in no way necessary to an effective magical working. Magic is available to you anytime, anywhere, with nothing more than the will necessary to bring it to fruition. Yet, tools have a very important place in our tradition, as they help us to focus our minds on something other than the mundane. Just as your knowledge allows you to fix the sink with the aid of a wrench, tools of magic simply give you a conduit for what is already part of you. Tools themselves are just instruments; you are the enabler, the responsible party for whatever energy is created.

The movements and words of a ritual (including dance and music) are believed to help bring the mind, body, and soul into a new awareness. Thus, understanding what items Witches have used in magic and why becomes important to furthering our understanding of the Craft as a whole. After you have this knowledge, you can decide for yourself which ones you would like to use, if any. In this way, the decentralized nature of Wicca allows us great personal diversity in our faith, and in the manner which we observe that faith.

Things which are commonly in the sacred space include a symbol of the God/dess, various colored candles, the athame (ritual knife), incense, salt, water, the chalice, ritual notes, ritual robe and symbolic representations of the various elements. It is easiest to explain each of these separately first, then as a group of harmoniously functioning tools.

To begin, you need to find a place that will act as an *altar*. In other words, a flat surface where you can lay out all of your tools, and one which will not be damaged by wax drippings. If you like, you can have a central altar for your tools, and four other mini-altars, each set up in one of the four elemental directions, as discussed in Circle Casting below. My altar is the top of a bookshelf which is high enough to elude both my son and my 5 cats.

My best friend uses the lid to a basket where everything is stored after ritual. Sometimes I use my dining room table! What is most important is that this area be secure so everything stays in place, and that it is consistently accessible for your ritual work. Even a window ledge will do, just so you have a place you can set things when not in use.

Your *God/dess symbol* can be almost anything. Some Witches use actual figurines, others employ pictures, posters or art and still others use natural objects such as flowers, interestingly shaped rocks, etc. I will very often change the type of God/dess symbol used in my sacred space to reflect the season or ritual more directly. An example of this can be found in Chapter Two, where I give directions on how to make the corn husk Goddess, who is adorned with colors and flowers according to the time of year it is.

It is good to mention here that your ritual cup and knife are also representations of the male/female energies, so if you want, they too can portray the Divine in your rituals. The idea here is simply to make a place in your sacred space for that special God/dess energy, symbolized by making a place for the God/dess image.

The *athame,* or ritual knife, is a personal thing. Instead of the athame, some Witches prefer to use a wooden or metal and crystal wand, others employ swords and staves to trace pentagrams and cast their magic circles. You can just use your hand, if you wish. The athame is customarily doubled-edged to remind us of the dual nature of our humanity, and thus to use our power with care. It is used for marking the boundary of a magic circle, for opening and closing entryways into that sacred space, and often for tracing magical sigils in the air.

In certain traditions, especially those of a more specialized nature, this knife is set aside and used for nothing other than magical workings. Others, however, have no objections to employing the knife to cut their herbs, or even to using it at the dinner table. Either way is correct depending on your viewpoint and feelings towards your tools.

I do recommend that you have a special wrapping or storage area in which to keep your athame and all your magical tools while not in use. This keeps people from handling them without thought, and also helps protect your tools from undesired energies. Good examples of protective storage are: wrapping in a white cotton or silk cloth (the color of protection), placing them in a cedar box, putting them in a pouch or drawer, or setting them back on your altar.

Incense is used in ritual for two reasons. First, I personally find the fresh smell helps me to center my attention on the matter at hand. In this respect, it creates a special atmosphere in which you can work. Second, and perhaps more important, is the magical significance of the ingredients in the incense. In Chapter Six of this book, I describe a little of the history of incense, how to make your own, and how to choose herbs according to their metaphysical attributes to help increase the effectiveness of your efforts. If you buy incense from a store, try to consider these attributes so that you have the "right tool for the right job." If you are allergic to smoke, you can simply have the incense or herbs on your altar, without burning them. It is not so much the burning of the incense as what the ingredients symbolize to you that is important. I should also note here that it is sometimes helpful to use the same incense each time you perform a specific ritual or spell because then it helps to subconsciously remind you of the purpose of your magical working.

Incense and burners come in many forms. In the context of this book, I am talking about using powdered incense to sprinkle over charcoal because that is the type of incense that I personally make. It allows me to use only as much as desired. No matter what form of incense you choose, be sure get the right type of holder, so that treasured items do not end up burned by ashes or sparks.

Candles are used in ritual in much the same way as incense is, for the ambiance they give. Their light is softer, easier on the eyes, and more conducive to aiding heightened awareness than that of florescent bulbs. Candles are often lit at the four elemental points, and are often different colors for this purpose. Red and orange are good for fire, blue and purple for water, brown and green for earth, yellow for air. A white candle is often used to represent the God/dess or the protective white-light spoken of in the following section of the book called "Creating a Sacred Space." Sometimes a Witch will "dress" the candle as a way of preparing it for ritual use. This is simply anointing it with a specially prepared, scented oil. Apply the oil to the center of the candle and rub it toward the top, then toward the bottom. The oil is chosen for its magical significance, depending on the purpose of the ritual.

In picking out candle holders, try to find ones which have a good base so that perfectly good altar cloths are not ruined by wax, or better yet, get dripless candles. Most importantly, be certain your flames are a safe distance from walls, dry flowers and any other flammable items. If you are renting space for ritual work, be sure to ask if "open flame" is allowed in their insurance codes. Safety and wisdom are part of magic too.

Salt and water are often used to represent the elements of Earth and Sea. Salt is specifically employed because of its association with cleansing and purification. In this manner, salt water (or just salt) may be sprinkled around the sacred space as a means of cleansing any negative energies and helping to protect the circle. Salt water may also be sprinkled on the participants of a circle for the same effect. Both the salt and water are usually placed in a silver or earthenware container, the latter often being held by the chalice, or small cauldron.

In the section on "Casting a Circle" (soon to follow in this chapter), I share the idea of the four elements and their role in a magical space, but I would like to take a moment to share a means to represent these elements in creative ways. For example, the table for the South often houses a red or orange candle, representing fire. If you do not have a candle, you could place a red or orange crystal, cloth, or floral arrangement there to represent that element. Other alternatives include a cauldron, some matches, fire coral, a child's fire engine or anything you associate with fire. Remember, the object itself is not as important as the connection it has to your perceptions. What's really nice about many of these objects is the fact that you can leave them out after ritual without anyone asking questions!

One last item I would like to tackle here is that of *ritual clothing*. I honestly don't know how a robe came to be the customary garment for magic, but I assume it had to do with some of our druidical history and roots in Medieval Europe. I believe, however, that wearing different clothing from your norm is a good idea. What you wear makes you feel different. When you have one special outfit set aside for a function, each time you put it on, it ques your thought process towards that specific function. Some groups do practice their rituals "sky clad" or without clothing because they feel it brings them closer to nature and releases them from the pretense of materially based images. However, you should not practice sky clad if you are uncomfortable with it. I have worn everything from a jeans and a robe to my pink drop-drawer pajamas and slippers for magic depending on the time and circumstances involved! Perhaps a kimono you find in an antique store, or a flowing blouse that was given to you by a dear friend will become your magical "robe." Whatever your choice, make sure you can sit, stand, dance and move comfortably in it (without falling).

Remember that clothing itself (or the lack thereof) will not determine the success of your undertaking except in the way it affects your attitude, so choose something you are at ease in, but which is also somehow special.

Creating Sacred Space

They tune their hearts, by far the noblest aim.
— Robert Burns

At first the thought of creating sacred space can seem rather intimidating. After all, the first images that come to mind are of lofty cathedrals where people are afraid to talk. But, when you get to the heart of the matter, creating sacred space is more a matter of your attitude than any number of actions or words. For example, when we entered a church as children, we were often quiet out of reverence. Likewise, when we set aside a place for our personal magical work, it needs to be treated with respect, be this area a bookshelf, living room, or forest glade. The same woods you might run through gaily on a picnic outing may need to be entered with softer steps when preparing for ritual. Your attitude toward the space has changed its function.

Once you have the right frame of mind, you can then begin to set up protection for your space. The reason for doing this is simply one of precaution. Metaphysical energy attracts a certain amount of attention from beings of a spiritual nature. Just as you wouldn't leave the front door of your house open to anyone who happened by, you likewise need to close "supernatural" doors. Commonly this is done in Wicca through what is called casting a circle, calling the quarters or watchtowers, and/or putting up white-light barriers.

The last is perhaps the easiest to explain. White light is considered as symbolic of pure, protective energy. To begin, sit quietly with your eyes closed, imagining a white light surrounding first you, and then the area where you are working in. Most people find it easiest to envision this coming from above them, like sunshine does. As you see this clearly in your mind, allow the light to grow brighter. With a little practice you may notice you feel warmer, the room seems quieter (or somehow different) after you begin. This is a pretty good indication that you have done it correctly.

If you find that the image of white light does not leave you feeling safe and secure, try instead projecting images in your mind of items or people on the walls and ceiling of the room which do make you feel protected. I have a friend who envisions classical paintings, her cat, and the face of a baby around her before she begins any work. Another companion sets out different crystals from her altar in sections of the room, picturing them pouring light throughout the space. These examples show you how experimenting can help you discover what works best, and that there is little to impede exactly what images/objects you use other than the limits of your own mind.

Casting a Circle

After you find the best way to protect your sacred area, then you can move on to actually casting the circle and calling the quarters. To do this, it is first important to understand the symbolism involved. The circle itself is forever returning to itself, being the emblem of our soul's passage from birth, life, and death to rebirth (reincarnation). Through science we know that energy cannot be created or destroyed, it simply changes form, so it is for the soul, which is our spiritual energy, the essence which makes us unique individuals.

The four quarters, directions, winds or watchtowers (depending on your nomenclature) are replete with symbolism. It is believed that these four points of your circle have guardians, which are comparable to angelic beings, that are welcomed into the sacred space to protect and bless the workings. These beings may simply be called "guardians," but if you prefer you can use some of the names associated with the quarters given below.

In Wicca, North represents the element of earth, midnight, winter, the sense of touch, and the angelic spirit of Gabriel. South is the balance of the North, being fire, noon, summer, energy, and the sense of sight guarded by the angel Ariel. East is the place of dawn, spring, any magic dealing with the mental or our sense of smell, something that is carried on the winds, and the angelic being Michael. West is water, emotions, intuition, twilight, fall, the sense of taste, and the angel Raphael. In some traditions, a fifth elemental point, that of the center, is added to represent the spirit, transformation, movement, and the sense of hearing. These four or five mini-altars (or points on your main altar) are set up to represent the outer barrier of your magical space, to protect it, and help establish a special energy area in which magic can be built. Each one of these elements is called and welcomed into the sacred space by the invocation, sometimes specifically by name, and other times by a general greeting.

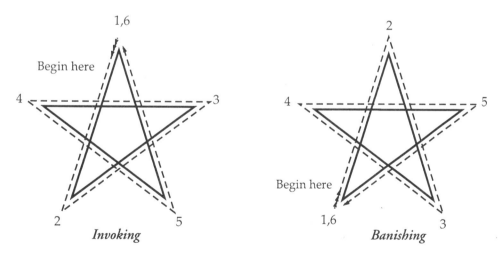

Invoking   *Banishing*

Then there is the all too often misunderstood pentagram. Interpretations of this symbol vary slightly depending on magical tradition, so I will give you my own to mull over. To me, the five points of this star represent the four basic elements of earth, air, fire and water, plus a fifth element of the self/spirit. The center of the pentagram is where all of these things work in perfect balance and harmony to create what is commonly called "magic." The image of the pentagram is often scribed in the air, over items, or near individuals for blessing and protection. Usually, when this is drawn, a visualization is also used to give it almost visible energy which can remain in that spot until released. In old days, sigils like this, which could be recognized by others of magical knowledge through trace energies, may have been called a wizard's mark. The two predominant types of pentagrams drawn in a circle are those for *invoking*, or welcoming energies, and those for dismissing or *banishing* energy (see diagram). The pentagram may be drawn in the air with a wand, athame (ritual knife), sword, staff or even one's hand.

There are actually many different ways to cast your circle, depending on with what you are most comfortable. There are times when I walk to my altar and welcome the powers by saying nothing more than, "Guardians of the four winds, please join me," if I get that formal. I often salute the Divine presence in a similar, unadorned manner. This approach is not lacking in respect, as I always settle my mind and heart first before I move towards magic. I just find that I prefer words and ways that are comfortable for the straight-forward homebody that I am. In my early days in Craft, however, I used more "conventional" methods until I found other ones which were more reflective of my Path. I would like to share two of these procedures here.

Circle Casting I

This first circle casting is designed for a small group of people. Begin by setting up your sacred space in one of two ways, depending on available room. Either have an altar in the center with all four elements represented on it, or have the central altar plus four small tables around the room which are placed in the appropriate directions. If you use the small tables, take whatever symbols you have chosen and place them on those tables.

Once the room is set up with plenty of space, have four members of the group walk to the four corners of the altar/room one at a time, beginning in the East, and either light the candles or place the symbols of the elements in their respective positions, speaking out loud some type of welcome to that Guardian power. An example for the Eastern point might be, "Greetings to the Powers of the Air, Thank you for blessing our sacred space. Protect us from all danger approaching from the East, and bring us the winds of change. So be it."

Depending on the tradition, sometimes an invoking pentagram is drawn in the air by the speaker during their salutation. I have also seen groups where the speaker walks clockwise once around the entire circle, with the candle or symbol in hand, providing a visual means of surrounding the space with that energy. The candle/symbol is then set on the table and they return to the Circle.

These actions and words are considered an invocation to summon that specific energy to your Circle. When writing or choosing your invocations, consider the people who will be saying them so that the words are comfortable on their lips. I personally recommend reasonably short invocations because they can be memorized. This allows the participants to concentrate on the feeling behind the words instead of a piece of paper in front of them. I have also found this makes for a much smoother ritual with fewer distractions. Other examples of invocations can be found in Chapter Three, "Celebrating the Seasons."

Once the invocation has been voiced to all four points and the individuals have returned to the Circle, the next step is to have the leader of the group bind them together in love and trust for the working. This is usually done by some type of summary invocation, my personal favorite goes as follows:

Children of this circle, braid ye to me, one by one
Till the golden flower blooms, and brings the light of suns
Let us join our hands, and bring the circle round
To share our magic with the land, all evil being bound.
We call the guardians of the winds, to wrap us in your arms
Keeping all within this Circle, safe from any harm.
So mote it be.

During this, all members of the circle should close their eyes and try to envision the words. When the speaker talks of "the light of suns" this is an opportunity to re-visualize the white light protection spoken of earlier this chapter. Hands should be joined to create a physical circle while saying the third verse. The term "so mote it be" is very much like the Christian "amen," meaning "so be it." It is simply an affirmation of belief. After this, you can proceed to sing, chant, meditate, study together, work a spell, or whatever else is planned for that gathering. By the way, this isn't Church. There is nothing wrong with shared laughter in your groups!

I should note at this point that magical Circles are considered to be "out of space, out of time," meaning that magic has no limits. I often recommend that watches be left outside the circle, or one person be responsible should someone need to get home by a specific hour. Your focus now should be on the spiritual, not the mundane. I also feel strongly that phones should be turned off or tended by an answering machine, and that the Circle should not be trampled through thoughtlessly. If someone needs to be excused from the circle, they should do so with proper respect for the magical space and the others in attendance.

When you are ready to leave, the process is basically reversed. The elemental quarters are thanked for their attendance and given a hearty farewell, this time ending with the East. In this instance the speaker for the East might say, "Watchtower of Air, we thank you for attending our Circle. Move now your winds to carry our work where it is needed. Farewell." After the four Guardians are dismissed, it is fairly traditional to close the meeting with a saying which goes, "Merry Meet, Merry Part, and Merry Meet Again." This phrase wraps up with eight words the joy of gathering with a common goal, and the fact that we are all part of a much greater Circle than the one we just attended.

Circle Casting II

Since I am a solitary practitioner of magic, I could spend days talking about working magic alone (and usually do with those willing to listen). To balance this, however, let me say that I hold no disdain for covens, it is just that formal group settings never seemed to work for me personally; the "spark" just wasn't there. Because of this, I have spent a fair amount of time and energy creating solitary rituals.

Even if you are part of a coven, there may still be times when you will want to work alone, especially if the magic concerns a private matter. In this instance, if you are reworking someone else's words or even the traditional rituals of your group, "I" is substituted for "We" throughout the text, and you are the one who will be performing the whole ceremony from beginning to end.

While rituals with a group have a special energy to them which comes from sharing, solitary rites can be just as moving and powerful, giving us the opportunity to work unhindered by any awkwardness we might feel with other people around. Solitary rites are where we can be 100% ourselves, working magic in the way our heart chooses to express it.

In preparation, you may not want to set up a full room with four cardinal points, but instead just arrange your personal altar. At home, I put the vacuum cleaner out of my range of sight, turn on some soft instrumental music, and spend time with the God/dess who lives inside and outside of myself. Once I feel settled and my mind is not thinking about the burnt roast or problems at work, I begin.

As with a group, you should create your sacred space and cast a circle, but this time instead of using the group's ritual form, you can choose to use your own. Again, I encourage trying it, there is a lot of freedom found in these moments. In the sample invocation which follows, the elements are called in the order of East, South, West and North, proceeding around your circle clockwise. The last two verses of the invocation are spoken in the center, to "set" the circle into place until you release it.

(East)
Of quiet time and lessons learned,
I want to sing of something found
Of passages that I have earned,
Books of life that I have bound.

(South)
Spirit guides and Masters all
Those that would to show me grace
Tis to you I come and call
While in this world I seek my place.

(West)
Of quiet thought and healing rest
I want to sing of something whole
Of times when men withstood the test
To find new freedom in their soul.

(North)
Spirit guides and Masters hear
Those that would to teach me love
Wash away the earth-worn tears
Release in me the peaceful dove.

(Center)
Of quiet joy and sights so rare
I want to sing of something grand
Of gifts revealed as mine to share
Of wonders carried by my hands.

Spirit guides and Masters see
Those that would to grant me flight
Tis with You I come to be
A God/dess flying wings of light.
So mote it be.

You can then proceed to work your spell or ritual, meditate, read, or whatever you want to accomplish during this time. Remember to dismiss and thank the guardians when you are ready to close, leaving the sacred space with the same respectful attitude as when you came.

Cleansing

When'er a sunny gleam appears
To brighten up our veil of tears . . .
— Sir Walter Scott

Before any object or tool is used as a focus for metaphysical energy, it is always a good idea to cleanse it. This way, any residue negativity which it may have "picked up" from its environment will not affect you or your magical efforts. By purifying your tools, you can then approach them fresh and make them completely yours through a process of claiming (described later in this chapter).

I recommend several different methods of cleansing objects. First is that of soaking the object in charged spring water mixed with a touch of salt. The salt and the water are symbolic of cleansing. As the object sits in the water, visualize any spiritual "dirt" being washed away until the item is almost like new again. This newness is not in appearance, but in the way it feels to you. If the article cannot be soaked in water because of its components, you may sprinkle the salt water around it, using the same imagery.

Another approach, which comes to us from our Celtic ancestors, is that of passing an object through smoke or flames. One of the most common traditions from May Day celebrations in Scotland was to walk the cattle through the smoke of the fires that morning, believing this would cleanse them of any sickness and keep them well for the following year. In many cultures, fire is seen as a purifier, quite literally burning away the old, leaving only an unblemished core. Now, obviously, you do not want to burn your tools or any other items that you are cleansing. To cleanse something, pass the item through the smoke of incense or a wood fire. If you like, you can even add traditional herbs of protection and cleansing (myrrh, rosemary, cloves, sandalwood, frankincense and cinnamon are all good choices) to the incense or hearth for added potency. Again, you should envision any soil leaving the item and being moved away with the smoke.

A third technique for cleansing utilizes rich soil as the focus. If the object you wished cleansed can sit in earth without it being damaged, this is a very effective means of cleansing. Pour your soil (potting soil or top soil is best) into an earthen-ware bowl, placing the object inside with equal amounts of soil all around it. Then hold the bowl in both hands, picturing white light pouring liberally into the soil as if it were water. As you do, also envision any negativity as dirt, which leaves the item and merges with the soil. You can then remove the object, and use this soil in your garden, for herbs or whatever you need. The white light you have poured into it will help your plants to grow.

The fourth method, the use of bundles of burning sage and cedar, comes to us through Native American traditions. These herbal wands, known commonly as smudge sticks, are often available at herb shops, cooperatives, and especially any place which sells Native American items. I do issue a little caution as they can spark unexpectedly when burned, however they are excellent to use in any environment to eliminate negative energy) or odors) and bring an increased sense of balance.

Charging

> *Religion is a great force;*
> *the only real motive force in the world.*
> —George Bernard Shaw

Similar to a battery, objects (especially crystals) used in magic can be charged with a specific type of power to increase the effectiveness of a spell/ritual, to place around the house for a special purpose, or to give to someone in need. For example, if a friend has been ill for a while, you may wish to give them a crystal filled with healing energy. Or, if you frequently use your wand to cast a circle, you may wish to saturate it with protective magic.

The way an object can be charged varies depending on its intended use. Perhaps the most common method is to leave the item in the light of the sun or moon during a particular time, season or phase, usually for a span of three days/nights. The light of the sun rising could be used to charge an object and then the object could be used to increase someone's physical strength, whereas a setting sun's rays might be used to help calm nervous energy. In magic, the sun is traditionally associated with matters of strength, virility, intellect, logic, law, and the masculine energy.

On the other hand, the moon is employed for energy pertaining to fertility, nurturing, creativity, intuition, and the feminine. One way of using the moon in a spell would be to set a covered bottle of water in the light of a Full Moon, then drink it before working on any artistic endeavor.

To take this idea one step further, I would like to add that you can combine traditional magical symbolism with this charging process. In the aforementioned examples, the basic correlations of dusk, dawn, and water were added for more refined results. Other ideas along these lines include charging a sprig of basil (which is magically associated with love) with a rising sun and giving it to your mate as a emblem of growing devotion and fire in your relationship. Or, you could place some caraway seeds (which are related to luck) in the light of a waxing moon then sew them into a little sachet to help increase your good fortune.

Use a little imagination and intuition and add a bit of research concerning the magical affiliations of various things. Then the useful nature of charging techniques becomes a limitless tool in your magical work.

Blessing

> *. . . finds tongues in trees,*
> *books in the running brooks,*
> *sermons in the stones,*
> *and good in everything . . .*
> — William Wordsworth

Blessing is a means to entreat Divine favor for a specific person or object. In magic, we sometimes bless people: a couple during their marriage, or a child when born. Witches also bless objects whose intended application is within the magical Circle or as a gift to someone we hold dear. A very old and venerated method for blessing is that of "laying on of hands." Throughout the history of religious observances, the hands have always been considered the conduit of Divine energy.

Blessing is really very simple. Begin by visualizing the white light spoken of before, only this time allow it to flow through you into the object or person. It is good at this point to speak the purpose of the blessing. This may be as simple as, "Divine powers, I ask that you grant this couple/child joy in life, and fill each day with light and love." However, if you are blessing an object, you may wish to state the intended function of the item at this time. For example, "Lord and Lady of Light, I ask that you bless this crystal with the energy of fire for use in the Southern point of my altar. By my will and Your power, so be it." In this way, you have not only invoked the Divine favor, but given your crystal a unique purpose for your magic, one which will only be enhanced by use.

Claiming

Just as not all people fit into a size ten shoe, not all magical tools "fit" everyone who comes across them. Sometimes you will sense that you should purchase a certain tool, yet feel slightly uncomfortable with it because of residual energy. In this case, you could cleanse the item. After doing this, you may wish to set the tool apart for your personal use only.

Some items you come across for your magical work may come to mean more to you than others, but as you collect your paraphernalia you should spend some amount of time getting familiar with each of them and charging them with your energy. If you think of your tools as if they were empty cups and your own energy as water, the more you pour into the cups, the more they become filled with your power.

Charging an item with personal energy can be as easy as carrying it with you on a very frequent basis. The more you use or carry an object, the more it will become "attuned" to your spiritual energy. However, if you have a special item which you want to keep separate and use for personal magic, you may want to actually have a claiming ritual to mark it for that function.

Again, create your sacred space, making the object the center of your altar. You will want to mark the tool in some way during this ritual, whether by carving or painting something on it, by rubbing it with your skin oil as an animal does to "scent" something, or by anointing it with a drop of your blood. This last method may seem a little archaic and distasteful to some, but to me blood is a powerful symbol of personal life force. By placing a drop on your private tools, you are endowing them with that same vitality. It is simple to do. A little rubbing alcohol and small pin to prick the skin work fine to achieve the desired amount! If this technique is uncomfortable for you, then use one of the alternatives. For example, if you paint or carve a symbol on the item, allow it to be one which you feel represents the best of your true self.

During this procedure, you may get a message from the item by way of a mental image, a feeling in your hands, a scent in the room, or whatever. Pay attention to these signals. They will help you to know how to employ the tool for best results, and may give you a clue to the object's preferred name. I had a friend once who was carving a magical staff for himself. While he worked, on three separate occasions dragonflies landed on the staff. He interpreted this to mean that the staff was best used for spells or rituals which used fire as a component, and that the name of the staff would be "dragonfly."

While it may seem at first rather silly to name an inanimate object, the power of names should not be overlooked in magic. They carry a special vibration and strength all their own (more information on magical names is given in Chapter Thirteen). Because of this, naming an object and "claiming" it often go hand in hand. What is the first thing you do when you bring an animal home from the pet shop? What is the most talked about issue regarding an expected baby? Somehow in the process of choosing a name, we are also taking an object/person/animal into the circle of our lives on an intimate level. It is because of this amity that names and claiming can be useful in your magic.

On Halloween a witch is seen
As she stirs her mystic brew,
She reads within the smoke that curls
What the future holds for you.

Definition of Spells vs. Rituals

It is sometimes difficult to define the difference between a spell and a ritual because they usually encompass many of the same techniques. In my own mind, I define a spell almost as a mini-ritual. Some spells come to us through oral history and others are born out of our creativity. If we remind ourselves that the purpose of magic is to bend and move energy towards a desired goal, then a spell is the tool/technique which can help make such movement possible.

An old folk spell I have used with some success helps illustrate this idea. According to the version I was given, if someone is gossiping or somehow causing you ill-will, you write their name on a piece of paper. Then, as you fold this paper three times, in three directions (three has always been a favorite number among mystics due to the correlation between body-mind-soul, Maiden-Mother-Crone) you envision a white bubble of light all around it. Bind this paper with a white thread, again to reinforce the idea of protection, and place it in water to freeze, thus literally cooling and immobilizing the negativity. This is a non-harmful, non-manipulative spell that does nothing other than stop untruth and reflect dissenting energy back to its source.

The actions of writing, folding, binding and freezing serve as ways to focus your mind, your purpose, and your desire toward a specific energy, that of protection. The symbolism of these things gives direction to the protection: that of restricting or "freezing." Finally, the ice itself becomes the token of a reflective force now wrapped around you. Because of this, the contrary energy is bounced back to the initiator.

So, it can be said that some rituals are like elongated spells with the added dimension of religious observation added to them. Spells may be done within or without the magic Circle, prayer being considered a form of a spell. A spell is simply a deliberate process for achieving a goal when the normal material means has had little impact.

In creating spells for yourself, it is good to try work within natural law, to be precise and never assume anything. Take care that your work does not harm or manipulate others, and remember that spells rely on the symbolism they create in our subconscious mind in order to work toward a changed reality. Never employ a spell which makes no sense to you, which is in a language you don't understand, or one which you feel is not ethical, as it will either end up as wasted energy, or worse yet, go awry. One of the first rules of magic, and I think the best one, is to keep your good wits and wisdom about you, like a trusted friend.

The outward shows of sky and earth,
Of hill and valley he has viewed,
And impulses of deeper birth
Have come to him in solitude.
— William Wordsworth

Summary

This has been only a brief overview of the technicalities of magic. Don't let it overwhelm or worry you, there is no way you can learn all there is to know about the Craft in one day, or even perhaps one lifetime. Like everything else, magic takes practice and patience. It is a thriving, changing faith that does not have the written bylaws of more customary religions, but relies greatly on the inspiration and vision shared by those magicians living before us, and those yet to come.

The most important thing you can do is take magic one step at a time. Allow this chapter to act as a building block for your personal creative magic. Once you have your foundations, you can become the pioneer for a religion that will grow with you, bringing new awareness every day. This spirit of endeavor, and the foresight to use that energy toward a better tomorrow, was part of the legacy given to us by our Victorian ancestors, a legacy which you, through this book, can begin to discover.

May the Powers of Light be with you on this tremendous journey.

For what is truth today may tomorrow be only partially so to a developing soul.
—Edgar Cayce

He shall have there to good talent
When he has a good taste
And has eaten a good repast
And supped of the brewis* a sup
Slept after a sweet drop
Through Goddis help and my counsail
Soon he shall be fresh and hail.
                    Sir Walter Scott

* Broth

APPENDIX C

Magical Goods and Services

The worst kind of vice is advice.
—Samuel Taylor Coleridge

In the last seven years, and especially since I began editing "The Magi," I have been able to sample a wide range of goods and services available in the magical community. In your own search for quality products, I heartily suggest shopping around. Like the supermarket, price does not always insure value. Ask people you know for recommendations, write for catalogs and compare until you find something that not only appeals to your higher senses, but also your pocketbook.

The places I have listed below are those that I am personally acquainted with, or have heard excellent things about. Delivery times, quality of the products and the spirit with which it is made are all of high caliber, so I feel fairly comfortable in passing them along to you.

ABYSS
34 Cottage Street, Box 69
E. Hampton, MA 01027
413-527-8765
   Notes: Crystals, jewelry, herbs, Wicca, Shamanism, Celtic traditions, and Egyptian pieces.

BREWER'S EMPORIUM
241 River Street
Depew, NY 14043
(See Hennessy Homebrew on next page for notes.)

HENNESSY HOMEBREW
470 N. Greenbush Road (Rte 4)
Rensselaer, NY 12144
   Notes: If you are planning to begin making your own magical wines for ritual use, these two companies (Brewer's Emporium and Hennessey Homebrew) have some of the best prices on basic supplies you can find. Kits and books available. Please send SASE for catalog.

CASTLE RISING
The Ethnic Market
P.O. Box 3127
Morgantown, WV 26505
   Notes: One of the largest and most unusual collection of sparkling powders, stick/liquid incense, and perfumed oils. The scents are incredible! I believe they also have a catalog of magical goods, including small cauldrons, cups, athames, etc. $3.00 for catalog.

CIRCLE NETWORK NEWS
Box 219
Mt. Horeb, WI 53572
   Notes: A long standing journal of magic with consistently excellent articles and artwork. Networking guides, books and much more.

EARTH CARE PAPER PRODUCTS
Box 7070
Madison, WI 53707
   Notes: 100% recycled paper products including stationary and note cards. Also carry a line of cellulose bags for use in the kitchen in place of plastic. These are biodegradable!

EARTH MAGIC PRODUCTIONS
2170 Broadway, Suite 16
New York, NY 10024
   Notes: Books and tapes by Marion Weinstein, author of *Positive Magic*.

HOURGLASS CREATIONS & MAILLE ORDER
256 Rhode Island
Buffalo, NY 14213
   Notes: Historical herbalism, soaps, oils, creams, powder, tinctures, powder incense, pomanders, wood work, chain maille and leather creations, graphics. SASE for catalog or price quotes. Custom work encouraged!

KURLUK CANDLE SHOP
P. O. Box 6186
Baltimore MD 21231

Notes: Loose herbs (in quantities as small as one ounce), Mo Jo bags, powder and stick incense, herbal teas, magickal oils, and candles (excellent prices). Catalog $1.50.

LLEWELLYN'S NEW WORLDS (formerly New Times)
Box 64383-784
St. Paul, MN 55164-0383

Notes: Continual updates on new reading materials available for the magical community. Comments by prominent authors on various issues, interviews, newsletter listings and more!

LOTUS LIGHT
Box 2
Wilmot, WI 53192
414-862-2395

Notes: Wonderful essential oils, bulk herbs of 1 pound and up, herbal and floral vitamins, bath salts and literally hundreds of other earth-safe products, including natural flea care for pets. Excellent delivery time, no minimum order.

MERMADE MAGICKAL ARTS
Box 33-402
Long Beach, CA 90801

Notes: Many unique gift items which are very well crafted. Catalog $2.00.

MOONCIRCLES
235 Lexington Avenue
Buffalo, NY 14222

Notes: Beautiful hand-painted dresses with Pagan themes, tapes, books, jewelry, runes, incense, smudge pots and much more. What they don't have, they can often find for you. Please enclose SASE for information requested.

NEW MOON CREATIONS
Fay Esan
4819 William Street
Lancaster, NY 14086

Notes: Custom-made ritual garb, including robes, capes, and cloaks. Please send a detailed description of the item you are interested in (with SASE) for price quote.

PAGAN FREE PRESS RESOURCE LISTING
Box 55223
Tulsa, OK 74155
Notes: Hundreds of listings on goods and services in the magical community. Catalog is $8.00.

RAINBOW'S END HERBS
Jackie Swift
10084 Hooker Hill Road
Perrysburg, NY 14129
Notes: Jackie has a farm where she grows many of her herbs. She carries bulk herbs and spices in small amounts, as well as various herbal products, including oils, bath bundles, tinctures and more. Please send SASE for any information needed.

RODALE PRESS
Emmaus, PA 18098
215-967-5171
Notes: A distributor of many excellent books on herbalism and natural health care. Full listing of titles available. Direct orders through the publishing house accepted.

ROWAN TREE NEWS SAMPLE PACKET
Box 383
Northridge, CA 91328
Notes: Contains copies of "Rowan Tree News," Mystery School information, "The Unicorn" and "The Littlest Unicorn." The last of these is a lovely journal for children. Catalog is $5.00.

SILVERRAVEN
Box 1392
Mechanicsburg, PA 17055
Notes: Custom-made pottery for ritual use, including cups, plates, and candle holders. SilverRaven is the coordinator of the Wiccan Pagan Press Alliance and can often help you find other goods and services. Please send SASE for requested information.

WARES FOR THE MAGICKAL ECOLOGIST
Nora Beeman Fiorella
Box 21915
Santa Barbara, CA 93121
Notes: Dream shields, beaded jewelry, sachets. I especially love her totem pouches. Nora has a real sensitivity for the natural world and her work reflects it. Please send SASE for goods list. Custom work is encouraged!

GLOSSARY

A Glossary of Magical Terms

An expert is one who knows more and more of less and less.
— Nicholas M. Buttler

For those of you reading this book without the advantage of a background in magic, this Glossary is included to help you understand the meanings of words which may be unfamiliar to you. Interestingly enough, in reviewing this list you will also probably discover that commonplace terms will take on new connotations.

The world of magic has endured nearly 2,000 years of bad press and misunderstanding. By defining our jargon, the hope is that future misconceptions can be avoided. In every faith there are expressions used to interpret energy, God, and the many mysteries of the world that are just beyond our normal range of understanding. When we look closely at the meanings of these words, we suddenly discover that most of the teachings of the world religions have much in common. The central and most important theme in all of them is love. Realistically, however, love cannot exist unless informed insights begin to replace fallacy.

So take a moment to read this section. Allow it to become a bridge between magic and your everyday world, a place where they can meet and enjoy each other's company in Victorian peacefulness.

Adept — Person working within a mystical tradition who has gained power and insight through various levels of initiation and self development. This person is believed to be wise and knowledgeable beyond the human norm, and is often regarded as a teacher figure.

Air — One of the four elements taught in Medieval Alchemy. Sylphs are considered air spirits and the astrological signs of Libra, Gemini, and Aquarius are considered governed by this element. Air is traditionally represented in the Eastern portion of magical rituals—sometimes by feathers, incense or fans. The element itself may be employed as a component for magic dealing with change, movement, the mind, intuition, and learning.

Altar — Central area of a ritual space, for most religions. The tools of that faith, which are used for ritual are placed upon it. Often symbols of the God/dess and other important icons of the religion are on the altar.

Amulet — A small object, worn or carried on a person, believed to act in a protective manner for its carrier. Stones, a rabbit's foot, astrological symbols, St. Christopher medals, and the Abracadabra of the Gnostics are examples of amulets. The symbolic nature of the item may lend itself to the final application of the amulet. For example, the paw of a sure-footed animal might be kept as a amulet against falling, or the feather of an owl displayed as an amulet of wisdom. Amulets tend to give the wearer a mental sense of well-being, and when given as a gift are a means of showing concern for safety and welfare.

Archetype — A common image or original model of experience found in the subconscious or collective unconscious which relates to humanity's basic emotions and states throughout the various phases of living. Tarot card images portray archetypes. The major arcana of the Tarot are believed to be paradigms of existence, personality types, and encounters.

Asperge — Sprinkling water or wine around the circumference of a circle to bless or purify the area. May also be done on objects and people for the same purpose.

Astrology — One of the most popular forms of divination, astrology centers around the belief that certain celestial bodies influence human life, and that the cosmic situations at the time of a person's birth can act as a prediction of their future and personality. Originally a means of mapping out the earth for travelers, it dates back to the Babylonians.

Athame — The ritual dagger of Witches used in ceremony, an athame is usually black handled and double edged. The two edges represent the balance in all things. The blade itself is sometimes etched with magical symbols which have personal meanings for the user.

Aura — This natural field of energy that surrounds all living things is most easily experienced through body heat, but it is visible to some sensitives. The color and texture of this field is believed to indicate health, states of mind, and even spiritual ability.

Balance — The belief that we need to keep our lives on an even keel, including that of the spirit. It means acknowledging the light and dark of all things, keeping a solid perspective, temperance.

Banishing — A ritual designed specifically to ward off or alleviate negative influences through ceremony and/or prayer.

Blessing — The moving of Divine energy to an item or person to grant special protection, care, and love. The words "blessed be" are often used among Witches as a greeting and farewell.

Book of Shadows — Like a Bible for a Witch, this book contains beliefs, rituals, charms, spells and incantations. Often hand-written and kept with care, this book may be passed down through covens or created by the solitary practitioner.

Censer — A vessel in which incense is burned during rituals and meditations. It would often be swung or hung from a chain.

Centering — A means of bringing yourself back into emotional, physical, or spiritual focus through meditation and visualization, often by drawing energy into your center of gravity.

Channeling — The ability to allow oneself to become a medium, or doorway for a spiritual entity or energy to communicate or move through. For example, one person may channel healing energy and another may channel a spirit guide.

Chanting — Not unlike prayer, except usually more repetitious in nature. It is meant to bring about a specific mental state to aid the movement of magical energy.

Charging — Using your mind to place energy into an object for use at a later time. It is not unlike "plugging in" a battery, except this is accomplished through psychic force.

Charm — Object or incantation believed to have a beneficial power. From the Latin word meaning song, its meaning varies according to usage. An object might have a charm (incantation) for friendship placed on it, for example. Certain verbal charms illustrate the believed power of rhyme and rhythm as seen in the child's verse, "rain, rain go away."

Circle — The area where magical workings are done. The term "casting a circle" is used to describe the process of making sacred space through prayer, meditation, incense, and other methods spoken of in Appendix B. It is also a casual reference to the organization or group of people with which you are associated and with whom you do magical work.

Commune — Not to be confused with channeling, this is the ability to communicate with spirits or the Divine without opening yourself to them. In this instance, the person with a gift for communing might act like a long distance operator recounting information.

Component — In spells, this is some type of verbal prologue, physical gesture, or material element used to help focus the magical energy.

Consecration — To bless or sanctify an object, person, or area. Consecration is usually done for magical tools, the ritual space, the altar, and sometimes for individuals on special occasions, in order to be certain all negative influences are removed.

Craft, The — The term Wicca originally meant the Wise Craft, shortened today to simply "The Craft" in magical jargon. It is in no way associated with Satanism, as is often the misconception.

Cycles (life, death, rebirth) — In Wicca and Paganism, there is a belief that all life follows the specific cycles manifested in nature: birth, life, death, and rebirth. On a less grand scale, these cycles can take on a more personal nature, through circumstances which help us to grow and learn, thus helping us to leave the old behind, and find new beginnings.

Dark Moon — Another name for the New Moon, usually a time of rest before new labors.

Dedication — For children, this is likened to the baptism. It is a time of thankfulness when a child is brought before friends and the God/dess to bless and name.

Divination — The art of foretelling by many different, and sometimes unusual, means. The interpretation of signs and omens. Included in this are divining rods, runes, Tarot cards, clouds, dust, dice, and hundreds of other means throughout history and various cultures.

Drawing Down the Moon — Not unlike the Christian tradition, which believes that the sacrament figuratively becomes the body and blood of Christ, this is the magical tradition of drawing the Divine presence into the priest or priestess so that they become the personified figure of the God/dess for a particular ritual.

Dressing a Candle — Anointing a candle, from the center outward, with scented oil for ritual use.

Druidical — The druids were originally a Celtic order of astronomers and healers. In recent days, people who have druidical callings are thought of as people with a strong understanding of and attachment to nature. They often have a strong desire to preserve it.

Earth — Another of the alchemical elements. Gnomes and goblins are considered Earth creatures. Taurus, Virgo and Capricorn are governed by this element. Earth is a grounding element. It is used to symbolize growth and stability in magic, and stands in the Northern point of a magical circle.

East — The place where most rituals begin for White Witches, East is the point of the morning star and new beginnings, thus a sign of illumination and new life. In the magical circle it is represented by the element of Air.

Elements, the — In the Middle Ages, the world was divided up by alchemists into four major elements: Earth, Air, Fire and Water. In the Tarot these are represented respectively by pentagrams, wands, swords and cups. In the Cabalistic tradition, the sacred name of God, YHVH likewise carried the elements in the order of Fire, Water, Air and Earth. The Hindu faith adds one more element, that of Spirit, or Ether, to represent the other four in perfect balance, the center of the pentagram, and the Void.

Esbats — A magical meeting which celebrates a particular phase of the moon, most often the Full Moon. Considered a good time to concentrate on magical teaching, especially as it pertains to intuition and creativity.

Familiar — Some form of animal which has a strong psychic link with a Witch. This animal is treated as a magical partner, and believed to lend energy and insight to the magic user. Was at one time believed to be an incarnated portion of the soul of the person who had the creature.

Fates — Destiny. In Greece, the three faces of Fate were: the one who governed birth and the thread of life, the one who determined the length of a life (the length of the thread), and the last who cut the thread at death. Likewise in the Craft, the Goddess has three aspects, personified by the Maiden, Mother and Crone.

Feminine — In magic, everything from plants to planets are divided by their traits, some being considered Yin, or feminine in nature, others being Yang, or masculine. Generally, feminine aspects have to do with intuition, instinct, love, healing, the moon, and gentle arts. Each polarity is venerated for its qualities, neither male nor female being greater, simply different. The feminine nature is often represented by the moon.

Fire — The third element of the alchemical tradition, fire is a purifier, an element of change. It stands in the Southern point of the magic circle, presumably because areas in the South tend to be hotter. Animals aligned with fire include lizards, many desert creatures, and the fabled dragon. Magic employing fire as a symbol is often centered around energy and the will.

Full Moon — In magic, the nights of a Full Moon are used to bring fruitfulness to any endeavor. It is a time of fertility and creativity. An excellent period to work magics dealing with drawing favorable energy into yourself, healing, love, etc.

God/dess — A way of writing a term for the Divine being which represents both male and female attributes.

Grail — From ancient traditions, especially the Celtic and European, this is a magical cup, cauldron, or horn which contains healing elixir and the water of life. In the Christian tradition, it was the cup which was used at the last supper, and which caught the blood of Christ at the crucifixion.

Grimoire — This originally referred to old textbooks of European magic written between the 17th and 18th centuries. These books contained information on spells, divinations, charms, recipes, etc. The name may have been a derivative of a Latin word for magic or a Norse term, grima, meaning specter. Today a grimoire is considered a collection of herbals, spells, rituals, and other useful magical information.

Grounding — A means of calming energy and dispersing it into the Earth. An especially good practice for jittery people is to sit up against a large tree, and allow their nervous energy to flow into the roots below them. Grounding is a way to compose one's mind and spirit.

Guardians — An alternative name for the four elements, the four directions and/or the four watchtowers. The term is also sometimes used to describe angelic beings which stand watch in these prescribed areas. It comes from a belief that the elements have at least symbolic power to protect against negative influences approaching from their quarter of influence.

Healing Magic — In early days, before the origins of disease were known, many turned to magical cures to ease the mind, and hopefully the body. In all instances of healing, both Christian and magical, touching or laying on of hands has been an important factor in imparting that blessing. Techniques included methods of attempting to transfer disease to an animal or other object. In some instances, these techniques seemed to work, which may be attributable to their psychological benefits. Today's methods include auric balancing, bio feedback, crystals, touch therapy, herbalism combined with magic, and many more.

Herbalism — The use of various plants to promote health or to make substances, such as creams, powder, deodorizers and other useful products. Modern science has shown that many of the old herbal techniques handed down to us from the middle ages and earlier do have value. Magical herbalism combines the symbolism of the plant with the known attributes and uses them as components for spells and rituals. Older beliefs centered on the ideas of like curing like. For example a round, smooth onion was thought to be a magical cure for baldness, and anything which had a bad smell could keep away evil spirits. Magical herbalism also uses planetary correspondences, special harvesting times, and astrology to aid the overall effectiveness of the outcome.

Hermetic — Hermetic texts date back to the early days of Christianity, and contain information on astrology, magic and other intellectual pursuits. These writings had a considerable effect on European thought, to the point where the study of mysticism could be perceived as scholarly. Hermetic orders tend to remain secluded in order to study. This symbolism is carried over into magic in many ways, not the least of which is the Hermit of the Tarot, who signals the need for retreat and introspection.

High Magic — As opposed to other forms of magic, this is a detailed, very ceremonial form, often based on Egyptian traditions.

Higher Self — The belief that within each person there is a Divine spark, a highly spiritual being whom we can listen to for guidance, not unlike a conscience.

Hourly Correspondence — In certain forms of magic, each hour has a significant effect on rituals and spell casting. This correspondence is often combined with those of the moon, sun and planets to augment the effect.

Icon — Object of uncritical devotion, sacred painting, mosaic or statue.

Initiation — Similar in some ways to a baptism into a Church, initiation marks the acknowledgement of a magical path and acceptance of certain tenets of that path. In certain traditions, there are levels of initiation which designate degrees of knowledge and adeptness.

Invoke — To call upon, appeal, or summon. Invocations in magic are usually done at the opening of a circle to bring protective powers and assist the overall, positive functioning of the sacred space being created for ritual.

Karma — Linked with the belief in reincarnation, karma is the law of cause and effect; the idea being that whatever you do in your life you are accountable for it, either now or in your next existence. For example, one who murders in this life might find themselves at the mercy of another in their next incarnation as a way of balancing that negative karma.

Kitchen Witch — Someone who takes a hearth and home approach to the mystical, and who takes tools from the home and employs them for magical ends. This is a very simple and personal form of magic meant to reflect a unique vision of the Divine and the individual's place in the greater scheme of things.

Libation — Pouring a little wine or other liquid on the ground during ritual as a way of thanking the Earth for her bounty.

Magic — The moving of universal energy by use of the will towards a specific use and function. Although considered by the common public as supernatural, most people involved in magic see it as an ability anyone can develop with time, patience, and study.

Magic Circle — A gathering of people (or even one person) where sacred space has been created for the working of magic.

Masculine — As opposed to feminine energy, this is the radiant sun, strength, intellect, and logic. The masculine form of the Goddess is the horned god (a type of Pan) who reminds us of our link to nature, and who is sometimes represented by the sun.

Medicine Pouch — Depending on the tradition, a medicine pouch may be one which is worn to hold special stones or other items which act together like an amulet or charm. In Native American traditions, a similar pouch is sometimes linked with the healer of the tribe and filled with useful herbs.

Meditation — A means of calming the mind and spirit through breathing techniques and introspection. Deliberate thoughtfulness on one subject to gain insight and perspective.

Moon Magic — Any magic using the moon phases as a component in its spells or rituals. Also magic dealing with the unconscious mind, instinct, psychic phenomena, healing, and the feminine aspects.

New Age — Considered to be a change in the overall vibration of the Earth, a New Age is marked by the movement of the Earth into a new sphere of the sky in astrology. It is believed that the present age is one which will bring increased awareness of the Earth, of psychic gifts and an increase in harmony among peoples.

Offering — The presentation of gifts to the God/dess in thankfulness, often first fruits of the garden, grain, etc.

Pagan — When the early Church came on the scene, the popularity of Pagan traditions proved to be a real problem. Saint's days replaced Pagan holidays in an attempt to displace the old gods as portray them as evil spirits. Similarly, magic wells and trees became Gospel Oaks and Holy Springs.

Today, Pagans usually follow a myriad of Divine images or believe that there are many faces and facets to the same God/dess. Their worship is diversified, often being based in nature.

Pentacle — Also known as the Star of Bethlehem, it was originally a symbol of health and life. It was probably derived from the pentagram shape which appears when you cut an apple core in half. Later, it became known as the Witch's cross and is believed to represent all four elements, (the fifth point being the self).

Planetary Correspondence — The placement of the planets and their astrological significances are sometimes used to create specific effects in magic. In this respect, a plant might be picked or a ritual might take place at a special time in order to help increase its effectiveness.

Poltergeist — Translated from two words meaning "uproar" and "ghost." These are mischievous and often unhappy spirits who make themselves known by noises or other means.

Psychic — Someone who is apparently able to understand or use powers outside the normal range of physical law. These abilities are believed to be linked with the mind.

Quarters — The four directions or elements used in creating a magic circle or sacred space.

Reincarnation — The belief that the soul or spirit of a person is immortal, and returns to physical existence after death. This cycle of life, death, and rebirth is repeated until the spirit has purified itself to the point of universal knowledge and understanding, thus returning to God/dess.

Ritual — Life itself is ritualistic in nature. The order in which religious services are performed is a ritual. In magic, basic elements of the ritual include preparing a sacred space, performing the purpose of the gathering, sharing of wine and cakes, then dismissing the circle.

Ritual Cup — A cup, bowl, horn or other drinking vessel which holds a liquid for use during the ritual. The liquid presented in the ritual cup is also usually symbolic in nature, having been prepared for the purpose of the gathering.

Runes — An early form of writing from Germany, runes were chiefly used for communication and magical markings. They were carved in places where the user thought they would be most effective. Today runes are cast as a means of divination, carved into objects for protection, and sometimes used in visualizations to bring their believed attributes into our lives.

Sabbat — The name given to the eight great festivals of the year, celebrating the movement of the sun through the sky, the turn of the seasons. (See also the magical calendar in Chapter Three).

Scribe a Circle — The act of drawing a protective circle, literally or figuratively, in a room to prepare the sacred space.

Shamanism — Usually a derivative of a Native American tradition, the shaman's role is often one of healing, teaching, and divining. Shamanism is a tradition which usually has emphasis on ancestral and natural spirits. Those with shamanistic callings often feel very closely linked to the Earth and its creatures.

Simples — An old term used for medicinal herbs. Also, a term sometimes applied to the recipes for herbal restoratives.

Sky Clad — Participating in a circle, ritual, or other magical activity without clothing. This is done in an effort to connect with nature and get away from the superficial. It is not necessary for any type of Wiccan worship, but is a matter of personal choice.

Smudge Stick — A bundle of herbs—most often including sage, cedar and/or lavender—which is lit. The smoke of these herbs is believed to alleviate negative influences and may be used to prepare a ritual space or to aid in other spiritual activities, such as meditation.

So Mote It Be — The way most rituals, prayers etc. are ended in magic circles. Like the Christian "Amen," meaning "so be it."

Spiritualist — One who believes that the dead can communicate with the living, especially through a medium or channel.

Sun Magic — Pertaining to the masculine attributes, any fire-based magics or any ritual that marks the passage of the sun through the sky, such as a solstice (when the sun is farthest from the equator). In comparison, an equinox is usually celebrated as a Moon or midnight festival. The sun has attributes of leadership, strength, etc.

Sunward — Clockwise, usually referring to movement around a circle in dance. Meant to mimic the motions of the heavens and bring positive energy to the working.

Talisman — Anything which is believed to bring good luck or protect from harm. May also be applied to various harbingers.

Telepathy — A mental ability that allows one to read minds and/or the emotions of others, sometimes with startling accuracy.

Vibration — In magic and many metaphysical traditions, each living thing (and sometimes even non-living items) carry with them a specific energy which acts like a signature or finger print. This signature is called a vibration which may be interpreted in sound, light, heat, or other forms by a psychic.

Visionary — One who has a gift for not only seeing the future, (in their mind's eye) but also seeing things being described to them, without foreknowledge of those things. Visionaries can be rather uncanny in their observations, sometimes making people uncomfortable with their ability to read beyond the surface of almost any situation.

Visualization — The use of creative mental images while meditating to bring about positive change or perspective in a situation.

Wand — While usually made out of wood, a wand may also be made of metal, crystal, or any other natural substance that has a long, baton-like shape. Used in many different types of magic, often to cast or scribe a circle.

Waning Moon — Decreasing in size, the period marked from Full Moon to New Moon. Magics worked during this time often have to do with releasing bad habits, any type of abatement, or even prudence.

Watchtowers — Another name for the Guardians or four major elements of the magic Circle, so named because they are believed to watch over the sacred space and protect all within from harm.

Water — The fourth element of the alchemical tradition, water is generally considered to have a feminine delineation. Animals included in this are fish, gulls, and beavers. Magic which employs water as a component often pertains to healing, calming, fertility, emotions, and replenishing inner strength.

Waxing Moon — The time period from the New Moon until the Full Moon, used in magic for bringing positive change, growth, and things you need into your life.

Wheel of the Year — Probably had its origins with the Roman God Fortuna (thus the Wheel of Fortune in the Tarot). The Wheel of the Year is basically a representation of the seasons, of the part fate plays in all things, and of ever changing life. It is represented in the Tarot by the tenth card in the Major Arcana, and is alluded to by the circular table of Arthurian legend.

Witch — One who practices a tradition of Wicca, the wise Craft. These traditions include, but are not limited to, Gardinarian, Celtic, European, Norse, Alexandrian, Dianic, Egyptian, and many more. Contrary to modern misconceptions, Witches do not consider themselves Satanists, as this entity has no place in the Divine order of Wiccan theology.

BIBLIOGRAPHY

References and Resources

A Century of American Illustration. New York: Brooklyn Museum, Sanders Printing, 1972.

Ainsworth, C.H. *Superstitions.* Buffalo, NY: University Press, 1973.

Anderson, Jay and Matelic, Candace. *Living History Farms.* Des Moines, IA: Living History Foundation, 1980.

Armstrong, N. *A Collectors History of Fans.* New York: Clarkson N. Potter Inc., 1974.

๛

Bach, M. *Questions on the Quest.* New York: Harper and Row, 1978.

Bartlett, Irving H. *The American Mind in the Mid-Nineteenth Century.* Arlington Heights, IL: AHM Publishing, 1967.

Bell, J. *Old Jewelry 1840-1950.* Florence, AL: Books Americana, 1982.

Beyerl, Paul. *Master Book of Herbalism.* Custer, WA: Phoenix, 1984.

Bishop, A. and Simpson, D. *The Victorian Seaside Cookbook.* Newark, NJ: New Jersery History Society, 1983.

Black, William G. *Folk Medicine.* New York: Burt Franklin Co., 1883.

Bramson, Ann. *Soap.* New York: Workman Publishing Co., 1972.

Bravo, Brett. *Crystal Healing Secrets.* New York: Warner Books, 1988.

Bricklin, Mark. *Natural Healing.* Emmaus, PA: Rodale Press, 1987.

Bridges, Hal. *American Mysticism.* New York: Harper & Row Publishing, 1970.

Buckland, Raymond, ed. *The 1991 Magickal Almanac.* St. Paul, MN: Llewellyn Publications, 1991.

_____. *Complete Book of Saxon Witchcraft.* New York: Weiser Co., 1974.

Budge, E.A. Wallis. *Amulets and Superstitions.* New York: Dover Publications, 1930.

Buffalo City Directory 1889, New York: Courier Co., 1889.

Byrne, R. *The 637 Best Things Anybody Ever Said.* New York: Antheneum Books, 1983.

Campanelli, Pauline and Dan. *Ancient Ways.* St. Paul, MN: Llewellyn Publications, 1991.

Cavendish, Richard, ed. *Man, Myth and Magic.* New York: BPC Publishing, 1983.

_____. *A History of Magic.* New York: Taplinger Publishing, 1977.

_____. *Illustrated Guide to the Supernatural.* Boston, MA: G.K. Hall & Co., 1986.

Chandenon, Ludo. *In Praise of Wild Herbs.* Santa Barbara, CA: Capra Press, 1975.

Chaundler, Christine. *The Book of Superstitions.* Secaucus, NJ: Citadel Press, 1970.

Clifton, C. *Edible Flowers.* New York: McGraw-Hill Publishing, 1976.

Coleman, E. ed. *Poems of Byron, Keats & Shelley.* New York: International Collectors Publishing, 1967.

Coleman, E.A. *Changing Fashions 1800-1970.* New York: Brooklyn Museum, 1982.

Collins, C. Cody. *Love of a Glove.* New York: Fairchild Publications, 1945.

Crawford, T.S. *History of the Umbrella.* New York: Taplinger Publishing Co., 1970.

Cross, Jean. *In Grandmother's Day.* Englewood Cliffs, NJ: Prentice Hall, 1980.

Culpeper's English Physician. Glenwood, IL: Wilshire Book Co, 1979.

Cunningham, Scott. *The Magic in Food.* St. Paul, MN: Llewellyn Publications, 1991.

_____. *Earth, Air, Fire & Water.* St. Paul, MN: Llewellyn Publications, 1991.

_____. *Magickal Herbalism.* St. Paul, MN: Llewellyn Publications, 1983.

_____. *The Magic of Incense, Oils & Brews.* St. Paul, MN: Llewellyn Publications, 1982.

Day, C.L. *Quipus & Witch's Knots.* Lawrence, KS: University of Kansas Press, 1967.

DeGivry, Grillot. *Witchcraft, Magic & Alchemy.* England: Spottiswood, Ballantyne & Co. LTD, 1931.

Drury, Nevill. *Dictionary of Mysticism & the Occult.* New York: Harper & Row Publishing, 1985.

Duval, William. *Collecting Postcards.* Poole, England: Blanford Press, 1978.

Ellis, Arthur J. *The Divining Rod: A History of Water Witching.* Washington Government Printing, US Department of Interior, 1917.

The Encyclopedia of Occultism & Parapsychology. 3rd Edition. New York: Gale Research Inc., 1991.

Epstein, Diana. *Buttons.* New York: Walker & Co., 1968.

Evaine, Lady Arwen. *The Complete Anachronism's Guide to Brewing.* Milpitas, CA: SCA Inc., 1990.

Evans, Susan. *Pomanders & Sweetbags.* New York: Falconwood Press, 1988.

❧

Farpid, B. and Lee, A. *Fairies.* New York: Souvenir Press, 1978.

Farrar, Janet and Stewart. Spells and How They Work. Custo, WA: Phoenix Publishing, 1990.

_____. *The Witch's God.* Custer, WA: Phoenix Publishing, 1989.

_____. *The Witch's Goddess.* Custer, WA: Phoenix Publishing, WA, 1987.

Fitzgerald, Edward. *Rubiayat of Omar Khayyam.* Boston: LC Page & Co., 1899.

Fox, William, M.D. *The Model Botanic Guide to Health.* Fargate: Sheffield Independent Press Ltd., 1907.

❧

Gayre, R. *Brewing Mead.* Boulder, CO: Brewer's Publishing, 1986.

Gems for the Fireside, A Treasury for the Home Circle. New York: A.W. Mills, Publisher, 1882.

Gernsheim, A. *Victorian and Edwardian Fashion.* New York: Dover Publications, 1963.

Gordon, L. *Green Magic.* New York: Viking Press, 1977.

Gorsline, D. *What People Wore.* New York: Bonanza Books Co., 1952.

❧

Hall, Manly P. *The Secret Teachings of All Ages.* Los Angeles: Philosophical Research Society, 1977.

Harp, Reba. *Edgar Cayce Encyclopedia of Health.* New York: Warner Books, 1986.

Harper Atlas of World History. New York: Harper & Row Co., 1986.

Hart, Ernest H. *Living with Pets.* New York: Vanguard Press, 1977.

Hechtlinger, Adelaide. *The Seasonal Hearth.* New York: Overlook Press, 1986.

Hobson, Phyllis. *Wine, Beer & Soft Drinks.* Charlotte, VT: Garden Way Publishing, 1976.

Holden, E. *Nature Notes of an Edwardian Lady.* New York: Arcade Publishing, 1989.

_____. *The Country Diary of an Edwardian Lady.* New York: Arcade Publishing, 1989.

Hopping, Jane W. *The Pioneer Lady's Country Kitchen.* New York: Villard Books, 1988.

Hull, Trade W. *History of the Glove.* London: Effingham Wildon Royal Exchange, 1854.

❧

Innes, Brian. *The Tarot.* New York: Crescent Books, 1976.

Isles, Joanna. *A Proper Tea.* New York: St. Martin's Press, 1987.

Kakuzo, Okakura. *The Book of Tea.* London: Prentice Hall, 1906.

Kowalchick, Claire and Hyloon, William, eds. *Rodale's Complete Illustrated Encyclopedia of Herbs.* Emmaus, PA: Rodale Publishing, 1987.

Kunz, G.F. *The Curious Lore of Precious Stones.* New York: Dover Publications, 1913.

Larson, J., *American Illustration 1890-1925.* Canada: Glenbow Museum, 1986.

Leighton, Ann. *American Gardens of the 19th Century.* University of Massachusetts Press, 1987.

Lichine, Alexis, ed. *New Encyclopedia of Wines & Spirits.* 5th ed. New York: Alfred A. Knopf Co., 1987.

Linton, R. *Halloween.* New York: Henry Schuman Inc., 1950.

Long, William J. *English Literature.* Boston, MA: Ginn & Co., 1919.

Lynes, Russell. *The Domesticated Americans.* New York: Harper & Row, 1957.

MacNicol, M. *The Art of Flower Cooking.* New York: Fleet Press, 1967.

McDowell, Josh. *Understanding the Occult.* San Bernadino, CA: Here's Life Publishers, 1982.

Mercatante, A. *The Magic Garden.* New York: Harper & Row, 1976.

Mercatante, A.S. *Zoo of the Gods.* New York: Harper & Row, 1974.

Mohr, Merilyn. *The Art of Soap Making.* Toronto: Firefly Books, 1979.

Murphy, Richard and Appenzeller, Tim, eds. *Fairies and Elves.* Virgina: Time Life books, 1984.

Nelson, John A. *Weather Vanes.* Harrisberg, PA: Stackpole Books, 1990.

Newall, Venetia. *The Encyclopedia of Witchcraft and Magic.* New York: Dial Press, 1974.

Northcote, Lady Rosaline. *The Book of Herb Lore.* New York: Dover Publications, 1912.

Oseterley, W. *The Sacred Dance.* New York: Cambridge University Press, 1923.

Palaiseul, Jean. *Grandmother's Secrets*. New York: G.P. Putnam's Sons, 1973.

Perrot, M., ed. *A History of Private Life*. Cambridge, MA: Balknap Press of Harvard University, 1987.

Peter, M. *Collecting Victorian Jewelry*. New York: Emerson Books, 1970.

Plat, Sir Hugh. *Delights for Ladies*. New York: Falconwood Press, 1988.

Pratt, James. *Tea Lover's Treasury*. San Francisco, CA: 101 Productions, 1982.

༄

Riotte, Louise. *Sleeping with a Sunflower*. Pownal, VT: Gardenway Publishing, 1987.

Rohde, Eleanor S. *Olde English Herbals*. New York: Dover Publications, 1922.

Rose, Jeanne. Kitchen Cosmetics. San Francisco, CA: Aris Books, 1978.

Ryall, Rhiannon. *West County Wicca*. Custer, WA: Phoenix, 1989.

༄

Sams, Jamie and Carson, David. *Medicine Cards*. Sante Fe, NM: Bear & Co., 1988.

Sanecki, Kay N. *The Complete Book of Herbs*. MacMillan Publishing, NY, 1974.

Schapira, Joel, David and Karl. *The Book of Coffee and Tea*. New York: St. Martin Press, 1906.

Scourse, Nicollette. *The Victorians and their Flowers*. Portland, OR: Timber Press, 1983.

Sculley, Bradley, ed. *American Tradition in Literature*. Vol. II. New York: Random House Publishing, 1981.

Sears & Roebuck Co. Consumer Guide. Fall 1900. Chicago, IL: DBI Books Inc., reprinted 1968.

Seligmann, Kurt. *The Mirror of Magic*. New York: Pantheon Books, 1948.

Seymour, John. *Forgotten Household Crafts*. New York: Alfred A. Knopf, 1987.

Shaudys, P.V. *Herbal Treasures*. Pownal VT: Garden Way Publishing, 1990.

Showers, Paul. *Fortune Telling*. Pennsylvania: Blakiston Company, 1942.

Singer, C. *From Magic to Science*. New York: Dover Publications, 1958.

Smith, Elson C. *Treasury of Name Lore*. New York: Harper & Row Publishing, 1967.

Starhawk. *The Spiral Dance*. San Francisco: Harper & Row, 1989.

Starke, D. *Poise and How to Attain it*. New York: Funk & Wagnall, 1916.

Steele, P. *Ozark Tales & Superstitions*. Gretna, LA: Pelican Publishing Co., 1983.

Stewart, George. *American Given Names*. New York: Oxford University Press, 1979.

Summer Rain, Mary. *Earthway*. New York: Pocket books, 1990.

Swarthout, Doris. *An Age of Flowers*. Greenwich, CT: Chatham Press, 1975.

༄

Tekulsky, Matthew. *The Butterfly Garden*. Massachusetts: Harvard Common Press, 1985.

Thomas, Mai. *Grannie's Remedies*. New York: James H. Heineman, Inc., 1965.

Thompson, Frances. *Antiques from the Country Kitchen*. Illinois: Wallace Homestead Company, 1985.

Thompson, R., ed. *Penny Merriments of Samuel Peppy*. New York: Columbia University Press, 1977.

Tillona, P. *Feast of Flowers*. New York: Funk & Wagnall, 1969.

Tuleja, Tad. *Curious Customs*. New York: Harmony Books, 1987.

Turgeon, C. ed. *The Encyclopedia of Creative Cooking*. New York: Weathervane Books, 1982.

Valiente, Doreen. *Rebirth of Witchcraft*. Custer, WA: Phoenix, 1989.

Von Boehn, Max. *Modes & Manners of Ornaments*. Toronto: J.M. Dent & Sons, 1927.

Walker, Barbara. *Woman's Dictionary of Symbols and Sacred Objects*. San Francisco: Harper & Row, 1988.

Waltner, W. *Heritage Hobby Craft*. New York: Lantern Press, 1977.

Weed, Susun. *Healing Wise*. New York: Ash Tree Publishing, 1989.

Whiteside, Robert L. *Animal Language*. New York: Frederick Fell Publishing, 1981.

Whitney, Dr. Leon F. *First Aid for Pets*. Toronto: Copp-Clark Company, 1954.

Wiseman, E.J. *Victorian Do it Yourself*. North Pomfret, VT: David & Charles Inc., 1976.

Wootton, A. *Animal Folklore, Myth and Legend*. New York: Blandford Press, 1986.

Zook, J. *Hexology*. Paradise, PA: Publisher unknown, 1964.

INDEX

Index of Key Words

The only way round is through.
— Robert Frost

STAY IN TOUCH

On the following pages you will find listed, with their current prices, some of the books now available on related subjects. Your book dealer stocks most of these and will stock new titles in the Llewellyn series as they become available. We urge your patronage.

To obtain our full catalog, to keep informed about new titles as they are released and to benefit from informative articles and helpful news, you are invited to write for our bimonthly news magazine/catalog, *Llewellyn's New Worlds of Mind and Spirit*. A sample copy is free, and it will continue coming to you at no cost as long as you are an active mail customer. Or you may subscribe for just $7.00 in the U.S.A. and Canada ($20.00 overseas, first class mail). Many bookstores also have *New Worlds* available to their customers. Ask for it.

Stay in touch! In *New Worlds'* pages you will find news and features about new books, tapes and services, announcements of meetings and seminars, articles helpful to our readers, news of authors, products and services, special money-making opportunities, and much more.

Llewellyn's New Worlds of Mind and Spirit
P.O. Box 64383-784, St. Paul, MN 55164-0383, U.S.A.

* * *

TO ORDER BOOKS AND TAPES

If your book dealer does not have the books described on the following pages readily available, you may order them directly from the publisher by sending full price in U.S. funds, plus $3.00 for postage and handling for orders *under* $10.00; $4.00 for orders *over* $10.00. There are no postage and handling charges for orders over $50.00. Postage and handling rates are subject to change. We ship UPS whenever possible. Delivery guaranteed. Provide your street address as UPS does not deliver to P.O. Boxes. UPS to Canada requires a $50.00 minimum order. Allow 4–6 weeks for delivery. Orders outside the U.S.A. and Canada: Airmail—add retail price of book; add $5.00 for each non-book item (tapes, etc.); add $1.00 per item for surface mail.

FOR GROUP STUDY AND PURCHASE

Because there is a great deal of interest in group discussion and study of the subject matter of this book, we feel that we should encourage the adoption and use of this particular book by such groups by offering a special quantity price to group leaders or agents.

Our Special Quantity Price for a minimum order of five copies of *A Victorian Grimoire* is $44.85 cash-with-order. This price includes postage and handling within the United States. Minnesota residents must add 6.5% sales tax. For additional quantities, please order in multiples of five. For Canadian and foreign orders, add postage and handling charges as above. Credit card (VISA, MasterCard, American Express) orders are accepted. Charge card orders only ($15.00 minimum order) may be phoned in free within the U.S.A. or Canada by dialing 1-800-THE-MOON. For customer service, call 1-612-291-1970. Mail orders to:

LLEWELLYN PUBLICATIONS
P.O. Box 64383-784, St. Paul, MN 55164-0383, U.S.A.

Prices subject to change without notice.

JUDE'S HERBAL HOME REMEDIES
Natural Health, Beauty & Home-Care Secrets
by Jude C. Williams, M.H.

There's a pharmacy—in your spice cabinet! In the course of daily life we all encounter problems that can be easily remedied through the use of common herbs—headaches, dandruff, insomnia, colds, muscle aches, burns—and a host of other afflictions known to humankind. *Jude's Herbal Home Remedies* is a simple guide to self care that will benefit beginning or experienced herbalists with its wealth of practical advice. Most of the herbs listed are easy to obtain.

Discover how cayenne pepper promotes hair growth, why cranberry juice is a good treatment for asthma attacks, how to make a potent juice to flush out fat, how to make your own deodorants and perfumes, what herbs will get fleas off your pet, how to keep cut flowers fresh longer ... the remedies and hints go on and on!

This book gives you instructions for teas, salves, tinctures, tonics, poultices, along with addresses for obtaining the herbs. Dangerous and controversial herbs are also discussed.

Grab this book and a cup of herbal tea, and discover from a Master Herbalist more than 800 ways to a simpler, more natural way of life.

0-87542-869-X, 240 pgs., 6 x 9, illus., softcover $9.95

THE MAGIC IN FOOD
Legends, Lore & Spells
by Scott Cunningham

Foods are storehouses of natural energies. Choosing specific foods, properly preparing them, eating with a magical goal in mind: these are the secrets of *The Magic in Food*, an age-old method of taking control of your life through your diet.

Though such exotic dishes as bird's-nest soup and saffron bread are included in this book, you'll find many old friends: peanut butter and jelly sandwiches ... scrambled eggs... tofu... beer. We've consumed them for years, but until we're aware of the energies contained within them, foods offer little more than nourishment and pleasure.

You'll learn the mystic qualities of everyday dishes, their preparation (if any) and the simple method of calling upon their powers. The author has included numerous magical diets, each designed to create a specific change within its user: increased health and happiness, deeper spirituality, enhanced sexual relations, protection, psychic awareness, success, love, prosperity—all through the hidden powers of food.

0-87542-130-X, 384 pgs., 6 x 9, illus., color plates, softcover $14.95

MAGICAL HERBALISM
The Secret Craft of the Wise
by Scott Cunningham

Certain plants are prized for the range of magical energies they possess. Magical herbalism unites the powers of plants and man to produce and direct change in accord with will and desire. In this book, author Scott Cunningham presents the magic of amulets, charms, sachets, incense, oils, simples, infusions, and anointments. He also includes full instructions, recipes as well as rituals and spells. And best of all, all of the herbs can be easily obtained— purchased in stores or by mail.

0-87542-120-2, 260 pgs., 5 1/4 x 8, illus., softcover $7.95

COSMIC KEYS
Fortunetelling for Fun and Self-Discovery
by M. Blackerby

This book invites those just starting out in the psychic mysteries to jump in and take a revealing and positive look inside themselves and the people around them. Through the hands-on application of the Cosmic Keys—Chinese astrology (combined with Sun sign astrology), numerology, palmistry, card reading and finally, the author's original Dream Key and Universal Coloring Test—readers come away with telling insights into their individual personalities and life situations. The illustrations and coloring mantra were created especially for the workbook, and readers are encouraged to color each as they move through the book, as well as record personal data found in each section.

0-87542-027-3, 200 pgs., 7 X 10, illus., softcover $12.95

Prices subject to change without notice.